STUDENT SOLUTIONS MANUAL

COST
ACCOUNTING
NINTH EDITION
A MANAGERIAL EMPHASIS

STUDENT SOLUTIONS MANUAL

COST

ACCOUNTING

NINTH EDITION

A MANAGERIAL EMPHASIS

HORNGREN • FOSTER • DATAR

Stanford University *Stanford University* *Stanford University*

PRENTICE HALL, Upper Saddle River, NJ 07458

Project editor: Richard Bretan
Acquisitions editor: P.J. Boardman
Associate editor: Diane deCastro
Manufacturing buyer: Paul Smolenski

© 1997 by Prentice Hall, Inc.
A Simon & Schuster Company
Upper Saddle River, New Jersey 07458

Printed in the United States of America

10 9 8 7 6 5 4 3

ISBN 0-13-567646-0

Prentice-Hall International (UK) Limited, *London*
Prentice-Hall of Australia Pty. Limited, *Sydney*
Prentice-Hall Canada Inc., *Toronto*
Prentice-Hall Hispanoamericana, S.A., *Mexico*
Prentice-Hall of India Private Limited, *New Delhi*
Prentice-Hall of Japan, Inc., *Tokyo*
Simon & Schuster Asia Pte. Ltd., *Singapore*
Editora Prentice-Hall do Brasil, Ltda., *Rio de Janeiro*

TABLE OF CONTENTS

CHAPTER 1
THE ACCOUNTANT'S ROLE IN THE ORGANIZATION

See the front matter of this Solutions Manual for suggestions regarding your choices of assignment material for each chapter.

1-2   **Management accounting** measures and reports financial as well as other types of information that assists managers in fulfilling the goals of the organization. **Financial accounting** focuses on external reporting that is guided by generally accepted accounting principles.

1-4   The business functions in the value chain are:

- **Research and development**--the generation of, and experimentation with, ideas related to new products, services, or processes.
- **Design of products, services, and processes**--the detailed planning and engineering of products, services, or processes.
- **Production**--the coordination and assembly of resources to produce a product or deliver a service.
- **Marketing**--the process by which individuals or groups (a) learn about and value the attributes of products or services and (b) purchase those products or services.
- **Distribution**--the mechanism by which products or services are delivered to the customer.
- **Customer service**--the support activities provided to customers.

1-6   Uses of feedback in a management control system includes:
- Changing goals
- Searching for alternative means of operating
- Changing methods for making decisions
- Making predictions
- Changing operations
- Changing the reward system

1-8   Yes. Drucker is advocating that accountants do more than scorekeeping, which is often interpreted as being a "cop on the beat" or a watchdog. It is also essential that accountants emphasize their attention-directing and problem-solving functions.

1-10   The IMA is the Institute of Management Accountants. It is the largest association of management accountants in the United States. The CMA (Certified Management Accountant) is the professional designation for management accountants and financial executives. It demonstrates that the holder has passed the admission criteria and demonstrated the competency of technical knowledge required by the IMA.

1-12   Steps to take when established written policies provide insufficient guidance are:
(a)   discuss problem with the immediate superior (except when it appears that the superior is involved).
(b)   clarify relevant concepts by confidential discussion with an objective advisor.
If (a) and (b) and other avenues do not resolve the situation, resignation from the organization should be considered.

1-14   Yes, management accountants have customers just as companies have customers who purchase their products or services. Management accountants provide information and advice to many line and staff people in the organization and to various external parties. It is essential that they provide information and advice that line and staff customers and external parties view as timely and relevant.

1-16   (15-20 min.) **Financial and management accounting.**

This problem can form the basis of an introductory discussion of the entire field of management accounting.

1.   The focus of management accounting is on helping internal users to make better decisions, whereas the focus of financial accounting is on helping external users to make better decisions. Management accounting helps in making most decisions, including pricing, product choices, investments in equipment, making or buying goods and services, and manager rewards.

2.   Generally accepted accounting principles affect both management accounting and financial accounting. However, an organization's management accounting system is not governed by generally accepted accounting principles. For example, if an organization wants to account for assets on the basis of replacement costs for internal purposes, no outside agency can prohibit such accounting.

1-18 (15 min.) **Purposes of accounting systems.**

1.

Report Statement	Purpose
a	Performance measurement of . . . people
b	Meeting external regulatory . . .
c	Formulating overall strategies . . .
d	Cost planning and cost control
e	Product/customer emphasis decisions

2.   A report developed for financial reporting is constrained by generally accepted accounting principles. GAAP does not constrain any of the other 4 purposes. For example, report (c) (ten-year projections of revenues, costs and investments . . .) can include recognition of uncertainties that are not permitted under GAAP. Similarly, (e) (report comparing profitability of soft drink sales in retail outlets . . .) can use non-GAAP permitted adjustments for leases and other operating differences across the outlets to increase comparability across units. For example, GAAP distinctions between capital leases and operating leases need not be adhered to in the (e) report.

1-20   (15 min.)   **Value chain and classification of costs, pharmaceutical company.**

Cost Item	Value Chain Business Function
a.	Design
b.	Marketing
c.	Customer service
d.	Research and Development
e.	Marketing
f.	Production
g.	Marketing
h.	Distribution

1-22 (15 min.) **Scorekeeping, attention directing, and problem solving.**

Because the accountant's duties are often not sharply defined, some of these answers might be challenged.
a. Scorekeeping
b. Attention directing
c. Scorekeeping
d. Problem solving
e. Attention directing
f. Attention directing
g. Problem solving
h. Scorekeeping, depending on the extent of the report
i. This question is intentionally vague. The give-and-take of the budgetary process usually encompasses all three functions, but it emphasizes scorekeeping the least. The main function is attention directing, but problem solving is also involved.
j. Problem solving

1-24 (15 min.) **Changes in management and changes in management accounting.**

Change in Management Accounting	Key Theme in Newly Evolving Management Approach
a.	Total value-chain analysis
b.	Key success factors (quality) or Total value-chain analysis
c.	Dual external/internal focus
d.	Continuous improvement
e.	Customer satisfaction is priority one

1-26 (20-30 min.) **Responsibility for analysis of performance.**

This problem raises plenty of thought-provoking questions. Unfortunately, there are no pat answers. The generalizations about these relationships are difficult to formulate.

1. Apparently, the controller's performance-analysis staff have not won the confidence or respect of Whisler and other line officers. Whisler regards these accountants as interlopers who are unqualified for their analytical tasks on two counts: (a) the task is Whisler's, not the accountants'; and (b) Whisler better understands his own problems. It is unlikely that the controller's performance-analysis staff has maintained a day-to-day relationship with line personnel in Division C.

2. Phillipson should point out that the work is being done by her performance-analysis staff in order to enable Whisler to better concentrate on his other work. The detached analyses by her staff should help Whisler better understand and improve his own performance.

Furthermore, Phillipson should point out that Whisler would need his own divisional accounting staff in order to prepare the necessary analysis of performance if Phillipson's group did not support him. More uniform reporting formats and procedures and more objective appraisals potentially could occur if the performance-analysis staff remains as part of the corporate controller's group.

3. Two approaches within the existing organization reporting relationships are:
(a) Placing higher priority on having her performance-analysis staff view the division personnel as important customers and actively seeking out ways to increase customer satisfaction.
(b) Encouraging greater use of teams in which division personnel and corporate control personnel are members. Hopefully, mutual respect will increase by this close interaction.

A more extreme approach would be to change the organization's reporting relationships and staff assignments. For example, each division manager could have his or her own performance-analysis staff member as part of the plant controller's group.

1-28 (30 min.) Software procurement decisions, ethics.

1.   Companies with "codes of conduct" frequently have a "supplier clause" that prohibits their employees from accepting "material" (in some cases, any) gifts from suppliers. The motivations include:

(a)   Integrity/conflict of interest. Suppose Michaels recommends that a Horizon 1-2-3 product subsequently be purchased by Fiesta. This recommendation could be because he felt he owed them an obligation as his trip to the Cancun conference was fully paid by Horizon.

(b)   The appearance of a conflict of interest. Even if the Horizon 1-2-3 product is the superior one at that time, other suppliers likely will have a different opinion. They may believe that the way to sell products to Fiesta is via "fully-paid junkets to resorts." Those not wanting to do business this way may down-play future business activities with Fiesta even though Fiesta may gain much from such activities.

Some executives view the meeting as "suspect" from the start given the Caribbean location and its "rest and recreation" tone.

2.   Pros of attending user meeting

(a)   Able to learn more about the software products of Horizon.
(b)   Able to interact with other possible purchasers and get their opinions.
(c)   Able to influence the future product development plans of Horizon in a way that will benefit Fiesta. An example is Horizon subsequently developing software modules tailored to food product companies.
(d)   Saves Fiesta money. Visiting suppliers and their customers typically costs money, whereas Horizon is paying for the Cancun conference.

Cons of Attending
(a)   The ethical issues raised in requirement 1.
(b)   Negative moral effects on other Fiesta employees who do not get to attend the Cancun conference. These employees may reduce their trust and respect for Michaels' judgment, arguing he has been on a "supplier-paid vacation."

Conditions on Attending Fiesta Might Impose
(a)   Sizable part of time in Cancun has to be devoted to business rather than recreation.
(b)   Decision on which Fiesta executive attends is not made by the person who attends (this reduces the appearance of a conflict of interest).
(c)   Person attending (Michaels) does not have final say on purchase decision (this reduces the appearance of a conflict of interest).
(d)   Fiesta executives go only when a new major purchase is being contemplated (to avoid the conference becoming a regular "vacation").

1-28 (Cont'd)

A Conference Board publication on <u>Corporate Ethics</u> asked executives about a comparable situation:
- 76% said Fiesta and Michaels face an ethical consideration in deciding whether to attend.
- 71% said Michaels should not attend, as the payment of expenses is a "gift" within the meaning of a credible corporate ethics policy.

3.   <u>Pros of having a written code</u>
        The Conference Board outlines the following reasons why companies adopt codes of ethics
(a)   Signals commitment of senior management to ethics.
(b)   Promotes public trust in the credibility of the company and its employees.
(c)   Signals the managerial professionalism of its employees.
(d)   Provides guidance to employees as to how difficult problems are to be handled. If adhered to, employees will avoid many actions that are unethical or appear to be unethical.

(e)   Drafting of the policy (and its redrafting in the light of ambiguities) can assist management in anticipating and preparing for ethical issues not yet encountered.

<u>Cons of having a written code</u>

(a)   Can give appearance that all issues have been covered. Issues not covered may appear to be "acceptable" even when they are not.
(b)   Can constrain the entrepreneurial activities of employees. Forces people to always "behave by the book."
(c)   Cost of developing code can be "high" if it consumes a lot of employee time.

1-30 (30-40 min.) **Responding to allegations of fraud.**

Broad Street has several issues to consider:

Issue 1: Are the allegations true that "last year's reported earnings for the bond-trading division are fictitious"?

Issue 2: Is the head of bond trading promoting a culture where illegal behavior is acceptable?

Issue 3: How to handle any adverse publicity, even if issues 1 & 2 are found to be groundless.

The "anonymous letter" itself should be examined first. Is it from a person who has written many prior letters alleging similar illegal behaviors. If these prior letters have been investigated and found to be groundless, then the Board may decide not to pursue the matter further unless pressed to by an outside party. Corporations get a variety of "crank" letters, (many, apparently from the same source) most of which have no foundation. It is not typically possible to conduct a detailed investigation of every such letter that a company receives.

Issue 1

The letter asserts that "the head of bond trading has been inventing bond trades that are supposed to be highly profitable. They are not." Several groups could assist in any investigation of the allegation.

CHAPTER 2
AN INTRODUCTION TO COST TERMS AND PURPOSES

2-2   **Cost assignment** is a general term that encompasses both (1) tracing accumulated costs to a cost object, and (2) allocating accumulated costs to a cost object.
Cost tracing is the assigning of direct costs to a chosen cost object.
Cost allocation is the assigning of indirect costs to a chosen cost object.
    The relationship between these terms is as follows:

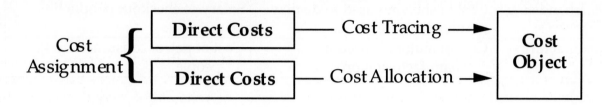

2-4   Consider a supervisor's salary in a maintenance department of a telephone company. If the cost object is the department, the salary is a direct cost. If the cost object is a telephone call by a customer, the salary is an indirect cost.

2-6   Cost reduction efforts frequently focus on:

1.   doing only value-added activities, and
2.   efficiently managing the use of the cost drivers in those value-added activities.

2-8   **A variable cost** is a cost that changes in total in proportion to changes in the quantity of a cost driver.
    A **fixed cost** is a cost that does not change in total despite changes in the quantity of a cost driver.

Suppose the cost object is a Ford motor vehicle. A dashboard is a variable cost of the motor vehicle. The annual lease of the plant in which the vehicle is assembled illustrates a fixed cost for that year.

2-10   A unit cost is computed by dividing some total cost (the numerator) by some number of units (the denominator). In many cases, the numerator will include a fixed cost that will not change despite changes in the number of units to be assembled. It is erroneous in those cases to multiply the unit cost by volume changes to predict changes in total costs at different volume levels.

2-12 **Capitalized costs** are costs that are first recorded as an asset (capitalized) when they are incurred. These costs are presumed to provide future benefits to the company. Examples are costs to acquire computer equipment and motor vehicles. **Noncapitalized costs** are costs that are recorded as expenses of the accounting period when they are incurred. Examples are salaries:

	Capitalized Costs	**Noncapitalized Costs**
Service	Cost to purchase computer equipment	Cost of telephone calls
Merchandising	Cost of shelving used to display merchandise	Salary of checkout people
Manufacturing	Cost of materials used in manufacturing process	Cost of petrol consumed by sales people

2-14 **Direct materials costs:** The acquisition costs of all materials that eventually become part of the cost object (say, units finished or in process) and that can be traced to that cost object in an economically feasible way. Acquisition costs of direct materials include freight-in (inward delivery) charges, sales taxes, and custom duties.

Direct manufacturing labor costs: The compensation of all manufacturing labor that is specifically identified with the cost object (say, units finished or in process) and that can be traced to the cost object in an economically feasible way. Examples include wages and fringe benefits paid to machine operators and assembly-line workers.

Indirect manufacturing costs: All manufacturing costs considered to be part of the cost object (say, units finished or in process) but that cannot be individually traced to that cost object in an economically feasible way. Examples include power, supplies, indirect materials, indirect manufacturing labor, plant rent, plant insurance, property taxes on plants, plant depreciation, and the compensation of plant managers.

Prime costs: All direct manufacturing costs. In the two-part classification of manufacturing costs, prime costs would comprise direct materials costs. In the three-part classification, prime costs would comprise direct materials costs and direct manufacturing labor costs.

Conversion costs: All manufacturing costs other than direct materials costs.

2-16 (10 min.) **Total costs and unit costs.**

1. Total cost, $4,000. Unit cost per person, $4,000 ÷ 500 = $8.00

2. Total cost, $4,000. Unit cost per person, $4,000 ÷ 2,000 = $2.00

3. The main lesson of this problem is to alert the student early in the course to the desirability of thinking in terms of total costs rather than unit costs wherever feasible. Changes in the number of cost driver units will affect <u>total</u> variable costs but not <u>total</u> fixed costs. In our example, it would be perilous to use either the $8.00 or the $2.00 unit cost to predict the total cost because the total costs are not affected by the attendance. Instead, the student association should use the $4,000 total cost. Obviously, if the musical group agreed to work for, say, $4.00 per person, such a unit variable cost could be used to predict the total cost.

2-18 (10 min.) **Total costs and unit costs.**
1. Unit cost = Total costs ÷ Number of units

	<u>Total costs</u>	<u>Number of units</u>	<u>Unit cost</u>
(a)	$60,000	200	$300
(b)	60,000	250	240
(c)	60,000	300	200

2. The unit-cost figures per passenger computed in requirement 1 should play no role in predicting the total air-flight costs to be paid next month. Golden Holidays pays Global on a per round-trip flight basis, not on a per passenger basis. Hence the cost driver for next month is the number of round-trip flights not the number of passengers.

2-20 (15 min.) **Cost drivers and the value chain.**

1.

	Business Function Area	Representative Cost Driver
A.	Research and Development	Number of research scientists
B.	Design of Products/Processes	Hours of computer-aided design (CAD) work
C.	Production	Number of machine assembly hours
D.	Marketing	Number of sales personnel
E.	Distribution	Weight of cars shipped
F.	Customer Service	Number of cars recalled for defective parts

2.

	Business Function Area	Representative Cost Driver
A.	Research and Development	• Square feet of R&D laboratory space • Number of new models being developed
B.	Design of Products/Processes	• Number of focus groups on alternative color combinations • Hours of process engineering time on retooling assembly equipment
C.	Production	• Direct manufacturing labor hours • Kilowatt hours of energy consumed
D.	Marketing	• Number of advertisements on television • Number of total mailings to existing customers about new model
E.	Distribution	• Number of vehicles shipped • Number of distributors in sales area
F.	Customer Service	• Number of personnel on toll-free customer phone lines • Number of packages mailed about safety complaints with existing model

2-22 (15-20 min.) **Classification of costs, service sector.**

Cost object: Each individual focus group

Cost variability: With respect to changes in the number of focus groups

There may be some debate over classifications of individual items. Debate is more likely as regards cost variability.

Cost Item	D or I	V or F
A	D	V
B	I	F
C	I	V[a]
D	I	F
E	D	V
F	I	F
G	D	V
H	I	V[b]

[a] Some students will note that phone call costs are variable when each call has a separate charge. It may be a fixed cost if Consumer Focus has a flat monthly charge for a line, irrespective of the amount of usage.

[b] Gasoline costs are likely to vary with the number of focus groups. However, vehicles likely serve multiple purposes, and detailed records may be required to examine how costs vary with changes in one of the many purposes served.

2-24 (15-20 min.) **Classification of costs, manufacturing sector.**

Cost object: Type of car assembled (Corolla or Geo Prism)

Cost variability: With respect to changes in the number of cars assembled

There may be some debate over classifications of individual items. Debate is more likely as regards cost variability.

Cost Item	D or I	V or F
A	D	V
B	I	F
C	D	F
D	D	F
E	D	V
F	I	V
G	D	V
H	I	F

2-26 (20-25 min.) **Computing cost of goods manufactured and cost of goods sold.**

Schedule of Cost of Goods Manufactured
for the Year Ended December 31, 19_7
(in thousands)

Direct materials used		$ 87,000
Direct manufacturing labor costs		34,000
Indirect manufacturing costs:		
Property tax on plant building	$ 3,000	
Plant utilities	17,000	
Depreciation of plant building	9,000	
Depreciation of plant equipment	11,000	
Plant repairs and maintenance	16,000	
Indirect manufacturing labor costs	23,000	
Indirect materials used	11,000	
Miscellaneous plant overhead	4,000	94,000
Manufacturing costs incurred during 19_7		215,000
Add beginning work in process inventory, Jan. 1, 19_7		20,000
Total manufacturing costs to account for		235,000
Deduct ending work in process inventory, Dec. 31, 19_7		26,000
Cost of goods manufactured		$209,000

Schedule of Cost of Goods Sold
for the Year Ended December 31, 19_7
(in thousands)

Beginning finished goods, Jan. 1, 19_7	$ 27,000
Cost of goods manufactured (above)	209,000
Cost of goods available for sale	236,000
Ending finished goods, Dec. 31, 19_7	34,000
Cost of goods sold	$202,000

2-28 (30-40 min.) **Cost of goods manufactured.**

Canesco Company
Schedule of Cost of Goods Manufactured for the Year Ended December 31, 19_7
(in thousands)

1.

Direct materials costs:		
Beginning inventory, Jan. 1, 19_7	$22,000	
Purchases of direct materials	75,000	
Cost of direct materials available for use	97,000	
Ending inventory, Dec. 31, 19_7	26,000	
Direct materials used		$ 71,000
Direct manufacturing labor costs		25,000
Indirect manufacturing costs:		
Indirect manufacturing labor costs	$15,000	
Plant insurance	9,000	
Depreciation—plant building and equipment	11,000	
Repairs and maintenance—plant	4,000	39,000
Manufacturing costs incurred during 19_7		135,000
Add beginning work in process inventory, Jan. 1, 19_7		21,000
Total manufacturing costs to account for		156,000
Deduct ending work in process inventory, Dec. 31, 19_7		20,000
Cost of goods manufactured		$136,000

2.

Canesco Company
Income Statement for the Year Ended December 31, 19_7
(in thousands)

Revenues		$300,000
Cost of goods sold:		
Beginning finished goods, Jan. 1, 19_7	$ 18,000	
Cost of goods manufactured (Requirement 1)	136,000	
Cost of goods available for sale	154,000	
Ending finished goods, Dec. 31, 19_7	23,000	131,000
Gross margin		169,000
Operating costs:		
Marketing, distribution, and customer service	$ 93,000	
General and administrative	29,000	122,000
Operating income		$ 47,000

2-30 (15-20 min.) Interpretation of statements.

1. The schedule in 2-29 can become a Schedule of Cost of Goods Manufactured and Sold simply by including the beginning and ending finished goods inventory figures in the supporting schedule, rather than directly in the body of the income statement. Note that the term cost of goods manufactured refers to the cost of goods brought to completion (finished) during the accounting period, whether they were started before or during the current accounting period. Some of the manufacturing costs incurred are held back as costs of the ending work in process; similarly, the costs of the beginning work in process inventory become a part of the cost of goods manufactured for 19_7.

2. The sales manager's salary would be charged as a marketing cost as incurred by both manufacturing and merchandising companies. It is basically an operating cost that appears below the gross margin line on an income statement. In contrast, an assembler's wages would be assigned to the products worked on. Thus, the wages cost would be charged to Work in Process and would not be expensed until the product is transferred through Finished Goods Inventory to Cost of Goods Sold as the product is sold.

3. The direct-indirect distinction can be resolved only with respect to a particular cost object. For example, in defense contracting, the cost object may be defined as a contract. Then, a plant supervisor's salary may be charged directly and wholly to that single contract.

4.   Direct materials used   = \$320,000,000 ÷ 1,000,000 units = \$320 per unit
        Depreciation   = \$ 80,000,000 ÷ 1,000,000 units = \$ 80 per unit

5. Direct materials unit cost would be unchanged at \$320. Depreciation unit cost would be \$80,000,000 ÷ 1,200,000 = \$66.67 per unit. Total direct materials costs would rise by 20% to \$384,000,000, whereas total depreciation would be unaffected at \$80,000,000.

6. Unit costs are averages, and they must be interpreted with caution. The \$320 direct materials unit cost is valid for predicting total costs because direct materials is a variable cost; total direct materials costs indeed change as output levels change. However, fixed costs like depreciation must be interpreted quite differently from variable costs. A common error in cost analysis is to regard all unit costs as one--as if all the total costs to which they are related are variable costs. Changes in output levels (the denominator) will affect total variable costs, but not total fixed costs. Graphs of the two costs may clarify this point; it is safer to think in terms of total costs rather than in terms of unit costs.

2-32 (15-20 min.) **Interpretation of statements.**

1.   The schedule in 2-31 can become a Schedule of Cost of Goods Manufactured and Sold simply by including the beginning and ending finished goods inventory figures in the supporting schedule, rather than directly in the body of the income statement. Note that the term <u>cost of goods manufactured</u> refers to the cost of goods brought to completion (finished) during the accounting period, whether they were started before or during the current accounting period. Some of the manufacturing costs incurred are held back as costs of the ending work in process; similarly, the costs of the beginning work in process inventory become a part of the cost of goods manufactured for 19_7.

2.   The sales manager's salary would be charged as a marketing cost as incurred by both manufacturing and merchandising companies. It is basically an operating cost that appears below the gross margin line on an income statement. In contrast, an assembler's wages would be assigned to the products worked on. Thus, the wages cost would be charged to Work in Process and would not be expensed until the product is transferred through Finished Goods Inventory to Cost of Goods Sold as the product is sold.

3.   The direct-indirect distinction can be resolved only with respect to a particular cost object. For example, in defense contracting, the cost object may be defined as a contract. Then, a plant supervisor's salary may be charged directly and wholly to that single contract.

4.   Direct materials used   = $105,000,000 ÷ 1,000,000 units = $105 per unit
      Depreciation   = $ 9,000,000 ÷ 1,000,000 units = $ 9 per unit

5.   Direct materials unit cost would be unchanged at $105. Depreciation unit cost would be $9,000,000 ÷ 1,500,000 = $6 per unit. Total direct materials costs would rise by 50% to $157,500,000 ($105 × 1,500,000). Total depreciation cost of $9,000,000 would remain unchanged.

6.   Unit costs are averages, and they must be interpreted with caution. The $105 direct materials unit cost is valid for predicting total costs because direct materials is a variable cost; total direct materials costs indeed change as output levels change. However, fixed costs like depreciation must be interpreted quite differently from variable costs. A common error in cost analysis is to regard all unit costs as one--as if all the total costs to which they are related are variable costs. Changes in output levels (the denominator) will affect <u>total</u> variable costs, but not <u>total</u> fixed costs. Graphs of the two costs may clarify this point; it is safer to think in terms of total costs rather than in terms of unit costs.

2-34 (20-25 min.) **Finding unknown balances.**

Let G = given, I = inferred

Step 1: Use gross margin formula	CASE 1	CASE 2
Revenues	$ 32,000 G	$ 31,800 G
Cost of goods sold	A 20,700 I	20,000 G
Gross margin	11,300 G	C $11,800 I

Step 2: Use schedule of cost of goods manufactured formula

Direct materials used	$ 8,000 G	$ 12,000 G
Direct manufacturing labor costs	3,000 G	5,000 G
Indirect manufacturing costs	7,000 G	D 6,500 I
Manufacturing costs incurred	18,000 I	23,500 I
Add beginning work in process, 1/1	0 G	800 G
Total manufacturing costs to account for	18,000 I	24,300 I
Deduct ending work in process, 12/31	0 G	3,000 G
Cost of goods manufactured	$ 18,000 I	$ 21,300 I

Step 3: Use cost of goods sold formula

Beginning finished goods inventory, 1/1	$ 4,000 G	4,000 G
Cost of goods manufactured	18,000 I	21,300 I
Cost of goods available for sale	22,000 I	25,300 I
Ending finished goods inventory, 12/31	B 1,300 I	5,300 G
Cost of goods sold	$ 20,700 I	$20,000 G

For case 1, do steps 1, 2 and 3 in order.

For case 2, do steps 1, 3 and then 2.

2-36 (30 min.) Comprehensive problem on unit costs, product costs.

1. If 2 pounds of direct materials are used to make each unit of finished product, 100,000 units × 2 lbs., or 200,000 lbs. were used at $0.70 per pound of direct materials ($140,000 ÷ 200,000 lbs). Therefore, the ending inventory of direct materials is 2,000 lbs. × $0.70 = $1,400.

2.

	Manufacturing Costs for 100,000 units		
	Variable	Fixed	Total
Direct materials costs	$140,000	$ –	$140,000
Direct manufacturing labor costs	30,000	–	30,000
Plant energy costs	5,000	–	5,000
Indirect manufacturing labor costs	10,000	16,000	26,000
Other indirect manufacturing costs	8,000	24,000	32,000
Cost of goods manufactured	$193,000	$40,000	$233,000

Average unit manufacturing cost: $233,000 ÷ 100,000 units
= $2.33 per unit

Finished goods inventory in units: $= \dfrac{\$20,970 \text{ (given)}}{\$2.33 \text{ per unit}}$
= 9,000 units

3. Units sold in 19_7   = Beginning inventory + Production – Ending inventory
= 0 + 100,000 – 9,000 = 91,000 units

Selling price per unit in 19_7   = $436,800 ÷ 91,000
= $4.80 per unit

4.

Revenues (91,000 units sold × $4.80)		$436,800
Cost of units sold:		
Beginning finished goods, Jan. 1, 19_7	$ 0	
Cost of goods manufactured	233,000	
Cost of goods available for sale	233,000	
Ending finished goods, Dec. 31, 19_7	20,970	212,030
Gross margin		224,770
Operating costs:		
Marketing, distribution, and customer-service costs	162,850	
Administrative costs	50,000	212,850
Operating income		$ 11,920

Note: Although not required, the full set of unit variable costs is:

Direct materials costs	$1.40	⎫
Direct manufacturing labor costs	0.30	⎪
Plant energy costs	0.05	⎬ per unit manufactured
Indirect manufacturing labor costs	0.10	⎪
Other indirect manufacturing costs	0.08	⎭
Marketing, distribution, and customer-service costs	1.35	⎬ per unit sold

2-38 (25-30 min.) **Revenue and cost recording and classifications, ethics.**

1.   Concerns include:

(a)   Total payments made by Country Outfitters do not "appear" to be adequately described. Elements of "total compensation" appear to be:
• $12 million payment to Jeans West in Caribe
• $4.8 million payment to Jeans West subsidiary in Switzerland
• Assistance with life insurance plans for "Jeans West executives at rates much more favorable than those available in Caribe"

One possible motivation for restricting the payment in the Caribe to $12 million is to avoid showing higher profits in Caribe. A second motivation could be that the Swiss subsidiary is siphoning to Jeans West senior executives revenues that should be paid to Jeans West. This could arise if the Jeans West Swiss subsidiary is "owned" by the senior executives of Jeans West rather than being a 100% subsidiary of Jeans West.

The Conference Board in <u>Corporate Ethics Practices</u> (1992) has a discussion case where several Latin American distributors ask a U.S. company for some payments to be made to a Swiss bank account because "local taxes are confiscatory and the local exchange rates make it very difficult to achieve profitable results." A survey of over 200 executives recommended:

• Deny the request because what is unethical in one country
  cannot be ethical in another   90%

• Accede to the request because it does not violate
  the local distributors' standard business practices   10%

Those in the 10% included comments such as "we must play by the local rules," "it is arrogant to suggest home ethics are superior to local ethics," and "I'm not sure we can force our view of right and wrong on the whole world." Country Outfitters could have faced an ultimatum from Jeans West that part of the payment be sent to Switzerland and have been told "that everybody does it in Caribe."

The assistance with the insurance plans is in the gray area. If Jeans West is willing to accept a lower price in return for CO assisting with the insurance plans, it may be a judicious economic decision by CO. CO is not hurt economically in this scenario. The concern is whether CO is assisting the senior executives diverting "defacto payments" to themselves.

(b)   Product design costs of CO include $4.8 million for "own product design." It is stated that the Director of Product Design views it "as an 'off-statement' item that historically he has no responsibility for nor any say about" and that "to his knowledge, Jeans West uses only CO designs with either zero or minimal changes." It may be that the $4.8 million payment is a hidden payment made to avoid Caribe taxation. However, the result is incorrect classification of product design costs at CO.

2-38 (Cont'd)

(c)   Jeans West receives from CO the margin between $16.8 million ($12 million + $4.8 million) and the $3.0 million payment for denim—i.e., $13.8 million. Note that CO can assist Jeans West to meet the 25% ratio of "domestic labor costs to total costs." Charging $6.00 million for denim and receiving $19.8 million for jeans will result in the same $13.8 million margin, but will mean Jeans West will not meet the 25% test, as total costs will now be $13 million instead of $10 million. CO has to ensure it takes an arms-length in its approach to supply contracts and purchase contracts or else it may be accused by the Caribe government of assisting Jeans West avoid local taxes.

Note: Some students will ask whether Jeans West should be able to classify labor fringe benefits as domestic labor cost. This is not Roberts' domain given she is Controller of CO. Her concern with the Caribe tax rebate is whether CO is being "pressured" to adjust its billing amounts to facilitate Jeans West having a ratio of "domestic labor costs to total costs" exceeding 25%. If you want to discuss this issue, point out that labor fringe benefits are typically an integral part of labor costs. Hence, if they can be traced, Jeans West is justified by including them in domestic labor costs.

2.   There are a variety of ethical issues relating primarily to competence and integrity that Roberts faces:

(a)   Is CO assisting Jeans West to avoid income taxes in Caribe either
• by funneling $4.8 million to a Swiss company rather than to Jeans West in Caribe, or
• by understating both the $3.000 million denim supply cost and the $16.8 total revenue amount?

(b)   Is CO assisting senior executives of Jeans West to enrich themselves at the expense of the shareholders of Jeans West?

(c)   Are the accounting records of CO properly reflecting the underlying activities?

3.   Steps Roberts could take include:

(a)   Seeking further information on why the $4.8 million payment is being made to the Swiss subsidiary. This should be done first internally and then by speaking to Jeans West executives.

(b)   Ensure product design costs at CO reflect actual product design work. So-called "off-statement" items should be eliminated if no adequate explanation can be given for them.

(c)   Ensure CO personnel follow any company guidelines about supply relations or customer relations. There is nothing inherently wrong with assisting Jeans West negotiate a better insurance package for its executives. The concern is whether developing a "too cozy" relationship will lead to more questionable practices being overlooked.

CHAPTER 3
COST-VOLUME-PROFIT RELATIONSHIPS

3-2 Examples of revenue drivers other than units of output sold (or manufactured) are selling prices and the level of marketing costs.

3-4 **Operating income** is total revenues from operations for the accounting period minus total costs from operations (excluding income taxes):

Operating income = Total revenues – Total costs

Net income is operating income plus nonoperating revenues (such as interest revenue) minus nonoperating costs (such as interest cost) minus income taxes. Chapter 3 assumes nonoperating revenues and nonoperating costs are zero. Thus, Chapter 3 computes net income as:

Net income = Operating income – Income taxes

3-6 The assumptions underlying the CVP analysis outlined in Chapter 3 are:

1. Total costs can be divided into a fixed component and a component that is variable with respect to the level of output.
2. The behavior of total revenues and total costs is linear (straight-line) in relation to output units within the relevant range.
3. The unit selling price, unit variable costs, and fixed costs are known.
4. The analysis either covers a single product or assumes that a given revenue mix of products will remain constant as the level of total units sold changes.
5. All revenues and costs can be added and compared without taking into account the time value of money.

3-8 CVP certainly is simple, with its assumption of a single revenue driver, a single cost driver, and linear revenue and cost relationships. Whether these assumptions make it simplistic depends on the decision context. In some cases, these assumptions may be sufficiently accurate for CVP to provide useful insights. The examples in Chapter 3 (the software package context in the text and the travel agency example in the Problem for Self-Study) illustrate how CVP can provide such insights. In more complex cases, the general case can be used in a computer planning model.

3-10 **Contribution margin** is computed as revenues minus all costs that vary with respect to the output level.

   Gross margin is computed as revenues minus cost of goods sold.

   Contribution-margin percentage is the total contribution margin divided by revenues.

   Variable-cost percentage is the total variable costs (with respect to units of output) divided by revenues.

   Margin of safety is the excess of budgeted revenues over breakeven revenues.

3-12 Examples include:

   Manufacturing—subcontracting a component to a supplier on a per unit basis to avoid purchasing a machine with a high fixed depreciation cost.

   Marketing—changing a sales compensation plan from a fixed salary to percent of sales dollars basis.

   Customer service—hiring a subcontractor to do customer service on a per visit basis rather than an annual retainer basis.

3-14 A company with multiple products can compute a breakeven point by assuming there is a constant mix of products at different levels of total revenue.

3-16 (10 min.) **CVP computations.**

	Revenues	Variable Costs	Fixed Costs	Total Costs	Operating Income	Contribution Margin	Contribution Margin %
a.	$2,000	$ 500	$300	$ 800	$1,200	$1,500	75.0%
b.	2,000	1,500	300	1,800	200	500	25.0%
c.	1,000	700	300	1,000	0	300	30.0%
d.	1,500	900	300	1,200	300	600	40.0%

3-18 (15–20 min.) **CVP, changing revenues and costs.**

1. $\quad$ USP $\quad = \quad 8\% \times \$1,000 = \$80$
    $\quad$ UVC $\quad = \quad \$35\ (\$17 + \$18)$
    $\quad$ UCM $\quad = \quad \$45$
    $\quad$ FC $\quad = \quad \$22,000$ a month

(a) $\quad Q \quad = \quad \dfrac{FC}{UCM} \quad = \quad \dfrac{\$22,000}{\$45}$

$\qquad\qquad\quad = \quad 489$ tickets (rounded-up)

(b) $\quad Q \quad = \quad \dfrac{FC + TOI}{UCM} = \dfrac{\$22,000 + \$10,000}{\$45}$

$\qquad\qquad\qquad\quad = \quad \dfrac{\$32,000}{\$45}$

$\qquad\qquad\qquad\quad = \quad 712$ tickets (rounded up)

2. $\quad$ USP $\quad = \quad \$80$
    $\quad$ UVC $\quad = \quad \$29\ (\$17 + \$12)$
    $\quad$ UCM $\quad = \quad \$51$
    $\quad$ FC $\quad = \quad \$22,000$ a month

(a) $\quad Q \quad = \quad \dfrac{FC}{UCM} \quad = \quad \dfrac{\$22,000}{\$51}$

$\qquad\qquad\qquad\quad = \quad 432$ tickets (rounded-up)

(b) $\quad Q \quad = \quad \dfrac{FC + TOI}{UCM} = \dfrac{\$22,000 + \$10,000}{\$51}$

$\qquad\qquad\qquad\quad = \quad \dfrac{\$32,000}{\$51}$

$\qquad\qquad\qquad\quad = \quad 628$ tickets (rounded-up)

3-20 (20 min.) **CVP exercises.**

	Revenues	Variable Costs	Contribution Margin	Fixed Costs	Budgeted Operating Income
Orig.	$10,000,000[G]	$8,200,000[G]	$1,800,000	$1,700,000[G]	$100,000
1.	10,000,000	8,020,000	1,980,000	1,700,000	280,000
2.	10,000,000	8,380,000	1,620,000	1,700,000	(80,000)
3.	10,000,000	8,200,000	1,800,000	1,785,000	15,000
4.	10,000,000	8,200,000	1,800,000	1,615,000	185,000
5.	10,800,000	8,856,000	1,944,000	1,700,000	244,000
6.	9,200,000	7,544,000	1,656,000	1,700,000	(44,000)
7.	11,000,000	9,020,000	1,980,000	1,870,000	110,000
8.	10,000,000	7,790,000	2,210,000	1,785,000	425,000

[G] stands for given.

3-22 (5–10 min.)   **CVP, changing cost inputs.**

1.
$$\text{Revenues} - \begin{array}{c}\text{Variable}\\\text{Costs}\end{array} - \begin{array}{c}\text{Fixed}\\\text{Costs}\end{array} = \begin{array}{c}\text{Target}\\\text{Operating Income}\end{array}$$

Let Q = number of units to yield target operating income.
For target operating income of $0:

$$\begin{aligned}\$15Q - \$6Q - \$450 &= \$0\\ \$9Q &= \$450\\ Q &= 50 \text{ units}\end{aligned}$$

2.
$$\begin{aligned}\$15Q - \$5Q - \$450 &= \$0\\ \$10Q &= \$450\\ Q &= 45 \text{ units}\end{aligned}$$

3-24 (10 min.)   **CVP, international cost structure differences.**

1.

	Annual Fixed Costs	Selling Price	Variable Manuf. Costs per Sweater	Variable Mark/Dist Costs per Sweater	Unit Contrib. Margin	Breakeven Point in units
Singapore	$ 6,500,000	$32	$ 8.00	$11.00	$13	500,000
Thailand	4,500,000	32	5.50	11.50	15	300,000
U.S.	12,000,000	32	13.00	9.00	10	1,200,000

	(a) Breakeven point in units sold	(b) Breakeven point in revenues
Singapore	500,000	$16,000,000
Thailand	300,000	9,600,000
U.S.	1,200,000	38,400,000

2.

	Revenues	Variable Costs	Fixed Costs	Operating Income
Singapore	$25,600,000	$15,200,000	$6,500,000	$3,900,000
Thailand	25,600,000	13,600,000	4,500,000	7,500,000
U.S.	25,600,000	17,600,000	12,000,000	–4,000,000

Thailand has the lowest breakeven point—it has both the lowest fixed costs ($4,500,000) and the lowest variable cost per unit ($17.00). Hence, for a given selling price, Thailand will always have a higher operating income (or a lower operating loss) than Singapore or the U.S.

The U.S. breakeven point is 1,200,000 units. Hence, with sales of 800,000 units, it has an operating loss of $4,000,000.

3-26 (10–15 min.) **CVP, income taxes.**

1. Operating income $= $ Net income $\div$ (1 – tax rate)
$\qquad\qquad\qquad$ $= \$84,000 \div (1 - 0.40) \quad = \$140,000$

2. Contribution margin – Fixed costs = Operating income
Contribution margin – \$300,000 = \$140,000
Contribution margin = \$440,000

3. Revenues – 0.80 Revenues = Contribution margin
$\qquad\qquad$ 0.20 Revenues = \$440,000
$\qquad\qquad\qquad$ Revenues = \$2,200,000

4. Breakeven point = Fixed costs $\div$ Contribution margin percentage
Breakeven point = \$300,000 $\div$ 0.20
$\qquad\qquad\qquad$ = \$1,500,000

3-28 (15–20 min.) **Appendix, uncertainty, CVP**

1. King pays Foreman \$2 million plus \$4 (25% of \$16) for every home purchasing the pay-per-view. The expected value of the variable component is:

Demand (1)	Payment (2) = (1) × \$4	Probability (3)	Expected payment (4)
100,000	\$ 400,000	0.05	\$ 20,000
200,000	800,000	0.10	80,000
300,000	1,200,000	0.30	360,000
400,000	1,600,000	0.35	560,000
500,000	2,000,000	0.15	300,000
1,000,000	4,000,000	0.05	200,000
			\$1,520,000

The expected value of King's payment is \$3,520,000 (\$2,000,000 fixed fee + \$1,520,000).

2. USP $\;=\;$ \$16
UVC $\;=\;$ \$ 6 (\$4 payment to Foreman + \$2 variable cost)
UCM $=$ \$10
FC $\quad=\;$ \$2,000,000 + \$1,000,000 = \$3,000,000

$$Q \;=\; \frac{FC}{UCM}$$
$$\;=\; \frac{\$3,000,000}{\$10}$$
$$\;=\; 300,000$$

If 300,000 homes purchase the pay-per-view, King will break even.

3-30   (10 min.)   **CVP, movie production.**

1.   Fixed costs = $5,000,000 (production cost)
     Unit variable cost = $0.20 per $1 revenue (marketing fee)
     Unit contribution margin = $0.80 per $1 revenue

   (a) Breakeven point in revenues $= \dfrac{\text{Fixed costs}}{\text{Unit contribution margin per \$1 revenue}}$

$$= \frac{\$5,000,000}{\$0.80}$$

$$= \$6,250,000$$

   (b)   Royal Rumble receives 62.5% of box-office receipts. Box-office receipts of $10,000,000 translate to $6,250,000 in revenues to Royal Rumble.

2. | | |
     |---|---:|
     | Revenues, 0.625 × $300,000,000 | $187,500,000 |
     | Variable costs, 0.20 × $187,500,000 | 37,500,000 |
     | Contribution margin | 150,000,000 |
     | Fixed costs | 5,000,000 |
     | Operating income | $145,000,000 |

3-32   (30 min.)   **CVP, sensitivity analysis.**

1.   USP   = $30.00 × (1 − 0.30 margin to bookstore)
              = $30.00 × 0.70 = $21.00

     UVC   = $ 4.00   variable production and marketing cost
                  3.15   variable author royalty cost (0.15 × $30.00 × 0.70)
              $ 7.15

     UCM   = $21.00 − $7.15 = $13.85

     FC   = $ 500,000   fixed production and marketing cost
                  3,000,000   up-front payment to Washington
              $3,500,000

   Exhibit 3-32 A shows the PV graph.

EXHIBIT 3-32A
PV Graph for Media Publishers

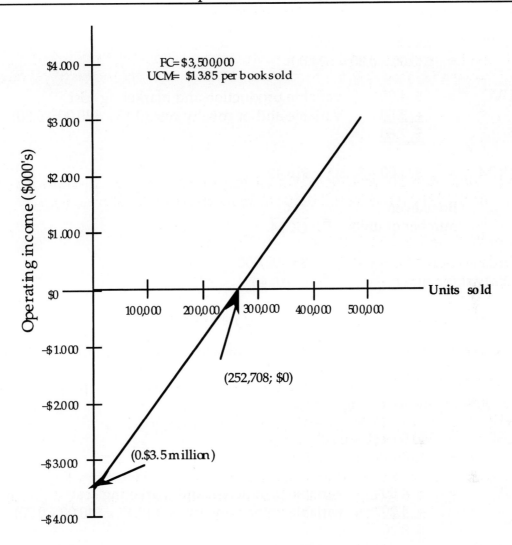

2. (a) Breakeven number of units

$$= \frac{FC}{UCM}$$

$$= \frac{\$3,500,000}{\$13.85}$$

$$= 252,708 \text{ copies sold (rounded)}$$

(b) Target OI

$$= \frac{FC + OI}{UCM}$$

$$= \frac{\$3,500,000 + \$2,000,000}{\$13.85}$$

$$= \frac{\$5,500,000}{\$13.85}$$

$$= 397,112 \text{ copies sold (rounded)}$$

3-32 (Cont'd

3. (a) Decreasing the normal bookstore margin to 20% of the listed bookstore price of $30 has the following effects:
3-32 (Cont'd.)

$$USP = \$30.00 \times (1 - 0.20)$$
$$= \$30.00 \times 0.80 = \$24.00$$

$$UVC = \begin{array}{l} \$\ 4.00 \\ +\ 3.60 \\ \hline \$\ 7.60 \end{array} \quad \begin{array}{l} \text{variable production and marketing cost} \\ \text{variable author royalty cost } (0.15 \times \$30.00 \times 0.80) \end{array}$$

$$UCM = \$24.00 - \$7.60 = \$16.40$$

$$\text{Breakeven number of units} = \frac{FC}{UCM}$$

$$= \frac{\$3,500,000}{\$16.40}$$

$$= 213,415 \text{ copies sold (rounded)}$$

The breakeven point decreases from 397,112 copies in requirement 2 to 213,415 copies.

(b) Increasing the listed bookstore price to $40 while keeping the bookstore margin at 30% has the following effects:

$$USP = \$40.00 \times (1 - 0.30)$$
$$= \$40.00 \times 0.70 = \$28.00$$

$$UVC = \begin{array}{l} \$\ 4.00 \\ +\ 4.20 \\ \hline \$\ 8.20 \end{array} \quad \begin{array}{l} \text{variable production and marketing cost} \\ \text{variable author royalty cost } (0.15 \times \$40.00 \times 0.70) \end{array}$$

$$UCM = \$28.00 - \$8.20 = \$19.80$$

$$\text{Breakeven number of units} = \frac{\$3,500,000}{\$19.80}$$

$$= 176,768 \text{ copies sold (rounded)}$$

The breakeven point decreases from 397,112 copies in requirement 2 to 176,768 copies.

3-34 (20–30 min.) **CVP, shoe stores.**

1. In number of pairs:

$$\frac{\text{Fixed costs}}{\text{Contribution margin per pair}} = \frac{\$360,000}{\$9.00} = 40,000 \text{ pairs}$$

In revenues:

$$\frac{\text{Fixed costs}}{\text{Contribution margin \% per dollar}} = \frac{\$360,000}{100\% - 70\%} = \$1,200,000$$

2.
Revenues, $30 × 35,000	$1,050,000
Variable costs, $21 × 35,000	735,000
Contribution margin	315,000
Fixed costs	360,000
Operating income (loss)	$ (45,000)

An alternative approach is that 35,000 units is 5,000 units below the breakeven point, and the unit contribution margin is $9.00:

$9.00 × 5,000 = $45,000 below the breakeven point

3. Fixed costs: $360,000 + $81,000 = $441,000
   Contribution margin per pair = $10.50

   (a) Breakeven point in units $= \dfrac{\$441,000}{\$10.50} = 42,000 \text{ pairs}$

   (b) Breakeven point in revenues = $30 × 42,000 = $1,260,000

4. Fixed costs = $360,000
   Contribution margin per pair = $8.70

   (a) Breakeven point in units $= \dfrac{\$360,000}{\$8.70} = 41,380 \text{ pairs (rounded up)}$

   (b) Breakeven point in revenues = $30 × 41,380 = $1,241,400

5. Breakeven point = 40,000 pairs
   Store manager receives commission on 10,000 pairs.
   Cost of commission = $0.30 × 10,000 = $3,000

Revenues, $30 × 50,000		$1,500,000
Variable costs:		
Cost of shoes	$975,000	
Salespeople commission	75,000	
Manager commission	3,000	1,053,000
Contribution margin		447,000
Fixed costs		360,000
Operating income		$ 87,000

An alternative approach is 10,000 units × $8.70 = $87,000.

3-36 (10-20 min.) **Sensitivity and inflation** (continuation of 3-35).

1. Revenues, $30 × 48,000 $1,440,000
                 $18 × 2,000   36,000 $1,476,000
    Variable costs:
        Goods sold $19.50 × 50,000   975,000
        Commission, 5% × $1,476,000   73,800   1,048,800
    Contribution margin   427,200
    Fixed costs   360,000
    Operating income $ 67,200

An alternative approach is:

    Contribution margin on 48,000 pairs × $9.00 $432,000
    Deduct negative contribution margin on unsold pairs,
        2,000 × [$18.00 − ($19.50 + $.90* commission)]   4,800
    Contribution margin   427,200
    Fixed costs   360,000
    Operating income $ 67,200

    *5% of $18.00 = $.90

2.   Optimal operating income, given perfect knowledge, would be the $432,000 contribution computed above, minus $360,000 fixed costs, or $72,000.

3.   The point of indifference is where the operating incomes are equal. Let X = unit cost per pair that would produce the identical operating income of $67,200. Then:

$$48,000[\$30.00 - (X + \$1.50)] - \$360,000 \ = \ \$ 67,200$$
$$48,000(\$28.50 - X) - \$360,000 \ = \ \$ 67,200$$
$$\$1,368,000 - 48,000X - \$360,000 \ = \ \$ 67,200$$
$$48,000X \ = \ \$940,800$$
$$X \ = \ \$19.60$$

Therefore, any rise in purchase cost in excess of $19.60 per pair increases the operating income benefit of signing the long-term contract.

In a short-cut solution, you could take the $4,800 difference between the "ideal" operating income (of $72,000) at the current cost per pair and the operating income under the contract (of $67,200) and divide it by 48,000 units to get 10 cents per pair difference.

3-38   (20–25 min.)   **Revenue mix, three products.**

1.   Operating income   = 80,000($2) + 100,000($3) + 20,000($6) – $406,000
     Operating income   = $160,000 + $300,000 + $120,000 – $406,000
     Operating income   = $174,000

   Let K = Number of units of Product K to break even
      5K = Number of units of Product J to break even
      4K = Number of units of Product H to break even

Revenues – Variable costs – Fixed costs	=	Zero operating income
Contribution margin – Fixed costs =		0
$2(4K) + $3(5K) + $6K – $406,000 =		0
$29K =		$406,000
K =		14,000 units of K
5K =		70,000 units of J
4K =		56,000 units of H
Total =		140,000 units

   The breakeven point is 14,000 K, 70,000 J and 56,000 H, a grand total of 140,000 units.

2.   Operating income would rise, because the higher-margin goods (K) would be substituting for lower-margin goods (J) in the sales mix:

   Operating income = 80,000($2) + 80,000($3) + 40,000($6) – $406,000
   Operating income = $160,000 + $240,000 + $240,000 – $406,000
   Operating income = $234,000

   Let K   = Number of units of Product K to break even
      2K = Number of units of J and H to break even

$2(2K) + $3(2K) +$6K – $406,000 =		0
$16K =		$406,000
K =		25,375 units of K
2K =		50,750 units of J
2K =		50,750 units of H
Total =		126,875 units

   The breakeven point of 140,000 units would decline to 25,375 K, 50,750 J, and 50,750 H, a grand total of 126,875 units.

3-40 (30 min.) **CVP, nonprofit event planning.**

1. Computation of fixed costs.

	Golf Club	Town Hall
Rental cost of venue	$2,000	$ 6,600
Chamber administration/marketing	3,500	3,500
Band	2,500	2,500
	$8,000	$12,600

Computation of contribution margin per person:

	Golf Club	Town Hall
Selling (ticket) price per person	$120	$120
Catering cost per person	80	60
Contribution margin per person	$ 40	$ 60

$$\text{Breakeven point} = \frac{\text{Fixed costs}}{\text{Unit contribution margin}}$$

$$\text{Breakeven point for Golf Club venue} = \frac{\$8,000}{\$40} = 200 \text{ tickets}$$

$$\text{Breakeven point for Town Hall venue} = \frac{\$12,600}{\$60} = 210 \text{ tickets}$$

2. Operating income = Revenues − Variable costs − Fixed costs

Let Q = Number of tickets sold
OI = Operating income

Golf Club Venue

$$OI = \$120Q - \$80Q - \$8,000$$

When Q = 150: OI = ($120 × 150) − ($80 × 150) − $8,000
= $18,000 − $12,000 − $8,000
= − $2,000

When Q = 300: OI = ($120 × 300) − ($80 × 300) − $8,000
= $36,000 − $24,000 − $8,000
= $4,000

Town Hall Venue

$$OI = \$120Q - \$60Q - \$12,600$$

When Q = 150: OI = ($120 × 150) − ($60 × 150) − $12,600
= $18,000 − $9,000 − $12,600
= − $3,600

When Q = 300: OI = ($120 × 300) − ($60 × 300) − $12,600
= $36,000 − $18,000 − $12,600
= $5,400

3-40 (Cont'd.)

      The Golf Club venue has higher variable costs per person and lower fixed costs. In contrast, the Town Hall venue has lower variable costs per person and higher fixed costs.

3.   Requirement 2 gives the operating income equation for each venue. Setting these two equations equal and solving for Q, gives 230 as the level of ticket sales at which the operating incomes for the two venues are equal:

$$
\begin{aligned}
\$120Q - \$80Q - \$8{,}000 &= \$120Q - \$60Q - \$12{,}600 \\
\$40Q - \$60Q &= \$8{,}000 - \$12{,}600 \\
\$20Q &= \$4{,}600 \\
Q &= 230
\end{aligned}
$$

Above 230, the Town Hall venue will yield higher operating income than the Golf Club venue.

3-42 (30-40 min.) **CVP, Income taxes.**

1. Revenues – Variable costs – Fixed costs = $\dfrac{\text{Target net income}}{1 - \text{Tax rate}}$

   Let X = Net income for 19_7

   $$20{,}000(\$25.00) - 20{,}000(\$13.75) - \$135{,}000 = \dfrac{X}{1 - 0.40}$$

   $$\$500{,}000 - \$275{,}000 - \$135{,}000 = \dfrac{X}{0.60}$$

   $$\$300{,}000 - \$165{,}000 - \$81{,}000 = X$$

   $$X = \$54{,}000$$

2. Let Q = Number of units to break even

   $$\$25.00Q - \$13.75Q - \$135{,}000 = 0$$

   $$Q = \$135{,}000 \div \$11.25 = 12{,}000 \text{ units}$$

3. Let X = Net income for 19_8

   $$22{,}000(\$25.00) - 22{,}000(\$13.75) - (\$135{,}000 + \$11{,}250) = \dfrac{X}{1 - 0.40}$$

   $$\$550{,}000 - \$302{,}500 - \$146{,}250 = \dfrac{X}{0.60}$$

   $$\$101{,}250 = \dfrac{X}{0.60}$$

   X = $60,7504. Let Q = Number of units to break even with new fixed costs of $146,250

   $$\$25.00Q - \$13.75Q - \$146{,}250 = 0$$

   $$Q = \$146{,}250 \div \$11.25 = 13{,}000 \text{ units}$$

   $$\text{Revenues} = 13{,}000(\$25.00) = \$325{,}000$$

   Alternatively, the computation could be $146,250 divided by the contribution margin percentage of 45% to obtain $325,000.

5. Let S = Required sales units to equal 19_7 net income

   $$\$25.00S - \$13.75S - \$146{,}250 = \dfrac{\$54{,}000}{0.6}$$

   $$\$11.25S = \$236{,}250$$

   $$S = 21{,}000 \text{ units}$$

   $$\text{Revenues} = 21{,}000 \text{ units} \times \$25.00 = \$525{,}000$$

6. Let A = Amount spent for advertising in 19_8

   $$\$550{,}000 - \$302{,}500 - (\$135{,}000 + A) = \dfrac{\$60{,}000}{0.6}$$

   $$\$550{,}000 - \$302{,}500 - \$135{,}000 - A = \$100{,}000$$

   $$\$550{,}000 - \$537{,}500 = A$$

   $$A = \$12{,}500$$

3-44   (20-30 min.)   **Appendix, CVP under uncertainty.**

1.   (a)   At a selling price of $100, the unit contribution margin is ($100 − $50) = $50, and it will require the sale of ($200,000 ÷ $50) = 4,000 units to break even. The sales in dollars is $400,000 and there is a 2/3 probability of equaling or exceeding this sales level.

1.   (b)   At a selling price of $70, the unit contribution margin is ($70 − $50) = $20, and it will require the sale of ($200,000 ÷ $20) = 10,000 units to break even. At the lower price, this sales in dollars is $700,000 and there is a 2/3 probability of equaling or exceeding this sales volume.

Therefore, if you seek to maximize the probability of showing an operating income, you are indifferent between the two strategies.

2. $$\text{Expected operating income} = \left[\left(\text{Selling price per unit} - \text{Variable costs per unit}\right) \times \left(\text{Expected sales level}\right)\right] - \left(\text{Fixed costs}\right)$$

<u>At a selling price of $100</u>:

      Expected revenues   = $450,000 ($100 × 4,500)

      Expected operating income = [($100 − $50) × 4,500] − $200,000
                                        = $25,000

<u>At a selling price of $70</u>:

      Expected revenues   = $750,000 ($70 × 10,715)

      Expected operating income = [($70 − $50) × 10,715] − $200,000
                                          = $14,300

A selling price of $100 will maximize the expected operating income.

3-46 (20–25 min.) **Ethics, CVP, cost analysis.**

1. (a) USP = $55
        UVC = $22 ($14 + $8)
        UCM = $33
        FC   = $20,000,000

        $$Q = \frac{FC}{UCM} = \frac{\$20,000,000}{\$33}$$

           = 606,061 monthly treatments (rounded up)

    (b) USP = $55
        UVC = $14
        UCM = $41
        FC   = $20,000,000

        $$Q = \frac{FC}{UCM} = \frac{\$20,000,000}{\$41}$$

           = 487,805 monthly treatments (rounded up)

2.   Allen believes that $8 per monthly visit should be included in the variable costs per visit. His argument is that a product like "Vital Hair" has a positive probability of attracting product litigation. By excluding any allowance for the possible event, the assumption is that it will be zero.

      Allen faces an integrity issue. His report to the Executive Committee will understate his expected cost estimates when he takes Kelly's advice. His report likely will be seen by those not attending the Executive Committee meeting. Moreover, even those attending the meeting may not remember any verbal comments Allen makes at the meeting.

      One possibility Allen should have explored is reporting the $14 per treatment variable cost in the breakeven computations but also include qualifications in the report about possible product litigation costs.

3.   Allen likely has been placed in a compromised situation. He may feel Kelly deliberately set him up to avoid the $8 amount being reported to the Executive Committee. At a minimum, he should directly confront Kelly with his concerns. If she is unresponsive, he faces a very tough dilemma. His options are:

(a)   Stay in his current position and be more determined next time to have his concerns registered.
(b)   Report his concerns to Kelly's immediate superior.
(c)   Resign

If he selects (a), it would be useful to show Kelly the *Standards of Ethical Conduct for Management Accountants* and stress how her behavior has put him in a difficult ethical situation.

CHAPTER 4
COSTING SYSTEMS AND ACTIVITY-BASED COSTING (1):
SERVICE AND MERCHANDISING APPLICATIONS

4-2 No. For most service-sector companies, labor is the single largest cost category. For example, labor costs comprise over 70% of the total costs of many law firms.

4-4 An advertising campaign for Pepsi is likely to be very specific to that individual client. Job costing enables all the specific aspects of each job to be identified. In contrast, the processing of checking account withdrawals is similar for many customers. Here, process costing can be used to compute the cost of each checking account withdrawal.

4-6 An accounting firm can use job cost information (a) to determine the profitability of individual jobs, (b) to assist in bidding on future jobs, and (c) to evaluate professionals who are in charge of managing individual jobs.

4-8 Two reasons for using six-month or annual budget periods are:
a. The numerator reason—the longer the time period, the less the influence of seasonal patterns, and
b. The denominator reason—the longer the time period, the less the effect of variations in output levels on the allocation of fixed costs.

4-10 *Peanut-butter costing* describes a costing approach that uses broad averages to uniformly assign the cost of resources to cost objects when the individual products, services, or customers in fact use those resources in a nonuniform way.

One way of determining if peanut-butter costing is occurring is to separately examine how individual products (services, customers, etc.) use the resources of the organization and to compare the results with the way the accounting system represents that usage.

4-12 *Costing system refinement* means making changes to an existing costing system that results in a better measure of the way that jobs, products, customers, and so on differentially use the resources of the organization.

Three guidelines for refinement are:
a. Classify as many of the total costs as direct costs as is economically feasible.
b. Select the number of indirect cost pools on the basis of homogeneity.
c. Use cost drivers as the chosen allocation bases.

4-14   Increasing the number of indirect-cost pools does NOT guarantee increased accuracy of product, service, or customer costs. If the existing cost pool is already homogeneous, increasing the number of cost pools will not increase accuracy. If the existing cost pool is not homogeneous, accuracy will increase only if the increased cost pools themselves increase in homogeneity vis-a-vis the single cost pool.

4-16   (20-30 min.) **Job costing; fill in the blanks.**
Key to filling in the unknowns on the Hogsbreath job is to follow Exhibit 4-4:

	Actual Costing		Normal Costing		Extended Normal Costing	
Direct job costs	$3,850	($55 × 70)	$3,850	($55 × 70)	$4,200	($60 × 70)
Indirect job costs	2,660	($38 × 70)	2,800	($40 × 70)	2,800	($40 × 70)
Total job costs	$6,510		$6,650		$7,000	

The road map to computing these amounts is (g = given)

$$\$3{,}850^{⑤} \; (\$55^{g} \times 70^{g}) \qquad \$3{,}850^{⑥} \; (\$55^{g} \times 70^{g}) \qquad \$4{,}200^{③} \; (\$60^{④} \times 70^{g})$$

$$\$2{,}660^{g} \; (\$38^{⑦} \times 70^{g}) \qquad \$2{,}800 \; (\$40^{①} \times 70^{g}) \qquad \$2{,}800^{②} \; (\$40^{②} \times 70^{g})$$

① Budgeted indirect cost rate (NC) = $2,800 ÷ 70 = $40 per hour
② $2,800 ($40 × 70)—same as for indirect job costs for normal costing
③ Direct job costs (ENC) = $4,200 ($7,000^{g} – $2,800^{②})
④ Budgeted direct cost rate (ENC) = $60 ($4,200^{③} ÷ 70^{g})
⑤ Direct job costs (AC) = $3,850 ($55^{g} × 70^{g})
⑥ Direct job costs (NC) = $3,850 ($55 × 70^{g})—same as for direct job costs for actual costing.
⑦ Indirect job costs (AC) = $38.00 ($2,660^{g} ÷ 70^{g})

2.   From requirement 1, we have calculated:

	Actual Rate	Budgeted Rate
Direct cost rate	$55	$60
Indirect cost rate	38	40

Hence, the unknowns for McBain for 19_8 are:

	Actual Amounts for 19_8	Budgeted Amounts for 19_8
Consulting labor compensation	$1,155,000	$1,080,000
Consulting labor hours	21,000 hours	18,000 hours
Consulting support costs	$798,000	$720,000

4-16 (cont'd)

The road map to computing these amounts is:

$\$1,155,000^{\text{②}}$ $21,000 \text{ hours}^{\text{①}}$ $\$798,000^{g}$	$\$1,080,000^{\text{③}}$ $18,000^{g}$ $\$720,000^{\text{④}}$

①   Consulting labor hours (A)   = $\$798,000^{g} \div \$38$

②   Consulting labor compensation (A)   = $\$1,155,000 \ (\$55 \times 21,000^{\text{①}})$

③   Consulting labor compensation (B)   = $\$1,080,000 \ (\$60 \times 18,000^{g})$

④   Consulting support costs (B)   = $\$720,000 \ (\$40 \times 18,000^{g})$

An overview of the McBain job-costing system is:

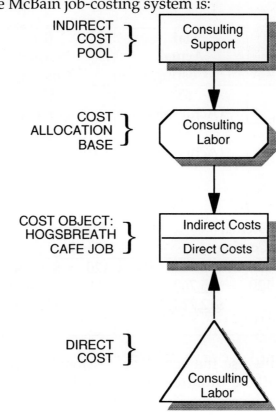

4-18   (20-30 min.) **Job costing; actual, normal, and extended normal costing.**

1.   Actual direct cost rate = $58 per professional labor-hour

Actual indirect cost rate $= \dfrac{\$744,000}{15,500 \text{ hours}} =$ $48 per professional labor-hour

Budgeted direct cost rate $= \dfrac{\$960,000}{16,000 \text{ hours}} =$ $60 per professional labor-hour

Budgeted indirect cost rate $= \dfrac{\$720,000}{16,000 \text{ hours}} =$ $45 per professional labor-hour

	(a) Actual Costing	(b) Normal Costing	(c) Extended Normal Costing
Direct Cost Rate	$58 (Actual rate)	$58 (Actual rate)	$60 (Budgeted rate)
Indirect Cost Rate	$48 (Actual rate)	$45 (Budgeted rate)	$45 (Budgeted rate)

2.

	(a) Actual Costing	(b) Normal Costing	(c) Extended Normal Costing
Direct Costs	$58 × 120 = $ 6,960	$58 × 120 = $ 6,960	$60 × 120 = $ 7,200
Indirect Costs	48 × 120 = 5,760	45 × 120 = 5,400	45 × 120 = 5,400
Total Job Costs	$12,720	$12,360	$12,600

All three costing systems use the actual professional labor time of 120 hours. The budgeted 110 hours for the Montreal Expos audit job is not used in job costing. However, Chirac may have used the 110 hour number in bidding for the audit.

The actual costing figure of $12,720 exceeds the normal costing figure of $12,360, because the actual indirect cost rate ($48) exceeds the budgeted indirect cost rate ($45). The normal costing figure of $12,360 is less than the extended normal costing figure of $12,600, because the actual direct cost rate ($58) is less than the budgeted direct cost rate ($60).

4-18 (Cont'd.)

An overview of the Chirac job-costing system is:

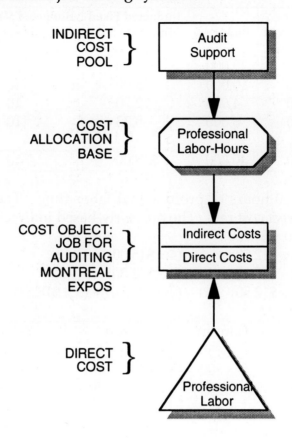

4-20 (20-30 min.) **Computing indirect-cost rates, job costing.**

1.

a.

	Budgeted Fixed Indirect Costs	Budgeted Hours	Budgeted Fixed Indirect Cost Rate Per Hour	Budgeted Variable Indirect Cost Rate Per Hour	Budgeted Total Indirect Cost Rate Per Hour
Jan.-March	$50,000	20,000	$ 2.50	$10	$12.50
April-June	50,000	10,000	5.00	10	15.00
July-Sept.	50,000	4,000	12.50	10	22.50
Oct.-Dec.	50,000	6,000	8.33	10	18.33
b.	$200,000	40,000	$ 5.00	$10	$15.00

2a. All four jobs use 10 hours of professional labor time. The only difference in job costing is the indirect cost rate. The quarterly-based indirect job cost rates are:

Hansen:	$(10 \times \$12.50)$	=		$125.00
Kai:	$(6 \times \$12.50)$	$+ \quad (4 \times \$15.00)$	=	$135.00
Patera:	$(4 \times \$15.00)$	$+ \quad (6 \times \$22.50)$	=	$195.00
Stevens:	$(5 \times \$12.50)$	$+ \quad (2 \times \$22.50) + (3 \times \$18.33)$	=	$162.50

	Hansen	**Kai**	**Patera**	**Stevens**
Revenues, 65×10	$650	$650	$650	$650.00
Direct costs, 30×10	300	300	300	300.00
Indirect costs	125	135	195	162.50
Total costs	425	435	495	462.50
Operating income	$225	$215	$155	$187.50

b. Using annual-based indirect job cost rates, all four customers will have the same operating income:

Revenues, 65×10	$650
Direct costs, 30×10	300
Indirect costs, 15×10	150
Total costs	450
Operating income	$200

3. All four jobs use 10 hours of professional labor time. Using the quarterly-based indirect cost rates, there are four different operating incomes as the work done on them is completed in different quarters. In contrast, using the annual indirect cost rate, all four customers have the same operating income. All these different operating income figures for jobs with the same number of professional labor-hours are due to the allocation of fixed indirect costs.

An overview of the Tax Assist job-costing system is:

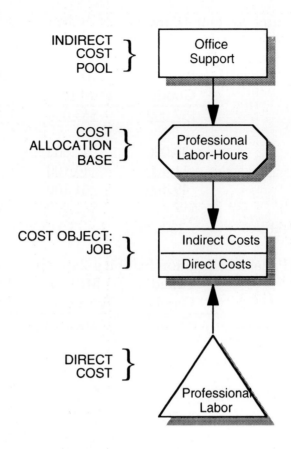

4-22 (15-20 min.) **Computing direct-cost rates, consulting firm.**

1. and 2.

	(a) Average Salary + Average Fringe Benefits	(b) Billable Time For Clients	(c) Total Time	(d) = (a) ÷ (b) Rate Per Billable Hour	(e)=(a)÷(c) Rate Per Total Hour
Director	$200,000	1,600	2,000	$125.00	$100
Partner	150,000	1,600	2,000	93.75	75
Associate	80,000	1,600	2,000	50.00	40
Assistant	50,000	1,600	2,000	31.25	25

3. The difference between requirements 1 and 2 is the denominator. Using only billable time as the denominator results in the hours associated with vacation, sick leave, and professional development being built into the direct cost rate for professional labor.

Including vacation, sick leave, and professional development in the denominator results in part of the total labor compensation not being assigned to jobs as part of the professional labor cost. In most cases where this approach is used, the costs associated with vacation, sick leave, and professional development are included in the indirect costs assigned to jobs.

4-24 (30 min.) **ABC, retail product-line profitability.**

1. The previous costing system (Panel A of Solution Exhibit 4-24) reports the following:

	Baked Goods	Milk & Fruit Juice	Frozen Products	Total
Revenues	$57,000	$63,000	$52,000	$172,000
Costs				
Cost of goods sold	38,000	47,000	35,000	120,000
Store support	11,400	14,100	10,500	36,000
Total costs	49,400	61,100	45,500	156,000
Operating income	$ 7,600	$ 1,900	$ 6,500	$ 16,000
Operating income ÷ Revenues	13.33%	3.02%	12.50%	9.30%

2. The ABC system (Panel B of Solution Exhibit 4-24) reports the following:

	Baked Goods	Milk & Fruit Juice	Frozen Products	Total
Revenues	$57,000	$63,000	$52,000	$172,000
Costs				
Cost of goods sold	38,000	47,000	35,000	120,000
Ordering	3,000	2,500	1,300	6,800
Delivery	7,840	2,880	2,240	12,960
Shelf-stocking	3,660	3,320	480	7,460
Customer support	3,100	4,100	1,580	8,780
Total costs	55,600	59,800	40,600	156,000
Operating income	$ 1,400	$ 3,200	$11,400	$ 16,000
Operating income ÷ Revenues	2.46%	5.08%	21.92%	9.30%

These activity costs are based on the following:

Activity	Cost Allocation Rate	Baked Goods	Milk & Fruit Juice	Frozen Products
Ordering	$100 per purchase order	30	25	13
Delivery	$80 per delivery	98	36	28
Shelf-stocking	$20 per hour	183	166	24
Customer support	$0.20 per item sold	15,500	20,500	7,900

The rankings of products in terms of relative profitability are:

	Previous Costing System		ABC System	
1.	Baked goods	13.33%	Frozen products	21.92%
2.	Frozen products	12.50	Milk & fruit juice	5.08
3.	Milk & fruit juice	3.02	Baked goods	2.46

The percentage revenue, COGS, and activity costs for each product-line are:

	Baked Goods	Milk & Fruit Juice	Frozen Products	Total
Revenues	33.14	36.63	30.23	100.00
COGS	31.67	39.17	29.16	100.00
Activity areas:				
Ordering	44.12	36.76	19.12	100.00
Delivery	60.49	22.22	17.28	100.00
Shelf-stocking	49.06	44.50	6.44	100.00
Customer support	35.31	46.70	17.99	100.00

3.   The baked good line drops sizably in profitability when the ABC is used. Although it constitutes 31.67% of COGS, it uses a higher % of total resources in each activity area, especially the high cost delivery activity area. In contrast, frozen products draws a much lower % of total resources used in each activity area than its % of total COGS. Hence, under ABC, frozen products is much more profitable.

Family Supermarkets may want to explore ways to increase sales of frozen products. It may also want to explore price increases on baked goods.

4-24 (Cont'd)

SOLUTION EXHIBIT 4-24

Product-Costing Overviews of Family Supermarkets

PANEL A: PREVIOUS COSTING SYSTEM

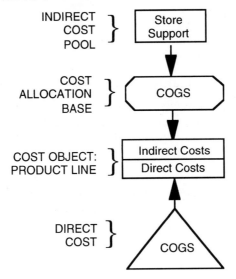

PANEL B: ABC COSTING SYSTEM

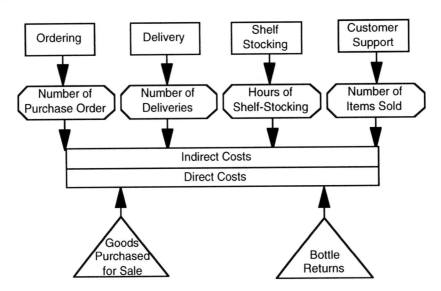

4-26   (20-35 min.) **Job costing, engineering consulting firm.**

1.

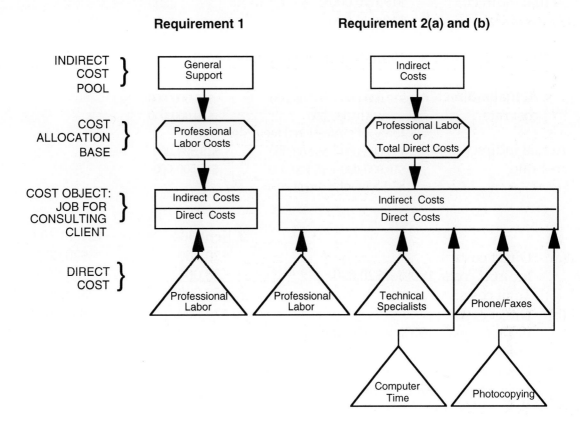

4-26 (Cont'd)

$$\text{Actual indirect cost rate} = \frac{\$19,000,000}{\$10,000,000}$$

$$= \text{190\% of professional labor-dollars.}$$

2. (a) $\text{Actual indirect cost rate} = \frac{\$19,000,000 - \$5,500,000}{\$10,000,000} = \frac{\$13,500,000}{\$10,000,000}$

$\qquad = \text{135\% of professional labor-dollars}$

(b) $\text{Actual indirect cost rate} = \frac{\$19,000,000 - \$5,500,000}{\$10,000,000 + \$5,500,000} = \frac{\$13,500,000}{\$15,500,000}$

$\qquad = \text{87.1\% of total direct costs}$

			Client 304	Client 308
3.	(a)	Direct costs	$20,000	$20,000
		Indirect costs, 190% × $20,000	38,000	38,000
		Total costs	$58,000	$58,000
	(b)	Direct costs	$26,000	$34,000
		Indirect costs, 135% × $20,000	27,000	27,000
		Total costs	$53,000	$61,000
	(c)	Direct costs	$26,000	$34,000
		Indirect costs, 87.1% × direct costs	22,646	29,614
		Total costs	$48,646	$63,614

			Client 304	Client 308
4.				
	(a)	Total costs	$58,000	$58,000
		Billings, 120% × total costs	69,600	69,600
	(b)	Total costs	$53,000	$61,000
		Billings, 120% × total costs	63,600	73,200
	(c)	Total costs	$48,646	$63,614
		Billings, 120% × total costs	58,375	76,337

5. Three guidelines for costing system refinement are:
   (i)   Direct cost tracing. Costing systems (b) and (c) increase the % of total costs that are directly traced to the cost object. Other things being equal, (b) or (c) is preferred to (a).
   (ii) Indirect cost pools. Costing systems (b) and (c) have the same single indirect cost pool, and, hence, this guideline does not assist in choosing between them.
   (iii) Cost allocation bases. Analysis could be made of whether professional labor costs or total direct costs is the cost driver of the costs in the indirect cost pool. Note that this analysis may lead to more than one indirect cost pool being selected. That is, costing system (b) and (c) may be further refined.

4-28 (15-20 min.) **Job costing, law firm.**

1.

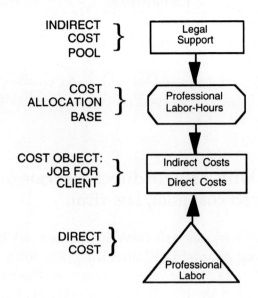

2.

Budgeted professional labor-hour direct cost rate	=	$\dfrac{\text{Budgeted total direct labor compensation}}{\text{Budgeted total direct labor-hours}}$
	=	$\dfrac{\$104,000}{1,600 \text{ hours}}$
	=	\$65 per professional labor-hour

3.

Budgeted indirect cost rate	=	$\dfrac{\text{Budgeted total costs in indirect cost pool}}{\text{Budgeted total professional labor-hours}}$
	=	$\dfrac{\$2,200,000}{1,600 \text{ hours} \times 25}$
	=	$\dfrac{\$2,200,000}{40,000 \text{ hours}}$
	=	\$55 per professional labor-hour

4-28 (Cont'd.)

4.	Richardson	Punch
Direct costs:		
Professional labor, $65 × 100;150	$ 6,500	$ 9,750
Indirect costs:		
Legal support, $55 × 100; 150	5,500	8,250
	$12,000	$18,000

4-30 (15-20 min.) **Job costing with a single direct-cost category, single indirect cost pool, law firm.**

1.   Pricing decisions at Wigan Associates are heavily influenced by reported cost numbers. Suppose Wigan is bidding against Hull and Kingston for a client with a job similar to that of Widnes Coal. If the costing system overstates the costs of these jobs, Wigan may bid too high and fail to land the client. If the costing system understates the costs of these jobs, Wigan may bid low, land the client, and then lose money in handling the case.

2.   Panel A of Solution Exhibit 4-30/4-31/4-32 at the end of this question presents an overview of the single direct/single indirect (SD/SI) costing approach

3.	Widnes Coal	St. Helens Glass	Total
Direct professional labor,			
$70 × 104; 96	$ 7,280	$ 6,720	$14,000
Indirect costs allocated,			
$105 × 104; 96	10,920	10,080	21,000
Total costs to be billed	$18,200	$16,800	$35,000

SOLUTION EXHIBIT 4-30/4-31/4-32
Alternative Job-Costing Approaches for Wigan Associates*

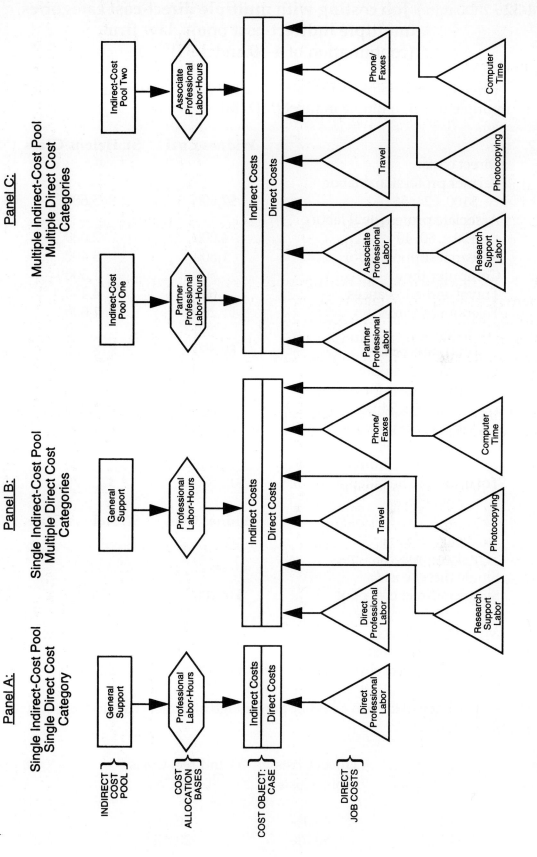

Panel A:
Single Indirect-Cost Pool
Single Direct Cost
Category

Panel B:
Single Indirect-Cost Pool
Multiple Direct Cost
Categories

Panel C:
Multiple Indirect-Cost Pool
Multiple Direct Cost
Categories

*Job = case

4-32 (30 min.) **Job costing with multiple direct-cost categories, multiple indirect-cost pools, law firm.**
(continuation of 4-30 and 4-31)

1. Panel C of the Solution Exhibit to 4-30/4-31/4-32 presents the costing overview for the multiple direct/multiple indirect (MD/MI) approach.

2.

	Widnes Coal	St. Helens Glass	Total
Direct costs:			
Partner professional labor,			
$100 × 24; 56	$2,400	$ 5,600	$ 8,000
Associate professional labor,			
$50 × 80; 40	4,000	2,000	6,000
Research support labor	1,600	3,400	5,000
Computer time	500	1,300	1,800
Travel and allowances	600	4,400	5,000
Telephones/faxes	200	1,000	1,200
Photocopying	250	750	1,000
Total direct costs	$9,550	$18,450	$28,000
Indirect costs allocated:			
Indirect costs for partners,			
$57.50 × 24; 56	1,380	3,220	4,600
Indirect costs for associates,			
$20 × 80; 40	1,600	800	2,400
Total indirect costs	2,980	4,020	7,000
Total costs to be billed	$12,530	$22,470	$35,000

	Widnes Coal	St. Helens Glass	Total
Summary of data:			
SD/SI Approach			
Single direct cost/			
Single indirect cost pool	$18,200	$16,800	$35,000
MD/MI Approach			
Multiple direct costs/			
Multiple indirect cost pools	$12,530	$22,470	$35,000

The MD/MI approach has a higher percentage of direct costs to total costs than does the SD/SI approach:

	Direct Costs / Total Costs	Indirect Costs / Total Costs
SD/SI	40.0%	60.0%
MD/MI	80.0%	20.0%

4-32 (Cont'd.)

The higher the percentage of costs directly traced to each case, the more accurate the product cost of each individual case.

The Widnes and St. Helens cases differ in how they use "resource areas" of Wigan Associates:

	Widnes Coal	St. Helens Glass
Partner professional labor	30.0%	70.0%
Associate professional labor	66.7	33.3
Research support labor	32.0	68.0
Computer time	27.8	72.2
Travel and allowances	12.0	88.0
Telephones/faxes	16.7	83.3
Photocopying	25.0	75.0

The Widnes Coal case makes relatively low use of the higher-cost partners but relatively higher use of the lower-cost associates than does St. Helens Glass. The Widnes Coal case also makes relatively lower use of the support labor, computer time, travel, phones/faxes, and photocopying resource areas than does the St. Helens Glass case.

The SD/SI approach imposes an averaging of the resources used in several (or all) of the seven "resource areas" recognized in MD/MI. The assumed use of resources in each of the seven "resource areas" by the SD/SI and MD/MI approaches are:

	SD/SI		MD/MI	
	Widnes	St. Helens	Widnes	St.Helens
Partners prof. labor	52.0%	48.0%	30.0%	70.0%
Associate prof. labor	52.0	48.0	66.7	33.3
Research support labor	52.0	48.0	32.0	68.0
Computer time	52.0	48.0	27.8	72.2
Travel and allowances	52.0	48.0	12.0	88.0
Telephones/faxes	52.0	48.0	16.7	83.3
Photocopying	52.0	48.0	25.0	75.0

3.   The specific areas where the MD/MI approach can provide better information for decisions at Wigan Associates include:

a.   *Pricing and product (case) emphasis decisions.* In a bidding situation using SD/SI data, Wigan may win legal cases on which it will subsequently lose money. It may also not win legal cases on which it would make money with a lower-priced bid. MD/MI signals to senior managers those legal cases that are the most profitable; these signals can be used in decisions where Wigan should increase their business development efforts.

4-32 (Cont'd.)

From a strategic viewpoint, SD/SI exposes Wigan Associates to cherry-picking by competitors. Other law firms may focus exclusively on Widnes Coal-type cases and take sizable amounts of "profitable" business from Wigan Associates. MD/MI reduces the likelihood of Wigan Associates losing cases on which they would have made money.

b. *Client relationships.* MD/MI provides a better "road map" for clients to understand how costs are accumulated at Wigan Associates. Wigan can use this road map when meeting with clients to plan the work to be done on a case <u>before</u> it commences. Clients can negotiate ways to get a lower-cost case from Wigan, given the information in MD/MI—for example, (a) use a higher proportion of associate labor time and a lower proportion of a partner time, and (b) use fax machines more and air travel less. If clients are informed in advance how costs will be accumulated, there is less likelihood of disputes about bills submitted to them <u>after</u> the work is done.

c. *Cost control.* The MD/MI approach better highlights the individual cost areas at Wigan Associates than does the SD/SI approach:

	MD/MI	SD/SI
Number of direct cost categories	7	1
Number of indirect cost categories	2	1
Total	9	2

MD/MI is more likely to promote better cost-control practices than SD/SI (as the nine cost categories in MD/MI may differ in terms of how to effectively manage costs).

4-34   (30 min.) **Legal billing practices, ethics.**

1.   The $250 rate was based on budgeted 19_7 compensation for Smith of $500,000 divided by 2,000 budgeted hours. The actual cost rate for Smith in 19_7 is:

$$\frac{\text{Actual compensation}}{\text{Actual hours worked}}$$

There are differences of opinion as to both the numerator and the denominator.

Numerator: Smith is paid $500,000 plus a $1 million bonus. The bonus could be due to many factors including his high-revenue billings, his attraction of major clients, or his being the founder of the firm. Presumably the government auditor will exclude the bonus payment as being not related to government work. However, the total $1.6 million may be what is required to retain Smith, and thus some would view this as total compensation.

4-34 (Cont'd.)

Denominator: The budgeted number of hours of 2,000 is relatively high for a senior partner of a law firm. New client development, upgrading of skills, and vacations/sick-leave all typically cause hours charged to clients to be below 2,000 per year (50 weeks × 40 hours per week). However, in Smith's case, he billed clients for 5,000 hours. As off-scale as this amount seems (365 days a year × 13.7 hours per day = 5,000), it is based on an actual situation.

Main Alternatives

(a)   Using the $600,000 numerator and the 5,000-hour denominator gives a labor cost rate of $120 per hour for Smith:

Billings to Department of Commerce
$120 × 1.60 × 125 hours = $24,000

(b)   Using the $600,000 numerator and the 2,000-hour denominator gives a labor cost rate of $300 per hour for Smith:

Billings to Department of Commerce
$300 × 1.60 × 125 hours = $60,000

The government auditor likely will argue for the $120 per hour rate. Smith may feel that this approach penalizes the firm for his well-above-average workload.

2.   Adams should raise several issues with Young. A key area is competence. Young's approach to reimbursing Smith is not in keeping with professional standards. Smith provides no documentation for individual line items on the credit card monthly bill. The appropriate approach is to require each reimbursable expenditure to be documented with some receipt (except for minor items, say, below $25, that are often reimbursed without documentation). Young is exposing the law firm to a third-party audit showing Smith charging many personal items to the firm and its clients.

Adams also should discuss integrity and objectivity concerns. If Young is in charge of developing job bills from Smith's time sheets, she should have observed his billing more than 24 hours a day on some days. On at least 20 days, Smith billed (in total) 30 hours per day across several clients. This she knows is overbilling. Her explanation that "she felt Smith's time was best spent on billable hours for clients rather than on justifying individual expense accounts" is unacceptable. A government audit would exclude many expenses Smith may have been reimbursed for without better justification.

Overbilling and very loose reimbursement practices can bring much disrepute onto Smith and Frank if it is discovered.

3.   Adams needs to be very direct and firm with Smith. The integrity of Smith and Frank is at stake. Any publicity about overbilling can cause some existing clients to leave and cause many potential clients to not consider Smith and Frank.

Adam should ask Smith to document his billing in more detail and to explain how he can bill 30 hours per day. He also must ask Smith to adequately document his expenses. No longer will it be appropriate to use the current "loose" practice of reimbursement of all but identified personal expenses. If Smith does not give adequate explanations, Adams must call a meeting of all partners to discuss whether Smith should be asked to resign. Moreover, there is also the troublesome issue of repaying clients of Smith for his potential overbilling.

CHAPTER 5
COSTING SYSTEMS AND ACTIVITY-BASED COSTING (2): MANUFACTURING APPLICATIONS

5-2   Examples of specific manufacturing overhead cost items are indirect manufacturing labor, plant engineer salaries, indirect materials, depreciation on plant and equipment, and energy costs.

5-4   The two major goals of a job-costing system are (i) to assist in the cost management of departments, and (ii) to determine the cost of individual jobs.

5-6   Credit entries to the Materials Control general ledger represent decreases in materials inventory. One set of credit entries is for transfers of direct materials to a Work-in-Process Control account. Another set of credit entries is for transfers of indirect materials to a Manufacturing Overhead Control.

5-8   Underallocation or overallocation of indirect (overhead) costs can arise because of: (a) Numerator reason—the actual overhead costs differ from the budgeted overhead costs, and (b) Denominator reason—the actual quantity used of the allocation base differs from the budgeted quantity.

5-10   The adjusted allocation rate approach results in the most accurate record of individual job costs. It also gives the same ending balances of work in process, finished goods, and cost of goods sold that would have been reported had an actual indirect-cost rate been used. Proration approaches do not make any adjustment to individual job cost records. Companies wanting an accurate record of job costs for pricing purposes, product profitability purposes, and evaluating managers of those jobs will prefer the adjusted allocation rate approach.

5-12   Four levels of a manufacturing cost hierarchy are:
(i)   Output unit-level costs
(ii)   Batch-level costs
(iii)   Product-sustaining costs
(iv)   Facility-sustaining costs.

5-14   An ABC approach focuses on activities as the fundamental cost objects. The costs of these activities are built up to compute the costs of products, services and customers, and so on. The traditional approach seeks to have one or a few indirect cost pools, irrespective of the heterogeneity in the facility. An ABC approach attempts to use cost drivers as the allocation base, whereas the traditional approach is less clear on this issue.

5-16   (20 -30 min.) **Job costing, normal and actual costing.**

1. $\dfrac{\text{Budgeted indirect}}{\text{cost rate}} = \dfrac{\text{Budgeted indirect costs}}{\text{Budgeted direct labor-hours}} = \dfrac{\$8,000,000}{160,000 \text{ hours}}$

   = $50 per direct labor-hour

   $\dfrac{\text{Actual indirect}}{\text{cost rate}} = \dfrac{\text{Actual indirect costs}}{\text{Actual direct labor-hours}} = \dfrac{\$6,888,000}{164,000 \text{ hours}}$

   = $42 per direct labor-hour

2.

	Laguna Model	Mission Model
(a) Normal costing		
Direct costs		
Direct materials	$106,450	$127,604
Direct labor	36,276	41,410
	142,726	169,014
Indirect costs		
Assembly support ($50 × 900; 1,010)	45,000	50,500
	45,000	50,500
Total costs	$187,726	$219,514
(b) Normal costing		
Direct costs		
Direct materials	$106,450	$127,604
Direct labor	36,276	41,410
	142,726	169,014
Indirect costs		
Assembly support ($42 × 900; 1,010)	37,800	42,420
	37,800	42,420
Total costs	$180,526	$211,434

3.   Normal costing enables Anderson to report a job cost as soon as the job is completed, assuming that both the direct materials and direct labor costs are known at the time of use/work. Once the 900 direct labor-hours are known for the Laguna Model (June 19_8), Anderson can compute the $187,726 cost figure using normal costing. In contrast, Anderson has to wait until the December 19_8 year end to compute the $180,526 cost figure using actual costing.

INDIRECT
COST
POOL }

COST
ALLOCATION
BASE }

COST OBJECT:
RESIDENTIAL
HOME }

DIRECT
COSTS }

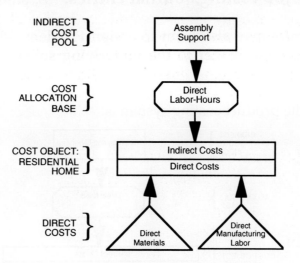

5-18 (35 - 45 min.) **Job costing, journal entries.**

Some instructors may also want to assign Problem 5-19. It demonstrates the relationships of the general ledger to the underlying subsidiary ledgers and source documents.

1. An overview of the product costing system is:

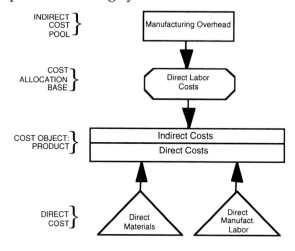

2.
(1)	Materials Control		$ 800	
	Accounts Payable Control			$ 800
(2)	Work in Process Control		$ 710	
	Materials Control			$ 710
(3)	Manufacturing Overhead Control		$ 100	
	Materials Control			$ 100
(4)	Work in Process Control		$1,300	
	Manufacturing Overhead Control		900	
	Wages Payable Control			$2,200
(5)	Manufacturing Overhead Control		$ 400	
	Accumulated—buildings and manufacturing equipment			$ 400
(6)	Manufacturing Overhead Control		$ 550	
	Miscellaneous accounts			$ 550
(7)	Work in Process Control		$2,080	
	Manufacturing Overhead Allocated			$2,080
	(1.60 × $1,300 = $2,080)			
(8)	Finished Goods Control		$4,120	
	Work in Process Control			$4,120
(9)	Accounts Receivable Control (or Cash)		$8,000	
	Revenues			$8,000
(10)	Cost of Goods Sold		$4,020	
	Finished Goods Control			$4,020
(11)	Manufacturing Overhead Allocated		$2,080	
	Manufacturing Overhead Control			$1,950
	Cost of Goods Sold			130

5-18 (Cont'd)

3.

Materials Control

Bal. 12/31_7	100	(2)	Issues	710
(1) Purchases	800	(3)	Issues	100
Bal. 12/31_8	90			

Work in Process Control

Bal. 12/31_7	60	(8)	Goods completed	4,120
(2) Direct materials	710			
(4) Direct manuf. labor	1,300			
(7) Manuf. overhead				
allocated	2,080			
	4,150			
Bal. 12/31_8	30			

Finished Goods Control

Bal. 12/31_7	500	(10)	Goods sold	4,020
(8) Goods completed	4,120			
Bal. 12/31_8	600			

Cost of Goods Sold

(10) Goods sold	4,020	(11) Adjust for over- allocation	130
Bal. 12/31_8	3,890		

Manufacturing Overhead Control

(3) Supplies	100	(11) To close	1,950
(4) Indirect manuf. labor	900		
(5) Depreciation	400		
(6) Miscellaneous	550		
	1,950		
Bal.	0		

Manufacturing Overhead Allocated

(11)	2,080	(7)	2,080
		Bal.	0

5-20 (45 min.) Job costing, journal entries.

Some instructors may wish to assign Problem 5-21. It demonstrates the relationships of journal entries, general ledger, subsidiary ledgers, and source documents.

1. An overview of the product-costing system is:

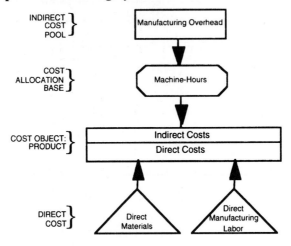

2. Amounts in millions.

(1)	Materials Control	$150	
	Accounts Payable Control		$150
(2)	Work in Process Control	$145	
	Materials Control		$145
(3)	Manufacturing Department Overhead Control	$ 10	
	Materials Control		$ 10
(4)	Work in Process Control	$ 90	
	Wages Payable Control		$ 90
(5)	Manufacturing Department Overhead Control	$ 30	
	Wages Payable Control		$ 30
(6)	Manufacturing Department Overhead Control	$ 19	
	Accumulated Depreciation		$ 19
(7)	Manufacturing Department Overhead Control	$ 9	
	Various liabilities		$ 9
(8)	Work in Process Control	$ 63	
	Manufacturing Overhead Allocated		$ 63
(9)	Finished Goods Control	$294	
	Work in Process Control		$294
(10a)	Cost of Goods Sold	$292	
	Finished Goods Control		$292
(10b)	Accounts Receivable Control (or Cash)	$400	
	Revenues		$400

5-20 (Cont'd)

The posting of entries to T-accounts is:

Materials Control			
Bal.	12	(2)	145
(1)	150	(3)	10

Work in Process Control			
Bal.	2	(9)	294
(2)	145		
(4)	90		
(8)	63		
Bal.	6		

Finished Goods Control			
Bal.	6	(10a)	292
(9)	294		

Cost of Goods Sold			
(10a)	292		
(11)	5		

Manufacturing Department Overhead Control			
(3)	10	(11)	68
(5)	30		
(6)	19		
(7)	9		

Manufacturing Overhead Allocated			
(11)	63	(8)	63

Accounts Payable Control			
		(1)	150

Wages Payable Control			
		(4)	90
		(5)	30

Accumulated Depreciation			
		(6)	19

Various Liabilities			
		(7)	9

Accounts Receivable Control			
(10b)	400		

Revenues			
		(10b)	400

The ending balance of Work-in-Process Control is $6.

3. (11) Manufacturing Overhead Allocated $63
        Cost of Goods Sold   5
           Manufacturing Department Overhead Control $68

5-22 (10-15 min.) **Accounting for manufacturing overhead.**

1. Budgeted manufacturing overhead rate $= \dfrac{\$7,000,000}{200,000}$

    $= \$35$ per machine-hour

2. Work in Process Control $6,825,000
       Manufacturing Overhead Allocated $6,825,000
    (195,000 machine-hours $\times$ $35 = $6,825,000)

3. $6,825,000 – $6,800,000 = $25,000 overallocated, an insignificant amount

    Manufacturing Overhead Allocated $6,825,000
       Manufacturing Department Overhead Control $6,800,000
       Cost of Goods Sold
                                                               25,000

5-24 (30 min.) **ABC, product-cost cross-subsidization.**

1. Direct costs
        Direct materials $150,000 $150,000
    Indirect costs
        Product support   983,000   983,000
        Total costs $1,133,000

    Cost per pound of potato cuts $= \dfrac{\$1,133,000}{1,000,000}$

    $= \$1.133$

2.	**Retail Potato Cuts**		**Institutional Potato Cuts**	
Direct costs				
Direct materials	$135,000		$15,000	
Packaging	180,000	315,000	8,000	23,000
Indirect costs				
Cleaning				
($0.120 × 900,000)	108,000			
($0.120 × 100,000)			12,000	
Cutting				
($0.24 × 900,000)	216,000			
($0.15 × 100,000)			15,000	
Packaging				
($0.48 × 900,000)	432,000			
($0.12 × 100,000)		756,000	12,000	39,000
Total costs		$1,071,000		$62,000
Units produced		900,000		100,000
Cost per unit		$1.19		$0.62

Note: The total costs of $1,133,000 ($1,071,000 + $62,000) are the same as those in Requirement 1.

3.   There is much evidence of product-cost cross-subsidization.

	Retail	Institutional
Current system	$1.133	$1.133
ABC system	$1.190	$0.620

Assuming the ABC numbers are more accurate, retail is undercosted by approximate 5% ($1.133) $1.19 = 0.95), while institutional is overcosted by 83% ($1.133) $0.620 = 1.83). The current system assumes each product uses all the activity areas in a homogeneous way. This is not the case. Institutional sales use sizably less resources in the cutting area and the packaging area. The percentage of total costs for each cost category are:

5-24 (Cont'd.)

	Retail	Institutional	Total
Direct costs			
Direct materials	90.0%	10.0%	100.0%
Packaging	95.7	4.3	100.0
Indirect costs			
Cleaning	90.0	10.0	100.0
Cutting	93.5	6.5	100.0
Packaging	97.3	2.7	100.0
Units produced	90.0%	10.0%	100.0%

Idaho can use the revised cost information for a variety of purposes:

(a) *Pricing/product emphasis decisions.* The sizable drop in the reported cost of institutional potatoes makes it possible that Idaho was overpricing potato products in this market. It lost the bid for a large institutional contract with a bid 30% above the winning bid. With its revised product cost dropping from $1.133 to $0.620, Idaho could have bid much lower and still made a profit. An increased emphasis on the institutional market appears warranted.

(b) *Product design decisions.* ABC provides a road map as to how to reduce the costs of individual products. The relative components of costs are:

	Retail	Institutional
Direct costs		
Direct materials	12.6%	24.2%
Packaging	16.8	12.9
Indirect costs		
Cleaning	10.1	19.3
Cutting	20.2	24.2
Packaging	40.3	19.3
Total costs	100.0%	100.0%

Packaging-related costs constitute 57.1% (16.8% + 40.3%) of total costs of the retail product line. Design efforts that reduce packaging costs can have a big impact on reducing total unit costs for retail.

(c) *Process improvements.* Each activity area is now highlighted as a separate cost. The three indirect cost areas are over 60% of total costs for each product, indicating the upside from improvements in the efficiency of processes in these activity areas.

5-26 (30 min.) **Cost hierarchies, unit cost analysis.**

1.   A.   Product-sustaining costs
     B.   Output unit-level costs
     C.   Output unit-level costs
     D.   (a)   Output unit-level costs
          (b)   Batch-level costs
     E.   Output unit-level costs
     F.   Facility-sustaining costs.

Each of the output unit-level costs (B, C, D(a) and E) increase or decrease as the number of cans of soft drink bottled increase or decrease. The $795,000 for setups is a function of the number of product line switches which is determined by how Thirst Quencher batches its production. The $1,228,000 cost for new product development aims to enhance the next generation of products. The $1,246,000 cost for plant supervision and safety costs is incurred, irrespective of individual volume levels at the plant, how production is batched, or what new products are developed.

2.   Output unit-level costs

Incoming material handling costs	$ 867,000	
Incoming materials purchase costs	4,426,000	
Production-line labor costs	2,421,000	
Energy costs	343,000	$ 8,057,000
Batch-level costs		
Product-line labor costs	795,000	795,000
Product-sustaining costs		
New product development	1,228,000	1,228,000
Facility-sustaining costs		
Plant supervision and safety	1,246,000	1,246,000
Total costs		$11,326,000

Output unit-level cost $= \dfrac{\$8,057,000}{20,000,000 \text{ cans}} = \$0.40285$ per can

Total unit cost $= \dfrac{\$11,326,000}{20,000,000 \text{ can}} = \$0.5663$ per can

   Thirst Quencher can use the unit costs at the output level for budgeting at different output levels and when evaluating the performance of plant managers. Inventory valuation for financial reporting requires total unit costs be computed. (Note that inventory valuation restricts itself to manufacturing costs. Some costs, such as R&D or distribution, may be excluded irrespective of where in the cost hierarchy they are found.)

5-26 (Cont'd.)

3.   The cost hierarchy is based on categorizing costs into different cost pools on the basis of different classes of cost drivers or different degrees of difficulty in determining cause-and-effect or benefits-received relationships. When budgeting costs at different output levels, the cost hierarchy points to the different types of cost drivers to examine. Similarly, when examining variances, the cost hierarchy can help guide the search for explanations.

5-28   (40-55 min.)   **Overview of general-ledger relationships.**

1& 3.   An effective approach to this problem is to draw T-accounts and insert all the known figures. Then, working with T-account relationships, solve for the unknown figures (here coded by the letter X for beginning inventory figures and Y for ending inventory figures).

Materials Control

X	15,000	(1)	70,000
Purchases	85,000		
	100,000		70,000
Y	30,000		

Work in Process Control

X		10,000	(4)	305,000
(1) DM	70,000			
(2) DL	150,000			
(3) Overhead	90,000	310,000		
		320,000		305,000
(a)		5,000		
(c)		3,000		
Y		23,000		

Finished Goods Control

X	20,000	(5)	300,000
(4)	305,000		
	325,000		300,000
Y	25,000		

Cost of Goods Sold

(5)	300,000	(d)	6,000

Manufacturing Department Overhead Control

	85,000	(d)	87,000
(a)	1,000		
(b)	1,000		

Manufacturing Overhead Allocated

(d)	93,000	(3)	90,000
		(c)	3,000

Manufacturing overhead cost rate = $90,000 ÷ $150,000 = 60%

Wages Payable Control

		(a)	6,000

Various Accounts

		(b)	1,000

2.   Adjusting and closing entries:

(a)   Work in Process Control $5,000
       Manufacturing Department Overhead Control 1,000
            Wages Payable Control $6,000
       To recognize payroll costs

(b)   Manufacturing Department Overhead Control $1,000
            Various accounts $1,000
       To recognize miscellaneous manufacturing overhead

(c)   Work in Process Control $3,000
            Manufacturing Overhead Allocated $3,000
       To allocate manufacturing overhead

<u>Note</u>: Students tend either to forget entry (c) entirely. Stress that a budgeted overhead allocation rate is used consistently throughout the year. This point is a major feature of this problem.

(d)   Manufacturing Overhead Allocated $93,000
            Manufacturing Department Overhead Control $87,000
            Cost of Goods Sold 6,000
       To close manufacturing overhead accounts and over-
       allocated overhead to cost of goods sold
   An overview of the product-costing system is:

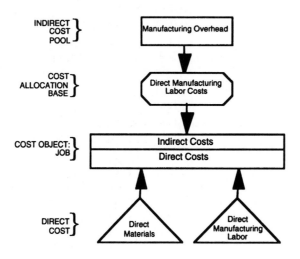

3.   See the answer to 1.

5-30 (30-40 min.) **Activity-based costing, product cost cross-subsidization.**

The motivation for 5-30 came from "ABC Minicase: Let them Eat Cake," *Cost Management Update* (Issue No. 31).

1.
$$\text{Budgeted MOH rate in 19\_7} = \frac{\$210,800}{200,000 \text{ units}}$$

= $1.054 per one-pound unit of cake

	Raisin Cake		Layered Carrot Cake	
Unit direct manufacturing cost				
Direct materials	$0.600		$0.900	
Direct manufacturing labor	0.140	$0.740	0.200	$1.100
Unit indirect manufacturing cost				
Manufacturing overhead				
($1.054 × 1, 1)	$1.054	1.054	$1.054	1.054
Unit total manufacturing cost		$1.794		$2.154

2.	Raisin Cake		Layered Carrot Cake	
Unit indirect manufacturing cost				
Direct materials	$0.600		$0.900	
Direct manufacturing labor	0.140	$0.740	0.200	$1.100
Unit indirect manufacturing cost				
Mixing ($0.04 × 5,8)	$0.200		$0.320	
Cooking ($0.14 × 2,3)	0.280		0.420	
Cooling ($0.02 × 3,5)	0.060		0.100	
Creaming/Icing ($0.25 × 0,3)	0.000		0.750	
Packaging ($0.08 × 3,7)	0.240	0.780	0.560	2.150
Unit total manufacturing cost		$1.520		$3.250

3.   The unit product costs in requirements 1 and 2 differ only in the assignment of indirect costs to individual products. The assumed usage of indirect cost areas under each costing system is:

	Existing System		ABC System	
	Raisin Cake	Layered Carrot Cake	Raisin Cake	Layered Carrot Cake
Mixing	50%	50%	38.5%	61.5%
Cooking	50	50	40.0	60.0
Cooling	50	50	37.5	62.5
Creaming/Icing	50	50	0.0	100.0
Packaging	50	50	30.0	70.0

The ABC system recognizes the substantial difference in usage of individual activity areas between raisin cake and layered carrot cake. The existing costing system erroneously assumes equal usage of activity areas by a pound of raisin cake and a pound of layered carrot cake.

5-30 (Cont'd.)

4.   Uses of activity-based cost numbers include:

(a)   Pricing decisions. BD can use the ABC data to decide preliminary prices for negotiating with its customers. Raisin cake is currently overcosted, while layered carrot cake is undercosted. Actual production of layered carrot cake is 100% more than budgeted. One explanation could be the underpricing of layered carrot cake.

(b)   Product emphasis. BD has more accurate product margins with ABC. BD can use this information for deciding which products to push (especially if there are production constraints).

(c)   Product design. ABC provides a road map on how a change in product design can reduce costs. The % breakdown of total indirect costs for each product are:

	Raisin Cake	Layered Carrot Cake
Mixing	25.6% ($0.20/$0.78)	14.9% ($0.32/$2.15)
Cooking	35.9	19.5
Cooling	7.7	4.7
Creaming/Icing	0.0	34.9
Packaging	30.8	26.0
	100.0%	100.0%

BD can reduce the cost of either cake by reducing its usage of each activity area. For example, BD can reduce raisin cake's cost by sizably reducing its cooking time or packaging time. Similarly, a sizable reduction in creaming/icing will have a marked reduction in layered carrot cake costs.

(d)   Process improvements. Improvements in how activity areas are configured will cause a reduction in the costs of products that use those activity areas.

(e)   Cost planning and flexible budgeting. ABC provides a more refined model to forecast costs of BD and to explain why actual costs differ from budgeted costs.

5-32 (20-30 min.) **Activity-based job-costing system.**

1. Solution Exhibit 5-32 presents costing overviews of the previous job-costing system and the refined activity-based job-costing system.

2. Direct manufacturing costs:

Direct materials		$3,000
Indirect manufacturing costs:		
Materials handling, $8 × 50	$ 400	
Machining, $68 × 12	816	
Assembly, $75 × 15	1,125	
Inspection, $104 × 4	416	2,757
Total manufacturing costs		$5,757

Total manufacturing costs = $5,757 × 50 = $287,850

3. A direct cost is a cost that is related to the particular cost object and that can be traced to it in an economically-feasible way. Denver may differ from its competitor in several ways.
   (a) Denver uses a more automated production approach with the result that manufacturing labor provides support to the machines.
   (b) Denver uses a less sophisticated information tracking system for manufacturing labor than its competitors.
Manufacturing labor costs are included in the individual indirect manufacturing (overhead) cost pools.

4. The refined activity-based costing system can provide information to:

   (a) Product designers—the indirect cost rates in each of the four indirect cost areas can guide decisions about how much (say) machine-hours to use versus assembly line hours when designing packaging machines.
   (b) Manufacturing personnel—decisions about productivity and cost management can focus on ways to reduce the indirect cost rates (such as decisions on how to make more efficient use of machines).
   (c) Marketing personnel—the ABC approach can help guide pricing decisions and negotiations with potential customers on ways to manufacture a lower-cost packaging machine.

5-32 (Cont'd.)

SOLUTION EXHIBIT 5-32
Job Costing Systems for Denver Company

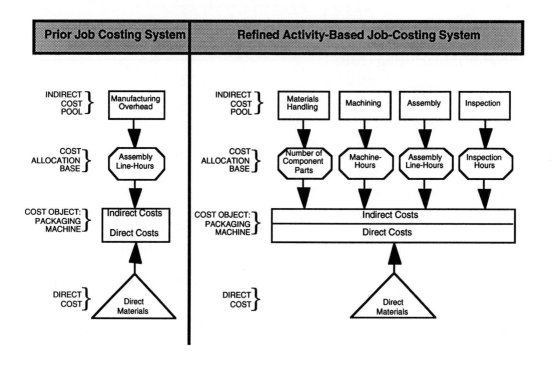

5-34 (15 min.) **Activity-based job costing.**

1. An overview of the product-costing system is:

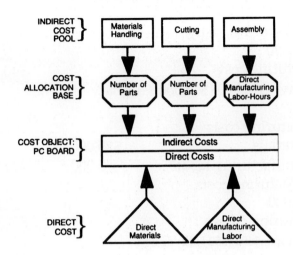

	Executive Chair	Chairman Chair
Direct manufacturing costs:		
Direct materials	$ 600,000	$25,000
Direct manufacturing labor,		
$20 × 7,500; 500	150,000	10,000
Direct manufacturing costs	750,000	35,000
Indirect manufacturing costs:		
Materials handling,		
$0.25 × 100,000; 3,500	25,000	875
Cutting,		
$2.50 × 100,000; 3,500	250,000	8,750
Assembly,		
$25.00 × 7,500; 500	187,500	12,500
	462,500	22,125
Indirect manufacturing costs	$1,212,500	$57,125
Total manufacturing costs		

Unit Costs
    Executive chair: $1,212,500 ÷ 5,000 = $242.50
    Chairman chair: $57,125 ÷ 100 = $571.25

2.

	Executive Chair	Chairman Chair
Upstream costs	$ 60.00	$146.00
Manufacturing costs	242.50	571.25
Downstream costs	110.00	236.00
Total costs	$412.50	$953.25

5-36   (20 min.)   **Job costing, contracting, ethics.**

1.   Direct manufacturing costs:

Direct materials	$25,000	
Direct manufacturing labor	6,000	$31,000
Indirect manufacturing costs,		
150% × $6,000		9,000
Total manufacturing costs		$40,000

Aerospace bills the Navy $52,000 ($40,000 × 130%).

2.   Direct manufacturing costs:

Direct materials	$25,000	
Direct manufacturing labor[a]	5,000	$30,000
Indirect manufacturing costs,		
150% × $5,000		7,500
Total manufacturing costs		$37,500

[a] $6,000 – $400 ($25 × 16) setup – $600 ($50 × 12) design

Aerospace should have billed the Navy $48,750 ($37,500 × 130%).

3.   The problems the letter highlights (assuming it is correct) include:

(a)   Costs included that should be excluded (design costs),
(b)   Costs double-counted (setup included as both a direct cost and in an indirect cost pool), and
(c)   Possible conflict of interest in Aerospace Comfort purchasing materials from a family-related company.

Steps the Navy could undertake include:
(i)   Use only contractors with a reputation for ethical behavior as well as quality products or services.
(ii)   Issue guidelines detailing acceptable and unacceptable billing practices by contractors. For example, prohibiting the use of double-counting cost allocation methods by contractors.
(iii) Issue guidelines detailing acceptable and unacceptable procurement practices by contractors. For example, if a contractor purchases from a family-related company, require that the contractor obtain quotes from at least two other bidders.
(iv)   Employ auditors who aggressively monitor the bills submitted by contractors.

CHAPTER 6
MASTER BUDGET AND RESPONSIBILITY ACCOUNTING

6-2   The budgeting cycle includes the following elements:
a.   Planning the performance of the organization as a whole as well as its subunits. The entire management team agrees as to what is expected.
b.   Providing a frame of reference, a set of specific expectations against which the actual results can be compared.
c.   Investigating variations from the plans. If necessary, corrective action follows investigation.
d.   Planning again, considering feedback and changed conditions.

6-4   Budgeted performance is better than past performance for judging managers. Why? Mainly because inefficiencies included in past results can be detected and eliminated in budgeting. Also, new opportunities in the future, which did not exist in the past, may be ignored if past performance is used.

6-6   Budgets may be a vehicle for communication, but sometimes the vehicle breaks down. As an example, the budget staff often finds it is unable to obtain line management participation in developing budgets. In some cases, line people tend to relinquish line budget responsibilities to the budget staff. Line personnel simply do not wish to be bothered with the budget. This indicates a lack of good communication.

6-8   A *rolling budget* is a budget or plan that is always available for a specified future period by adding a month, quarter, or year in the future as the month, quarter, or year just ended is dropped. *Pro forma statements* are budgeted or forecasted financial statements.

6-10   Pressure for budgeted revenues (costs) to be overstated (understated) can occur when managers use the budget to pressure employees to make above-average effort. The term "challenge budget" is sometimes used to describe this situation.
      Pressure for budgeted revenues (costs) to be understated (overstated) can occur when employees pad their estimates to make budgeted targets more easily achievable.

6-12   Benefits companies report from using activity-based budgeting include:
   1. ability to set more realistic budgets,
   2. better identification of resource needs,
   3. linking of costs to outputs,
   4. clearer linking of costs with staff responsibilities, and
   5. identification of budgetary slack.

6-14   The choice of a responsibility center type guides the variables to be included in the budgeting exercise. For example, if a revenue center is chosen, the focus will be on variables that assist in forecasting revenue. Factors related to, say, costs of the investment base will be considered only if they assist in forecasting revenue.

6-16 (15 min.) **Production budget (in units), fill in the missing numbers.**

	Model 101	Model 201	Model 301
Budgeted sales	180[G]	193[c]	867[G]
Add target ending FGI	14[a]	6[G]	33[G]
Total requirements	194[G]	199[G]	900[e]
Deduct beginning FGI	11[G]	8[G]	45[f]
Units to be produced	183[b]	191[d]	855[G]

[a] $194 - 180 = 14$ [d] $199 - 8 = 191$ G = given
[b] $194 - 11 = 183$ [e] $867 + 33 = 900$
[c] $199 - 6 = 193$ [f] $900 - 855 = 45$

6-18 (5 min.) **Sales and production purchases budget.**

Budgeted sales in units	100,000
Add target ending finished goods inventory	11,000
Total requirements	111,000
Deduct beginning finished goods inventory	7,000
Units to be produced	104,000

6-20 (5 min.) **Direct materials purchases budget.**

Direct materials to be used in production (bottles)	1,500,000
Add target ending direct materials inventory (bottles)	50,000
Total requirements (bottles)	1,550,000
Deduct beginning direct materials inventory (bottles)	20,000
Direct materials to be purchased (bottles)	1,530,000

6-22 (15-20 min.) **Budgeting revenue, cost of goods sold, and gross margin.**

Centrum Gift Shop
Budgeted Gross Margin
For the Quarter Ending December 31

	October	November	December	Total for the Quarter
Cash sales	$10,000	$11,000	$16,000	$37,000
Credit card sales:				
$ 7,000 × 0.96	6,720			
$ 8,000 × 0.96		7,680		
$12,000 × 0.96			11,520	25,920
Net sales	16,720	18,680	27,520	62,920
Cost of goods sold, at 40% of net sales	6,688	7,472	11,008	25,168
Gross margin	$10,032	$11,208	$16,512	$37,752

Some students may think that a 60% gross margin is high. However, this gross margin is before deducting many operating costs such as rent, advertising, and sales commissions.

6-24   (15-25 min.) **Budget for production and direct manufacturing labor.**

Roletter Company
Budget for Production and Direct Manufacturing Labor
For the Quarter Ended March 31, 19_8

	January	February	March	Quarter
Budgeted sales (units)	10,000	12,000	8,000	30,000
Add target ending finished goods inventory* (units)	16,000	12,500	13,500	13,500
Total requirements (units)	26,000	24,500	21,500	43,500
Deduct beginning finished goods inventory (units)	16,000	16,000	12,500	16,000
Units to be produced	10,000	8,500	9,000	27,500
Direct manufacturing labor-hours (DMLH) per unit	×2.0	× 2.0	× 1.5	
Total hours of direct manufacturing labor time needed	20,000	17,000	13,500	50,500
Direct manufacturing labor costs:				
Wages ($10.00 per DMLH)	$200,000	$170,000	$135,000	$505,000
Pension contributions ($0.50 per DMLH)	10,000	8,500	6,750	25,250
Workers' compensation insurance ($0.15 per DMLH)	3,000	2,550	2,025	7,575
Employee medical insurance ($0.40 per DMLH)	8,000	6,800	5,400	20,200
Social Security tax (employer's share) ($10.00 × 0.075 = $0.75 per DMLH)	15,000	12,750	10,125	37,875
Total direct manufacturing labor costs	$236,000	$200,600	$159,300	$595,900

*100% of the first following month's sales plus 50% of the second following month's sales.

Note that the employee Social Security tax of 7.5% is irrelevant. Such taxes are withheld from employees' wages and paid to the government by the employer on behalf of the employees; therefore, the 7.5% amounts are not additional costs to the employer.

6-26 (20-30 min.) **Kaizen approach to activity-based budgeting.**
(continuation of 6-25)

1.   March 19_8 rates

	January	February	March
Ordering	$90	$89.820	$89.64
Delivery	82	81.836	81.67
Shelf-stocking	21	20.958	20.92
Customer support	0.18	0.17964	0.179

These March 19_8 rates can be used to compute the total budgeted cost for each activity area:

	Soft Drinks	Fresh Produce	Packaged Food	Total
Ordering				
$89.64 × 14; 24; 14	$1,255	$2,151	$1,255	$ 4,661
Delivery				
$81.67 × 12; 62; 19	980	5,063	1,552	7,595
Shelf-stocking				
$20.92 × 16; 172; 94	335	3,598	1,966	5,899
Customer support				
$0.179 × 4,600; 34,200; 10,750	823	6,122	1,924	8,869
	$3,393	$16,934	$6,697	$27,024

2.   A Kaizen budgeting approach signals management's commitment to systematic cost reduction. Compare the budgeted costs from Question 6-25 and 6-26.

	Ordering	Delivery	Shelf-Stocking	Customer Support
Question 6-25	$4,680	$7,626	$5,922	$8,919
Question 6-26 (Kaizen)	4,661	7,595	5,899	8,869

The Kaizen budget number will show unfavorable variances for managers whose activities do not meet the required monthly cost reductions. This likely will put more pressure on managers to creatively seek out cost reductions by working "better" within FS or by having "better" interactions with suppliers or customers.

One limitation of Kaizen budgeting, as illustrated in this question, is that it assumes small incremental improvements each month. It is possible that some cost improvements arise from large discontinuous changes in operating processes, supplier networks, or customer interactions. Companies need to highlight the importance of seeking these large discontinuous improvements as well as the small incremental improvements.

6-28 (20 min.) **Continuous improvement, budgeting.**
(continuation of 6-27)

Areas where continuous improvement might be incorporated into the budgeting process:

(a)   Direct materials. Either an improvement in usage or price could be budgeted. For example, the budgeted usage amounts could be related to the maximum improvement of 1 square foot for either desk:

- Executive: 16 square feet – 15 square feet minimum = 1 square foot
- Chairman: 25 square feet – 24 square feet minimum = 1 square foot

Thus, a 1% reduction target per month could be:

- Executive: 15 square feet + (0.99 × 1) = 15.99
- Chairman: 24 square feet + (0.99 × 1) = 24.99

Some students suggested the 1% be applied to the 16 and 25 square foot amounts. This is incorrect as after several improvement cycles, the budgeted amount would be less than the minimum desk requirements

(b)   Direct manufacturing labor. The budgeted usage of 3 hours/5 hours could be continuously revised on a monthly basis. Similarly, the manufacturing labor cost per hour of $30 could be continuously revised down. The former appears more feasible than the latter.

(c)   Variable manufacturing overhead. By budgeting more efficient use of the allocation base, a signal is given for continuous improvement. A second approach is to budget continuous improvement in the budgeted variable overhead cost per unit of the allocation base.

(d)   Fixed manufacturing overhead. The approach here is to budget for reductions in the year-to-year amounts of fixed overhead. If these costs are appropriately classified as fixed, then they are more difficult to adjust down on a monthly basis.

6-30 (30 min.) **Budgeted income statement.**

Easecom Company
Budgeted Income Statement for 19_8
(in thousands)

Net sales		
Equipment ($6,000 × 1.06 × 1.10)	$6,996	
Maintenance contracts ($1,800 × 1.06)	<u>1,908</u>	
Total net sales		$8,904
Cost of goods sold ($4,600 × 1.03 × 1.06)		<u>5,022</u>
Gross margin		3,882
Operating costs:		
Marketing costs ($600 + $250)	850	
Distribution costs ($150 × 1.06)	159	
Customer maintenance costs ($1,000 + $130)	1,130	
Administrative costs	<u>900</u>	
Total operating costs		<u>3,039</u>
Operating income		<u>$ 843</u>

Note that the lost contribution margin of $1,000 is rarely accounted for in ordinary accounting systems. If measured at all, it would appear as an underachieved budgeted contribution margin; that is, actual would be less than budgeted by $1,000.

The essence of this case is to demonstrate the limitations of responsibility accounting and the futility of a "blame-setting" theme in implementing responsibility accounting.

The theory of responsibility accounting is straightforward--link each cost ultimately to the one person in the organization who has the most day-to-day influence over its total amount. Repair and maintenance costs provide one of the most difficult illustrations of implementing the theory. The total cost of the repair job, by itself, is the responsibility of the repair shop manager. The manager has the most influence over the total amount incurred at the instant of repair. However, in the eyes of many observers, the department is only an intermediate cost objective because it services other departments.

Most students will probably maintain that the utility department should bear the $2,600 cost because its failure to maintain specified clearances led to this incident. Some students will feel that the sanitation department should bear the extra costs above the $2,000 original proposal.

Decisions regarding these disputes are inherently contextual, so students should be properly uneasy about choosing a course of action for the controller. The controller has dealt with all parties before and will interact with them again and again, so he must measure the effects of his present decision against a whole series of decisions about the running of the control system. The key is to prevent a similar occurrence in this or other areas.

Given these precautions, the controller might avoid the issue of "fixing blame" by not charging any department (or by charging the controller's department). All the managers seem to have partial responsibility. The controller should learn from this incident and take action to:

1.   Pinpoint responsibility for preventive maintenance of utility lines in the future. Decide how future costs should be allocated to provide the best set of coordinated goals and incentives.

2.   Have a meeting of all department heads involved to improve mutual understanding of responsibilities.

6-34 (50-60 min.) **Comprehensive review of budgeting.**

1. **Schedule 1 : Revenue Budget**
    For the Year Ended December 31, 19_9

	Units (Lots)	Selling Price	Total Sales
Lemonade	1,080	$9,000	$ 9,720,000
Diet Lemonade	540	8,500	4,590,000
Total			$14,310,000

2. **Schedule 2 : Production Budget In Units**
    For the Year Ended December 31, 19_9

	Products	
	Lemonade	Diet Lemonade
Budgeted sales (Schedule 1)	1,080	540
Add target ending finished goods inventory	20	10
Total requirements	1,100	550
Deduct beginning finished goods inventory	100	50
Units to be produced	1,000	500

3. **Schedule 3A : Direct Materials Usage Budget in Units and Dollars**
   For the Year Ended December 31, 19_9

	Syrup-Lemon.	Syrup-Diet Lem.	Containers	Packaging	Total
Units of direct materials to be used for production of Lemonade (1,000 lots × 1)	1,000	-	1,000	1,000	
Units of direct materials to be used for production of Diet Lemonade (500 lots ×1)	-	500	500	500	
Total direct materials to be used (in units)	1,000	500	1,500	1,500	
Units of direct material to be used from beginning inventory (under FIFO)	80	70	200	400	
Multiply by cost per unit of beginning inventory	$ 1,100	$ 1,000	$ 950	$ 900	
Cost of direct materials to be used from beginning inventory (a)	$ 88,000	$ 70,000	$ 190,000	$ 360,000	$ 708,000
Units of direct materials to be used from purchases (1,000 – 80; 500 – 70; (1,500 – 200; 1,500 – 400)	920	430	1,300	1,100	
Multiply by cost per unit of purchased materials	$ 1,200	$ 1,100	$ 1,000	$ 800	
Cost of direct materials to be used from purchases (b)	$1,104,000	$473,000	$1,300,000	$ 880,000	3,757,000
Total costs of direct materials to be used(a + b)	$1,192,000	$543,000	$1,490,000	$1,240,000	$4,465,000

6-34 (Cont'd.)

4. **Schedule 3B : Direct Materials Purchases Budget in Units and Dollars**
    For the Year Ended December 31, 19_9

	Syrup-Lemon.	Syrup-Diet Lem.	Containers	Packaging	Total
Direct materials to be used in production (in units) from Schedule 3A	1,000	500	1,500	1,500	
Add target ending direct materials inventory in units	30	20	100	200	
Total requirements in units	1,030	520	1,600	1,700	
Deduct beginning direct materials inventory in units	80	70	200	400	
Units of direct materials to be purchased	950	450	1,400	1,300	
Multiply by cost/unit of purchased materials	$ 1,200	$ 1,100	$ 1,000	$ 800	
Direct materials purchase costs	$1,140,000	$495,000	$1,400,000	$1,040,000	$4,075,000

5. **Schedule 4 : Direct Manufacturing Labor Budget**
    For the Year Ended December 31, 19_9

	Output Units Produced (Schedule 2)	Direct Manufacturing Labor Hours per Unit	Total Hours	Hourly Rate	Total
Lemonade	1,000	20	20,000	$25	$500,000
Diet Lemonade	500	20	10,000	25	250,000
Total			30,000		$750,000

6. **Schedule 5 : Manufacturing Overhead Costs Budget**
    For the Year Ended December 31, 19_9

Variable manufacturing overhead costs:

Lemonade [$600 × 2 hours per lot × 1,000 lots (Schedule 2)]	$1,200,000
Diet Lemonade [$600 × 2 hours per lot × 500 lots (Schedule 2)]	600,000
Variable manufacturing overhead costs	1,800,000
Fixed manufacturing overhead costs	1,200,000
Total manufacturing overhead costs	$3,000,000

Fixed manufacturing overhead per bottling hour = $1,200,000 ÷ 3,000 = $400. Note that the total number of bottling hours is 3,000 hours : 2,000 hours for Lemonade (2 hours per lot × 1,000 lots) plus 1,000 hours for Diet Lemonade (2 hours per lot × 500 lots).

7. **Schedule 6A : Ending Inventory Budget**
    December 31, 19_9

	Units (Lots)	Cost per Unit (Lot)	Total	
Direct materials:				
Syrup for Lemonade	30	$1,200	$ 36,000	
Syrup for Diet Lemonade	20	1,100	22,000	
Containers	100	1,000	100,000	
Packaging	200	800	160,000	$318,000

	Units	Cost per Unit		
Finished goods:				
Lemonade	20	$5,500*	$110,000	
Diet Lemonade	10	5,400*	54,000	164,000
Total ending inventory				$482,000

*From Schedule 6B

Schedule 6B : Computation of Unit Costs of Manufacturing Finished Goods
For the Year Ended December 31, 19_9

	Cost Per Unit (Lot) or Hour of Input	Lemonade Inputs in Units (Lots) or Hours	Amount	Diet Lemonade Inputs in Units (Lots) or Hours	Hour
Syrup			$1,200		$1,100
Containers			1,000		1,000
Packaging			800		800
Direct manufacturing labor	$ 25	20	500	20	500
Variable manufacturing overhead*	600	2	1,200	2	1,200
Fixed manufacturing overhead*	400	2	800	2	800
Total			$5,500		$5,400

*Variable manufacturing overhead varies with bottling hours (2 hours per lot for both Lemonade and Diet Lemonade). Fixed manufacturing overhead is allocated on the basis of bottling hours at the rate of $400 per bottling hour calculated in Schedule 5.

8. ### Schedule 7 : Cost of Goods Sold Budget
    For the Year Ended December 31, 19_9

	From Schedule		Total
Beginning finished goods inventory, January 1, 19_9	Given*		$ 790,000
Direct materials used	3A	$4,465,000	
Direct manufacturing labor	4	750,000	
Manufacturing overhead	5	3,000,000	
Cost of goods manufactured			8,215,000
Cost of goods available for sale			9,005,000
Deduct ending finished goods inventory, December 31, 19_9	6		164,000
Cost of goods sold			$8,841,000

* Given in description of basic data and requirements (Lemonade, $5,300 × 100; Diet Lemonade, $5,200 × 50)

9. **Schedule 8 : Marketing Costs Budget**
For the Year Ended December 31, 19_9
Marketing costs, 12% × Sales, $14,310,000 $1,717,200

10. **Schedule 9 : Distribution Costs Budget**
For the Year Ended December 31, 19_9
Distribution costs, 8% × Sales, $14,310,000 $1,144,800

11. **Schedule 10 : Administration Costs Budget**
For the Year Ended December 31, 19_9
Administration costs
   10% × Cost of goods manufactured, $8,215,000 $821,500

12. **Budgeted Income Statement**
For the Year Ended December 31, 19_9

Sales	Schedule 1		$14,310,000
Cost of goods sold	Schedule 7		8,841,000
Gross margin			5,469,000
Operating costs:			
Marketing costs	Schedule 8	$1,717,200	
Distribution costs	Schedule 9	1,144,800	
Administration costs	Schedule 10	821,500	
Total operating costs			3,683,500
Operating income			$ 1,785,500

6-36 (40 min.) **Appendix, cash budgeting for distributor.**

1.   The pro forma cash budget for Alpha-Tech for the second quarter of 19_7 is presented below. Supporting calculations are presented on the next page.

Alpha-Tech Cash Budget
For the Second Quarter 19_7

	April	May	June
Beginning balance	$ 500,000	$ 500,000	$1,230,000
Collections[1]			
February sales	4,000,000		
March sales	5,400,000	3,600,000	
April sales		6,900,000	4,600,000
May sales			7,500,000
Total receipts	9,400,000	10,500,000	12,100,000
Total cash available	9,900,000	11,000,000	13,330,000
Disbursements			
Accounts payable	4,155,000	4,735,000	5,285,000
Wages[2]	3,450,000	3,750,000	4,200,000
General & Administrative[3]	900,000	900,000	900,000
Property taxes			340,000
Income taxes[4]	1,280,000		
Total disbursements	9,785,000	9,385,000	10,725,000
Cash balance	115,000	1,615,000	2,605,000
Cash borrow	385,000		
Cash repaid		(385,000)	
Ending balance	$ 500,000	$1,230,000	$ 2,605,000

[1] 60% of sales in first month; 40% of sales in second month.

[2] 30% of current month sales.

[3] (Total less property taxes and depreciation) ÷ 12.

[4] 40% × $3,200,000

Supporting Calculations

Accounts payable-parts received:

Cost of goods sold

Month	40% of revenues	Timing	February	March	April	May	June
February	$4,000,000	.30	$1,200,000				
March	3,600,000	.70	2,520,000				
March	3,600,000	.30		$1,080,000			
April	4,600,000	.70		3,220,000			
April	4,600,000	.30			$1,380,000		
May	5,000,000	.70			3,500,000		
May	5,000,000	.30				$1,500,000	
June	5,600,000	.70				3,920,000	
			$3,720,000	$4,300,000	$4,880,000	$5,420,000	

Payment							
February	$3,720,000	.25			$ 930,000		
March	4,300,000	.75			3,225,000		
March	4,300,000	.25				$1,075,000	
April	4,880,000	.75				3,660,000	
April	4,880,000	.25					$1,220,000
May	5,420,000	.75					4,065,000
			$ 0	$ 0	$4,155,000	$4,735,000	$5,285,000

2.   Cash budgeting is important for Alpha-Tech, because, as sales grow, so will expenditures for input factors. Since these expenditures generally precede cash receipts, the company must plan for possible financing to cover the gap between payments and receipts. The cash budget shows the probable cash position at certain points in time, allowing the company to plan for borrowing, as Alpha-Tech must do in April.

Cash budgeting also facilitates the control of excess cash. The company may be losing investment opportunities, if excess cash is left idle in a checking account. The cash budget alerts management to periods when there will be excess cash available for investment, thus facilitating financial planning and cash control.

6-38   (60-75 min.) **Comprehensive budget; fill in schedules.**

1.   Schedule A: Budgeted Monthly Cash Receipts

Item	September	October	November	December
Total sales	$40,000*	$48,000*	$60,000*	$80,000*
Credit sales (25%)	10,000*	12,000*	15,000	20,000
Cash sales (75%)	$30,000	$36,000	$45,000	$60,000
Receipts:				
Cash sales		$36,000*	$45,000	$60,000
Collections on accounts receivable		10,000*	12,000	15,000
Total		$46,000*	$57,000	$75,000

*Given.

2.   Schedule B: Budgeted Monthly Cash Disbursements for Purchases

Item	October	November	December	4th Quarter
Purchases	$42,000*	$56,000	$25,200	$123,200
Deduct 2% cash discount	840*	1,120	504	2,464
Disbursements	$41,160*	$54,880	$24,696	$120,736

*Given. Note that purchases are 0.7 of next month's sales given a gross margin of 30%.

3.   Schedule C: Budgeted Monthly Cash Disbursements for Operating Costs

Item	October	November	December	4th Quarter
Salaries and wages				
(15% of sales)	$ 7,200*	$ 9,000	$12,000	$28,200
Rent (5% of sales)	2,400*	3,000	4,000	9,400
Other cash operating costs				
(4% of sales)	1,920*	2,400	3,200	7,520
Total	$11,520*	$14,400	$19,200	$45,120

*Given.

6-38 (Cont'd.)

4.   Schedule D: Budgeted Total Monthly Cash Disbursements

Item	October	November	December	4th Quarter
Purchases	$41,160*	$54,880	$24,696	$120,736
Cash operating costs	11,520*	14,400	19,200	45,120
Light fixtures	600*	400	--	1,000
Total	$53,280*	$69,680	$43,896	$166,856

*Given.

5.   Schedule E: Budgeted Cash Receipts and Disbursements

Item	October	November	December	4th Quarter
Receipts	$46,000*	$57,000	$75,000	$178,000
Disbursements	53,280*	69,680	43,896	166,856
Net cash increase			$31,104	$ 11,144
Net cash decrease	$ 7,280*	$12,680		

*Given

6.   Schedule F: Financing Required

Item	October	November	December	4th Quarter
Beginning cash balance	$12,000*	$ 8,720*	$ 8,040	$12,000
Net cash increase			31,104	11,144
Net cash decrease	7,280*	12,680		
Cash position before borrowing (a)	4,720*	(3,960)	39,144	23,144
Minimum cash balance required	8,000*	8,000	8,000	8,000
Excess (Deficiency)	(3,280)*	(11,960)	31,144	15,144
Borrowing required (b)	4,000*	12,000		16,000
Interest payments (c)			540	540
Borrowing repaid(d)			16,000	16,000
Ending cash balance (a+b–c–d)	$ 8,720*	$ 8,040	$22,604	$22,604

*Given.

Interest computation:
$ 4,000 @ 18% for 3 months   = $180
$12,000 @ 18% for 2 months   =   360
Total interest expense $540

6-38 (Cont'd.)

7. Short-term, self-liquidating financing is best. The schedules clearly demonstrate the mechanics of a "self-liquidating" loan. The need for such a loan arises because of the seasonal nature of many businesses. When sales soar, the payroll and suppliers must be paid in cash. The basic source of cash is proceeds from sales. However, the credit extended to customers creates a lag between the sale and the collection of cash. When the cash is collected, it in turn may be used to repay the loan. The amount of the loan and the timing of the repayment are heavily dependent on the credit terms that pertain to both the purchasing and selling functions of the business. Somewhat strangely, in seasonal businesses, the squeeze on cash is often heaviest in the months of peak sales and is lightest in the months of low sales.

8.

Newport Stationery Store
Budgeted Income Statement
For the Quarter Ending December 31, 19__

Revenues—Schedule A		$188,000
Cost of goods sold (70% of sales)		131,600*
Gross margin		56,400
Operating costs		
Salaries and wages—Schedule C	$28,200	
Rent—Schedule C	9,400	
Other cash operating costs—Schedule C	7,520	
Depreciation ($1,000 × 3 months)	3,000	48,120
Operating income		8,280
Deduct interest expense— Schedule F		540
Add purchase discounts— Schedule B		2,464
Net income (before taxes)		$ 10,204

*Note: Ending inventory and proof of cost of goods sold:

Inventory, September 30	$ 63,600	
Add purchases—Schedule B	123,200	$186,800
Deduct inventory, December 31:		
Basic inventory	30,000	
December purchases—Schedule B	25,200	55,200
Cost of goods sold		$131,600

6-38 (Cont'd.)

Newport Stationery Store
Budgeted Balance Sheet
December 31, 19__

Assets:
   Current assets:
      Cash—Schedule F $ 22,604
      Accounts receivable
         December credit sales—Schedule A   20,000
      Inventory (see Note above)   55,200
         Total current assets   97,804
   Equipment and fixtures:
      Equipment—net ($100,000 – $3,000 depreciation) $97,000
      Fixtures—Schedule D   1,000   98,000
        Total $195,804

Liabilities and Owners' Equity:
   Liabilities   None
   Owners' equity $195,804*
      Total $195,804

*Owners' equity, September 30:
  $12,000 + $63,600 + $10,000 + $100,000 (Given) $185,600
  Net income, quarter ended December 31   10,204
  Owners' equity, December 31 $195,804

9.   All of the transactions have been simplified--for example, no bad debts are considered. Also, many businesses face wide fluctuation of cash flows within a month. For example, perhaps customer receipts lag and are bunched together near the end of a month and disbursements are due evenly throughout the month or are bunched near the beginning of the month. Cash needs would then need to be evaluated on a weekly and perhaps daily basis rather than on a monthly basis.

6-40   (60 min.)   **Athletic department of a university, budget revision options.**

This exercise illustrates the difficulty of budgeting issues in universities. There are multiple stakeholders––student-athletes, student non-athletes, coaches, sports administrators, university faculty, university administrators, and alumni. Actions that benefit one type of stakeholder can "gore the ox" of other stakeholders.

The general options that groups could examine are outlined below.

<u>Increasing Revenues</u>

There are at least two approaches to "increase" revenues:

(a)   Increase revenues from outside sources. For example, sell more tickets to football, basketball, etc. This is heavily driven by success. Reddy's concerns about academic standards likely will constrain Connolly's flexibility to recruit any athlete he believes to be a major star.

Some universities have been innovative in terms of increasing cable television revenues from coverage of college sporting games.

The tax status of universities needs to be considered in any revenue-increasing strategy. For example, holding non-university-related events at athletic facilities (e.g., a SuperBowl) can endanger the tax-exempt status of a university.

Connolly could propose direct fundraising for the Athletic Department. This could run into problems with Reddy, as she may require all fundraising to be coordinated at the University level.

(b)   Increase the "revenues" attributed to the Athletic Department. Connolly could argue that a successful athletic program has many positive externalities for Pacific University, many of which increase P.U. revenues.

- Alumni are more likely to give money and other contributions when they are stimulated by being on campus to watch a nationally-ranked team or viewing a successful P.U. team on television. Many universities use tickets to athletic events and invitations to related social functions as a thank-you to major donors.

- Athletic officials (especially nationally prominent coaches) are expected to assist Reddy and her senior officers in promoting P.U. to potential donors, parents of future students, etc. For example, the coach of a number-one-ranked football team may attend over 50 dinners/functions a year on behalf of the university. Some of these dinners are "one-on-one" with potential large donors.

- Merchandising revenue sold to alumni and other supporters is likely to increase when P.U.'s athletic teams achieve national success. These include sweaters, towels, and rings.

The current budgeting process gives zero recognition to these externalities, which may well exceed the projected $3.010 million deficit.

Decreasing Costs

Connolly can always cut costs to meet any level Reddy may impose. However, the ways to achieve any substantive reduction will be relatively painful.

(a)   Reduce scholarships (either number or amount) to students. This can take time to achieve bottom-line reductions, as existing students may have three more years of scholarship remaining. Unless Connolly cuts existing scholarships, he is restricted to cutting back on scholarships to new students. This option will be very painful. One consequence will be lower-quality levels of student athletes which will have implications for the sporting competitiveness of P.U. The option of cutting back on already committed existing scholarships would be traumatic (but it has occurred).

Connolly could undertake across-the-board cuts or target the reductions to some sports. For example, sports that do not draw sizable crowds may be candidates for reduction. One difficulty here is that Connolly is faced with both reducing total costs <u>and</u> increasing the relative % of scholarships to women. The scholarship breakdown is:

	Men's Program	Women's Program	Total
Football	37	–	37
Basketball	21	11	32
Swimming	6	4	10
Other	4	2	6
Total	68	17	85

The largest percentage of scholarships are for the two highly successful programs--men's football (37/85 = 44%) and men's basketball (21/85 = 25%). There is little room for cutbacks in the second-tier sports at P.U.

(b)   Reduce sports sponsored by the athletic department. Cut out support for all but a few targeted sporting programs. This will cause morale problems for students in these sporting programs (such as rugby, soccer and volleyball).

(c)   Reduce salaries and other costs of the athletic department. The salary for Bill Madden is an obvious target for Connolly's cost reduction. However, Madden may have a multi-year contract that leaves P.U. little room for cost reduction. Moreover, if cost reduction is attempted, Madden may leave, which could have negative general effects on morale and university finances. Connolly could approach alumni or sponsors to cover Madden's salary and other costs. This would address Reddy's budget balance concerns but not her concern as to the level of Madden's salary vis-a-vis leading academics.

Cost reductions could be achieved by reducing the number of assistant coaches, and the number of support officials. The effect of these reductions on student morale and P.U. athletic achievements is difficult to measure.

6-40 (Cont'd)

Gender Issues

Based on dollar expenditures and scholarships, Reddy has evidence to support her concerns. The men's programs get the "lion's share" of the expenditures and student scholarships.

	Men's Program	Women's Program
Costs	$11.040 million	$2.800 million
Full student scholarships	68	17

Connolly could respond by noting that the men's programs have a lower deficit based on revenues minus assigned costs (in millions):

	Men's Program	Women's Program
Revenues	$10.350	$0.780
Assigned costs	11.040	2.800
Contribution	$(0.690)	$(2.020)

This lower deficit reflects, in part, the large revenue-drawing capacity of their successful men's football and athletic departments.

Reddy's demands for a balanced budget, more gender equality, and higher academic standards leaves Connolly's in an unenviable position.

CHAPTER 7
FLEXIBLE BUDGETS, VARIANCES, AND
MANAGEMENT CONTROL: I

7-2 A *favorable variance*–denoted F– is a variance that increases operating income relative to the budgeted amount. An *unfavorable variance*–denoted U–is a variance that decreases operating income relative to the budgeted amount.

7-4 A Level 2 flexible-budget analysis enables a manager to distinguish how much the difference between an actual result and a budgeted amount is due to (a) differences between actual and budgeted output levels, and (b) differences between actual and budgeted selling prices, variable costs, and fixed costs.

7-6 *Effectiveness* is the degree to which a predetermined objective or target is met. *Efficiency* is the relative amount of inputs used to achieve a given level of output. Assume the objective is to deliver a package to a customer by 10 a.m. the next day. Effective performance would be making the delivery before 10 a.m. Efficient performance would be making the delivery using the least amount of resources (time, gasoline, and so on).

7-8 A manager should decompose the flexible-budget variance for direct materials into a price variance and an efficiency variance. The individual causes of these variances can then be investigated, recognizing possible interdependencies across these individual causes.

7-10 Direct materials price variances are often computed at the time of purchase, while direct materials efficiency variances are often computed at the time of usage. Purchasing managers are typically responsible for price variances, while production managers are typically responsible for usage variances.

7-12 Budgeted costs can be successively reduced over consecutive time periods to incorporate continuous improvement. The chapter uses the phrase continuous improvement standard costs to describe this approach.

7-14 The plant supervisor likely has good grounds for complaint if the plant accountant puts excessive emphasis on using variances to pin blame. The key value of variances is to help understand why actual results differ from budgeted amounts and then to use that knowledge to promote learning and continuous improvement.

7-16 (20-30 min.) **Flexible budget.**

	Actual Results (1)	Flexible-Budget Variances (2) = (1) – (3)	Flexible Budget (3)	Sales-Volume Variances (4) =(3)–(5)	Static Budget (5)
Units sold	2,800^G	–	2,800		3,000^G
Revenues	$313,600^a	5,600 F	$308,000^b	$22,000 U	$330,000^c
Variable costs	229,600^d	22,400 U	207,200^e	14,800 F	222,000^f
Contribution margin	84,000	16,800 U	100,800	7,200 U	108,000
Fixed costs	50,000^G	4,000 F	54,000^G	0	54,000^G
Operating income	$ 34,000	$12,800 U	$ 46,800	$ 7,200 U	$ 54,000

↑_____$12,800 U_____↑_____$ 7,200 U_____↑

Total flexible-budget variance Total sales-volume variance

↑_____$20,000 U_____↑

Total static-budget variance

^{a} $112 × 2,800 = $313,600
^{b} $110 × 2,800 = $308,000
^{c} $110 × 3,000 = $330,000
^{d} Given. Unit variable cost = $229,600 ÷ 2,800 = $82 per tire
^{e} $74 × 2,800 = $207,200
^{f} $74 × 3,000 = $222,000
^{G} Given

2.   The key information items are:

	Actual	Budgeted
Units	2,800	3,000
Unit selling price	$ 112	$ 110
Unit variable cost	$ 82	$ 74
Fixed costs	$50,000	$54,000

The total static-budget variance in operating income is $20,000 U. There is both an unfavorable total flexible-budget variance ($12,800) and an unfavorable sales-volume variance ($7,200).

The unfavorable sales-volume variance arises solely because actual units manufactured and sold were 200 less than the budgeted 3,000 units. The unfavorable static-budget variance of $12,800 in operating income is due primarily to the $8 increase in unit variable costs. This increase in unit variable costs is only partially offset by the $2 increase in unit selling price and the $4,000 decrease in fixed costs.

7-18 (20-30 min.) **Price and efficiency variances.**

1.   The key information items are:

	Actual	Budgeted
Output units (scones)	60,800	60,000
Input units	16,000	15,000
Cost per input unit	$0.82	$0.89

Peterson budgets to obtain 4 pumpkin scones from each pound of pumpkin.

   The flexible-budget variance is $408F.

	Actual Results (1)	Flexible-Budget Variance (2) = (1) – (3)	Flexible Budget (3)	Sales-Volume Variance (4) = (3) – (5)	Static Budget (5)
Pumpkin costs	13,120[a]	$408 F	$13,528[b]	$178 U	$13,350[c]

[a] 16,000 × $ 0.82 = $13,120
[b] 60,800 × 0.25 × $0.89 = $13,528
[c] 60,000 × 0.25 × $0.89 = $13,350

2.

Actual Costs Incurred (Actual Input × Actual Price)	Actual Input × Budgeted Price	Flexible Budget (Budgeted Input Allowed for Actual Output Achieved × Budgeted Price)
$13,120[a]	$14,240[b]	$13,528[c]

↑_____$1,120 F_____↑_____$712 U_____↑
      Price variance   Efficiency variance

↑_____$408 F_____↑
                  Flexible-budget variance

[a] 16,000 × $0.82 = $13,120
[b] 16,000 × $0.89 = $14,240
[c] 60,800 × 0.25 × $0.89 = $13,528

3.   The favorable flexible-budget variance of $408 has two offsetting components:

   (a)   favorable price variance of $1,120—reflects the $0.82 actual purchase cost being lower than the $0.89 budgeted purchase cost per pound.

   (b)   unfavorable efficiency variance of $712—reflects the actual materials yield of 3.80 scones per pound of pumpkin (60,800 ÷ 16,000 = 3.80) being less than the budgeted yield of 4.00 (60,000 ÷ 15,000 = 4.00).

One explanation is that Peterson purchased lower quality pumpkins at a lower cost per pound.

7-20 (30 min.)   **Flexible budget, fill in the blanks.**

	Actual Results	Flexible-Budget Variances	Flexible Budget	Sales-Volume Variances	Static Budget
Units produced and sold	20,000[G]	–	20,000	1,000	19,000[j]
Revenues	$40,000[a]	$1,000 U[G]	$41,000[e]	$2,050 F	$38,950
Variable costs	25,000[b]	400 U	24,600[f]	1,230 U	23,370[k]
Contribution margin	15,000[c]	1,400 U	16,400[h]	820 F	15,580[l]
Fixed costs	10,000[d]	200 U	9,800[G]	0 U	9,800[G]
Operating income	$ 5,000[G]	$1,600 U	$ 6,600[i]	$ 820 F	$5,780[m]

[G]Given

[a] $2.00[G] × 20,000 = $40,000

[b] $1.25[G] × 20,000 = $25,000

[c] $40,000 – $25,000 = $15,000

[d] $15,000 – $5,000 = $10,000

[e] $40,000 + $1,000 U[G] = $41,000;
   Actual selling price per unit = $2.05 ($41,000 ÷ 20,000)

[f] ($2.05 – VC) = $0.82; VC = $1.23 per unit
   $1.23 × 20,000 = $24,600

[h] $41,000 – $24,600 = $16,400

[i] $16,400 – $9,800 = $6,600

[j] $38,950 ÷ $2.05 = 19,000 units

[k] $1.23 × 19,000 = $23,370

[i] $38,950 – $23,370 = $15,580

[m] $15,580 – $9,800 = $5,780

The key inputs for explaining the unfavorable static-budget variance of $780 in operating income are:

	Actual	Budget
Units produced and sold	20,000	19,000
Selling price per unit	$2.00	$2.05
Variable cost per unit	$1.25	$1.23
Fixed costs	$10,000	$9,800

There was (a) a $0.05 reduction in the selling price per unit, (b) an $0.02 increase in variable cost per unit, and (c) an increase in $200 of fixed costs per week. The operating income effect of (a), (b), and (c) is $1,600 unfavorable. This $1,600 unfavorable flexible-budget variance exceeds the favorable sales-volume variance of $820.

7-22 (30-40 min.) **Comprehensive variance analysis.**

1.

Direct Materials	Actual Costs Incurred (Actual Input × Actual Price	Actual Input × Budgeted Price	Flexible Budget (Budgeted Input Allowed for Actual Output Achieved × Budgeted Price)
Purchase	(12,640 × $20.50) $259,120 ↑_____	(12,640 × $20) $252,800 ↑	
		$6,320 U Price Variance	

| | | (750 × 15.8 × $20) $237,000 ↑_____ | (750 × 16 × $20) $240,000 ↑ |
| Usage | | | $3,000 F Efficiency Variance |

| Direct Manufacturing Labor | (750 × 3.1 × $31.00) $72,075 ↑_____ | (750 × 3.1 × $30) $69,750 ↑_____ | (750 × 3.0 × $30.00) $67,500 ↑ |
| | | $2,325 U Price Variance | $2,250 U Efficiency Variance |

2.   **Direct Materials Price Variance** ($6,320U, due to actual price of $20.50 exceeding budgeted price of $20.00)

- Standard wrongly (unrealistically) set
- Poor price negotiation
- Purchase of higher quality wood
- Materials price unexpectedly increased due to external shocks (e.g., a natural disaster in major forest areas)
- Purchased in smaller lot sizes than budgeted and did not get quantity discounts
- Change in supplier when lower-priced supplier went out of business

7-22 (Cont'd.)

Direct Materials Efficiency Variance ($3,000 F, due to actual usage of 15.8 square feet per desk, compared to budgeted 16.0 square feet)

- Standard wrongly (unrealistically) set
- Increased skills of workers
- Use of more automated machinery (e.g., laser cutting)
- Workers did more extensive planning and scheduling for materials usage
- Economies of scale in production

Direct Manufacturing Labor Price Variance ($2,325 U, due to actual rate of $31.00 compared to budgeted $30.00)

- Standard wrongly (unrealistically) set
- Use of higher skill mix than budgeted
- Poor negotiations with labor
- Overtime may have been necessary to produce the extra 50 decks more than budgeted
- Unexpected labor shortage due to external factors

Direct Manufacturing Labor Efficiency Variance ($2,250 U, due to actual time being 3.1 hours compared to budgeted 3.0 hours per desk)

- Standard wrongly (unrealistically) set
- Labor may be less efficient at higher output levels due to tiredness
- Scheduler assigned less skilled workers to desk production
- Machine breakdowns required more use of labor
- Lower quality wood purchased requiring more labor input to finish desks

7-24 (25-30 min.) **Flexible budget preparation and analysis.**

1. Variance Analysis for Bank Management Printers for September 19_7
    Level 1 Analysis

	Actual Results (1)	Static-Budget Variances (2) = (1) – (3)	Static Budget (3)
Units sold	12,000	3,000 U	15,000
Revenue	$252,000[a]	$ 48,000 U	$300,000[c]
Variable costs	84,000[d]	36,000 F	120,000[f]
Contribution margin	168,000	12,000 U	180,000
Fixed costs	150,000	5,000 U	145,000
Operating income	$ 18,000	$ 17,000 U	$ 35,000

    ↑_____$17,000 U_____↑
Total static-budget variance

2. Level 2 Analysis

	Actual Results (1)	Flexible-Budget Variances (2) = (1) – (3)	Flexible Budget (3)	Sales Volume Variances (4) = (3) – (5)	Static Budget (5)
Units sold	12,000	0	12,000	3,000 U	15,000
Revenue	$252,000[a]	$12,000 F	$240,000[b]	$60,000 U	$300,000[c]
Variable costs	84,000[d]	12,000 F	96,000[e]	24,000 F	120,000[f]
Contribution margin	168,000	24,000 F	144,000	36,000 U	180,000
Fixed costs	150,000	5,000 U	145,000	0	145,000
Operating income	$ 18,000	$19,000 F	$ (1,000)	$36,000 U	$ 35,000

    ↑_____$19,000 F_____↑_____$36,000 U_____↑
    Total flexible-budget   Total sales-volume
    variance   variance

    ↑_____$17,000 U_____↑
Total static-budget variance

[a] $12,000 \times \$21 = \$252,000$ [d] $12,000 \times \$7 = \$ 84,000$
[b] $12,000 \times \$20 = \$240,000$ [e] $12,000 \times \$8 = \$ 96,000$
[c] $15,000 \times \$20 = \$300,000$ [f] $15,000 \times \$8 = \$120,000$

3. Level 2 analysis provides a breakdown of the static-budget variance into a flexible-budget variance and a sales-volume variance. The primary reason for the static-budget variance being unfavorable ($17,000 U) is the reduction in unit volume from the budgeted 15,000 to an actual 12,000. One explanation for this reduction is the increase in selling price from a budgeted $20 to an actual $21. Operating management was able to reduce variable costs by $12,000 relative to the flexible budget. This reduction could be a sign of efficient management. Alternatively, it could be due to using lower quality materials (which in turn adversely affected unit volume).

7-26 (20 min.) **Continuous improvement.** (continuation of 7-25)

1. Standard quantity input amounts per output unit are:

	Direct Materials	Direct Manufacturing Labor
January	10.0000	0.5000
February (Jan. × 0.997	9.9700	0.4985
March (Feb. × 0.997)	9.9400	0.4970

2. The answer to requirement 1 of Question 7-25 is identical except for the flexible-budget amount.

	Actual Costs Incurred (Actual Input × Actual Price)	Actual Input × Budgeted Price		Flexible Budget (Budgeted Input Allowed for Actual Output Achieved × Budgeted Price)
		Purchases	Usage	
Direct Materials	(100,000 × $3.10*) $310,000	(100,000 × $3.00) $300,000	(98,073 × $3.00) $294,219	(9,810 × 9.940 × $3.00) $292,534

$\uparrow$_____$10,000 U$_____$\uparrow$ $\uparrow$_____$1,685 U$_____$\uparrow$

Price variance   Efficiency variance

Direct Manufacturing Labor	(4,900 × $21**) $102,900	(4,900 × $20) $98,000		(9,810 × 0.497 × $20) $97,511

$\uparrow$_____$4,900 U$_____$\uparrow$ _____$489 U$_____$\uparrow$

Price variance   Efficiency variance

 * $310,000 ÷ 100,000 = $3.10
** $102,900 ÷ 4,900 = $21

Using continuous improvement standards sets a tougher benchmark. The efficiency variances for January (from Exercise 7-25) and March (from Exercise 7-26) are:

	January	March
Direct materials	$ 81 F	$1,685 U
Direct manufacturing labor	$100 F	$ 489 U

Note that the question assumes the continuous improvement applies only to quantity inputs. An alternative approach is to have continuous improvement apply to budgeted input cost per output unit ($30 for direct materials in January and $10 for direct manufacturing labor in January). This approach is more difficult to incorporate in a Level 2 variance analysis, as Level 2 requires separate amounts for quantity inputs and the cost per input.

7-28 (15-25 min.) **Journal entries and T-accounts.** (continuation of 7-27)

a.
Work in Process Control	$400,000	
Direct Materials Price Variance	7,400	
Direct Materials Efficiency Variance		$ 30,000
Materials Control		377,400
To record direct materials used		

b.
Work in Process Control	$200,000	
Direct Manufacturing Labor Price Variance		$ 3,600
Direct Manufacturing Labor Efficiency Variance		20,000
Wages Payable Control		176,400
To record liability and allocation of direct labor costs		

Materials Control		Direct Materials Price Variance		Direct Materials Efficiency Variance	
	(a) $377,400	(a) 7,400			(a) 30,000

Work in Process Control		Direct Manufacturing Labor Price Variance		Direct Manufacturing Labor Efficiency Variance	
(a) 400,000			(b) 3,600		(b) 20,000
(b) 200,000					

Wages Payable Control	
	(b) 176,400

The following journal entries pertain to the measurement of price variances when materials are purchased:

a1.
Materials Control	$600,000	
Direct Materials Price Variance	12,000	
Accounts Payable Control		$612,000
To record direct materials purchased		

a2.
Work in Process Control	$400,000	
Materials Control		$370,000
Direct Materials Efficiency Variance		30,000
To record direct materials used		

Materials Control		Direct Materials Price Variance	
(a1) 600,000	(a2) 370,000	(a1) 12,000	

Accounts Payable Control		Work in Process Control	
	(a1) 612,000	(a2) 400,000	

Direct Materials Efficiency Variance	
	(a2) 30,000

7-28 (Cont'd.)

The difference between standard costing and normal costing for direct cost items is:

	Standard Costs	Normal Costs
Direct Costs	Standard price(s) × Standard input allowed for actual outputs achieved	Actual price(s) × Actual input

These journal entries differ from the normal costing entries because Work in Process Control is no longer carried at "actual" costs. Furthermore, Materials Control can also be carried at standard unit prices rather than actual unit prices. Finally, variances appear for direct materials and direct manufacturing labor under standard costing but not under normal costing.

7-30 (30 min.) **Flexible budget preparation, service sector.**

1. • Budgeted selling price (revenue per loan application)

    1/2% × budgeted average loan amount = 1/2% × $200,000 = $1,000
    • Budgeted variable costs per output unit are:

Professional labor (6 × $40)	$240
Loan filing fees	100
Credit-worthiness checks	120
Courier mailings	50
Budgeted variable costs	$510

    • Budgeted fixed costs = $31,000 per month.

The static budget for the 90 loan applicant level (and the flexible budget for the 120 loan application level in Requirement 2) are:

	Requirement 1 90 Loan Applications	Requirement 2 120 Loan Applications
Budgeted revenue (90, 120 × $1,000)	$90,000	$120,000
Budgeted variable costs (90, 120 × $510)	45,900	61,200
Contribution margin	44,100	58,800
Fixed costs	31,000	31,000
Operating income	$13,100	$ 27,800

2. The actual results are:

Revenue (120 × 1/2% × $224,000)		$134,400
Variable costs:		
Professional labor (120 × 7.2 × $42)	$36,288	
Loan filing fees (120 × $100)	12,000	
Credit-worthiness checks (120 × $125)	15,000	
Courier mailings (120 × $54)	6,480	69,768
Contribution margin		64,632
Fixed costs		33,500
Operating income		$ 31,132

These actual results can be analyzed in a Level 2 variance analysis.

7-30 (Cont'd.)

Level 2 Analysis

	Actual Results (1)	Flexible-Budget Variances (2) = (1) – (3)	Flexible Budget (3)	Sales-Volume Variances (4) = (3) – (5)	Static Budget (5)
Units sold	120	0	120	30 F	90
Revenue	$134,400	$14,400 F	$120,000	$30,000 F	$90,000
Variable costs	69,768	8,568 U	61,200	15,300 U	45,900
Contribution margin	64,632	5,832 F	58,800	14,700 F	44,100
Fixed costs	33,500	2,500 U	31,000	0	31,000
Operating income	$ 31,132	$ 3,332 F	$ 27,800	$14,700 F	$13,100

↑_____$3,332 F_____↑_____$14,700 F_____↑
Total flexible-budget variance   Total sales-volume variance

↑_____$18,032 F_____↑
Total static-budget variance

   Note that the $18,032 favorable static-budget variance is largely the result of an increase in loan applications from a budgeted 90 to an actual 120. In addition, the average size of a loan increased from a budgeted $200,000 to $224,000, which explains the flexible-budget variance of $14,400 F for revenues ($0.5\% \times \$24,000 \times 120 = \$14,400$).

   One possible explanation is a rapid decrease in interest rates leading to an increase in demand for loan refinancing.

7-32 (30-40 min.) **Direct materials variances, long-term agreement with supplier.**

1.

Month (1)	Total Actual Direct Materials Usage in Dollars (2)	Average Actual Direct Materials Purchase Price per Pound of Metal (3)	Total Actual Quantity of Direct Materials in Pounds (4) = (2) ÷ (3)	Number of Machining Systems Produced (5)	Actual Direct Materials Input in Pounds per Machining System (6) = (4) ÷ (5)
January	$242,400	$120	2,020	10	202
February	286,560	120	2,388	12	199
March	442,260	126	3,510	18	195
April	395,264	128	3,088	16	193
May	253,440	120	2,112	11	192

Materials Price Variance

Month (1)	Actual Costs Incurred: Actual Input × Actual Price (2)	Actual Input (3)	Budgeted Price per Unit of Input (4)	Actual Input × Budgeted Price (5) = (3) × (4)	Direct Materials Price Variance (6) = (2) − (5)
January	$242,400	2,020	$120	$242,400	$ 0
February	286,560	2,388	120	286,560	0
March	442,260	3,510	120	421,200	21,060 U
April	395,264	3,088	120	370,560	24,704 U
May	253,440	2,112	120	253,440	0

Materials Efficiency Variance

Month (1)	Actual Input × Budgeted Price (2)	Budgeted Input per Unit of Output (3)	Actual Output Achieved (4)	Budgeted Price per Unit of Input (5)	Flexible Budget (Budgeted Input Allowed for Actual Output Achieved × Budgeted Price) (6) = (3) × (4) × (5)	Direct Materials Efficiency Variance (7) = (2) − (6)
January	$242,400	198	10	$120	$237,600	$4,800 U
February	286,560	198	12	120	285,120	1,440 U
March	421,200	198	18	120	427,680	6,480 F
April	370,560	198	16	120	380,160	9,600 F
May	253,440	198	11	120	261,360	7,920 F

2.   The unfavorable materials price variances in March and April imply that Mazak paid more than $120 per pound above the 2,400 pound contract amount.

Month (1)	Total Actual Costs Incurred (2)	Contract Amount for 2,400 lbs: 2,400 × $120 (3)	Cost For Purchases above 2,400 lbs. (4) = (2) – (3)	Quantity of Purchases above 2,400 lbs (5)	Actual Price per Pound of Purchases above 2,400 lbs. (6) = (4) ÷ (5)
March	$442,260	$288,000	$154,260	1,110	$138.97
April	395,264	288,000	107,264	688	155.91

The percentage price increases for the additional purchases above 2,400 pounds are:

	Actual Price	Standard Price	% Increase
March	$138.97	$120	15.8%
April	155.91	120	29.9

With a long-term agreement that has a fixed purchase-price clause for a set minimum quantity, no price variance will arise when the purchase amount is below the minimum quantity (assuming the budgeted price per unit is the contract price per unit). A price variance will occur only when the purchased amount exceeds the set minimum quantity. A price variance signals that the purchased amount exceeds this set minimum quantity (2,400 pounds per month).

It is likely that the supplier will charge a higher price (above $120) for purchases above the 2,400 base. If a lower price were charged, the purchaser might apply pressure to renegotiate the contract purchase price for the base amount. If the purchasing officer is able to negotiate only a small price increase for additional purchases above the base amount, the purchasing performance may well be "favorable" despite the materials price variance being labeled "unfavorable."

Mazak may see the advantage of a long-term contract in factors other than purchase price (for example, a higher quality of materials, a lower required level of inventories due to more frequent deliveries, and a guaranteed availability of materials). In general, the existence of a long-term agreement reduces the importance of materials price variances when evaluating the month-to-month performance of a purchasing officer.

7-34 (20-30 min.) **Flexible-budget preparation.**

1. Flexible budget data for Roan Music Box Fabricators for October 19_7.

	Budgeted Amount per Unit	Alternative Levels of Output		
		4,000 Units	5,000 Units	6,000 Units
Revenues	$ 77.00[a]	$308,000	$385,000	$462,000
Variable costs:				
Direct materials	22.00[b]	88,000	110,000	132,000
Direct manufacturing labor	15.00[c]	60,000	75,000	90,000
Variable manufacturing overhead	2.00[d]	8,000	10,000	12,000
Variable marketing cost	5.50[e]	22,000	27,500	33,000
Variable costs	44.50	178,000	222,500	267,000
Contribution margin	$32.50	130,000	162,500	195,000
Fixed costs:				
Manufacturing		51,700[f]	51,700	51,700
Marketing and administrative		82,600[g]	82,600	82,600
Fixed costs		134,300	134,300	134,300
Total costs		312,300	356,800	401,300
Operating income (loss)		$ (4,300)	$ 28,200	$ 60,700

[a] $70 + 10%($70) = $77
[b] $90,000 ÷ 4,500 = $20; $20 + 10%($20) = $22
[c] $67,500 ÷ 4,500 = $15
[d] given
[e] given
[f] $50,700 + ($12,000 ÷ 12) = $50,700 + $1,000 = $51,700
[g] $81,350 + ($15,000 ÷ 12) = $81,350 + $1,250 = $82,600

2. A flexible budget enables Roan to compute a richer set of variances than does a static budget. Roan will be able to compute a flexible-budget variance and a sales-volume variance. These additional variances provide more insight into **why** actual results differ from budgeted amounts.

7-36 (20–30 min.) **Direct materials and manufacturing labor variances, solving unknowns.**

All given items designated by an asterisk.

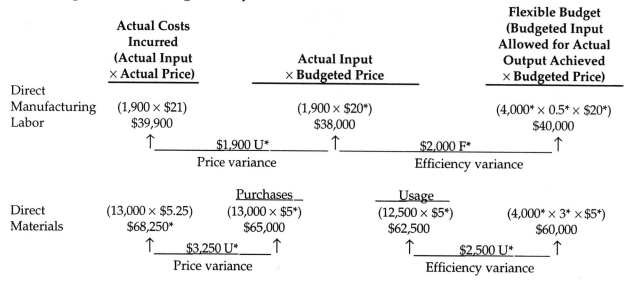

	Actual Costs Incurred (Actual Input × Actual Price)		Actual Input × Budgeted Price		Flexible Budget (Budgeted Input Allowed for Actual Output Achieved × Budgeted Price)
Direct Manufacturing Labor	(1,900 × $21) $39,900		(1,900 × $20*) $38,000		(4,000* × 0.5* × $20*) $40,000
	↑_____$1,900 U*_____↑ Price variance		↑_____$2,000 F*_____↑ Efficiency variance		

		Purchases		Usage		
Direct Materials	(13,000 × $5.25) $68,250*	(13,000 × $5*) $65,000	(12,500 × $5*) $62,500	(4,000* × 3* × $5*) $60,000		
	↑____$3,250 U*____↑ Price variance		↑____$2,500 U*____↑ Efficiency variance			

1. 4,000 × 0.5 = 2,000 hours
2. 1,900 hours
3. $21
4. 4,000 × 3 = 12,000 pounds
5. 12,500 pounds
6. 13,000 pounds
7. $5.25 per pound

7-38 (30 min.) **Comprehensive variance analysis.**

1.(a) Computing unit selling prices and unit costs of inputs:

$$\text{Actual selling price} = \$3,555,000 \div 450,000$$
$$= \$7.90$$

$$\text{Budgeting selling price} = \$3,200,000 \div 400,000$$
$$= \$8.00$$

$$\text{Selling-price variance} = \left(\begin{array}{c}\text{Actual} \\ \text{selling price}\end{array} - \begin{array}{c}\text{Budgeted} \\ \text{selling price}\end{array}\right) \times \begin{array}{c}\text{Actual} \\ \text{units sold}\end{array}$$

$$= \$7.90 - \$8.00) \times 450,000$$
$$= \$45,000 \text{ U}$$

(b) to (e)

The actual and budgeted unit costs are:

	Actual	Budgeted
Direct materials		
Cookie mix	$0.02	$0.02
Milk chocolate	0.20	0.15
Almonds	0.50	0.50
Direct labor		
Mixing	14.40	14.40
Baking	18.00	18.00

The actual output achieved is 450,000 pounds of chocolate nut supreme.

The direct cost price and efficiency variances are:

	Actual Costs Incurred (Actual Input × Actual Price) (1)	Price Variance (2)=(1)–(3)	Actual Input × Budgeted Prices (3)	Efficiency Variance (4)=(3)–(5)	Flex. Budget (Budgeted Input Allowed for Actual Output Achieved × Budgeted Price) (5)
Direct materials					
Cookie mix	$ 93,000	$ 0	$ 93,000[a]	$ 3,000 U	$ 90,000[h]
Milk chocolate	532,000	133,000 U	399,000[b]	61,500 U	337,500[i]
Almonds	240,000	0	240,000[c]	15,000 U	225,000[j]
	$865,000	$133,000 U	$732,000	$79,500 U	$652,500
Direct labor costs					
Mixing	$108,000	$ 0	$108,000[d]	$ 0	$108,000[k]
Baking	240,000	0	240,000[e]	30,000 F	270,000[l]
	$348,000	$ 0	$348,000	$30,000 F	$378,000

7-38 (Cont'd.)

[a] $\$0.02 \times 4{,}650{,}000 = \$93{,}000$
[b] $\$0.15 \times 2{,}660{,}000 = \$399{,}000$
[c] $\$0.50 \times 480{,}000 = \$240{,}000$
[d] $\$14.40 \times (450{,}000 \div 60) = \$108{,}000$
[e] $\$18.00 \times (800{,}000 \div 60) = \$240{,}000$

[h] $\$0.02 \times 10 \times 450{,}000 = \$90{,}000$
[i] $\$0.15 \times 5 \times 450{,}000 = \$337{,}500$
[j] $\$0.50 \times 1 \times 450{,}000 = \$225{,}000$
[k] $\$14.40 \times (1/60) \times 450{,}000 = \$108{,}000$
[l] $\$18.00 \times (2/60) \times 450{,}000 = \$270{,}000$

2. (a)   Selling price variance. This may arise from a proactive decision to reduce price to expand market share or from a reaction to a price reduction by a competitor. It could also arise from unplanned price discounting by salespeople.

   (b)   Material price variance. The $\$0.05$ increase in the price per ounce of milk chocolate could arise from uncontrollable market factors or from poor contract negotiations by Aunt Molly's.

   (c)   Material efficiency variance. For all three material inputs, usage is greater than budgeted. Possible reasons include lower quality inputs, use of lower quality workers, and the mixing and baking equipment not being maintained in a fully operational mode.

   (d)   Labor price variance. The zero variance is consistent with workers being on long-term contracts that are not renegotiated on a month-by-month basis.

   (e)   Labor efficiency variance. The favorable efficiency variance for baking could be due to workers eliminating non-value added steps in production.

7-40 (30 min.) **Price and efficiency variances, problems in standard setting, benchmarking.**

1. Budgeted materials input per shirt = 0.10 roll of cloth
    Budgeted manufacturing labor hours per shirt = 0.25 hours
    Budgeted materials cost = $50 per roll
    Budgeted manufacturing labor cost per hour = $18 per hour
    Actual output achieved = 4,488 shirts.

	Actual Costs Incurred (Actual Input × Actual Price)		Actual Input × Budgeted Price		Flexible Budget (Budgeted Input Allowed for Actual Output Achieved × Budgeted Price)
Direct Materials	$20,196		(408 × $50) $20,400		(4,488 × 0.10 × $50) $22,440
	↑_____$204 F_____	↑	_____$2,040 F_____		↑
	Price variance			Efficiency variance	
Direct Manufacturing Labor	$18,462		(1,020 × $18) $18,360		(4,488 × 0.25 × $18) $20,196
	↑_____$102 U_____	↑	_____$1,836 F_____		↑
	Price variance			Efficiency variance	

2. Actions employees may have taken include:
(a) Adding steps in working on a shirt that are not necessary.
(b) Taking more time on each step than is necessary.
(c) Creating problem situations so that the budgeted amount of average downtime will be overstated.
(d) Creating defects in shirts so that the budgeted amount of average rework will be overstated.

Employees may take these actions for several possible reasons.

(a) They may be paid on a piece-rate basis with incentives for above-budgeted production.
(b) They may want to create a relaxed work atmosphere, and less demanding standards can reduce stress.
(c) They may have a "them vs. us" mentality rather than a partnership perspective.

This behavior is unethical if it is deliberately designed to undermine the credibility of the standards used at Winston Fabrics.

7-40 (Cont'd.)

3. Savannah could use Benchmarking Clearing House information in several ways:
(a) For pricing and product emphasis purposes. Savannah should avoid getting into a pricing war with a competitor who has a sizably lower cost structure.
(b) As indicators of areas where Savannah is either highly cost-competitive or highly cost non-competitive.
(c) As performance targets for motivating and evaluating managers.

4. Main pros of Benchmarking Clearing House information:
(a) Highlights to Savannah in a direct way how it may or may not be cost competitive.
(b) Provides a "reality check" to many internal positions about efficiency or effectiveness.

Main cons are:
(a) Savannah may not be comparable to companies in the data base.
(b) Data about other company's costs may not be reliable.
(c) Cost of Benchmarking Clearing House reports.

CHAPTER 8
FLEXIBLE BUDGETS, VARIANCES,
AND MANAGEMENT CONTROL: II

8-2 At the start of an accounting period, a larger percentage of fixed overhead costs are locked-in than is the case with variable overhead costs.

8-4 Drivers of variable manufacturing overhead costs include:
- Machine-hours
- Direct manufacturing labor-hours or costs
- Number of production setups
- Number of parts per product
- Number of testing hours

8-6 Two factors affecting the spending variance for variable manufacturing overhead are:
a. Price inflation of individual items included in variable overhead.
b. Usage of individual items included in variable overhead.

8-8 A direct materials efficiency variance indicates whether more or less direct materials were used than was budgeted for the actual output achieved. A variable manufacturing overhead efficiency variance indicates whether more or less of the chosen allocation base was used than was budgeted for the actual output achieved.

8-10 The relationship for fixed-manufacturing overhead variances are:

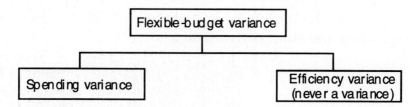

There is never an efficiency variance for fixed overhead, because managers cannot be more or less efficient in dealing with an amount that is fixed regardless of the output level. The result is that the flexible-budget variance amount is the same as the spending variance for fixed-manufacturing overhead.

8-12 There are two "never a variance" entries in the 4-Variance Analysis on p. 263:

- "Never a variance" for the production-volume variance for variable manufacturing overhead—the production volume variance applies only to fixed manufacturing overhead because a lump sum is to be allocated.

- "Never a variance" for the efficiency variance for fixed-manufacturing overhead—there can be no efficiency variance for fixed overhead because this amount is a lump sum regardless of the output level.

8-14 For planning and control purposes, fixed overhead costs are a lump sum amount that is not controlled on a per-unit basis. In contrast, for inventory costing purposes, fixed overhead costs are allocated to products on a per-unit basis. See Exhibit 8-4 (p.266) in the text.

8-16 (20 min.) **Variable manufacturing overhead, variance analysis.**

1.

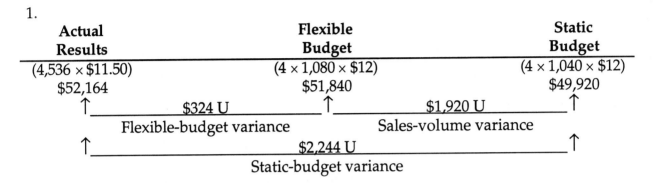

Actual Results	Flexible Budget	Static Budget
(4,536 × $11.50)	(4 × 1,080 × $12)	(4 × 1,040 × $12)
$52,164	$51,840	$49,920

$324 U — Flexible-budget variance

$1,920 U — Sales-volume variance

$2,244 U — Static-budget variance

2. Esquire manufactured an extra 40 suits than the 1,040 budgeted. This accounts for the unfavorable sales-volume variance of $1,920 for variable manufacturing overhead.

The actual variable manufacturing overhead of $52,164 exceeds the flexible budget amount of $51,840 for 1,080 suits by $324—hence the flexible budget variance is $324 U.

<u>NOT REQUIRED</u>

Further insight into the flexible-budget variance of $324 U for variable MOH is provided by the spending and efficiency variances:

Actual Costs Incurred	Actual Input × Budgeted Rate	Flexible Budget (Budgeted Input Allowed for Actual Output Achieved × Budgeted Rate)
(4,536 × $11.50)	(4,536 × $12)	(4 × 1,080 × $12)
$52,164	$54,432	$51,840

$2,268 F — Spending variance

$2,592 U — Efficiency variance

$324 U — Flexible-budget variance

Esquire had a favorable spending variance of $2,268, (the actual variable overhead rate was $11.50 per direct manufacturing labor-hour versus $12 budgeted). It had an unfavorable efficiency variance of $2,592 U (each suit averaged 4.2 labor-hours versus 4.00 budgeted).

8-18 (30-40 min.) Manufacturing overhead, variance analysis.

1. The summary analysis is:

	Spending Variance	Efficiency Variance	Production-Volume Variance
Variable Manufacturing Overhead	$40,700 F	$59,200 U	Never a variance
Fixed-Manufacturing Overhead	$23,420 U	Never a variance	$36,000 U

Variable Manufacturing Overhead

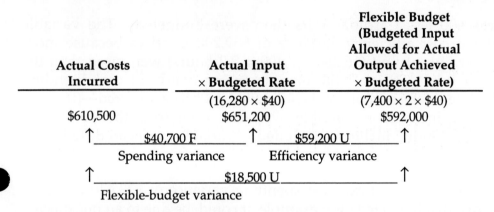

Actual Costs Incurred	Actual Input × Budgeted Rate	Flexible Budget (Budgeted Input Allowed for Actual Output Achieved × Budgeted Rate)
	(16,280 × $40)	(7,400 × 2 × $40)
$610,500	$651,200	$592,000

↑_____$40,700 F_____↑_____$59,200 U_____↑
      Spending variance   Efficiency variance

↑_____$18,500 U_____↑
    Flexible-budget variance

Fixed-Manufacturing Overhead

Actual Costs Incurred	Same Lump Sum Regardless of Output Level	Same Lump Sum Regardless of Output Level	Allocated (Budgeted Input Allowed for Actual Output Achieved × Budgeted Rate)
			(7,400 × 2 × $30.00)
$503,420	$480,000	$480,000	$444,000

↑_____$23,420 U_____↑_____↑_____$36,000 U_____↑
   Spending variance   Never a variance   Production volume variance

Summary information is:

	Actual	Flexible Budget	Static Budget
Output units	7,400	7,400	8,000
Allocation base (hours)	16,280	14,800[a]	16,000[b]
Allocation base per output unit	2.20	2.00	2.00
Variable MOH	$610,500	$592,000[c]	–
Variable MOH per hour	$37.50[d]	$40.00	–
Fixed MOH	$503,420	$480,000	$480,000
Fixed MOH per hour	$30.92[e]	–	$30.00[f]

[a] $7,400 \times 2.00 = 14,800$
[b] $8,000 \times 2.00 = 16,000$
[c] $7,400 \times 2 \times \$40 = \$592,000$
[d] $\$610,500 \div 16,280$ hours $= \$37.50$ per hour
[e] $\$503,420 \div 16,280$ hours $\simeq \$30.92$ per hour
[f] $\$480,000 \div 16,000$ hours $= \$30$ per hour

2.   Zyton produces 600 less CardioX units than were budgeted. The variable manufacturing overhead cost efficiency variance of $59,200 U arises because more assembly time hours per output unit (16,280 ÷ 7,400 = 2.2 hours) were used than the budgeted 2.0 hours per unit. The variable manufacturing overhead cost spending variance of $40,700 F indicates one or more of the following probably occurred—(i) actual prices of individual items included in variable overhead differ from their budgeted prices, or (ii) actual usage of individual items included in variable overhead differs from their budgeted usage.

    The fixed manufacturing overhead cost spending variance of $23,420 U means fixed overhead was above that budgeted. For example, it could be due to an unexpected increase in plant leasing costs. The unfavorable production-volume variance of $36,000 arises because actual output of 7,400 units is below the 8,000 units used in determining the $30.00 per assembly-hour budgeted rate.

3.   Planning and control of *variable* manufacturing overhead costs has both a long-run and a short-run focus. It involves Zyton planning to undertake only value-added overhead activities (a long-run view) and then managing the cost drivers of those activities in the most efficient way (a short-run view). Planning and control of *fixed* manufacturing overhead costs at Zyton has primarily a long-run focus. It involves undertaking only value-added fixed-overhead activities for a budgeted level of output. Zyton makes most of the key decisions that determine the level of fixed-overhead costs at the start of the accounting period.

8-20 (20-25 min.) **Spending and efficiency overhead variances, distribution.**

1. Budgeted variable overhead rate = $2 per hour of delivery time

    Budgeted fixed overhead rate $= \dfrac{\$120,000}{100,000 \times 0.25} = \dfrac{\$120,000}{25,000}$

    = $4.80 per hour of delivery time

A detailed comparison of actual and flexible budgeted amounts is:

	Actual	Flexible Budget	Static Budget
Output units (deliveries)	96,000	96,000	100,000
Allocation base (hours)	28,800	24,000[a]	25,000[b]
Allocation base per output unit	0.30[c]	0.25	0.25
Variable MOH	$60,000	$48,000[d]	–
Variable MOH per hour	$2.08[e]	$2.00	$2.00
Fixed MOH	$128,400	$120,000	$120,000
Fixed MOH per hour	$4.46[f]	–	$4.80[g]

[a] $96,000 \times 0.25 = 24,000$
[b] $100,000 \times 0.25 = 25,000$
[c] $28,800 \div 96,000 = 0.30$
[d] $96,000 \times 0.25 \times \$2.00 = \$48,000$
[e] $\$60,000 \div 28,800 = \$2.08$
[f] $\$128,400 \div 28,800 = \$4.46$
[g] $\$120,000 \div 25,000 = \$4.80$

The required variances are:

	Spending Variance	Efficiency Variance
Variable overhead	$2,400 U	$ 9,600 U
Fixed overhead	$8,400 U	—

These variances are computed as follows:

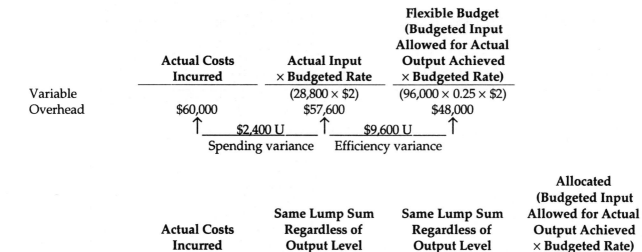

	Actual Costs Incurred	Actual Input × Budgeted Rate	Flexible Budget (Budgeted Input Allowed for Actual Output Achieved × Budgeted Rate)
Variable Overhead	$60,000	(28,800 × $2) $57,600	(96,000 × 0.25 × $2) $48,000
	↑___$2,400 U___↑ Spending variance	___$9,600 U___↑ Efficiency variance	

	Actual Costs Incurred	Same Lump Sum Regardless of Output Level	Same Lump Sum Regardless of Output Level	Allocated (Budgeted Input Allowed for Actual Output Achieved × Budgeted Rate)
Fixed Overhead	$128,400	$120,000	$120,000	(96,000 × 0.25 × $4.80) $115,200
	↑___$8,400 U___↑ Spending variance	↑ Never a variance	↑___$4,800 U___↑ Prodn. volume variance	

The spending variances for variable and fixed overhead are both unfavorable. This means that PPS had increases in either or both the cost of individual items (such as gasoline and truck maintenance) or higher-than-budgeted usage of these individual items per unit of the allocation base (delivery time). The unfavorable efficiency variance for variable overhead results from less efficient use of the cost allocation base—each delivery takes 0.30 hours versus a budgeted 0.25 hours.

2. The single direct cost category is delivery driver payments. The major problem in managing these costs is to restrain the rate of increase in the rate paid to drivers per delivery. PPS faces the challenge of having a low-cost delivery infrastructure. For example, purchasing delivery trucks with low fuel consumption will help reduce variable overhead costs. Purchasing vehicles with low annual maintenance will help reduce fixed overhead costs. Variable overhead costs are controlled by both cost planning, well prior to their incurrence, and day-to-day decisions. In contrast, most fixed overhead cost items are controlled by planning decisions made prior to the start of the year.

8-22 (10-15 min.) 4-variance analysis, fill in the blanks.

		Variable	Fixed
1.	Spending variance	$1,900 U	$1,000 U
2.	Efficiency variance	1,000 U	NEVER
3.	Production volume variance	NEVER	500 U
4.	Flexible budget variance	2,900 U	1,000 U
5.	Underallocated (overallocated) MOH	2,900 U	1,500 U

These relationships could be presented in the same way as in Exhibit 8-3 (variable overhead shown first):

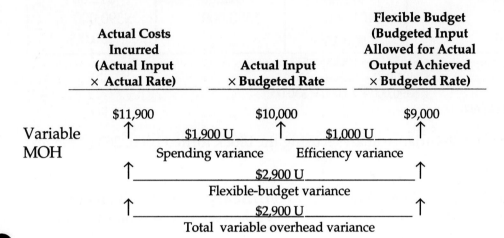

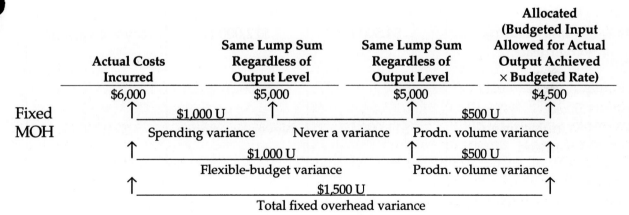

An overview of the 4 overhead variances using the block format on p. 263 of the text is:

4-Variance Analysis	Spending Variance	Efficiency Variance	Prodn. Volume Variance
Variable Overhead	$1,900 U	$1,000 U	Never a variance
Fixed Overhead	$1,000 U	Never a variance	$500 U

8-24 (30-40 min.) **Straightforward coverage of manufacturing overhead, standard-cost system.**

1. Solution Exhibit 8-24 shows the computations. Summary details are:

	Actual	Flexible Budget	Static Budget
Output units	41,000	41,000	43,333[a]
Allocation base (machine-hours)	13,300	12,300[b]	13,000
Allocation base per output unit	0.32[c]	0.30	0.30
Variable MOH	$155,100	$147,600[d]	–
Variable MOH per hour	$11.66[e]	$12.00	$12.00
Fixed MOH	$401,000	$390,000	$390,000
Fixed MOH per hour	$30.15[f]	–	$30.00[g]

a $13,000 \div 0.30 = 13,333$ e $155,100 \div 13,300 = 11.66
b $41,000 \times 0.30 = 12,300$ f $401,000 \div 13,300 = 30.15
c $13,300 \div 41,000 = 0.32$ g $390,000 \div 13,000 = 30.00
d $41,000 \times 0.30 \times $12 = $147,600$

An overview of the 4-variance analysis using the block format on p. 263 of the text is:

4-Variance Analysis	Spending Variance	Efficiency Variance	Production Volume Variance
Variable Manufacturing Overhead	$4,500 F	$12,000 U	Never a variance
Fixed Manufacturing Overhead	$11,000 U	Never a variance	$21,000 U

2. 1. Variable Manuf. Overhead Control $155,100
        Accounts Payable Control and other accounts $155,100

   2. Work in Process Control $147,600
        Variable Manuf. Overhead Allocated $147,600

   3. Fixed Manuf. Overhead Control $401,000
        Wages Payable Control, Accumulated
         Depreciation Control, etc. $401,000

   4. Work in Process Control $369,000
        Fixed Manuf. Overhead Allocated $369,000

8-24 (Cont'd)

3.   The control of variable manufacturing overhead requires the identification of the cost drivers for such items as energy, supplies, and repairs. Control often entails monitoring nonfinancial measures that affect each cost item, one by one. Examples are kilowatts used, quantities of lubricants used, and repair parts and hours used. The most convincing way to discover why overhead performance did not agree with a budget is to investigate possible causes, line item by line item.

Individual fixed manufacturing overhead items are not usually affected very much by day-to-day control. Instead, they are controlled periodically through planning decisions and budgeting procedures that may sometimes have horizons covering six months or a year (for example, management salaries) and sometimes covering many years (for example, long-term leases and depreciation on plant and equipment).

SOLUTION EXHIBIT 8-24

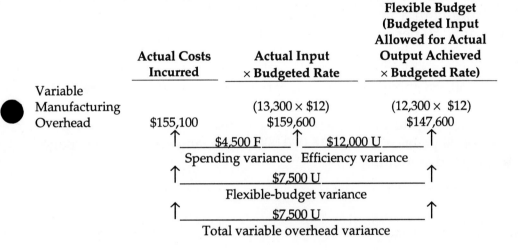

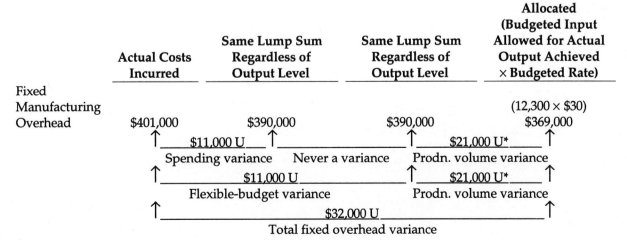

*Alternative computation:
13,000 denominator hours − 12,300 budgeted hours allowed = 700 hours
700 × $30 = $21,000 U

8-26 (15 min.) **Comprehensive review of Chapters 7 and 8, static budget.**

1.

	Actual Results (1)	Static-Budget Amounts (2)	Variances (3)
Revenues			
Circulation	$154,000	$140,000	$14,000 F
Advertising	394,600	360,000	34,600 F
	548,600	500,000	48,600 F
Costs			
Direct materials	224,640	180,000	44,640 U
Direct labor costs	50,112	45,000	5,112 U
Variable indirect costs	63,936	60,000	3,936 U
Fixed indirect costs	97,000	90,000	7,000 U
	435,688	375,000	60,688 U
Operating income	$112,912	$125,000	$12,088 U

2.   The *Monthly Herald* had an increase in total revenues of $48,600 above that budgeted. This arose from both a favorable circulation variance ($14,000 increase or 28,000 extra copies sold at $0.50 per copy) and a favorable advertising revenue variance of $34,600.

The actual costs are $60,688 above budget. The largest source of this increase comes from direct materials. The sources of this increase include (a) 20,000 extra copies printed, and (b) quality problems leading to many pages being unusable. The budgeted print pages for 320,000 copies of 50 pages each was 16,000,000 pages; an extra 1,280,000 pages were used above this budgeted amount.

8-28 (20 min.) **Engineered and discretionary overhead costs.**

1. Assuming full utilization of each worker, the budgeted labor cost per order is

$$\frac{\$15 \text{ per hour}}{2 \text{ articles} \times 0.2 \text{ hours per article}} = \frac{\$15}{0.4} = \$6 \text{ per order}$$

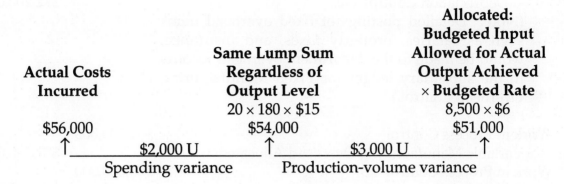

2.

	Actual Costs Incurred	Same Lump Sum Regardless of Output Level 20 × 180 × $15	Allocated: Budgeted Input Allowed for Actual Output Achieved × Budgeted Rate
	$56,000	$54,000	$54,000

↑_____$2,000 U_____↑_____$0_____↑
　　　Spending variance　　　　　Production-volume variance

3.   The engineered overhead cost approach assumes each order can have labor time assigned to it on a cause-and-effect basis. The $3,000 production-volume variance alerts management to the possibility of overstaffing and unused capacity.

The discretionary overhead cost approach assumes Quickserve cannot identify a cause-and-effect relation between the number of orders processed and labor costs. The control of labor costs is based on the manager's judgment and experience about likely workloads.

8-30   (20-30 min.) **Journal entries.** (continuation of 8-29)

a. Variable Manufacturing Overhead Control $36,100,000
    Accounts Control Payable and other accounts $36,100,000
    Fixed Manufacturing Overhead Control $72,200,000
      Wages Payable Control, Accumulated
        Depreciation Control, etc. $72,200,000
    (Note: Detailed postings of fixed overhead items
    such as salaries, property taxes, and insurance,
    would be made to the department overhead records
    in the subsidiary ledger for Fixed Manufacturing
    Overhead Control.)

b. Work in Process Control $31,500,000
    Variable Manufacturing Overhead Allocated $31,500,000
    Work in Process Control $63,000,000
      Fixed Manufacturing Overhead Allocated $63,000,000

c. Variable Manufacturing Overhead Allocated $31,500,000
    Variable Manufacturing Overhead Spending Variance   1,900,000
    Variable Manufacturing Overhead Efficiency Variance   2,700,000
      Variable Manufacturing Overhead Control $36,100,000

    Fixed Manufacturing Overhead Allocated $63,000,000
    Fixed Manufacturing Overhead Spending Variance   200,000
    Fixed Manufacturing Prodn. Volume Overhead Variance   9,000,000
      Fixed Manufacturing Overhead Control $72,200,000

    Cost of Goods Sold $4,600,000
      Variable Manufacturing Overhead Efficiency Variance $2,700,000
      Variable Manufacturing Overhead Spending Variance   1,900,000

    Cost of Goods Sold $9,200,000
      Fixed Manuf. Overhead Spending Variance $ 200,000
      Fixed Manuf. Prodn. Volume Overhead Variance   9,000,000

Of course, rather than being closed directly to Cost of Goods Sold, in certain cases the overhead variances may be prorated at year end, as is covered in Appendix A to Chapter 8.

8-32 (30-40 min.) **Working backward from given variances.**

1. Solution Exhibit 8-32 outlines the Chapter 7 and 8 framework underlying this solution.

(a) $\$176,000 \div \$1.10$ = 160,000 pounds
(b) $\$69,000 \div \$11.50$ = 6,000 pounds
(c) $\$10,350 - \$18,000$ = $\$7,650$ F
(d) Standard direct manufacturing labor rate
                            = $\$800,000 \div 40,000$ hours
                            = $\$20$ per hour

Actual direct manufacturing labor rate	= $\$20 + \$0.50 = \$20.50$
Actual direct manufacturing labor hours	= $\$552,750 \div \$20.50$
	= 25,500 hours

(e) Standard variable manufacturing overhead rate = $\$480,000 \div 40,000$
                                            = $\$12$ per direct manufacturing labor-hour

Variable manufacturing overhead efficiency variance of $\$18,000 \div \$12$	= 1,500 excess hours
Actual hours—Excess hours	= Standard hours allowed
25,500 – 1,500	= 24,000 hours

(f) Budgeted fixed manufacturing overhead rate = $\$640,000 \div 40,000$ hours
                                            = $\$16$ per direct manufacturing labor-hour

Fixed manufacturing overhead allocated	= $\$16 \times 24,000$ hours
	= $\$384,000$
Production volume variance	= $\$640,000 - \$384,000$
	= $\$256,000$ U

2. The control of variable manufacturing overhead requires the identification of the cost drivers for such items as energy, supplies, and repairs. Control often entails monitoring nonfinancial measures that affect each cost item, one by one. Examples are kilowatts used, quantities of lubricants used, and repair parts and hours used. The most convincing way to discover why overhead performance did not agree with a budget is to investigate possible causes, line item by line item.

Individual fixed overhead items are not usually affected very much by day-to-day control. Instead, they are controlled periodically through planning decisions and budgeting procedures that may sometimes have planning horizons covering six months or a year (for example, management salaries) and sometimes covering many years (for example, long-term leases and depreciation on plant and equipment

SOLUTION EXHIBIT 8-32

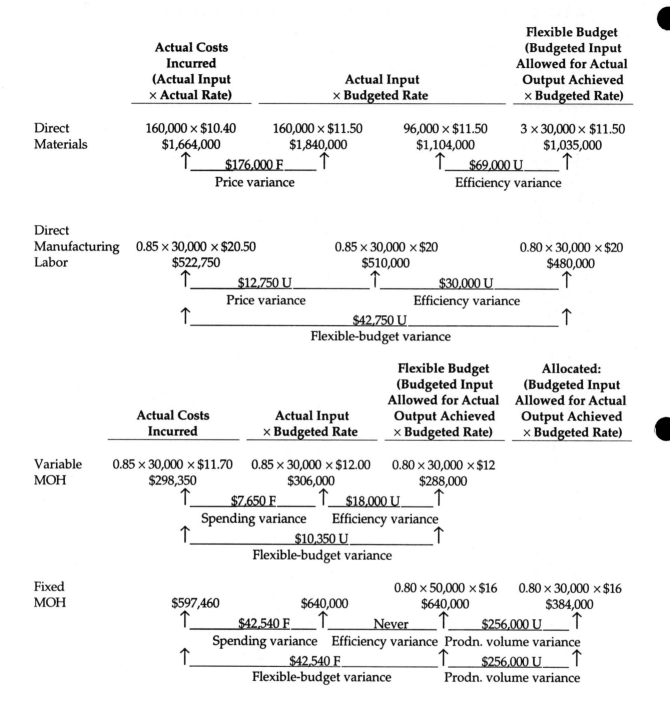

	Actual Costs Incurred (Actual Input × Actual Rate)	Actual Input × Budgeted Rate		Flexible Budget (Budgeted Input Allowed for Actual Output Achieved × Budgeted Rate)
Direct Materials	160,000 × $10.40 $1,664,000	160,000 × $11.50 $1,840,000	96,000 × $11.50 $1,104,000	3 × 30,000 × $11.50 $1,035,000
	↑___$176,000 F___↑ Price variance		↑___$69,000 U___↑ Efficiency variance	

Direct Manufacturing Labor	0.85 × 30,000 × $20.50 $522,750	0.85 × 30,000 × $20 $510,000	0.80 × 30,000 × $20 $480,000
	↑___$12,750 U___↑ Price variance	↑___$30,000 U___↑ Efficiency variance	
	↑___$42,750 U___↑ Flexible-budget variance		

	Actual Costs Incurred	Actual Input × Budgeted Rate	Flexible Budget (Budgeted Input Allowed for Actual Output Achieved × Budgeted Rate)	Allocated: (Budgeted Input Allowed for Actual Output Achieved × Budgeted Rate)
Variable MOH	0.85 × 30,000 × $11.70 $298,350	0.85 × 30,000 × $12.00 $306,000	0.80 × 30,000 × $12 $288,000	
	↑___$7,650 F___↑ Spending variance	↑___$18,000 U___↑ Efficiency variance		
	↑___$10,350 U___↑ Flexible-budget variance			
Fixed MOH	$597,460	$640,000	0.80 × 50,000 × $16 $640,000	0.80 × 30,000 × $16 $384,000
	↑___$42,540 F___↑ Spending variance	↑___Never___↑ Efficiency variance	↑___$256,000 U___↑ Prodn. volume variance	
	↑___$42,540 F___↑ Flexible-budget variance		↑___$256,000 U___↑ Prodn. volume variance	

8-34 (30-50 min.) Review of Chapters 7 and 8, 3- variance analysis.

1. Total standard production costs are based on 7,800 units of output.

Direct materials, 7,800 × $15.00	
(or 7,800 × 3 lbs. × $5.00 or 23,400 lbs. × $5.00)	117,0000
Direct manufacturing labor, 7,800 × $75.00	
(or 7,800 × 5 hrs. × $15.00 or 39,000 hrs. × $15.00)	585,000
Manufacturing overhead:	
Variable, 7,800 × $30.00 (or 39,000 hrs. × $6.00)	234,000
Fixed, 7,800 × $40.00 (or 39,000 hrs. × $8.00)	312,000
Total	$1,248,000

The following is for later use:

Fixed manufacturing overhead, a lump-sum budget $320,000*

$$\text{*Fixed manufacturing overhead rate} = \frac{\text{Budgeted fixed manufacturing overhead}}{\text{Denominator level}}$$

$$\$8.00 = \frac{\text{Budget}}{40,000 \text{ hrs.}}$$

$$\text{Budget} = 40,000 \text{ hrs.} \times \$8.00 = \$320,000$$

2. Solution Exhibit 8-34 presents a columnar presentation of the variances. An overview of the 3-variance analysis using the block format of the text is:

3-Variance Analysis	Spending Variance	Efficiency Variance	Production Volume Variance
Total Manufacturing Overhead	$39,400 U	$6,600 U	$8,000 U

SOLUTION EXHIBIT 8-34

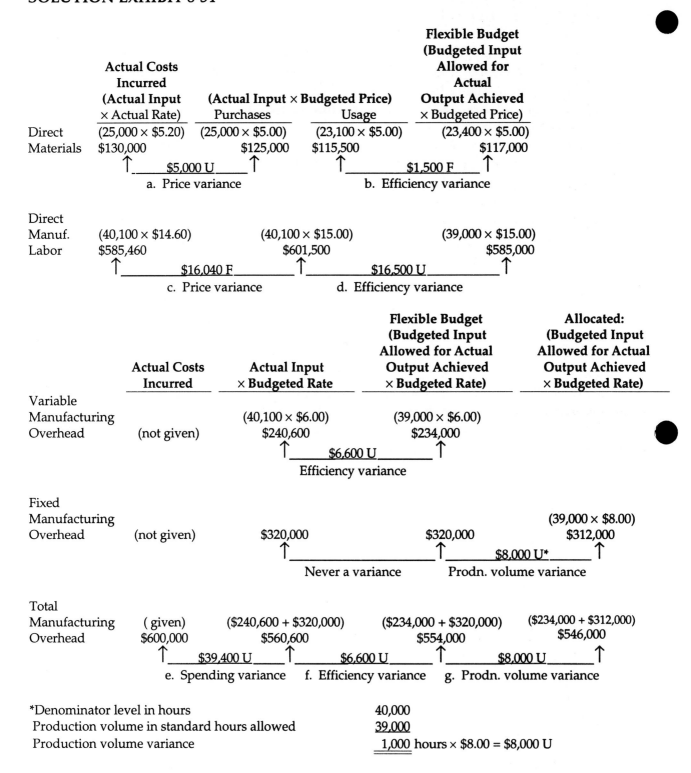

	Actual Costs Incurred (Actual Input × Actual Rate)	(Actual Input × Budgeted Price) Purchases	Usage	Flexible Budget (Budgeted Input Allowed for Actual Output Achieved × Budgeted Price)
Direct Materials	(25,000 × $5.20) $130,000	(25,000 × $5.00) $125,000	(23,100 × $5.00) $115,500	(23,400 × $5.00) $117,000

↑_____ $5,000 U _____↑   ↑_____ $1,500 F ____↑
a. Price variance   b. Efficiency variance

Direct Manuf. Labor	(40,100 × $14.60) $585,460	(40,100 × $15.00) $601,500	(39,000 × $15.00) $585,000

↑_____ $16,040 F _____↑   ↑_____ $16,500 U _____↑
c. Price variance   d. Efficiency variance

	Actual Costs Incurred	Actual Input × Budgeted Rate	Flexible Budget (Budgeted Input Allowed for Actual Output Achieved × Budgeted Rate)	Allocated: (Budgeted Input Allowed for Actual Output Achieved × Budgeted Rate)
Variable Manufacturing Overhead	(not given)	(40,100 × $6.00) $240,600	(39,000 × $6.00) $234,000	

↑_____ $6,600 U _____↑
Efficiency variance

Fixed Manufacturing Overhead	(not given)	$320,000	$320,000	(39,000 × $8.00) $312,000

↑_____↑_____ $8,000 U* _____↑
Never a variance   Prodn. volume variance

	Actual Costs Incurred	Actual Input × Budgeted Rate	Flexible Budget	Allocated
Total Manufacturing Overhead	(given) $600,000	($240,600 + $320,000) $560,600	($234,000 + $320,000) $554,000	($234,000 + $312,000) $546,000

↑____ $39,400 U ____↑____ $6,600 U _____↑____ $8,000 U _____↑
e. Spending variance   f. Efficiency variance   g. Prodn. volume variance

*Denominator level in hours 40,000
Production volume in standard hours allowed 39,000
Production volume variance .... 1,000 hours × $8.00 = $8,000 U

8-16

8-36 (15 min.) **Appendix, straightforward proration of manufacturing variances.**

1.

	Work in Process	Finished Goods	Cost of Goods Sold
Ending balances before proration ($1,800,000)	$180,000	$720,000	$ 900,000
Unfavorable net variances ($330,000 – $50,000 or $280,000); 10%, 40% and 50%	28,000	112,000	140,000
Ending balances after proration	$208,000	$832,000	$1,040,000

2.

Work in Process	$ 28,000	
Finished Goods	112,000	
Cost of Goods Sold	140,000	
Prodn. Volume Variance	50,000	
Other variances		$330,000

3.   The other variances undoubtedly include the direct materials purchase price variance, which should be prorated to Direct Materials Inventory, too. Failure to make such a proration here will affect the accuracy of the ending balances.

The information provided pertains to total ending balances, and not to the manufacturing overhead component of the total ending balances. Chapter 5 describes how the use of total ending balances can lead to inaccuracies when the overhead component is not constant over time.

8-38 (20-30 min.) **Engineered and discretionary overhead costs, customer service.**

1. The budgeted per call rate is:

$$\frac{\$3,000}{5 \times 20} \quad = \quad \$30 \text{ per call}$$

	Actual Costs Incurred	Same Lump Sum Regardless of Output Level	Allocated: (Budgeted Input Allowed for Actual Output Achieved × Budgeted Rate)
April	$24,600	$24,000[a]	$24,300[b]
May	$24,600	$24,000[a]	$19,500[c]

```
                    ↑_____ April $600 U  ↑____ April $300 F ____↑
                    ↑──── May $600 U ────↑──── May $4,500 U────↑
                       Spending variance   Production-volume variance
```

[a] $3,000 × 8 = $24,000
[b] $30 × 810 = $24,300
[c] $30 × 650 = $19,500

2.

	Actual Costs Incurred	Same Lump Sum Regardless of Output Level	Allocated: (Budgeted Input Allowed for Actual Output Achieved × Budgeted Rate)
April	$24,600	$24,000[a]	$24,400
May	$24,600	$24,000[a]	$24,000

```
                    ↑_____ April $600 U  ↑____ April $0 ____↑
                    ↑──── May $600 U ────↑──── May $0 ───────↑
                       Spending variance   Production-volume variance
```

3.   The engineered overhead cost approach highlights the possibility of overstaffing and unused capacity. It provides more insight for cost management than does the discretionary overhead cost approach if the assumption of cause-and-effect relationship between the level of service calls and labor costs is descriptive of hiring practices at Cable Galore.

8-40 (20 min.) **Standard-setting, benchmarking, ethics.**
(continuation of 8-39)

1.   Padding of standard costs and standard amounts for a billing operation can arise from:

    (i)   Deliberately taking longer time to process the bills when standards are being set.

    (ii)   Deliberately not taking advantage of information technology in the standard-setting period and then exploiting that technology later on.

    (iii)   Creating problems in billing for which solutions have already been worked out and using only those solutions in the non-standard-setting period.

    (iv)   Not purchasing items in the most economic way during the standard-setting period.

Reasons for padding include:

    (i)   Individual performance evaluation—individuals wish to look "good" for bonuses, promotion, etc. purposes.

    (ii)   Department performance evaluation—departments wish to retain autonomy which is more likely with favorable variances.

    (iii)   Defying authority and control systems—some individuals have an inherent opposition to "standards" and "controls"

2.   Stone can operate at several levels:

(a)   Best practice observation—MEG's report should be a catalyst to Sharon examining what other companies in the survey are doing and then using this best practice internally. MEG may be hired to facilitate field visits to other more efficient companies.

(b)   Operations—make flow charts of how billing occurs at Sharon, and eliminate all unnecessary steps.

(c)   Incentive systems—provide economic and other incentives to Sharon employees to implement efficiency and effectiveness improvements. The emphasis here should be on accuracy and timeliness of billing as well as the cost of billing.

(d)   Corporate culture—Sharon should emphasize that "padding" and the deliberate misrepresentation it entails is unacceptable. This could be done via in-house programs on ethics and culture or by making "examples" of those found deliberately undermining a culture of honesty and teamwork for Sharon.

CHAPTER 9
INCOME EFFECTS OF ALTERNATIVE
INVENTORY-COSTING METHODS

9-2 The term **direct costing** is a misnomer for variable costing for two reasons:

a. Variable costing does not include all direct costs as inventoriable costs. Only variable direct manufacturing costs are included. Any fixed direct manufacturing costs and any direct nonmanufacturing costs (either variable or fixed) are excluded from inventoriable costs.

b. Variable costing includes as inventoriable costs not only direct manufacturing costs but also some indirect costs (variable indirect manufacturing costs).

9-4 The main issue between variable costing and absorption costing is the proper timing of the release of fixed manufacturing costs as costs of the period:

a. at the time of incurrence, or

b. at the time the finished units to which the fixed overhead relates are sold.

Variable costing uses (a) and absorption costing uses (b).

9-6 Variable costing does not view fixed costs as unimportant or irrelevant, but it maintains that the distinction between behaviors of different costs is crucial for certain decisions. The planning and management of fixed costs is critical, irrespective of what inventory costing method is used.

9-8 The factors that affect the breakeven point under variable costing are:

1. Fixed costs.
2. Unit contribution margin.
3. Sales level in units.

9-10 Under throughput costing, only variable direct materials costs are inventoriable. This is only a subset of the costs inventoriable under variable costing—hence the term "super-variable costing." For example, variable direct manufacturing labor is a cost of the period in which they are incurred under throughput costing but an inventoriable cost under variable costing.

9-12 Approaches used to reduce the negative aspects associated with using absorption costing include:

a. Change the accounting system
- Adopt either variable or throughput costing, both of which reduce the incentives of managers to build for inventory.
- Adopt an inventory holding charge for managers who tie up funds in inventory.

b. Extend the time period used to evaluate performance. By evaluating performance over a longer time period (say, 3 to 5 years), the incentive to take short-run actions that reduce long-term income is lessened.

c. Include nonfinancial as well as financial variables in the measures used to evaluate performance.

9-14 The *theoretical capacity* and *practical capacity* denominator-level concepts emphasize what a plant can supply. The *normal utilization* and *master-budget utilization* concepts emphasize what customers demand for products produced by a plant.

9-16 (30 min.) **Variable and absorption costing, explaining operating income differences.**

1. Key inputs for income statement computations are:

	April	May
Beginning inventory	0	150
Production	500	400
Goods available for sale	500	550
Units sold	350	520
Ending inventory	150	30

The unit fixed and total manufacturing costs per unit under absorption costing are:

		April	May
(a)	Fixed manufacturing costs	$2,000,000	$2,000,000
(b)	Units produced	500	400
(c)=(a)÷(b)	Unit fixed manufacturing costs	$4,000	$5,000
(d)	Unit variable manufacturing costs	$10,000	$10,000
(e)=(c)+(d)	Unit total manufacturing costs	$14,000	$15,000

9-16 (Cont'd.)

(a) Variable costing

	April 19_7		May 19_7	
Revenues[a]		$8,400,000		$12,480,000
Variable costs				
Beginning inventory	$ 0		$1,500,000	
Variable cost of goods manufactured[b]	5,000,000		4,000,000	
Cost of goods available for sale	5,000,000		5,500,000	
Ending inventory[c]	1,500,000		300,000	
Variable manufacturing cost of goods sold	3,500,000		5,200,000	
Variable marketing costs	1,050,000		1,560,000	
Total variable costs		4,550,000		6,760,000
Contribution margin		3,850,000		5,720,000
Fixed costs				
Fixed manufacturing costs	2,000,000		2,000,000	
Fixed marketing costs	600,000		600,000	
Total fixed costs		2,600,000		2,600,000
Operating income		$1,250,000		$3,120,000

a. $24,000 × 350; 520
b $10,000 × 500; 400
c $10,000 × 150; 30

9-16 (Cont'd.)

(b)   Absorption costing

	April 19_7		May 19_7	
Revenues[a]		$8,400,000		$12,480,000
Cost of goods sold				
Beginning inventory	0		$2,100,000	
Variable manufacturing costs[b]	$5,000,000		4,000,000	
Fixed manufacturing costs[c]	2,000,000		2,000,000	
Cost of goods available for sale	7,000,000		8,100,000	
Ending inventory[d]	2,100,000		450,000	
Cost of goods sold		4,900,000		7,650,000
Gross margin		3,500,000		4,830,000
Marketing costs				
Variable marketing costs[e]	1,050,000		1,560,000	
Fixed marketing costs	600,000		600,000	
Total marketing costs		1,650,000		2,160,000
Operating income		$1,850,000		$ 2,670,000

[a] $24,000 × 350; 520

[b] $10,000 × 500; 400

[c] ($4,000 × 500); ($5,000 × 400)

[d] ($14,000 × 150; $15,000 × 30)

[e] ($3,000 × 350; $3,000 × 520)

2.
$$\begin{pmatrix} \text{Absorption-Costing} \\ \text{operating income} \end{pmatrix} - \begin{pmatrix} \text{Variable-costing} \\ \text{operating income} \end{pmatrix} = \begin{pmatrix} \text{Fixed manufacturing} \\ \text{costs in} \\ \text{ending inventory} \end{pmatrix} - \begin{pmatrix} \text{Fixed manufacturing} \\ \text{costs in} \\ \text{beginning inventory} \end{pmatrix}$$

April:

$$\begin{aligned}
\$1,850,000 - \$1,250,000 &= (\$4,000 \times 150) - (\$0) \\
\$600,000 &= \$600,000
\end{aligned}$$

May:

$$\begin{aligned}
\$2,670,000 - \$3,120,000 &= (\$5,000 \times 30) - (\$4,000 \times 150) \\
-\$450,000 &= \$150,000 - \$600,000 \\
-\$450,000 &= -\$450,000
\end{aligned}$$

The difference between absorption and variable costing is due solely to moving fixed manufacturing costs into inventories as inventories increase (as in April) and out of inventories as they decrease (as in May).

9-18   (40 min.)   **Variable and absorption costing, explaining operating income differences.**

1.   Key inputs for income statement computations are:

	January	February	March
Beginning inventory	0	300	300
Production	1,000	800	1,250
Goods available for sale	1,000	1,100	1,550
Units sold	700	800	1,500
Ending inventory	300	300	50

The unit fixed and total manufacturing costs per unit under absorption costing are:

		January	February	March
(a)	Fixed manufacturing costs	$400,000	$400,000	$400,000
(b)	Units produced	1,000	800	1,250
(c)=(a)÷(b)	Unit fixed manufacturing costs	$ 400	$ 500	$ 320
(d)	Unit variable manufacturing costs	$ 900	$ 900	$ 900
(e)=(c)+(d)	Unit total manufacturing costs	$ 1,300	$ 1,400	$ 1,220

9-18 (Cont'd.)

(a) Variable Costing

	January 19_8	February 19_8	March 19_8
Revenues[a]	$1,750,000	$2,000,000	$3,750,000
Variable costs			
Beginning inventory[b]	$ 0	$270,000	$ 270,000
Variable cost of goods manufactured[c]	900,000	720,000	1,125,000
Cost of goods available for sale	900,000	990,000	1,395,000
Ending inventory[d]	270,000	270,000	45,000
Variable manufacturing cost of goods sold	630,000	720,000	1,350,000
Variable marketing costs[e]	420,000	480,000	900,000
Total variable costs	1,050,000	1,200,000	2,250,000
Contribution margin	700,000	800,000	1,500,000
Fixed costs			
Fixed manufacturing costs	400,000	400,000	400,000
Fixed marketing costs	140,000	140,000	140,000
Total fixed costs	540,000	540,000	540,000
Operating income	$ 160,000	$ 260,000	$ 960,000

[a] $2,500 × 700; 800; 1,500
[b] $? × 0; $900 × 300; $900 × 300
[c] $900 × 1,000; 800; 1,250
[d] $900 × 300; 300; 50
[e] $600 × 700; 800; 1,500

9-18 (Cont'd.)

(b) Absorption Costing

	January 19_8	February 19_8	March 19_8
Revenues[a]	$1,750,000	$2,000,000	$3,750,000
Cost of goods sold			
Beginning inventory[b]	$ 0	$390,000	420,000
Variable manufacturing costs[c]	900,000	720,000	1,125,000
Fixed manufacturing costs[d]	400,000	400,000	400,000
Cost of goods available for sale	1,300,000	1,510,000	1,945,000
Ending inventory[e]	390,000	420,000	61,000
Cost of goods sold	910,000	1,090,000	1,884,000
Gross margin	840,000	910,000	1,866,000
Marketing costs			
Variable marketing costs[f]	420,000	480,000	900,000
Fixed marketing costs	140,000	140,000	140,000
Total marketing costs	560,000	620,000	1,040,000
Operating income	$280,000	$ 290,000	$ 826,000

[a] $2,500 × 700; 800; 1,500
[b] ($? × 0; $1,300 × 300; $1,400 × 300)
[c] $900 × 1,000, 800, 1,250
[d] ($400 × 1,000); ($500 × 800); ($320 × 1,250)
[e] ($1,300 × 300); ($1,400 × 300); ($1,220 × 50)
[f] $600 × 700; 800; 1,500

2.

$$\begin{pmatrix} \text{Absorption-costing} \\ \text{operating income} \end{pmatrix} - \begin{pmatrix} \text{Variable costing} \\ \text{operating income} \end{pmatrix} = \begin{pmatrix} \text{Fixed manufacturing} \\ \text{costs in} \\ \text{ending inventory} \end{pmatrix} - \begin{pmatrix} \text{Fixed manufacturing} \\ \text{costs in} \\ \text{beginning inventory} \end{pmatrix}$$

January: $280,000 − $160,000 = $120,000 − $0
                       $120,000 = $120,000

February: $290,000 − $260,000 = $150,000 − $120,000
                        $30,000 = $30,000

March: $826,000 − $960,000 = $16,000 − $150,000
                      − $134,000 = −$134,000

The difference between absorption and variable costing is due solely to moving fixed manufacturing costs into inventories as inventories increase (as in January) and out of inventories as they decrease (as in March).

9-20 (10 min.) **Absorption and variable costing.**

The answers are 1(a) and 2(c). Computations:

1. **Absorption Costing**:

Revenues[a]		$4,800,000
Cost of goods sold:		
Variable manufacturing costs[b]	$2,400,000	
Fixed manufacturing costs[c]	360,000	2,760,000
Gross margin		2,040,000
Marketing and administrative costs:		
Variable marketing and administrative[d]	1,200,000	
Fixed marketing and administrative	400,000	1,600,000
Operating income		$ 440,000

[a] $40 × 120,000
[b] $20 × 120,000
[c] Fixed manufacturing rate = $600,000 ÷ 200,000
                         = $3 per output unit
 $3 × 120,000
[d] $10 × 120,000

2. **Variable Costing**:

Revenues[a]		$4,800,000
Variable costs:		
Variable manufacturing costs of goods sold[b]	$2,400,000	
Variable marketing and administrative costs[c]	1,200,000	3,600,000
Contribution margin		1,200,000
Fixed costs:		
Fixed manufacturing costs	600,000	
Fixed marketing and administrative costs	400,000	1,000,000
Operating income		$ 200,000

[a] $40 × 120,000
[b] $20 × 120,000
[c] $10 × 120,000

9-22 (30-40 min.) **Income statements.**

1.   The Mass Company
       Income Statements For the Year 19_7
                                     (in thousands)

(a) **Variable Costing**:

Revenues (25,000 × $40)		$1,000
Variable costs:		
Beginning inventory (1,000 × $24)	$ 24	
Variable cost of goods manufactured (29,000 × $24)	696	
Cost of goods available for sale	720	
Ending inventory (5,000 × $24)	120	
Variable manufacturing cost of goods sold	600	
Variable marketing and administrative costs		
(25,000 × $1.20)	30	
Variable costs		630
Contribution margin		370
Fixed costs:		
Fixed manufacturing overhead costs	120	
Fixed marketing and admin. costs	190	
Fixed costs		310
Operating income		$ 60

(b) **Absorption Costing:**

Revenues (25,000 × $40)		$1,000
Cost of goods sold:		
Beginning inventory (1,000 × $28)	$ 28	
Variable manufacturing costs (29,000 × $24)	696	
Fixed manufacturing costs (given)	120	
Cost of goods available for sale	844	
Ending inventory (5,000 × $28)	140	
Cost of goods sold		704
Gross margin		296
Marketing and administrative costs:		
Variable marketing and admin. costs (25,000 × $1.20)	30	
Fixed marketing and admin. costs	190	
Marketing and admin. costs		220
Operating income		$ 76

2.
$$\begin{pmatrix} \text{Absorption} & \text{Variable} \\ \text{Costing} & \text{Costing} \\ \text{Operating} - \text{Operating} \\ \text{Income} & \text{Income} \end{pmatrix} = \begin{pmatrix} \text{Fixed} & \text{Fixed} \\ \text{manuf. costs} & \text{manuf. costs} \\ \text{in ending} - \text{in beginning} \\ \text{inventory} & \text{inventory} \end{pmatrix}$$

$$\$76,000 - \$60,000 = [(5,000 \times \$4) - (1,000 \times \$4)]$$
$$= \$20,000 - \$4,000$$
$$= \$16,000$$

The operating income figures differ because the amount of fixed manufacturing costs in the ending inventory differs from that in beginning inventory.

3. Advantages:

   a. The fixed costs are reported as period costs (and not allocated to inventory), thus increasing the likelihood of better control of these costs.
   b. Operating income is directly influenced by changes in unit sales (and not influenced by build-up of inventory).
   c. The impact of fixed costs on operating income is emphasized.
   d. The income statements are in the same form as used for cost-volume-profit analysis.
   e. Product line, territory, etc., contribution margins are emphasized and more readily ascertainable.

   Disadvantages:
   a. Total costs may be overlooked when considering operating problems.
   b. Distinction between fixed and variable costs is arbitrary for many costs.
   c. Emphasis on variable costs may cause some managers to ignore fixed costs.
   d. A new variable-costing system may be too costly to install unless top managers think that operating decisions will be improved collectively.

9-24 (10-20 min.) **Breakeven under absorption costing .**
(continuation of 9-23)

1.   The unit contribution margin is $5 – $3 – $1 = $1. Total fixed costs ($540,000) divided by the unit contribution margin ($1.00) equals 540,000 units. Therefore, under variable costing 540,000 units must be <u>sold</u> to break even.

2.   If there are no changes in inventory levels, the breakeven point can be the same, 540,000 units, under both variable costing and absorption costing. However, as the preceding problem demonstrates, under absorption costing, the breakeven point is not unique; operating income is a function of both sales and production. Some fixed overhead is "held back" when inventories rise (10,000 units × $0.70 = $7,000), so operating income is positive even though sales are at the breakeven level as commonly conceived.

$$\text{Breakeven sales in units} = \frac{\left(\begin{array}{c}\text{Total fixed}\\\text{costs}\end{array}\right) + \left[\left(\begin{array}{c}\text{Fixed manuf.}\\\text{overhead}\\\text{rate}\end{array}\right) \times \left(\begin{array}{c}\text{Breakeven}\\\text{sales in}\\\text{units}\end{array} - \begin{array}{c}\text{Units}\\\text{produced}\end{array}\right)\right]}{\text{Unit contribution margin}}$$

Let N   = Breakeven sales in units

$$N = \frac{\$540,000 + \$0.70(N - 550,000)}{\$1.00}$$

$$N = \frac{\$540,000 + \$0.70N - \$385,000}{\$1.00}$$

$$\$0.30N = \$155,000$$

$$N = 516,667 \text{ units (rounded)}$$

Therefore, under absorption costing, when 550,000 units are produced, 516,667 units must be sold for the income statement to report zero operating income.

Proof of 19_8 breakeven point:

Gross margin, 516,667 units × ($5.00 – $3.70)		$671,667
Output level MOH variance, as before	$ 35,000	
Marketing and administrative costs:		
Variable, 516,667 units × $1.00	516,667	
Fixed	120,000	671,667
Operating income		$ 0

3.   If no units are sold, variable costing will show an operating loss equal to the fixed manufacturing costs, \$420,000 in this instance. In contrast, the company would break even under absorption costing, although nothing was sold to customers. This is an extreme example of what has been called "selling fixed manufacturing overhead to inventory."

<u>A final note</u>: We find it helpful to place the following comparisons on the board, keyed to the three parts of this problem:

1. Breakeven = f (sales)
2. Breakeven = f (sales and production)
3. Breakeven = f (0 units sold and 540,000 units produced), an extreme case

9-26 (30 min.) **Operating income effects of alternative denominator-level concepts.**

1. Solution Exhibit 9-26 reports the operating income for each denominator-level concept. Computations include:

Denominator-Level Concept	Variable Manufacturing Cost*	Budgeted Fixed Manufacturing Overhead Cost Rate	Total Manufacturing Costs
Theoretical capacity	$46.30	$ 7.99	$54.29
Practical capacity	46.30	12.00	58.30
Normal capacity	46.30	15.00	61.30

* $120,380,000 ÷ 2,600,000 = $46.30 per barrel

The output-level overhead variance for each denominator-level concept is:

(a) Theoretical capacity: $40,632,000 − ($7.99 × 2,600,000)
    $40,632,000 − $20,774,000 = $19,858,000 U
(b) Practical capacity: $40,632,000 − ($12.00 × 2,600,000)
    $40,632,000 − $31,200,000 = $ 9,432,000 U
(c) Normal utilization: $40,632,000 − ($15.00 × 2,600,000)
    $40,632,000 − $39,000,000 = $ 1,632,000 U

Illustration of operating income differences:

Practical − Theoretical:	$13,848,000 −	$13,046,000	=	$ 802,000
Normal − Practical:	$14,448,000 −	$13,848,000	=	$ 600,000
Normal − Theoretical:	$14,448,000 −	$13,046,000	=	$1,402,000

The difference in operating income across the three denominator-level concepts is due solely to differences in fixed manufacturing overhead included in the ending 200,000 barrels of inventory:

Theoretical capacity: 200,000 × $ 7.99 = $1,598,000

}$802,000 difference

Practical capacity: 200,000 × $12.00 = $2,400,000

}$600,000 difference

Normal capacity: 200,000 × $15.00 = $3,000,000

9-26 (Cont'd.)

2. Given the data in this question, the theoretical capacity concept reports the lowest operating income and thus (other things being equal) the lowest tax bill for 19_8. Lucky Larger benefits by having deductions as early as possible. The theoretical capacity denominator-level concept maximizes the deductions for manufacturing costs.

3. The IRS may restrict the flexibility of a company in several ways.
   a. Restrict the denominator-level concept choice.
   b. Restrict the cost line items that can be expensed rather than inventoried.
   c. Restrict the ability of a company to use shorter write-off periods or more accelerated write-off periods for inventoriable costs.

SOLUTION EXHIBIT 9-26

	Theoretical Capacity	Practical Capacity	Normal Utilization
Revenues ($68 × 2,400,000)	$163,200,000	$163,200,000	$163,200,000
Cost of goods sold:			
Beginning inventory	0	0	0
Variable manufacturing costs,			
$46.30 × 2,600,000	120,380,000	120,380,000	120,380,000
Fixed manufacturing overhead costs,			
$7.99, $12, $15 × 2,600,000	20,774,000	31,200,000	39,000,000
Cost of goods available for sale	141,154,000	151,580,000	159,380,000
Ending inventory,			
$54.29, $58.30, $61.30 × 200,000	10,858,000	11,660,000	12,260,000
Total cost of goods sold (at budgeted costs)	130,296,000	139,920,000	147,120,000
Adjustment for variances	19,858,000[a]	9,432,000[a]	1,632,000[a]
Cost of goods sold	150,154,000	149,352,000	148,752,000
Gross margin	13,046,000	13,848,000	14,448,000
Other costs	0	0	0
Operating income	$ 13,046,000	$ 13,848,000	$ 14,448,000

[a] See the answer to requirement 1 for computation.

9-28 (40 min.) The All-Fixed Company in 19_9.

● This problem always generates active classroom discussion.

1. The treatment of fixed manufacturing overhead in absorption costing is affected primarily by what denominator level is selected as a base for allocating fixed manufacturing costs to units produced. In this case, is 10,000 tons per year, 20,000 tons, or some other denominator level the most appropriate base?

We usually place the following possibilities on the board or overhead projector and then ask the students to indicate by vote how many used one denominator level versus another. Incidentally, discussion tends to move more clearly if variable-costing income statements are discussed first, because there is little disagreement as to computations under variable costing.

a. Variable-Costing Income Statements:

		19_8	19_9	Together
Revenues (and contribution margin)		$300,000	$300,000	$600,000
Fixed costs:				
Manufacturing costs	$280,000			
Marketing and administrative cost	40,000	320,000	320,000	640,000
Operating income		$(20,000)	$(20,000)	$(40,000)

● b. Absorption Income Statements:

The ambiguity about the 10,000- or 20,000-unit denominator level is intentional. IF YOU WISH, THE AMBIGUITY MAY BE AVOIDED BY GIVING THE STUDENTS A SPECIFIC DENOMINATOR LEVEL IN ADVANCE.

Alternative 1. Use 20,000 units as a denominator; fixed manufacturing overhead per unit is $280,000 ÷ 20,000 = $14.

	19_8	19_9	Together
Revenues	$300,000	$ 300,000	$600,000
Manufacturing costs @ $14	280,000	--	280,000
Deduct ending inventory	140,000	--	--
Cost of goods sold	140,000	140,000*	280,000
Underallocated manuf. overhead--			
output level variance	--	280,000	280,000
Marketing and administrative costs	40,000	40,000	80,000
Total costs	180,000	460,000	640,000
Operating income	$120,000	$(160,000)	$(40,000)

* Inventory carried forward from 19_8 and sold in 19_9.

●

9-28 (Cont'd.)

<u>Alternative 2</u>.   Use 10,000 units as a denominator; fixed manufacturing overhead per unit is $280,000 ÷ 10,000 = $28.

	19_8	19_9	Together
Revenues	$300,000	$300,000	$600,000
Manufacturing costs @ $28	560,000	--	560,000
Deduct ending inventory	280,000	--	--
Cost of goods sold*	280,000	280,000	560,000
Underallocated manuf. overhead-- output level variance	--	280,000	--
Overallocated manuf. overhead -- output level variance	(280,000)	–	–
Marketing and administrative costs	40,000	40,000	80,000
Total costs	40,000	600,000	640,000
Operating income	$260,000	$(300,000)	$ (40,000)

*Inventory carried forward from 19_8 and sold in 19_9.

Note that operating income under variable costing follows sales and is not affected by inventory changes.

Note also that students will understand the variable-costing presentation much more easily than the alternatives presented under absorption costing.

2.   Breakeven point $= \dfrac{\text{Fixed costs}}{\text{Contribution margin per ton}} = \dfrac{\$320,000}{\$30}$

$=$ 10,667 tons per year or 21,333 for two years.

If the company could sell 667 more tons per year at $30 each, it could get the extra $20,000 contribution margin needed to break even.

Most students will say that the breakeven point is 10,667 tons per year under both absorption costing and variable costing. The logical question to ask a student who answers 10,667 tons for variable costing is: "What operating income do you show for 19_8 under absorption costing?" If a student answers $120,000 (alternative 1 above), or $260,000 (alternative 2 above), ask: "But you say your breakeven point is 10,667 tons. How can you show an operating income on only 10,000 tons sold during 1998?"

The answer to the above dilemma lies in the fact that operating income is affected by both sales and production under absorption costing.

9-28 (Cont'd.)

Optional: Given that sales would be 10,000 tons in 19_8, solve for the production level that will provide a breakeven level of zero operating income. Using the formula in the chapter, sales of 10,000 units, and a fixed manufacturing overhead rate of $14 (based on $280,000 ÷ 20,000 units denominator level = $14):

Let P = Production level

$$\text{Breakeven sales in units} = \frac{\left(\substack{\text{Total fixed} \\ \text{costs}}\right) + \left[\left(\substack{\text{Fixed manuf.} \\ \text{overhead} \\ \text{rate}}\right) \times \left(\substack{\text{Breakeven} \\ \text{sales in} \\ \text{units}} - \substack{\text{Units} \\ \text{produced}}\right)\right]}{\text{Unit contribution margin}}$$

$$10,000 \text{ tons} = \frac{\$320,000 + \$14(10,000 - P)}{\$30}$$

$300,000	=	$320,000 + $140,000 − $14P
$14P	=	$160,000
P	=	11,429 units (rounded)

Proof:

Gross margin, 10,000 × ($30 − $14)		$160,000
Output level variance, (20,000 − 11,429) × $14	$120,000	
Marketing and administrative costs	40,000	160,000
Operating income		$ 0

Given that production would be 20,000 tons in 19_8, solve for the breakeven unit sales level. Using the formula in the chapter and a fixed manufacturing overhead rate of $14 (based on a denominator level of 20,000 units):

Let N = Breakeven sales in units

$$N = \frac{\left(\substack{\text{Total fixed} \\ \text{costs}}\right) + \left[\left(\substack{\text{Fixed manuf.} \\ \text{overhead rate}}\right) \times \left(N - \substack{\text{Units} \\ \text{produced}}\right)\right]}{\text{Unit contribution margin}}$$

$$N = \frac{\$320,000 + \$14(N - 20,000)}{\$30}$$

$30N	=	$320,000 + $14N − $280,000
$16N	=	$40,000
N	=	2,500 units

9-28 (Cont'd.)

Proof:

Gross margin, 2,500 × ($30 – $14)		$40,000
Output level MOH variance	$ 0	
Marketing and administrative costs	40,000	40,000
Operating income		$ 0

We find it helpful to put the following comparisons on the board:

Variable costing breakeven = f(sales)
= 10,000 tons

Absorption-costing breakeven = f(sales and production)
= f(10,000 and 11,429)
= f(2,500 and 20,000)

3. Absorption costing inventory cost: Either $140,000 or $280,000 at the end of 19_8 and zero at the end of 19_9.

Variable costing: Zero at all times. This is a major criticism of variable costing and focuses on the issue of the definition of an asset.

4. Operating income is affected by both production and sales under absorption costing. Hence, most managers would prefer absorption costing because their performance in any given reporting period, at least in the short run, is influenced by how much production is scheduled near the end of a period.

9-30 (25-35 min.) **Comparison of variable costing and absorption costing.**

1. Operating income is a function of both sales and production under absorption costing, whereas it is a function only of sales under variable costing. Therefore, inventory changes can have dramatic effects on operating income under absorption costing. In this case, the severe decline in inventory has resulted in enormous fixed costs from beginning inventory being charged against 19_8 operations.

2. The income statement deliberately contains an ambiguity about whether the fixed manufacturing overhead of $1,000,000 is the budgeted or actual amount. Of course, it must be the budgeted amount, because the spending variance and the output level variance are shown separately. Therefore:

$$\begin{matrix} \text{Output level} \\ \text{Manuf. costs variance} \end{matrix} = \begin{matrix} \text{Budgeted fixed} \\ \text{manufacturing overhead} \end{matrix} - \begin{matrix} \text{Fixed manufacturing} \\ \text{overhead allocated} \end{matrix}$$

$$\$400,000 = \$1,000,000 - \text{Allocated}$$

$$\text{Allocated} = \$600,000, \text{ which is 60\% of denominator level}$$

3. Note that the answer to (3) is independent of (2). The difference in operating income of $315,000 ($600,000 − $285,000) is explained by the release of $315,000 of fixed manufacturing costs when the inventories were decreased during 19_8:

	Absorption Costing	Variable Costing	Fixed Manuf. Overhead in Inventory
Inventories:			
December 31, 19_7	$1,650,000	$1,320,000	$330,000
December 31, 19_8	75,000	60,000	15,000
Release of fixed manuf. costs			$315,000

The above schedule in this requirement is a formal presentation of the equation:

$$\left(\begin{matrix} \text{Absorpting} \\ \text{Costing} \\ \text{operating} \\ \text{income} \end{matrix} - \begin{matrix} \text{Variable} \\ \text{Costing} \\ \text{operating} \\ \text{income} \end{matrix} \right) = \left(\begin{matrix} \text{Fixed} \\ \text{manuf. costs in} \\ \text{ending} \\ \text{inventory} \end{matrix} - \begin{matrix} \text{Fixed} \\ \text{manuf. costs in} \\ \text{beginning} \\ \text{inventory} \end{matrix} \right)$$

$$(\$285,000 - \$600,000) = (\$15,000 - \$330,000)$$
$$= -\$315,000$$

Alternatively, the presence of fixed manufacturing overhead costs in each income statement can be analyzed:

Absorption costing,
  Fixed manuf. costs in cost of goods sold
    ($4,575,000 - $3,660,000) $ 915,000
  Output level MOH variance 400,000
    1,315,000

Variable costing, fixed manuf. costs charged to
  expense 1,000,000
Difference in operating income explained $ 315,000

Although it is not required, the following supplementary analysis may clarify the relationships:

	Absorption Costing	Variable Costing
Inventory, December 31, 19_7	$1,650,000	$1,320,000
Cost of goods manufactured*	3,000,000	2,400,000
Available for sale	4,650,000	3,720,000
Inventory, December 31, 19_8	75,000	60,000
Cost of goods sold	$4,575,000	$3,660,000

*Computed from the other data, which are given.

4. a. Absorption costing is more likely than variable costing to lead to inventory buildups. Under absorption costing, operating income in a given accounting period is increased because some fixed manufacturing overhead is accounted for as an asset (inventory) instead of an expense (fixed cost written off during the current period).

   b. Although variable costing will counteract undesirable inventory buildups, other measures can be used without abandoning absorption costing. Examples include budget targets and nonfinancial measures of performance such as maintaining specific inventory levels, inventory turnovers, delivery schedules, and equipment maintenance schedules.

9-32 (30-40 min.)   **Some additional requirements to problem 9-31; absorption costing and output-level variances.**

1. Revenues (1,070 × $1,000) $1,070,000
    Cost of goods sold:
        Beginning inventory (50 × $800) $ 40,000
        Variable manufacturing costs (1,180 × $200)   236,000
        Fixed manufacturing costs (1,180 × $600)   708,000
        Cost of goods available for sale   984,000
        Ending inventory (160 × $800)   128,000
            Cost of goods sold (at std. costs)   856,000
    Gross margin (at standard costs)   214,000
    Adjustment for variances[a]   12,000
    Gross margin   202,000
    Marketing and administrative costs:
        Variable marketing and admin. costs   53,500
        Fixed marketing and admin. costs   120,000
        Adjustment for variances   0
            Marketing and admin. costs   173,500
    Operating income $ 28,500

[a] Unfavorable output level (production volume)
    variance = 20 × $600 = $12,000

The decrease in operating income from $40,000 for Jan.–Nov. 19_7 to $28,500 for Jan.–Dec. 19_7 arises because:

Operating income through November 30, 19_7 $40,000
Additional revenues $70,000
Additional cost of goods sold $56,000
Additional other variable costs   3,500   59,500   10,500
                                                     50,500
Production-volume variance   12,000
Additional other fixed costs   10,000   22,000
Operating income for 19_7 $28,500

2. Fixed manufacturing overhead rate:
        Total fixed manufacturing overhead (1,200 units × $600) $720,000
        Divide by practical capacity (125 units × 12 months)   1,500
        Equals fixed manufacturing overhead rate $480 per unit
        Units produced during 19_7   1,180

        Production-volume variance: (1,500 – 1,180 units) × $480
                        320 units × $480   = $153,600 U

9-34 (30 min.) **Absorption costing, standard costs, management ethics.**

1.   Solution Exhibit 9-34 reports the absorption-costing operating income to be $2,006,000. The 19_7 operating income increase over 19_6 is 40.57%:

$$\frac{\$2,006,000}{\$1,427,010} = 40.57\% \text{ increase}$$

2.   The ending inventory of 30,000 crankshafts absorbs $540,000 of the standard fixed manufacturing costs. Thus, if the Flint Division had zero ending inventory, the operating income would have been $1,466,000 ($2,006,000 – $540,000). (Alternatively, if the Flint Division had ending inventory of 30,000 units but used variable costing, operating income would have been $540,000.) The 19_7 operating income increase over 19_6 would have been only

$$\frac{\$1,466,000}{\$1,427,010} = 2.73\% \text{ increase}$$

Easson may suspect Wood of "producing for inventory" because he has qualified himself for a 30% annual bonus by having 30,000 crankshafts in inventory. A policy of producing only to order (with zero inventories) would have resulted in Wood receiving a visit from the "IEC corporate consulting team."

   Assuming 250 working days a year, daily production averages 1,920. Hence, the ending inventory is approximately 15.625 days of production. Wood might argue that it is necessary to hold this inventory to meet any variation in demand. However, this position seems unlikely given that there has been a reduction in demand in the last four months of 19_7 (hence, excess capacity now probably exists) and the standard machining time per crankshaft is only 30 minutes. Another argument Wood might make is that there are economies of scale in large production runs of crankshafts. (Note that the data in the question assumes no economies of scale.)

3.   Easson should be careful in raising issues of management ethics with Wood. As a head of IEC corporate consulting, she is in an advisory role. She might make detailed suggestions about how IEC's costs could be reduced by holding less inventory. However, suggestions about Wood being unethical probably should come from those to whom Wood reports in a hard-line relationship.

SOLUTION EXHIBIT 9-34
Industrial Equity Company, Flint Division
Income Statement Using Absorption Costing for 19_7

Revenues ($66 × 450,000)		$29,700,000
Cost of goods sold		
Beginning inventory,	$ 0	
Variable manufacturing costs,		
$37^a × 480,000	17,760,000	
Fixed manufacturing costs,		
$18^b × 480,000	8,640,000	
Cost of goods available for sale	26,400,000	
Ending inventory,		
$55^c × 30,000	1,650,000	
Total cost of goods sold		
(at standard costs)	24,750,000	
Adjustment for variances	300,000 U	
Total cost of goods sold		25,050,000
Gross margin		4,650,000
Marketing costs		
Variable marketing costs:		
$4 × 450,000	1,800,000	
Fixed marketing costs	1,000,000	
Adjustment for variances	$ (156,000)	
Total marketing costs		2,644,000
Operating income		$ 2,006,000

[a] Standard variable manufacturing cost per crankshaft:

Direct materials	$20
Direct manufacturing labor	5
Manufacturing overhead	12
	$37

[b] Standard fixed manufacturing cost per crankshaft:
$9,000,000 ÷ 500,000 = $18.00 per crankshaft

[c] Standard absorption manufacturing cost per crankshaft:

Variable manufacturing cost	$37
Fixed manufacturing cost	18
	$55

9-36   (60 min.)   **Absorption, variable, and throughput costing.**

1.

(a)   Unit fixed manufacturing overhead cost

$$= \frac{\$7,500,000}{3,000 \text{ vehicles} \times 20 \text{ standard hours}}$$

$$= \frac{\$7,500,000}{60,000}$$

$$= \$125 \text{ per standard assembly hour}$$
or $2,500 per vehicle

(b)

Direct materials per unit	$6,000
Direct manufacturing labor per unit	1,800
Variable manufacturing overhead per unit	2,000
Fixed manufacturing overhead per unit	2,500
Total manufacturing cost per unit	$12,300

9-36 (Cont'd.)

2. Amounts in thousands.

	Absorption Costing		
	January	February	March
Revenues	$32,000	$46,400	$51,200
Cost of goods sold			
Beginning inventory	0	14,760	8,610
Variable manufacturing costs	31,360	23,520	37,240
Fixed manufacturing costs	8,000	6,000	9,500
Cost of goods available for sale	39,360	44,280	55,350
Ending inventory	14,760	8,610	15,990
Cost of goods sold (at standard cost)	24,600	35,670	39,360
Adjustment for variances	500 F	1,500 U	2,000 F
Total cost of goods sold	24,100	37,170	37,360
Gross margin	7,900	9,230	13,840
Marketing costs	0	0	0
Operating income	$ 7,900	$ 9,230	$13,840
Inventory Details (Units)			
Beginning inventory	0	1,200	700
Production	3,200	2,400	3,800
Goods available for sale	3,200	3,600	4,500
Sales	2,000	2,900	3,200
Ending inventory	1,200	700	1,300
Inventory Details ($12,300 per unit)			
Beginning inventory ($12,300 per unit)	$ 0	$14,760	$ 8,160
Ending inventory ($1,000s)	$14,760	$ 8,610	$15,990

Computation of Bonus	January	February	March
Operating income	$7,900,000	$9,230,000	$13,840,000
× 0.5%	$ 39,500	$46,150	$ 69,200

3. Amounts in thousands

	Variable Costing		
	January	**February**	**March**
Revenues	$32,000	$46,400	$51,200
Variable Costs			
Beginning inventory	0	11,760	6,860
Variable cost of goods manufactured	31,360	23,520	37,240
Cost of goods available for sale	31,360	35,280	44,100
Ending inventory	11,760	6,860	12,740
Variable manuf. COGS	19,600	28,420	31,360
Variable marketing costs	0	0	0
Variable costs (at standard cost)	19,600	28,420	31,360
Adjustment for variances	0	0	0
Total variable costs	19,600	28,420	31,360
Contribution margin	12,400	17,980	19,840
Fixed costs			
Fixed manuf. overhead costs	7,500	7,500	7,500
Fixed marketing costs	0	0	0
Fixed costs (at standard cost)	7,500	7,500	7,500
Adjustment for variances	0	0	0
Total fixed costs	7,500	7,500	7,500
Operating income	$ 4,900	$10,480	$12,340

Inventory details ($9,800 per unit)

	January	February	March
Beginning inventory (units)	0	1,200	700
Ending inventory (units)	1,200	700	1,300
Beginning inventory $000s	$0	$11,760	$ 6,860
Ending inventory ($000s)	$11,760	$ 6,860	$12,740

Computation of Bonus	**January**	**February**	**March**
Operating income	$4,900,000	$10,480,000	$12,340,000
× 0.5%	$ 24,500	$52,400	$ 61,700

4.

	January	February	March	Total
Absorption-Costing Bonus	$39,500	$46,150	$69,200	$154,850
Variable-Costing Bonus	24,500	52,400	61,700	138,600
Difference	$15,000	$ (6,250)	$ 7,500	$16,250

The difference between absorption and variable costing arises because of differences in production and sales:

	January	February	March	Total
Production	3,200	2,400	3,800	9,400
Sales	2,000	2,900	3,200	8,100
Δ in Inventory	1,200	(500)	600	1,300

9-36 (Cont'd.)

By building for inventory, Hart can capitalize $2,500 of fixed manufacturing overhead costs per unit. This will provide a bonus payment of $12.50 per unit, as operating income under absorption costing will exceed that under variable costing when production is greater than sales. Over the three-month period, the inventory buildup is 1,300 units giving a difference of $16,250 in bonus payments.

5.   Amounts in thousands

	Throughput Costing		
	January	February	March
Revenues	$32,000	$46,400	$51,200
Variable direct materials costs			
Beginning inventory	0	7,200	4,200
Direct materials in goods manufactured	19,200	14,400	22,800
Cost of goods available for sale	19,200	21,600	27,000
Ending inventory	7,200	4,200	7,800
Total variable direct materials costs	12,000	17,400	19,200
Throughput contribution	20,000	29,000	32,000
Other costs			
Manufacturing[a]	19,660	16,620	21,940
Marketing	0	0	0
Total other costs	19,660	16,620	21,940
Operating income	$ 340	$12,380	$10,060

[a] ($3,800 × 3,200) + $7,500,000
    ($3,800 × 2,400) + $7,500,000
    ($3,800 × 3,800) + $7,500,000

Computation of Bonus	January	February	March
Operating income	$340,000	$12,380,000	$10,060,000
× 0.5%	$ 1,700	$ 61,900	$ 50,300

A summary of the bonuses paid is:

	January	February	March	Total
Absorption Costing	$39,500	$46,150	$69,200	$154,850
Variable Costing	24,500	52,400	61,700	138,600
Throughput Costing	1,700	61,900	50,300	113,900

6.   Alternative approaches include:
  (a) Use an alternative income computation approach to absorption costing.
    (i) Variable costing
    (ii) Throughput costing
  (b) Use a financial charge for inventory buildup to reduce dysfunctional aspects of absorption costing—e.g., opportunity costs of funds tied up in inventory.
  (c) Adopt non-financial performance targets—e.g., attaining but not exceeding inventory levels.
  (d) Change the compensation package to have a longer-term focus using either an external variable (e.g., stock options) or an internal variable (e.g., five-year average income).

CHAPTER 10
DETERMINING HOW COSTS BEHAVE

10-2   The two assumptions are:
1.   Variations in the total costs of a cost object are explained by variations in a single cost driver.
2.   A linear cost function adequately approximates cost behavior within the relevant range of the cost driver.   A linear cost function is a cost function where, within the relevant range, the graph of total costs versus a single cost driver forms a straight line.

10-4   No.   High correlation merely indicates that the two variables move together in the data examined.   It is essential to also consider economic plausibility before making inferences about cause and effect.   Without any economic plausibility for a relationship, it is less likely that a high level of correlation observed in one set of data will be similarly found in other sets of data.

10-6   The conference method develops cost estimates on the basis of analysis and opinions gathered from various departments of an organization (purchasing, process engineering, manufacturing, employee relations, etc.).   Advantages of the conference method include:
1.   The speed with which cost estimates can be developed.
2.   The pooling of knowledge from experts across functional areas.
3.   The improved credibility of the cost function to all personnel.

10-8   The six steps are:
1.   Choose the dependent variable (the variable to be predicted, which is some type of cost).
2.   Identify the cost driver(s) (independent variables).
3.   Collect data on the dependent variable and the cost driver(s).
4.   Plot the data.
5.   Estimate the cost function.
6.   Evaluate the estimated cost function.

Step 3 typically is the most difficult for a cost analyst.

10-10   Criteria important when choosing among alternative cost functions are:
1.   Economic plausibility.
2.   Goodness of fit.
3.   Slope of the regression line.

10-12 A *learning curve* is a function that shows how labor-hours per unit decline as units of output are increased. Two models used to capture different forms of learning are:
1. Cumulative average-time learning model. The cumulative average time per unit declines by a constant percentage each time the cumulative quantity of units produced is doubled.
2. Incremental unit-time learning model. The incremental unit time (the time needed to produce the last unit) declines by a constant percentage each time the cumulative quantity of units produced is doubled.

10-14 No. A cost driver is any factor whose change causes a change in the total cost of a related cost object. A cause-and-effect relationship underlies selection of a cost driver. Some users of regression analysis include numerous independent variables in a regression model in an attempt to maximize goodness of fit, irrespective of the economic plausibility of the independent variables included. Some of the independent variables included may not be cost drivers.

10-16 (10 min.) **Estimating a cost function.**

1. Slope coefficient $= \dfrac{\text{Difference in costs}}{\text{Difference in machine-hours}}$

    $= \dfrac{\$3,900 - \$3,000}{7,000 - 4,000}$

    $= \dfrac{\$900}{3,000} = \$0.30$ per machine hour

    Constant $= $ Total cost $-$ (Slope coefficient $\times$ Quantity of cost driver)
    $= \$3,900 - (\$0.30 \times 7,000) = \$1,800$
    $= \$3,000 - (\$0.30 \times 4,000) = \$1,800$

The cost function based on the two observations is:

Maintenance costs $= \$1,800 + \$0.30$ (machine-hours)

2. The cost function in requirement 1 is an estimate of how costs behave within the relevant range, not at cost levels outside the relevant range. If there are no months with zero machine-hours represented in the maintenance account, data in that account cannot be used to estimate the fixed costs at the zero machine-hours level. Rather, the constant component of the cost function provides the best available starting point for a straight line that approximates how a cost behaves within the relevant range.

10-18 (20 min.) **Various cost-behavior patterns.**

1. K
2. B
3. G
4. J Note that A is incorrect because, although the cost per pound eventually equals a constant at $9.20, the total dollars of cost increases linearly from that point onward.
5. I The total costs will be the same regardless of the volume level.
6. L
7. F This is a classic step-function cost.
8. K
9. C

10-20 (20 min.) **Account analysis method.**

1.
Variable costs:

Car wash labor	$240,000
Soap, cloth, and supplies	32,000
Water	28,000
Power to move conveyor belt	72,000
Total variable costs	$372,000

Fixed costs:

Depreciation	$ 64,000
Supervision	30,000
Cashier	16,000
Total fixed costs	$110,000

Costs are classified as variable because the total costs in these categories change in proportion to the number of cars washed in Lorenzo's operation. Costs are classified as fixed because the total costs in these categories do not vary with the number of cars washed.

2. Variable costs per car $= \dfrac{\$372,000}{80,000} = \$4.65$ per car

Total costs estimated for 90,000 cars = $110,000 + ($4.65 \times 90,000) = $528,500

3. Average cost in 19_8 $= \dfrac{\$372,000 + \$110,000}{80,000} = \dfrac{\$482,000}{80,000} = \$6.025$

Average cost in 19_9 $= \dfrac{\$528,500}{90,000} = \$5.87$

10-20 (Cont'd.)

Some students may assume that power costs of running the continuously moving conveyor belt is a fixed cost. In this case, the variable costs in 19_8 will be $300,000 and the fixed costs $182,000.

The variable costs per car in 19_8 = $300,000 ÷ 80,000 cars = $3.75 per car

Total costs for 90,000 cars in 19_9 = $182,000 + ($3.75 × 90,000) = $519,500

The average cost of washing a car in 19_9 = $519,500 ÷ 90,000 = $5.77

10-22 (20 min.) **Estimating a cost function, high-low method.**

1.   See Solution Exhibit 10-22. There is a positive relationship between the number of service reports (a cost driver) and the customer-service department costs. This relationship is economically plausible.

2.

	Number Of Service Reports	Customer-Service Department Costs
Highest observation of cost driver	436	$21,890
Lowest observation of cost driver	122	12,941
Difference	314	$ 8,949

Customer-service department costs = $a + b$ (number of service reports)

$$\text{Slope coefficient } (b) = \frac{\$8,949}{314} = \$28.50 \text{ per service report}$$

Constant (a) = $21,890 – $28.50 (436) = $9,464
                = $12,941 – $28.50 (122) = $9,464

Customer-service
department costs = $9,464 + $28.50 (number of service reports)

3.   Other possible cost drivers of customer-service department costs are:
   (a) Number of products replaced with a new product (and the dollar value of the new products charged to the customer-service department).
   (b) Number of products repaired and the time and cost of repairs.

SOLUTION EXHIBIT 10-22
Plot of Number of Service Reports Versus
Customer-Service Costs for Capitol Products

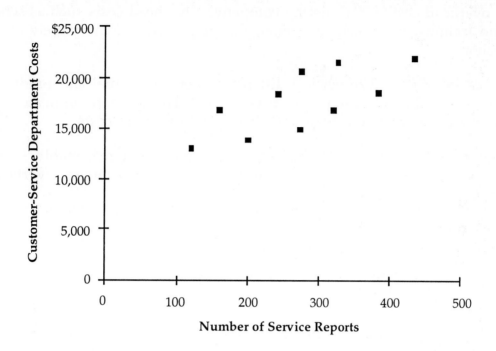

10-24 (25 min.)   **Regression analysis, service company.**

1a.   Solution Exhibit 10-24 plots the relationship between labor-hours and overhead costs and shows the regression line.

$$y = \$48,271 + \$3.93\ X$$

1b.   *Economic plausibility.* Labor-hours appears to be an economically plausible driver of overhead costs for a catering company. Overhead costs such as scheduling, hiring, and training of workers, and managing the workforce are largely incurred to support labor.

     Goodness of fit.   The vertical differences between actual and predicted costs are extremely small, indicating a very good fit.   The good fit indicates a strong relationship between the labor-hour cost driver and overhead costs.

     Slope of regression line. The regression line has a reasonably steep slope from left to right. The positive slope indicates that, on average, overhead costs increase as labor-hours increase.

2.   The regression analysis indicates that, within the relevant range of 2,500 to 7,500 labor-hours, the variable cost per person for a cocktail party equals:

Food and beverages	$15.00
Labor (0.5 hrs. × $10 per hour)	5.00
Variable overhead (0.5 hrs × $3.93 per labor-hour)	1.97
Total variable cost per person	$21.97

3.   To earn a positive contribution margin, the minimum bid for a 200-person cocktail party would be any amount greater that $4,394. This amount is calculated by multiplying the variable cost per person of $21.97 by the 200 people. At a price above the variable costs of $4,394, Bob Jones will be earning a contribution margin toward coverage of his fixed costs.

     Of course, Bob Jones will consider other factors in developing his bid including (a) an analysis of the competition—vigorous competition will limit Jones's ability to obtain a higher price (b) a determination of whether or not his bid will set a precedent for lower prices—overall, the prices Bob Jones charges should generate enough contribution to cover fixed costs and earn a reasonable profit, and (c) a judgment of how representative past historical data (used in the regression analysis) is about future costs.

SOLUTION EXHIBIT 10-24
Regression Line of Labor-Hours on Overhead Costs
for Bob Jones's Catering Company

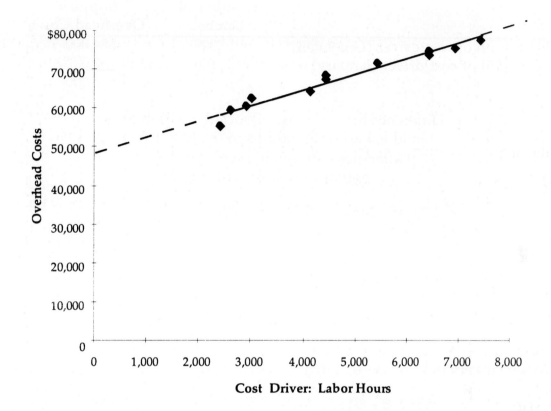

10-26 (25–30 min.) **High-low method, cost estimation, cost management.**

1a.   The high-low method estimates the cost function on the basis of only the highest and lowest observed values of the cost driver within the relevant range.

	Cost Driver: Number of Batches	Support Overhead Costs
Highest observation of cost driver (December)	309	$84,000
Lowest observation of cost driver (January)	106	57,000
Difference	203	$27,000

$$\text{Slope coefficient, } b = \frac{\text{Difference between costs associated with highest and lowest observations of the cost driver}}{\text{Difference between highest and lowest observations of the cost driver}}$$

$$= \ \$27,000 \div 203 = \$133.00 \text{ per batch}$$

The constant $a = y - bX$

At the highest observation of the cost driver,

$\quad$ Constant $a = \$84,000 - (\$133 \times 309) = \$84,000 - \$41,097 = \$42,903$

Alternatively, subject to rounding differences, the constant a could be computed using the lowest observation of the cost driver

$\quad$ Constant $a \quad = \quad \$57,000 - (\$133 \times 106) = \$57,000 - \$14,098 = \$42,902$

The high-low estimate of the cost function is

$$y \quad = \quad a + bX$$

$$y \quad = \quad \$42,903 + \$133 \times \text{Number of batches}$$

1b.   Solution Exhibit 10-26 plots the monthly data and the cost function estimated using the high-low method for support overhead costs and the number of batches.

1c.   Solution Exhibit 10-26 also plots the regression line for support overhead costs and the number of batches. Solution Exhibit 10-26 indicates clearly that the cost function represented by the regression line dominates the cost function estimated using the high-low method. The high-low cost function is not representative of, and does not "fit," the data—the high-low cost function line is on one side of the data with all data points lying below the high-low line. In contrast, the regression line goes through the data minimizing the squared vertical differences between actual and predicted costs.

The high-low cost function line exposes the obvious danger of relying on only two observations to estimate the cost relationship between number of batches and support overhead costs. For one thing, the highest and lowest cost driver value observations are not representative. Even if representative high and representative low observations are chosen, the high-low method suffers from the limitation of ignoring information from all but two observations when estimating the cost function.

Chu should definitely choose the regression line-based cost function $y = \$16,031 + \$197.30 \times$ Number of batches to estimate, manage and control costs.

2. Using the high-low cost function line $y = \$42,903 + \$133 \times$ Number of batches, for 300 batches, Chu would budget costs of

$$y = \$42,903 + \$133 \times 300 = \$42,903 + \$39,900 = \$82,803$$

Using the regression cost function line $y = \$16,031 + \$197.03 \times$ Number of batches for 300 batches, Chu would budget costs of

$$y = \$16,031 + \$197.30 \times 300 = \$16,031 + \$59,190 = \$75,221$$

3a.

	Budgeted Revenues and Costs for Next Month Using	
	High-Low Cost Function	Regression Cost Function
Costs other than support overhead	$125,000	$125,000
Support overhead costs	82,803	75,221
Total costs	207,803	200,221
Add margin of 20% of total costs	41,561	40,044
Target revenues	$249,364	$240,265

Estimating costs using the high-low cost function, rather than the regression cost function, will cause Chu to overestimate costs and choose higher target revenues and prices. If these markets are competitive, higher prices could cause Rohan Plastics to lose business. The regression cost function, which is a more accurate predictor of support overhead cost behavior, suggests that Rohan Plastics could charge lower prices, earn less revenue and still achieve the desired margin.

10-26 (Cont'd.)

3b.   Choosing the "wrong" cost function—the high-low cost function—will also have repercussions for cost management and cost control. Suppose Rohan Plastics budgets support overhead costs of $82,803 for next month using the high-low cost function. Suppose actual support overhead costs are $78,000. Based on the high-low prediction of $82,803, Rohan Plastics would conclude it has performed well, and would probably prompt the company to adopt similar practices in the future. But comparing the $78,000 performance with the $75,221 prediction of the regression model indicates poor control of costs that would instead cause Rohan Plastics to search for ways to improve its cost performance. Using the wrong cost function gives management misleading signals about how well it is managing and controlling costs.

SOLUTION EXHIBIT 10-26
Regression and High-Low Lines of Number of Batches
on Support Overhead Costs for Rohan Plastics

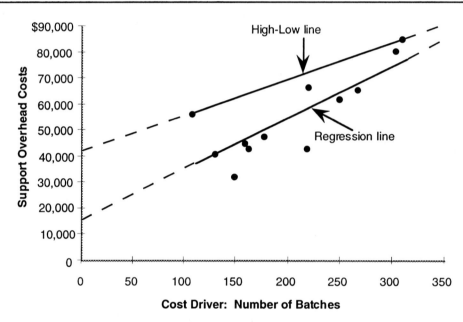

10-28 (20 min.) **Learning curve, incremental unit-time learning curve.**

1.   The direct manufacturing labor-hours (DMLH) required to produce the first 2, 3 and 4 units, given the assumption of an incremental unit-time learning curve of 90%, is as follows:

Cumulative Number of Units (1)	Individual Unit Time for Xth Unit (2)	Cumulative Total Time (3)
1	3,000	3,000
2	2,700 (3,000 × 0.90)	5,700
3	2,539	8,239
4	2,430 (2,700 × 0.90)	10,669

Values in column 2 are calculated using the formula $y = pX^q$

where p = 3,000, X = 2, 3 or 4 and $q = -0.1520$, which gives
  when X = 2, $y = 3,000 \times 2^{-0.1520} = 2,700$
  when X = 3, $y = 3,000 \times 3^{-0.1520} = 2,539$
  when X = 4, $y = 3,000 \times 4^{-0.1520} = 2,430$

	Variable costs of producing		
	2 units	3 units	4 units
Direct materials $80,000 × 2; 3; 4	$160,000	$240,000	$ 320,000
Direct manufacturing labor			
$25 × 5,700; 8,239; 10,669	142,500	205,975	266,725
Variable manufacturing overhead			
$15 × 5,700; 8,239; 10,669	85,500	123,585	160,035
Total variable costs	$388,000	$569,560	$746,760

2.

	Variable costs of producing	
	2 units	4 units
Incremental unit-time learning curve		
(from requirement 1)	$388,000	$746,760
Cumulative average-time learning curve		
(from Exercise 10-27)	376,000	708,800
Difference	$ 12,000	$ 37,960

Total variable costs for manufacturing 2 and 4 units are lower under the cumulative average-time learning curve relative to the incremental unit-time learning curve. Direct manufacturing labor-hours required to make additional units decline more slowly in the incremental unit-time learning curve relative to the cumulative average-time learning curve assuming the same 90% factor is used for both curves. The reason is that, in the incremental unit-time learning curve, as the number of units double, only the last unit produced has a cost of 90% of the initial cost. In the cumulative average-time model, doubling the number of units causes the average cost of *all* the additional units produced (not just the last unit) to be 90% of the initial cost.

10-30 (20–30 min.) **Cost estimation, incremental unit-time learning curve.**

1. Cost to Produce the Second through the Eighth Boats:

Direct materials, 7 × $100,000	$ 700,000
Direct manufacturing labor, 49,356* × $30	1,480,680
Variable overhead, 49,356 × $20	987,120
Other overhead, 25% of $1,480,680	370,170
Total costs	$3,537,970

*The direct labor hours to produce the second through the eighth boats can be calculated via a table format, given the assumption of an incremental unit-time learning curve of 85%:

Cumulative Number of Units	Individual Unit Time For Xth Unit (m)*	Cumulative Total Time
1	10,000	10,000
2	8,500	18,500
3	7,729	26,229
4	7,225	33,454
5	6,856	40,310
6	6,569	46,879
7	6,336	53,215
8	6,141	59,356

*Calculated as $m = pX^q$ where $p = 10,000$, $q = -0.2345$, and $X = 1, 2, 3, ..., 8$.

The direct manufacturing labor-hours to produce the second through the eighth boat is $59,356 - 10,000 = 49,356$ hours.

10-30 (Cont'd.)

2.   Difference in total costs to manufacture the second through the eighth boat under the incremental unit-time learning model and the cumulative average-time learning model is $3,537,970 (calculated in requirement 1 of this problem) – $2,949,975 (from requirement 1 of Problem 10-26) = $587,995.

The incremental unit-time learning curve has a slower decline in the reduction in time required to produce successive units than does the cumulative average-time learning curve (see Problem 10-29, requirement 1). Assuming the same 85% factor is used for both curves:

Cumulative Number of Units	Estimated Cumulative Direct Manufacturing Labor-Hours	
	Cumulative Average-Time Learning Model	Incremental Unit-Time Learning Model
1	10,000	10,000
2	17,000	18,500
4	28,900	33,454
8	49,130	59,356

Nautilus should examine its own internal records on past jobs and seek information from engineers, plant managers, and workers when deciding which learning curve better describes the behavior of direct manufacturing labor-hours on the production of the PT109 boats.

10-32 (30 min.) **Cost estimation, incremental unit-time learning curve.**

Cumulative Number of Lots (1)	Individual Direct Manufacturing Labor Cost per Unit in Each Lot (m)* (2)	Direct Manufacturing Labor Costs per Lot (3) = (2) × 30 units	Cumulative Total Cost
1	$40,000	$1,200,000	$1,200,000
2	36,000	1,080,000	2,280,000
3	33,848	1,015,440	3,295,440
4	32,400	972,000	4,267,440
5	31,320	939,600	5,207,040
6	30,464	913,920	6,120,960
7	29,760	892,800	7,013,760
8	29,160	874,800	7,888,560

* Calculated as $m = pX^q$ where $p = \$40,000$, $q = -0.1520$, and $X = 1, 2, 3, \ldots, 8$.

10-32 (Cont'd.)

Total variable costs of producing 240 units of new telecommunication equipment:

Direct materials, 240 units × $60,000	$14,400,000
Direct manufacturing labor	7,888,560
Variable manufacturing overhead, 60% of $7,888,560	4,733,136
Total variable manufacturing costs	$27,021,696

Difference in predicted costs:

Predicted cost under incremental unit-time learning curve model	$27,021,696
Predicted cost under cumulative average-time learning curve model (requirement 2 of Problem 10-31)	25,597,440
Difference in favor of cumulative average-time learning curve model	$ 1,424,256

When the same learning rate is assumed (90% in our example), the cumulative average learning curve model gives lower costs because the average time and cost per unit declines by 90% each time the cumulative quantity of units produced is doubled. In contrast, under the incremental unit learning curve model, only the time and cost to produce the last unit at the 2X production level is 90% of the time and cost needed to produce the last unit at the X production level.

10-34 (30–40 min.) **High-low and regression approaches.**

1.   Solution Exhibit 10-34 plots the relationship between machine-hours and power costs.

SOLUTION EXHIBIT 10-34
Plot of Machine-Hours Versus Power Costs

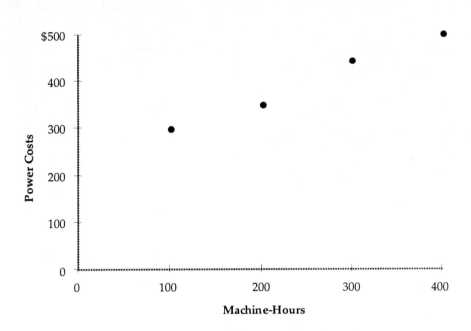

2a.

	Machine-Hours (X)	Power Costs (Y)
Highest observation of independent variable	400	$500
Lowest observation of independent variable	100	300
Difference	300	$200

Difference

$$\text{Slope coefficient} \quad = \frac{\$200}{300} = \$0.667 \text{ per machine-hour}$$

$$\text{Constant} \quad = \$500 - (\$0.667 \times 400) = \$233.20$$
$$= \$300 - (\$0.667 \times 100) = \$233.30$$
(difference in values are due to rounding errors)

Cost function estimated with high-low approach is:

$$y = \$233.20 + \$0.667X$$

10-34 (Cont'd.)

b.   One approach to computing a and b under the regression approach is to use the equations given in the chapter appendix.

Period (1)	Machine-Hours X (2)	Power Costs Y (3)	X^2 (4)	XY (5)
1	200	350	40,000	70,000
2	300	450	90,000	135,000
3	100	300	10,000	30,000
4	400	500	160,000	200,000
Total	1,000	1,600	300,000	435,000

$$\Sigma Y = na + b(\Sigma X)$$

$$\Sigma XY = a\,(\Sigma X) + b(\Sigma X)^2$$

That is,

1,600	=	$4a + 1{,}000b$	R_1
435,000	=	$1{,}000a + 300{,}000\,b$	R_2
400,000	=	$1{,}000a + 250{,}000\,b$	$R_3 = 250(R_1)$
35,000	=	$50{,}000\,b$	$R_4 = R_2 - R_3$

$$b = \frac{35{,}000}{50{,}000} = \$0.70$$

$$1{,}600 = 4a + 1{,}000\,(0.70)$$

$$900 = 4a$$

$$a = \frac{900}{4} = \$225$$

Cost function estimated with the regression approach is:

$$y = \$225 + \$0.70 \text{ (machine-hours)}$$

Alternatively, we can substitute directly by reexpressing into the normal equations symbolically as follows:

$$a = \frac{(\Sigma Y)(\Sigma X^2) - (\Sigma X)(\Sigma XY)}{n(\Sigma X^2) - (\Sigma X)(\Sigma X)}$$

$$\text{and } b = \frac{n(\Sigma XY) - (\Sigma X)(\Sigma Y)}{n(\Sigma X^2) - (\Sigma X)(\Sigma X)}$$

10-34 (Cont'd.)

Substituting, we get

$$a = \frac{(1,600)(300,000) - (1,000)(435,000)}{4(300,000) - (1,000)(1,000)} = \frac{45000,000}{200,000} = \$225$$

$$b = \frac{(4)(435,000) - (1,000)(1,600)}{4(300,000) - (1,000)(1,000)} = \frac{140,000}{200,000} = \$0.70$$

Another approach is to use a computer software package. Results are:

Variable	Coefficient	Standard Error	t-value
Constant	$225	$19.36	11.62
Independent Variable: Machine-hours	$0.70	$ 0.07	10.00

$r^2 = 0.98$; Durbin-Watson Statistic = 2.20

In this simple illustration, the high-low estimate, using only two observations, closely approximates the least squares regression approach that minimizes the sum of squares of the vertical deviations from the observations to the estimated regression line. The regression equation indicates that variable power costs are $0.70 per machine-hour against the high-low estimate of $0.667. The fixed component of power costs within the relevant range equals $225, while the high-low method estimates this component as $233.20. The high-low method gives good results in this case because all the data points fall very close to the regression line.

3. $\quad \bar{Y} = \Sigma Y \div 4 = \$1,600 \div 4 = \$400$

$$\Sigma(Y - \bar{Y})^2 = (350 - 400)^2 + (450 - 400)^2 + (300 - 400)^2 + (500 - 400)^2$$

$$= 2,500 + 2,500 + 10,000 + 10,000 = 25,000$$

Period	Y	$y = \$225 + \$0.70\,X$	Y – y	$(Y - y)^2$
1	350	365	−15	225
2	450	435	+15	225
3	300	295	+ 5	25
4	500	505	− 5	25
Total	1,600			500

$$r^2 = 1 - \frac{\text{Unexplained variation}}{\text{Total variation}} = 1 - \frac{\Sigma(Y - y)^2}{\Sigma(Y - \bar{Y})^2} = 1 - \frac{500}{25,000} = 0.98$$

10-34 (Cont'd.)

An r^2 of 0.98 indicates excellent goodness of fit. Only 2% of the variation in power costs is not explained by machine-hours. Since the relation between machine-hours and power costs is also economically plausible, Campi Corporation can be very confident of using the regression results to set its flexible budget for power costs. Machine-hours is a cost driver of power costs.

10-36 (30 min.) **Evaluating multiple regression models, not for profit.**

1. It is economically plausible that the correct form of the model of overhead costs includes both number of academic programs and number of enrolled students as cost drivers. The findings in Problem 10-35 indicate that each of the independent variables affects overhead costs. (Each regression has a significant r^2 and t-value on the independent variable.) Hanks could choose to divide overhead costs into two cost pools, (i) those overhead costs that are more closely related to number of academic program and (ii) those overhead costs more closely related to number of enrolled students, and rerun the simple regression analysis on each overhead cost pool. Alternatively, Hanks could run a multiple regression analysis with total overhead costs as the dependent variable and the number of academic programs and number of enrolled students as the two independent variables.

2. Solution Exhibit 10-36A evaluates the multiple regression model using the format of Exhibit 10-21. Hanks should use the multiple regression model over the two simple regression models of Problem 10-35. The multiple regression model appears economically plausible and the regression model performs very well when estimating overhead costs. It has an excellent goodness of fit, significant t-values on both independent variables, and meets all the specification assumptions for ordinary least squares regression.

There is some correlation between the two independent variables but multi-collinearity does not appear to be a problem here. The significance of both independent variables (despite some correlation between them) suggests that each variable is a driver of overhead cost. Of course, as the chapter describes, even if the independent variables exhibited multicollinearity, Hanks should still prefer to use the multiple regression model over the simple regression models of Problem 10-35. Omitting any one of the variables will cause the estimated coefficient of the independent variable, included in the model to be biased away from its true value.

3. Possible uses for the multiple regression results include:

a. Planning and budgeting at Southwestern University. The regression analysis indicates the variables (number of academic programs and number of enrolled students) that help predict changes in overhead costs.

b. Cost control and performance evaluation. Hanks could compare actual performance with budgeted or expected numbers and seek ways to improve the efficiency of the University operations, and evaluate the performance of managers responsible for controlling overhead costs.

10-36 (Cont'd.)

c. Cost management. If cost pressures increase, the University might save costs by closing down academic programs that have few students enrolled.

SOLUTION EXHIBIT 10-36A
Evaluation of Cost Function for Overhead Costs Estimated with Multiple Regression for Southwestern University

Criterion	Number of Academic Programs and Number of Enrolled Students as Independent Variables
1. Economic Plausibility	A positive relationship between overhead costs and number of academic programs and number of enrolled students is economically plausible at Southwestern University.
2. Goodness of Fit	$r^2 = 0.81$ Excellent goodness of fit.
3. Significance of Independent Variable(s)	t-values of 3.46 on number of academic programs and 2.03 on number of enrolled students are both significant.
4. Specification Analysis of Estimation Assumptions	The assumptions of linearity, constant variance, and normality of residuals hold, but inferences drawn from only 12 observations are not reliable; the Durbin Watson statistic = 1.84 indicates that independence of residuals holds.

10-38 (30–40 min.)   **Purchasing department cost drivers, multiple regression analysis.**

The problem reports the exact t-values from the computer runs of the data. Because the coefficients and standard errors given in the problem are rounded to three decimal places, dividing the coefficient by the standard error may yield slightly different t-values.

1.   Regression 4 is a well-specified regression model:

Economic plausibility: Both independent variables are plausible and are supported by the findings of the Couture Fabrics study.

Goodness of fit: The r^2 of 0.63 indicates an excellent goodness of fit.

Significance of independent variables: The t-value on # of POs is 2.14 while the t-statistic on # of Ss is 2.00.   These t-values are either significant or border on significance.

Specification analysis: Results are available to examine the independence of residuals assumption.   The Durbin-Watson statistic of 1.90 indicates that the assumption of independence is not rejected.

Regression 4 is consistent with the findings in Problem 10-37 that both the number of purchase orders and the number of suppliers are drivers of purchasing department costs.   Regressions 2, 3, and 4 all satisfy the four criteria outlined in the text.   Regression 4 has the best goodness of fit (0.63 for Regression 4 compared to 0.42 and 0.39 for Regressions 2 and 3, respectively). Most importantly, it is economically plausible that both the number of purchase orders and the number of suppliers drive purchasing department costs.   We would recommend that Lee use Regression 4 over Regressions 2 and 3.

2.   Regression 5 adds an additional independent variable (MP$) to the two independent variables in Regression 4.   This additional variable (MP$) has a t-value of –0.07, implying its slope coefficient is insignificantly different from zero.   The r^2 in Regression 5 (0.63) is the same as that in Regression 4 (0.63), implying the addition of this third independent variable adds close to zero explanatory power. In summary, Regression 5 adds very little to Regression 4.   We would recommend that Lee use Regression 4 over Regression 5.

3.   Budgeted purchasing department costs for the Baltimore store next year are:

$485,384 + ($123.22 × 3,900) + ($2,952 × 110) = $1,290,662

4.   Multicollinearity is a frequently encountered problem in cost accounting; it does not arise in simple regression because there is only one independent variable in a simple regression.   One consequence of multicollinearity is an increase in the standard errors of the coefficients of the individual variables.   This frequently shows up in reduced *t*-values in the multiple regression relative to their *t*-values in the simple regression:

Variables	*t*-value in Multiple Regression	*t*-value from Simple Regressions in Problem 10-37
Regression 4:		
# of POs	2.14	2.43
# of Ss	2.00	2.28
Regression 5:		
# of POs	1.95	2.43
# of Ss	1.80	2.28
MP$	–0.07	0.85

The decline in the *t*-values in the multiple regressions is consistent with some (but not very high) collinearity among the independent variables.   Pairwise correlations between the independent variables are:

	Correlation
# of POs / # of Ss	0.29
# of POs / MP$	0.27
# of Ss / MP$	0.34

5.   Decisions in which the regression results in Problems 10-37 and 10-38 could be used are:

Cost management decisions: Fashion Flair could restructure relationships with the suppliers so that fewer separate purchase orders are made. Alternatively, it may aggressively reduce the number of existing suppliers.

Purchasing policy decisions: Fashion Flair could set up an internal charge system for individual retail departments within each store. Separate charges to each department could be made for each purchase order and each new supplier added to the existing ones. These internal charges would signal to each department ways in which their own decisions affect the total costs of Fashion Flair.

Accounting system design decisions: Fashion Flair may want to discontinue allocating purchasing department costs on the basis of the dollar value of merchandise purchased. Allocation bases better capturing cause-and-effect relations at Fashion Flair are the number of purchase orders and the number of suppliers.

10-40 (40 min.) **High-low method, alternative regression functions, accrualaccounting adjustments.**

1. Solution Exhibit 10-40A presents the two data plots. The plot of engineering support reported costs and machine-hours shows two separate groups of data, each of which may be approximated by a separate cost function. The problem arises because the plant records materials and parts costs on an "as purchased," rather than an "as used," basis. The plot of engineering support restated costs and machine-hours shows a high positive correlation between the two variables (the coefficient of determination is 0.94); a single linear cost function provides a good fit to the data. Better estimates of the cost relation result because Kennedy adjusts the materials and parts costs to an accrual accounting basis.

2.

	Cost Driver Machine-Hours	Reported Engineering Support Costs
Highest observation of cost driver (August)	73	$617
Lowest observation of cost driver (September)	19	1,066
Difference	54	–$449

$$\text{Slope coefficient, } b = \frac{\text{Difference between costs associated with highest and lowest observations of the cost driver}}{\text{Difference between highest and lowest observations of the cost driver}}$$

$$= \frac{-\$449}{54} = -\$8.31 \text{ per machine hour}$$

Constant (at highest observation of cost driver) = $617 – (–$8.31)(73) = $1,224
Constant (at lowest observation of cost driver) = $1,066 – (–$8.31)(19) = $1,224

The estimated cost function is $y = \$1,224 - \$8.31X$

	Cost Driver Machine-Hours	Restated Engineering Support Costs
Highest observation of cost driver (August)	73	$966
Lowest observation of cost driver (September)	19	370
Difference	54	$596

$$\text{Slope coefficient, } b = \frac{\text{Difference between costs associated with highest and lowest observations of the cost driver}}{\text{Difference between highest and lowest observations of the cost driver}}$$

$$= \frac{596}{54} = \$11.04 \text{ per machine hour}$$

10-40 (Cont'd.)

Constant (at highest observation of cost driver)   = $ 966 – ($11.04)(73) = $160
Constant (at lowest observation of cost driver)   = $ 370 – ($11.04)(19) = $160

The estimated cost function is y = $160 + $11.04 X

3.   The cost function estimated with engineering support restated costs better approximates the regression analysis assumptions. See Solution Exhibit 10-40B for a comparison of the two regressions.

4.   Of all the cost functions estimated in requirements 2 and 3, Kennedy should choose Regression 2 using engineering support restated costs as best representing the relationship between engineering support costs and machine hours.   The cost functions estimated using engineering support reported costs are mispecified and not-economically plausible because materials and parts costs are reported on an "as purchased," rather than on an "as used," basis. With respect to engineering support restated costs, the high-low and regression approaches yield roughly similar estimates. The regression approach is technically superior because it determines the line that best fits all observations. In contrast, the high-low method only considers two points (observations with the highest and lowest cost drivers) when estimating the cost function. Solution Exhibit 10-40B shows that the cost function estimated using the regression approach has excellent goodness of fit (r^2 = 0.94) and appears to be well specified.

5.   Using the regression cost function estimated with restated costs, Kennedy should budget $748.38 as engineering support costs for December calculated as follows:
    Engineering support costs = $176.38 + ($11.44 per hour × 50 hours) = $748.38

6.   Problems Kennedy might encounter include:
    a.   A perpetual inventory system may not be used in this case; the amounts requisitioned likely will not permit an accurate matching of costs with the independent variable on a month-by-month basis.
    b.   Quality of the source records for usage by engineers may be relatively low; e.g., engineers may requisition materials and parts in batches, but not use them immediately.
    c.   Records may not distinguish materials and parts for maintenance from materials and parts used for repairs and breakdowns; separate cost functions may be appropriate for the two categories of materials and parts.
    d.   Year-end accounting adjustments to inventory may mask errors that gradually accumulate month-by-month.

10-40 (Cont'd.)

7.   Picking the correct cost function is important for cost prediction, cost management and performance evaluation. For example, had United Packaging used Regression 1 (engineering support reported costs) to estimate the cost function, it would erroneously conclude that engineering support costs decrease with machine hours. In a month with 60 machine-hours, regression 1 would predict costs of $1,393.20 − ($14.23 × 60) = $539.40. If actual costs turn out to be $800, management would conclude that changes should be made to reduce costs. In fact, on the basis of the preferred regression 2, support overhead costs are lower than the predicted amount of $176.38 + ($11.44 × 60) = $862.78—a performance that management should seek to replicate, not change.

On the other hand, if machine-hours worked in a month were low, say 25 hours, regression 1 would erroneously predict support overhead costs of $1,393.20 − ($14.23 × 25) = $1,037.45. If actual costs are $700, management would conclude that its performance has been very good. In fact, compared to the costs predicted by the preferred regression 2 of $176.38 + ($11.44 × 25) = $462.38, the actual performance is rather poor. Using regression 1, management may feel costs are being managed very well when in fact they are much higher than what they should be and need to be managed "down."

10-40 (Cont'd.)

Plots and Regression Lines for Engineering Support
Reported Costs and Engineering Support Restated Costs

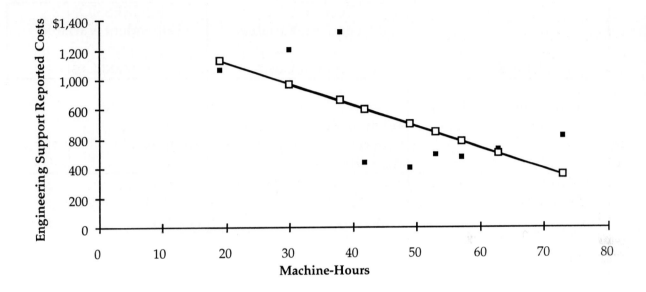

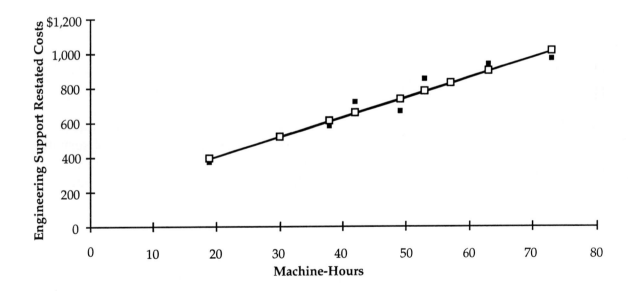

10-40 (Cont'd)

SOLUTION EXHIBIT 10-40B
Comparison of Alternative Cost Functions for Engineering Support Costs
at United Packaging

CRITERION	REGRESSION 1 Dependent Variable: Engineering Support Reported Costs	REGRESSION 2 Dependent Variable: Engineering Support Restated Costs
1. Economic Plausibility	Negative slope relationship is economically implausible over the long run.	Positive slope relationship is economically plausible.
2. Goodness of Fit	$r^2 = 0.43$. Moderate goodness of fit.	$r^2 = 0.94$. Excellent goodness of fit.
3. Significance of Independent Variables	t-statistic on machine hours is statistically significant (t = –2.31), albeit economically implausible.	t-statistic on machine hours is highly statistically significant (t=10.59).
4. Specification Analysis: A. Linearity	Linearity does not describe data very well.	Linearity describes data very well.
B. Constant variance of residuals	Appears questionable, although 12 observations do not facilitate the drawing of reliable inferences.	Appears reasonable, although 12 observations do not facilitate the drawing of reliable inferences.
C. Independence of residuals	Durbin-Watson = 2.26. Residuals serially uncorrelated.	Durbin-Watson = 1.31. Some evidence of serial correlation in the residuals.
D. Normality of residuals	Data base too small to make reliable inferences.	Data base too small to make reliable inferences.

CHAPTER 11
RELEVANT REVENUES, RELEVANT COSTS,
AND THE DECISION PROCESS

11-2   *Relevant costs* are those expected future costs that differ among alternative courses of action. Historical costs are irrelevant because they are past costs and, therefore, cannot differ among alternative future courses of action.

11-4   *Quantitative factors* are outcomes that are measured in numerical terms. Some quantitative factors are financial—that is, they can be easily expressed in financial terms. Direct materials is an example of a quantitative financial factor. *Qualitative factors* are factors that are not measured in numerical terms. An example is employee morale.

11-6   No. Some variable costs may not differ among the alternatives under consideration and, hence, will be irrelevant. Some fixed costs may differ among the alternatives and, hence, will be relevant.

11-8   *Opportunity cost* is the contribution to income that is forgone (rejected) by not using a limited resource in its next-best alternative use.

11-10   No. Managers should aim to get the highest contribution margin per unit of the constraining (that is, scarce, limiting, or critical) factor. The constraining factor is what restricts or limits the production or sale of a given product (for example, availability of machine-hours).

11-12   No. Managers tend to favor the alternative that makes their performance look best so they focus on the measures used in the performance-evaluation model. If the performance-evaluation model does not emphasize maximizing operating income or minimizing costs, managers will most likely not choose the alternative that maximizes operating income or minimizes costs.

11-14   The three steps in solving a linear programming problem are:
1.   Determine the objective.
2.   Specify the constraints.
3.   Compute the optimal solution.

11-16 (20 min.) **Disposal of assets.**

1.   This is an unfortunate situation, yet the $80,000 costs are irrelevant regarding the decision to remachine or scrap. The only relevant factors are the future revenues and future costs. By ignoring the accumulated costs and deciding on the basis of expected future costs, operating income will be maximized (or losses minimized). The difference in favor of remachining is $3,000:

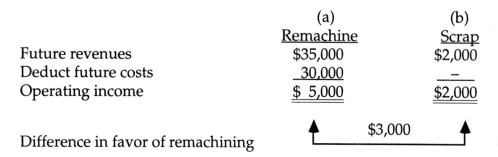

	(a) Remachine	(b) Scrap
Future revenues	$35,000	$2,000
Deduct future costs	30,000	–
Operating income	$ 5,000	$2,000

Difference in favor of remachining $3,000

2.   This, too, is an unfortunate situation. But the $100,000 original cost is irrelevant to this decision. The difference in favor of rebuilding is $7,000:

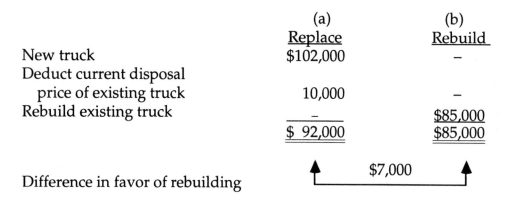

	(a) Replace	(b) Rebuild
New truck	$102,000	–
Deduct current disposal price of existing truck	10,000	–
Rebuild existing truck	–	$85,000
	$ 92,000	$85,000

Difference in favor of rebuilding $7,000

Note, here, that the current disposal price of $10,000 is relevant, but the original cost (or book value, if the truck were not brand new) is irrelevant.

11-18 (15 min.) **Multiple choice.**

1. (b)

Special order price per unit	$6.00	
Variable manufacturing costs per unit	4.50	
Contribution margin per unit	$1.50	

Effect on operating income = $1.50 × 20,000 units
                            = $30,000 increase

2. (b)

Costs of purchases, 20,000 units × $60		$1,200,000
Total relevant costs of making:		
Variable manufacturing costs, $64 – $16	$48	
Fixed costs eliminated	9	
Costs saved by not making	$57	
Multiply by 20,000 units, so total		
costs saved are $57 × 20,000		1,140,000
Extra costs of purchasing outside		60,000
Minimum savings necessary for Part No. 575		25,000
Necessary relevant costs that would have		
to be saved in manufacturing Part No. 575		$ 85,000

11-3

11-20 (30 min.) Make versus buy, activity-based costing.

1. The expected manufacturing cost per unit of CMCBs in 19_8 is as follows:

	Total manufacturing costs of CMCB (1)	Manufacturing cost per unit (2) = (1) ÷ 10,000
Direct materials $170 × 10,000	$1,700,000	$170
Direct manufacturing labor $45 × 10,000	450,000	45
Variable batch manufacturing costs $1,500 × 80	120,000	12
Fixed manufacturing costs		
Avoidable fixed manufacturing costs	320,000	32
Unavoidable fixed manufacturing costs	800,000	80
Total manufacturing costs	$3,390,000	$339

2. The following table identifies the incremental costs in 19_8 if Svenson (a) made CMCBs and (b) purchased CMCBs from Minton.

	Total Incremental Costs		Per-Unit Incremental Costs	
Incremental Items	Make	Buy	Make	Buy
Cost of purchasing CMCBs from				
Minton		$ 3,000,000		$300
Direct materials	$1,700,000		$170	
Direct manufacturing labor	450,000		45	
Variable batch manufacturing costs	120,000		12	
Avoidable fixed manufacturing costs	320,000		32	
Total incremental costs	$2,590,000	$3,000,000	$259	$300
Difference in favor of making	↑ $410,000 ↑		↑ $41 ↑	

Note that the opportunity cost of using capacity to make CMCBs is zero since Svenson would keep this capacity idle if it purchases CMCBs from Minton.

Svenson should continue to manufacture the CMCBs internally since the incremental costs to manufacture are $259 per unit compared to the $300 per unit that Minton has quoted. Note that the unavoidable fixed manufacturing costs of $800,000 ($80 per unit) will continue to be incurred whether Svenson makes or buys CMCBs. These are not incremental costs under either the make or the buy alternative and are, hence, irrelevant.

3. Svenson should continue to make CMCBs. The simplest way to solve this problem is to recognize that Svenson would prefer to keep any excess capacity idle rather than use it to make CB3s. Why? Because expected incremental future revenues from CB3s ($2,000,000) are less than expected incremental future costs ($2,150,000). If Svenson keeps its capacity idle, we know from requirement 2 that it should make CMCBs rather than buy them.

An important point to note is that, because Svenson forgoes no contribution by not being able to make and sell CB3s, the opportunity cost of using its facilities to make CMCBs is zero. It is, therefore, not forgoing any profits by using the capacity to manufacture CMCBs. If it does not manufacture CMCBs, rather than lose money on CB3s, Svenson will keep capacity idle.

A longer and more detailed approach is to use the total alternatives or opportunity cost analyses shown in Exhibit 11-7 of the chapter.

TOTAL-ALTERNATIVES APPROACH TO MAKE-OR-BUY DECISIONS

	Choices for Svenson		
Relevant Items	**Make CMCBs and Do Not Make CB3s**	**Buy CMCBs and Do Not Make CB3s**	**Buy CMCBs and Make CB3s**
Total incremental costs of making/buying CMCBs (from requirement 2)	$2,590,000	$3,000,000	$3,000,000
Excess of future costs over future revenues from CB3s	0	0	150,000
Total relevant costs	$2,590,000	$3,000,000	$3,150,000

Svenson will minimize manufacturing costs by making CMCBs.

OPPORTUNITY-COST APPROACH TO MAKE-OR-BUY DECISIONS

	Choices for Svenson	
Relevant Items	**Make CMCB**	**Buy CMCB**
Total incremental costs of making/buying CMCBs (from requirement 2)	$2,590,000	$3,000,000
Opportunity cost: profit contribution forgone because capacity cannot be used to make CB3s	0*	0
Total relevant costs	$2,590,000	$3,000,000
	↑_____↑	
Difference in favor of making CMCBs	$410,000	

* Opportunity cost is 0 because Svenson does not give up anything by manufacturing CMCBs. Had it not manufactured CMCBs, it would be best off leaving the capacity idle (rather than manufacturing and selling CB3s).

11-22 (10 min.) **Inventory decision, opportunity cost.**

1. Unit cost, orders of 20,000 $8.00
    Unit cost, order of 240,000 (0.95 × $8.00) $7.60

    Alternatives under consideration:
    (a)   Buy 240,000 units at start of year.
    (b)   Buy 20,000 units at start of each month.

    Average investment in inventory:
    (a)   (240,000 × $7.60) ÷ 2 $912,000
    (b)   (20,000 × $8.00) ÷ 2   80,000
    Difference in average investment $832,000

Opportunity cost of interest forgone from 240,000-unit purchase at start of year
= $832,000 × 0.08 = $66,560

2.   No. The $66,560 is an opportunity cost rather than an incremental or outlay cost. No actual transaction records the $66,560 as an entry in the accounting system.

3.   The following table presents the two alternatives:

	Alternative A: Purchase 240,000 spark plugs at beginning of year (1)	Alternative B: Purchase 20,000 spark plugs at beginning of each month (2)	Difference (3)=(1)–(2)
Annual purchase (incremental) costs			
(240,000 × $7.60; 240,000 × $8)	$1,824,000	$1,920,000	$(96,000)
Annual interest income that could be earned if			
investment in inventory were invested			
(opportunity cost)			
(8% × $912,000; 8% × $80,000)	72,960	6,400	66,560
Relevant costs	$1,896,960	$1,926,400	$(29,440)

Column (3) indicates that purchasing 240,000 spark plugs at the beginning of the year is preferred relative to purchasing 20,000 spark plugs at the beginning of each month because the lower purchase cost exceeds the opportunity cost of holding larger inventory. If other incremental benefits of holding lower inventory such as lower insurance, materials handling, storage, obsolescence, and breakage costs were considered, the costs under Alternative A would have been higher, and Alternative B may have been preferred.

11-24 (10 min.) **Selection of most profitable product.**

Only Model 14 should be produced. The key to this problem is the relationship of manufacturing overhead to product. Note that it takes twice as long to produce Model 9; machine-hours for Model 9 are twice that for Model 14. Management should choose the product mix that maximizes operating income for a given production capacity (the scarce resource in this situation). In this case, Model 14 will yield a $19.00 contribution to fixed costs per unit of machine time, and Model 9 will yield $18.00:

	Model 9	Model 14
Selling price per unit	$100.00	$70.00
Variable costs per unit	82.00	60.50
Contribution margin per unit	$ 18.00	$ 9.50
Relative use of machine-hours per unit of product	× 1	× 2
Contribution margin per unit of machine time	$ 18.00	$19.00

11-26 (20–25 min.) **Customer profitability, choosing customers.**

1. Broadway should not drop the Kelly Corporation business, as the following analysis shows.

Loss in revenues from dropping Kelly	$(80,000)
Savings in costs:	
Variable costs	48,000
Fixed costs 20% × $100,000	20,000
Total savings in costs	68,000
Effect on operating income	$(12,000)

Broadway Printers would be worse off by $12,000 if it drops the Kelly Corporation business.

2. If Broadway accepts the additional business from Kelly, it would take an additional 500 hours of machine time. If Broadway accepts all of Kelly's and Taylor's business for February, it would require 2,500 hours of machine time (1,500 hours for Taylor and 1,000 hours for Kelly). Broadway only has 2,000 hours of machine capacity. It must, therefore, choose how much of the Taylor or Kelly business to accept. If Broadway accepts any additional business from Kelly, it must forgo some of Taylor's business.

To maximize operating income, Broadway should maximize contribution margin per unit of the constrained resource. (Fixed costs will remain unchanged at $100,000 regardless of the business Broadway chooses to accept in February, and is, therefore, irrelevant.) The contribution margin per unit of the constrained resource for each customer in January is:

11-26 (Cont'd.)

	Taylor Corporation	Kelly Corporation
Revenues	$120,000	$80,000
Variable costs	42,000	48,000
Contribution margin	$ 78,000	$32,000

Contribution margin per machine hour

$$\frac{\$78,000}{1,500} = \$52 \qquad \frac{\$32,000}{500} = \$64$$

Since the $80,000 of additional Kelly business in February is identical to jobs done in January, it will also have a contribution margin of $64 per machine-hour, which is greater than the contribution margin of $52 per machine-hour from Taylor. To maximize operating income, Broadway should first allocate all the capacity needed to take the Kelly Corporation business (1,000 machine-hours) and then allocate the remaining 1,000 (2,000 – 1,000) machine-hours to Taylor. Broadway's operating income in February would then be $16,000, which is greater than the $10,000 operating income in January.

	Taylor Corporation	Kelly Corporation	Total
Contribution margin per machine-hour	$52	$64	
Machine-hours to be worked	1,000	1,000	
Contribution margin	$52,000	$64,000	$116,000
Fixed costs			100,000
Operating income			$ 16,000

Alternatively, we could present Broadway's operating income by taking 2/3rds (1,000 ÷ 1,500 machine-hours) of Taylor's January revenues and variable costs, and doubling (1,000 ÷ 500 machine-hours) Kelly's January revenues and variable costs.

	Taylor Corporation	Kelly Corporation	Total
Revenues	$80,000	$160,000	$240,000
Variable costs	28,000	96,000	124,000
Contribution margin	52,000	64,000	116,000
Fixed costs			100,000
Operating income			$ 16,000

The problem indicated that Broadway could choose to accept as much of the Taylor and Kelly business for February as it wants. However, some students may raise the question that Broadway should think more strategically before deciding what to do. For example, how would Taylor react to Broadway's inability to satisfy its needs? Will Kelly continue to give Broadway $160,000 of business each month or is the additional $80,000 of business in February a special order? For example, if Kelly's additional work in February is only a special order and Broadway wants to maintain a long-term relationship with Taylor, it may, in fact, prefer to turn down the additional Kelly business. It may feel that the additional $6,000 in operating income in February is not worth jeopardizing Taylor's long-term relationship. Other students may raise the possibility of Broadway accepting all the Taylor and Kelly business for February if it can subcontract some of it to another reliable, high-quality printer.

11-28   (30 min.)   **Equipment upgrade versus replacement.**

1.   Solution Exhibit 11-28 presents a cost comparison of the upgrade and replacement alternatives for the three years taken together. It indicates that Pacifica Corporation should replace the production line because it is better off by $180,000 by replacing rather than upgrading.

2a.   Suppose the capital expenditure to replace the production line is $X. Using data from Solution Exhibit 11-28, the cost of replacing the production line is equal to $1,620,000 – $90,000 + $X. Using data from Solution Exhibit 11-28, the cost of upgrading the production line is equal to $2,160,000 + $300,000 = $2,460,000. We want to find $X such that

$$\$1,620,000 - \$90,000 + \$X = \$2,460,000$$

that is, $$\$1,530,000 + \$X = \$2,460,000$$
that is, $$\$X = \$2,460,000 - \$1,530,000$$
or $$\$X = \$ \ 930,000$$

Pacifica would prefer replacing, rather than upgrading, the existing line if the replacement cost of the new line does not exceed $930,000.

2b.   Suppose the units produced and sold each year equal y. Using data from Solution Exhibit 11-28, the cost of replacing the production line is $9y – $90,000 + $750,000, while the cost of upgrading is $12y + $300,000. We solve for the y at which the two costs are the same.

$$\$9y - \$90,000 + \$750,000 = \$12y + \$300,000$$
$$\$9y + \$660,000 = \$12y + \$300,000$$
$$\$3y = \$360,000$$
$$y = 120,000 \text{ units}$$

For expected production and sales of less than 120,000 units over 3 years (40,000 units per year), the upgrade alternative is cheaper. When production and sales are low, the higher operating costs of upgrading are more than offset by the significant savings in capital costs when upgrading relative to replacing. For expected production and sales exceeding 120,000 units over 3 years, the replace alternative is cheaper. For high output, the benefits of the lower operating costs of replacing, relative to upgrading, exceed the higher capital costs.

11-28 (Cont'd.)

SOLUTION EXHIBIT 11-28
Comparing Upgrade and Replace Alternatives

	Three Years Together		
	Upgrade (1)	Replace (2)	Difference (3) = (1) – (2)
Cash-operating costs $12; $9 × 180,000	$2,160,000	$1,620,000	$ 540,000
Current disposal price		(90,000)	90,000
One-time capital costs, written off periodically as depreciation	300,000	750,000	(450,000)
Total relevant costs	$2,460,000	$2,280,000	$ 180,000

Note that sales and book value of the existing machine are the same under both alternatives and, hence, irrelevant.

3.   Operating income for the first year under the upgrade and replace alternatives are as follows:

	Upgrade	Replace
Sales $25 × 60,000	$1,500,000	$1,500,000
Cash-operating costs $12; $9 × 60,000	720,000	540,000
Depreciation	220,000[a]	250,000[b]
Loss on disposal of old production line	—	270,000[c]
Total costs	940,000	1,060,000
Operating income	$ 560,000	$ 440,000

[a] $360,000 + $300,000 ÷ 3 = $220,000   [b] $750,000 ÷ 3 = $250,000
[c] Book value – current disposal price = $360,000 – $90,000 = $270,000

First-year operating income is higher by $120,000 under the upgrade alternative. If first year's operating income is an important component of Azinger's bonus, he would prefer the upgrade over the replace alternative even though the decision model in requirement 1 prefers the replace to the upgrade alternative. This exercise illustrates the conflict between the decision model and the performance evaluation model (requirement 3)

11-30 (20 min.) **Opportunity cost.**

1.   The opportunity cost to Wolverine of producing the 2,000 units of Orangebo is the contribution margin lost on the 2,000 units of Rosebo that would have to be forgone, as computed below:

Revenue per unit		$20
Variable costs per unit:		
Direct materials	$ 2	
Direct manufacturing labor	3	
Variable manufacturing overhead	2	
Variable nonmanufacturing costs	4	11
Contribution margin per unit		$ 9
Contribution margin for 2,000 units		$ 18,000

The opportunity cost is $18,000. Opportunity cost is the maximum contribution to operating income that is forgone (rejected) by not using a limited resource in its next-best alternative use.

2.   Contribution margin from manufacturing 2,000 units of Orangebo and purchasing 2,000 units of Rosebo from Buckeye is $16,000, as follows:

	Manufacture Orangebo	Purchase Rosebo	Total
Revenue per unit	$15	$20	
Variable costs per unit:			
Purchase costs	–	14	
Direct materials	2		
Direct manufacturing labor	3		
Variable manufacturing overhead	2		
Variable non manufacturing overhead	2	4	
Variable costs per unit	9	18	
Contribution margin per unit	$ 6	$ 2	
Contribution margin from selling 2,000 units of Orangebo and 2,000 units of Rosebo	$12,000	$4,000	$16,000

As calculated in requirement 1, Wolverine's contribution margin from continuing to manufacture 2,000 units of Rosebo is $18,000. Accepting the Miami Company and Buckeye offer will cost Wolverine $2,000 ($16,000 – $18,000). Hence, Wolverine should refuse the Miami Company and Buckeye Corporation's offers.

3.   The minimum price would be $9, the sum of the incremental costs as computed in requirement 2. This follows because, if Wolverine has surplus capacity, the opportunity cost = $0. For the short-run decision of whether to accept Orangebo's offer, fixed costs of Wolverine are irrelevant. Only the incremental costs need to be covered for it to be worthwhile for Wovlerine to accept the Orangebo offer.

11-32 (30–40 min.) **Make or buy, unknown level of volume.**

1.   Let X = 1 starter assembly. The variable costs required to manufacture 150,000X are:

Direct materials	$200,000
Direct manufacturing labor	150,000
Variable manufacturing overhead	100,000
Total variable costs	$450,000

The variable costs per unit is $450,000 ÷ 150,000 = $3.00 per unit.

The data can be presented in both "all data" and "relevant data" formats:

	All Data		Relevant Data	
	Alternative 1: Make	**Alternative 2: Buy**	**Alternative 1: Make**	**Alternative 2: Buy**
Variable manufacturing costs	$ 3X	–	$ 3X	–
Fixed general manufacturing overhead	150,000	$150,000	–	–
Fixed overhead, avoidable	100,000	–	100,000	–
Division 2 manager's salary	40,000	50,000	40,000	$50,000
Division 3 manager's salary	50,000	–	50,000	–
Purchase cost, if bought from Tidnish Electronics	–	4X	–	4X
Total	$340,000 + $ 3X	$200,000 + $ 4X	$190,000 + $ 3X	$50,000 + $ 4X

The number of units at which the costs of make and buy are equivalent is:

All data analysis: $340,000 + $3X = $200,000 + $4X
                                    X = 140,000

or

Relevant data analysis: $190,000 + $3X = $50,000 + $4X
                                        X = 140,000

Assuming cost minimization is the objective, then:
- If production is expected to be less than 140,000 units, it is preferable to buy units from Tidnish.
- If production is expected to exceed 140,000 units, it is preferable to manufacture internally (make) the units.
- If production is expected to be 140,000 units, this is the indifference point between buying units from Tidnish and internally manufacturing (making) the units.

11-32 (Cont'd.)

2.   The information on the storage cost, which is avoidable if self-manufacture is discontinued, is relevant; these storage charges represent current outlays that are avoidable if self-manufacture is discontinued. Assume these $50,000 charges are represented as an opportunity cost of the make alternative. The costs of internal manufacture that incorporate this $50,000 opportunity cost are:

All data analysis: $390,000 + $3X

Relevant data analysis: $240,000 + $3X

The number of units at which the costs of make and buy are equivalent is:

All data analysis: $390,000 + $3X $=$ $200,000 + $4X
                                          X $=$ 190,000

Relevant data analysis: $240,000 + $3X $=$ $50,000 + $4X
                                          X $=$ 190,000

If production is expected to be less than 190,000, it is preferable to buy units from Tidnish. If production is expected to exceed 190,000, it is preferable to manufacture the units internally.

11-34 (30–40 min.) Relevant cost of materials.

1. Hernandez Corporation has already purchased the 10,000 pounds of the special cement that it needs so it will incur no incremental costs. Alternatively stated, the costs of materials are past (sunk) costs.

If Hernandez obtained Contract No. 2 a month from now, it would cost $21,000 in substitute material (10,000 pounds x $2.10 per pound). There is, therefore, a cost (lost benefit) of $21,000 by using the special cement on Contract No. 1 now. Alternatively, Hernandez could sell the special cement immediately for $16,000. The opportunity cost that Hernandez should use is the benefit it would get in the next best alternative should it not use the cement in Contract No. 1. The greater of these two benefits is using the cement in Contract No. 2. The opportunity cost is $21,000. The relevant costs that Gomez should use when bidding on Contract No. 1 is:

Incremental cost	$ 0
Plus Opportunity cost	21,000
Relevant cost	$21,000

2. As in Question 1, the incremental costs of acquiring the special cement for use on Contract No. 1 are zero because Hernandez has already purchased the material. If Hernandez does not land Contract No. 2, then the opportunity cost of using the special cement for Contract No. 1 is $15,000 (10,000 pounds × $1.50 per pound), the amount Hernandez would get if it sold the special cement one month from now.

Gomez assesses a probability of 0.7 that the special cement will be used on Contract No. 2 and a probability of 0.3 that the special cement will be sold.

The expected benefit of holding the special cement and not using it on Contract No. 1 is

$$= \quad 0.7 \times \$21,000^* + 0.3 \times \$15,000^{**}$$
$$= \quad \$14,700 + \$4,500 = \$19,200$$

* relevant cost if special cement is used in Contract No. 2 (see requirement 1)
** relevant cost if special cement is sold one month from now

Alternatively, the special cement can be sold right away and fetch $16,000. The opportunity cost is the greater of these two benefits and, hence, equals $19,200. When bidding on the contract, Gomez should use:

Incremental cost	$ 0
Plus Opportunity cost	19,200
Relevant cost	$19,200

3. In this case, the benefit of selling the cement now is $23,000, while the benefit of using the cement in Contract No. 2 is $21,000. The opportunity cost of using the cement in Contract No. 1 is the greater of these two numbers, $23,000.

Incremental cost	$ 0
Plus Opportunity cost	23,000
Relevant cost	$23,000

11-36 (30–40 min.) **Considering three alternatives.**

1. The 5% surcharge is irrelevant.

	Sell to Kaytell as Special Order	Convert to Standard Model	Sell as Special Order As Is
Selling price	$68,400	$62,500	$52,000
Deduct cash discount	–	1,250	–
Net selling price	68,400	61,250	52,000
Additional manufacturing costs:			
Direct materials	6,200	2,850	–
Direct manufacturing labor	4,200	3,300	–
Variable manufacturing overhead	2,100	1,650	–
Total additional manufacturing costs	12,500	7,800	–
Commissions	2,052	1,225	1,560
Total costs	14,552	9,025	1,560
Contribution to operating income	$53,848	$52,225	$50,440

2.

Kaytell contribution	$53,848
Next-best alternative:	
Standard model contribution	52,225
Change in contribution to operating income	$ 1,623

$$\text{Change in net sales price} = \frac{\text{Change in contribution}}{1 - \text{Commission \%}}$$

$$= \frac{\$1,623}{1 - 0.03} = \frac{\$1,623}{0.97}$$

$$= \$1,673 \text{ (rounded)}$$

Original Kaytell price	$68,400
Reduction in contribution permissible before Auer switches to the next-best alternative	1,673
Minimum price Auer should accept from Kaytell and be indifferent between standard model and Kaytell offer	$66,727

3. Fixed manufacturing overhead should have no influence on the selling price quoted by Auer Company for (one-time-only) special orders:

    a. Auer Company should accept special orders whenever the company is operating substantially below capacity, including below the breakeven point, if incremental revenue from an order exceeds incremental cost. Normally, this approach would mean that the order should be accepted as long as the selling price of the order exceeds the variable manufacturing costs. The special order will result in a positive contribution toward fixed costs. The fixed manufacturing overhead is not considered in the pricing because it will be incurred whether the order is accepted or not.

11-36 (Cont'd.)

b.   If Auer Company is operating above its breakeven point and if a special order will allow the company to utilize unused capacity efficiently, the special order should be accepted as long as incremental revenue exceeds incremental cost, or, in most cases, the selling price exceeds the variable manufacturing costs. If the selling price exceeds the variable manufacturing costs, the order will yield a positive contribution toward the company's fixed costs. Fixed manufacturing overhead is not considered because it will be incurred whether the order is accepted or not. The only time the fixed manufacturing overhead would be relevant would be if Auer were near capacity and additional fixed costs would have to be incurred to complete the order. If this situation occurred, Auer's incremental costs would be higher, and they would have to be covered by the selling price.

11-38 (15 min.) **Make or buy.**

The maximum price Class Company should be willing to pay is $3.9417 per unit.

Expected unit production and sales of new product must be half of the old product (1/2 × 240,000 = 120,000) because the fixed manufacturing overhead rate for the new product is twice that of the fixed manufacturing overhead rate for the old product.

| | | Proposed | | |
| | | Make New Product | Old Product | |
	Present			Total
Sales	$1,440,000	$1,080,000	$1,440,000	$2,520,000
Variable (or purchase) costs:				
Manufacturing	720,000	600,000	946,000*	1,546,000
Marketing and other	360,000	240,000	288,000	528,000
Total variable costs	1,080,000	840,000	1,234,000	2,074,000
Contribution margin	360,000	240,000	206,000	446,000
Fixed costs:				
Manufacturing	120,000	120,000	–	120,000
Marketing and other	216,000	60,000	216,000	276,000
Total fixed costs	336,000	180,000	216,000	396,000
Operating income	$ 24,000	$ 60,000	$ –10,000	$ 50,000

*This is an example of opportunity costs, whereby subcontracting at a price well above the $3.50 current manufacturing (absorption) cost is still desirable because the old product will be displaced in manufacturing by a new product that is more profitable.

Because the new product promises an operating income of $60,000 (ignoring the irrelevant problems of how fixed marketing costs may be newly reallocated between products), the old product can sustain up to a $10,000 loss and still help accomplish management's overall objectives. Maximum costs that can be incurred on the old product are $1,440,000 plus the $10,000 loss, or $1,450,000. Maximum purchase cost: $1,450,000 – ($288,000 + $216,000) = $946,000. Maximum purchase cost per unit: $946,000 ÷ 240,000 units = $3.9417 per unit.

Alternative Computation

Operating income is $9.00 – $8.50 = $0.50 per unit		
for 120,000 new units	$60,000	
Target operating income	50,000	
Maximum loss allowed on old product	$10,000	
Maximum loss per unit allowed on old product,		
$10,000 ÷ 240,000 =		$0.0417
Sales price of old product		$6.0000
Allowance for loss		0.0417
Total costs allowed per unit		6.0417
Continuing costs for old product other than purchase cost:		
Fixed manufacturing costs—all transferred to		
new product	$ –	
Variable marketing costs	1.20	
Fixed marketing costs	0.90	2.1000
Maximum purchase cost per unit		$3.9417

11-40 (30–40 min.) **Optimal sales mix for a retailer, sensitivity analysis.**

1. Let G = floor space of grocery products carried
   D = floor space of dairy products carried

The LP formula of the decision is:

Maximize: $10G + $3D
Subject to: G + D ≤ 40,000
             G   ≥ 10,000
                    D ≥   8,000

2. Always Open may wish to maintain its reputation as a full-service food store carrying both grocery and dairy products. Customers may not be attracted if Always Open carries only the product line with the highest unit contribution margins. (Marketing and economics courses examine this issue under the label of interdependencies in the demand for products.)

3. Solution Exhibit 11-40 presents the graphic solution. The optimal solution is 32,000 square feet of grocery products and 8,000 square feet of dairy products.

The trial-and-error solution approach is:

Trial	Corner (G; D)	TCM = $10G + $3D		
1	(10,000; 8,000)	$10(10,000) + $3(8,000)	=	$124,000
2	(10,000; 30,000)	10(10,000) + 3(30,000)	=	190,000
3	(32,000; 8,000)	10(32,000) + 3(8,000)	=	344,000*

* Optimal solution is G = 32,000 and D = 8,000.

4. The optimal mix determined in requirement 3 will not change if the contribution margins per square foot change to grocery products, $8, and dairy products, $5. To avoid cluttering the graphic solution in Solution Exhibit 11-40, we demonstrate this using the trial-and-error solution approach.

Trial	Corner (G; D)	TCM = $8G + $5D	
1	(10,000; 8,000)	$8(10,000) + $5 (8,000)	= $120,000
2	(10,000; 30,000)	$8(10,000) + $5 (30,000)	= $230,000
3	(32,000; 8,000)	$8(32,000) + $5 (8,000)	= $296,000*

* Optimal solution is still G = 32,000 and D = 8,000.

The student can also verify by drawing lines parallel to the line through G = 5,000 and D = 8,000 (the equal contribution line for $40,000) that the furthest point where the equal contribution line intersects the feasible region is the point G = 32,000 and D = 8,000.

SOLUTION EXHIBIT 11-40
Graphic Solution to Find Optimal Mix, Always Open, Inc.

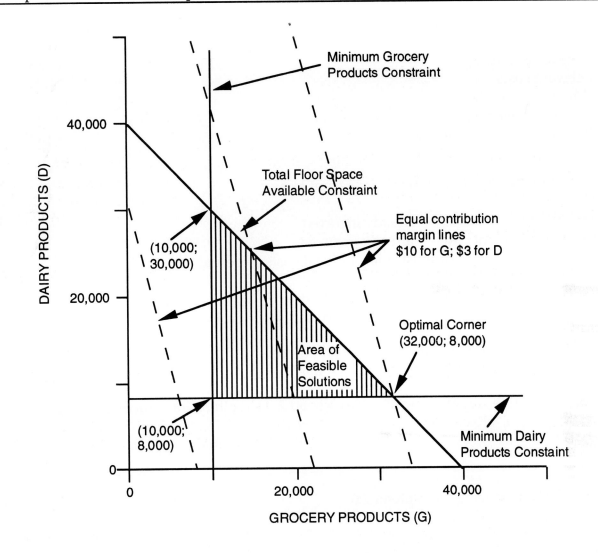

11-42 (30–40 min.) Relevant costs, opportunity costs.

1. Easyspread 2.0 has a higher relevant operating income than Easyspread 1.0. Based on this analysis, Easyspread 2.0 should be introduced immediately:

	Easyspread 1.0	Easyspread 2.0
Relevant revenues	$150	$185
Relevant costs:		
Manuals, diskettes	$ 0	$25
Total relevant costs	0	25
Relevant operating income	$150	$160

Reasons for other cost items being irrelevant are:

Easyspread 1.0
- Manuals, diskettes — already incurred
- Development costs — already incurred
- Marketing and administration — fixed costs of period

Easyspread 2.0
- Development costs — already incurred
- Marketing and administration — fixed costs of period

Note that total marketing and administration costs will not change whether Easyspread 2.0 is introduced on July 1, 19_8 or on October 1, 19_8.

An alternative way to show that Easyspread 2.0 should be introduced immediately is:

	Total (1)	Per Unit (2) = (1) ÷ 60,000
Incremental revenues from July–September 19_8 by introducing Easyspread 2.0 immediately on July 1, 19_8	$11,100,000[a]	$185
Incremental costs of manuals and diskettes in July–September 19_8 if Easyspread 2.0 is introduced on July 1, 19_8	1,500,000[b]	25
Incremental increase in operating income	9,600,000	160
Opportunity cost of selling Easyspread 2.0 is the lost revenue from not selling the existing stock of 60,000 units of Easyspread 1.0 (recall that there are no further costs to be incurred to sell Easyspread 1.0)	9,000,000[c]	150
Net relevant benefit	$ 600,000	$ 10

[a] $11,100,000 = $185 × 60,000   [b] $1,500,000 = $25 × 60,000   [c] $9,000,000 = $150 × 60,000

2. Other factors to be considered:

    a. Customer satisfaction. If 2.0 is significantly better than 1.0 for its customers, a customer-driven organization would immediately introduce it unless other factors offset this bias towards "do what is best for the customer."

    b. Quality level of Easyspread 2.0. It is critical for new software products to be fully debugged. Easyspread 2.0 must be error-free. Only consider an immediate release if 2.0 passes all quality tests and can be fully supported by the salesforce.

    c. Importance of being perceived to be a market leader. Being first in the market with a new product can give Basil Software a "first-mover advantage," e.g., capturing an initial large share of the market that, in itself, causes future potential customers to lean towards purchasing Easyspread 2.0. Moreover, by introducing 2.0 earlier, Basil can get quick feedback from users about ways to further refine the software while its competitors are still working on their own first versions. Moreover, by locking in early customers, you may increase the likelihood of these customers also buying future upgrades of Easyspread 2.0.

    d. Morale of developers. These are key people at Basil Software. Delaying introduction of a new product can hurt their morale, especially if a competitor then preempts Basil from being viewed as a market leader.

    e. Development of business relationships with distributors. There are pros and cons here. The pro is that, with 2.0, they will have a new product that will generate many sales at a higher selling price. Moreover, if rumors arise about 2.0 being planned, sales of 1.0 may plummet as people hold off buying until the new product is introduced. A possible con is that distributors may be stuck with unsold versions of 1.0. Will Basil be willing to take these units back as a credit against supplying 2.0?

    f. Alternative ways of disposing of Easyspread 1.0. One student suggested Basil donate all 60,000 Easyspread 1.0 packages to public schools and claim a tax deduction. Another student suggested there may be costs of disposing of Easyspread 1.0 (e.g., shredding the packages).

    g. Incentive compensation scheme at Basil Software. How will the writeoff (if any) on Easyspread 1.0 packages affect the compensation plan? Management at Basil may not view the costs of Easyspread 1.0 as a sunk cost if their bonus will be affected by a writeoff on Easyspread 1.0.

CHAPTER 12
PRICING DECISIONS, PRODUCT PROFITABILITY DECISIONS, AND COST MANAGEMENT

12-2   Not necessarily. For a one-time-only special order the relevant costs are only those costs that will change as a result of accepting the order. In this case, full product costs will rarely be relevant. It is more likely that full product costs will be relevant costs for long-run pricing decisions.

12-4   Activity-based costing helps managers in pricing decisions in two ways.
1.   It gives managers more accurate product-cost information for making pricing decisions.
2.   It helps managers to manage costs during value engineering by identifying the cost impact of eliminating, reducing or changing various activities.

12-6   A target cost per unit is the estimated long-run cost per unit of a product (or service) that, when sold at the target price, enables the company to achieve the targeted operating income per unit.

12-8   A value-added cost is a cost that customers perceive as adding value, or utility, to a product or service. Examples are costs of materials, direct labor, tools, and machinery. Examples of nonvalue-added costs are costs of rework, scrap, expediting, and breakdown maintenance.

12-10   Cost-plus pricing is a pricing approach in which managers add a markup to cost in order to determine price.

12-12   Two examples where the difference in the incremental or outlay costs of two products or services are much smaller than the differences in their prices follow:
1.   The difference in prices charged for a telephone call, hotel room, or car rental during busy versus slack periods is often much greater than the difference in costs to provide these services.
2.   The difference in incremental or outlay costs for an airplane seat sold to a passenger traveling on business or a passenger traveling for pleasure is roughly the same. However, airline companies routinely charge business travelers—those who are likely to start and complete their travel during the same week excluding the weekend—a much higher price than pleasure travelers who generally stay at their destinations over at least one weekend.

12-14   Three benefits of using a product life-cycle reporting format are:
1.   The full set of revenues and costs associated with each product becomes more visible.
2.   Differences among products in the percentage of total costs committed at early stages in the life cycle are highlighted.

3.   Interrelationships among business function cost categories are highlighted.

12-16 (20–30 min.) **Relevant-cost approach to pricing decisions, special order.**

1.

Relevant revenues, $3.80 × 1,000		$3,800
Relevant costs		
• Direct materials, $1.50 × 1,000	$1,500	
• Direct manufacturing labor, $0.80 × 1,000	800	
• Variable manufacturing overhead, $0.70 × 1,000	700	
• Variable selling costs, 0.05 × $3,800	190	
Total		3,190
Increase in operating income		$ 610

This calculation assumes that:
(a) The monthly fixed manufacturing overhead of $150,000 and $65,000 of monthly fixed marketing costs will be unchanged by acceptance of the 1,000 unit order.
(b) The price charged and the volumes sold to other customers are not affected by the special order.

Chapter 12 uses the phrase "one-time-only special order" to describe this special case.

2. The president's reasoning is defective on at least two counts:
(a) The inclusion of irrelevant costs—assuming the monthly fixed manufacturing overhead of $150,000 will be unchanged; it is irrelevant to the decision.
(b) The exclusion of relevant costs—variable selling costs (5% of the selling price) are excluded.

3. Key issues are:
(a) Will the existing customer base demand price reductions? If this 1,000-tape order is not independent of other sales, cutting the price from $5.00 to $3.80 can have a large negative effect on total revenues.
(b) Is the 1,000-tape order a one-time-only order, or is there the possibility of sales in subsequent months? The fact that the customer is not in Dill Company's "normal marketing channels" does not necessarily mean it is a one-time-only order. Indeed, the sale could well open a new marketing channel. Dill Company should be reluctant to consider only short-run variable costs for pricing long-run business.

12-18 (25 min.) Short-run pricing, capacity constraints.

1.   With no constraints on availability of Pyrone or on plant capacity, Boutique would want to charge a minimum price for Seltium that would cover its incremental costs to manufacture Seltium. (Because there is excess capacity, there is no opportunity cost.) In this case, the incremental costs are the variable costs to manufacture a kilogram of Seltium:

Pyrone (2 kilograms × $4 per kilogram)	$ 8
Direct manufacturing labor	4
Variable manufacturing overhead costs	3
Total variable manufacturing costs	$15

Hence, the minimum price that Boutique should charge to manufacture Seltium is $15 per kilogram. For 3,000 kilograms of Seltium, it should charge a minimum of $45,000 ($15 × 3,000).

2.   Now Pyrone is in short supply. Using it to make Seltium reduces the Bolzene that Boutique can make and sell. There is, therefore, an opportunity cost of manufacturing Seltium, the lost contribution from using the Pyrone to manufacture Bolzene. To make 3,000 kilograms of Seltium requires 6,000 (2 × 3,000) kilograms of Pyrone.

The 6,000 kilograms of Pyrone can be used to manufacture 4,000 (6,000 ÷ 1.5) kilograms of Bolzene, since each kilogram of Bolzene requires 1.5 kilograms of Pyrone.

The contribution margin from 4,000 kilograms of Bolzene is $24,000 ($6 per kilogram × 4,000 kilograms). This is the opportunity cost of using Pyrone to manufacture Seltium. The minimum price that Boutique should charge to manufacture Seltium should cover not only the incremental (variable) costs of manufacturing Seltium but also the opportunity cost:

	Costs of manufacturing Seltium	
	Total for 3,000 kilograms (1)	Per kilogram (2) = (1) ÷ 3,000
Relevant costs		
Incremental (variable) costs of manufacturing Seltium	$45,000	$15
Opportunity cost of forgoing manufacture and sale of Bolzene	24,000	8
Minimum cost of order	$69,000	$23

The minimum price per kilogram that Boutique should charge for Seltium is $23 per kilogram. For 3,000 kilograms of Seltium, Boutique should charge a minimum of $69,000 ($23 × 3,000 kgs).

12-20 (20–30 min.) **Value-added versus nonvalue-added cost classifications.**

1a. The classification of a cost as value-added or nonvalue-added is based on whether the cost can be eliminated without the customer perceiving a deterioration in the performance, function, or other quality of a product.

1b. There is room for much disagreement on these classifications, especially between the gray area and the nonvalue-added categories:

Value-added:
    b.   Assembling the tumbler unit.
    d.   Assembling the control panel.
    e.   Inserting the owner's manual and instruction guide in the dryer package.

Gray area:
    g.   Testing the operating capabilities of the assembled unit.
    h.   Packaging the clothes dryer in a breakage-resistant box.

Nonvalue-added:
    a.   Moving component parts from warehouse to assembly line.
    c.   Expediting materials to the door-assembly area because of a stock-balance error.
    f.   Reworking faulty latches on clothes-dryer doors.

2. Johns can use the classifications to guide her cost management decisions. Those costs falling in the nonvalue-added category are prime candidates for reduction or diminution. For example, the operations could be reconfigured to reduce the need to move materials from a warehouse to the assembly line. In some plants, warehouses have been eliminated and component parts are delivered directly to the assembly line. Errors can be eliminated to reduce expediting and reworking costs.

3. One question to ask is whether the motivations for introducing the value-added/nonvalue-added distinction can be achieved with other components of the management accounting system. For example, standards could be continuously revised to promote a cost-reduction mentality at the Home Appliance plant. Alternatively, Home Appliance could emphasize quality and productivity improvement programs that also seek to eliminate nonvalue-added costs and improve overall profitability.

12-22 (20 min.)   **Cost-plus target return on investment pricing.**

1.   Target operating income = target return on investment × invested capital

Target operating income , 25% of $960,000	$240,000
Total fixed costs	352,000
Target contribution margin	$592,000

Target contribution per room, ($592,000 ÷ 16,000)	$37
Add variable costs per room	3
Price to be charged per room	$40

Proof

Total room revenues ($40 × 16,000 rooms)		$640,000
Total costs:		
Variable costs ($3 × 16,000)	$ 48,000	
Fixed costs	352,000	
Total costs		400,000
Operating income		$240,000

The full cost of a room = variable cost per room + fixed cost per room
The full cost of a room = $3 + ($352,000 ÷ 16,000) = $3 + $22 = $25

Markup per room   =   Rental price per room – Full cost of a room
                     = $40 – $25 = $15
Markup percentage as a fraction of full cost = $15 ÷ $25 = 60%

2.   If price is reduced by 10%, the number of rooms Beck could rent would increase by 10%.

The new price per room would be 90% of $40	=	$36
The number of rooms Beck expects to rent is 110% of 16,000	=	17,600
The contribution margin per room would be $36 – $3	=	$33
Contribution margin = $33 × 17,600	=	$580,800

Since the contribution margin at the reduced price of $36 is less than the contribution margin at a price of $40, Beck should not reduce the price of the rooms. Note that the fixed costs of $352,000 will be the same under the $40 and the $36 price alternatives and are, hence, irrelevant to the analysis.

12-24 (15 min.) Considerations other than cost in pricing.

1.   No. We would expect the incremental or outlay costs to carry passengers to be no different in peak versus off-peak hours. Most costs of running the train network are fixed costs that are the same in peak and off-peak periods. In fact, the unit cost per passenger is likely to be higher during off-peak hours when fewer people travel. Yet the prices charged for peak hour travel are higher than the prices charged for off-peak travel.

2.   Charging higher prices for peak hour travel is an example of price discrimination. Price discrimination occurs because office-goers are relatively more price insensitive— they must use the London Underground to get to work, since an alternative such as driving to work may be even more expensive. Charging a higher price for peak hour travel maximizes the London Underground's operating income. Charging higher prices for peak hour travel is also an example of peak-load pricing. Because capacity is limited, London Underground raises prices to levels that the market will bear when demand is high.

   Other reasons that the London Underground may charge higher prices during peak hours is to encourage people who can travel at other times to do so. If the objective, however, is to encourage use of public transportation over private cars (to conserve energy, reduce environmental pollution, and road congestion), then there is a limit to how much the London Underground can charge during peak hours—charging too high a price for public transportation may encourage people to use private modes of transport.

12-26 (30–40 min.) Life-cycle product costing, product emphasis.

1. A life-cycle income statement traces revenue and costs of each individual software package from its initial research and development to its final customer servicing and support in the marketplace. The two main differences from a calendar-based income statement are:
   (a) Costs incurred in different calendar periods are included in the same statement.
   (b) Costs and revenue of each package are reported separately rather than aggregated into company-wide categories.

   The benefits of using a product life-cycle report are:
   (a) The full set of revenues and costs associated with each product becomes visible.
   (b) Differences among products in the percentage of total costs committed at early stages in the life cycle are highlighted.
   (c) Interrelationships among business function cost categories are highlighted. What is the effect, for example, of cutting back on R&D and product-design cost categories on customer-service costs in subsequent years?

2.

	EE-46		ME-83		IE-17	
Revenue ($000s)		$2,500		$1,500		$1,600
Costs ($000s)						
Research & development	$700		$450		$240	
Design	200		120		96	
Production	300		210		208	
Marketing	500		270		448	
Distribution	75		60		96	
Customer service	375	2,150	150	1,260	608	1,696
Operating income ($000s)		$ 350		$ 240		$ (96)

As emphasized in this chapter, the time value of money is not taken into account when summing life-cycle revenue or life-cycle costs. Chapters 22 and 23 discuss this topic in detail.

Rankings of the three packages on profitability (and relative profitability) are:

Operating income	Operating income / Revenues
1. EE-46: $350,000	1. ME-83: 16.0%
2. ME-83: $240,000	2. EE-46: 14.0%
3. IE-17: $ (96,000)	3. IE-17: (6.0%)

The EE-46 and ME-83 packages should be emphasized, and the IE-17 package should be de-emphasized. It is interesting that IE-17 had the lowest R&D costs but was the least profitable.

12-26 (Cont'd.)

3.   The cost structures of the three software packages are:

	EE-46	ME-83	IE-17
Research & development	32.5%	35.7%	14.1%
Design	9.3	9.5	5.7
Production	14.0	16.7	12.3
Marketing	23.3	21.4	26.4
Distribution	3.5	4.8	5.7
Customer service	17.4	11.9	35.8
	100.0%	100.0%	100.0%

The major differences are:
   a.   EE-46 and ME-83 have over 40% of their costs in the R&D/product design categories, compared to less than 20% (19.8%) for IE-17.
   b.   IE-17 has 35.8% of its costs in the customer-service category, compared to 17.4% for EE-46 and 11.9% for ME-83.

There are several explanations for these differences:
   a.   EE-46 and ME-83 differ sizably from IE-17 in their R&D/product design intensity. For example, EE-46 and ME-83 may require considerably (a) more interaction with users, and (b) more experimentation with software algorithms than does IE-17.
   b.   The software division should have invested more in the R&D/product design categories for IE-17. The high percentage for customer service could reflect the correcting of problems that should have been corrected prior to manufacture. Life-cycle reports highlight possible causal relationships among cost categories.

12-28 (30 min.)   **Relevant-cost approach to pricing decisions.**

1.	Revenues (1,000 crates at $100 per crate)		$100,000
	Variable costs:		
	Manufacturing	$40,000	
	Marketing	14,000	
	Total variable costs		54,000
	Contribution margin		46,000
	Fixed costs:		
	Manufacturing	$20,000	
	Marketing	16,000	
	Total fixed costs		36,000
	Operating income		$ 10,000

Normal markup percentage: $46,000 ÷ $54,000 = 85.19% of total variable costs.

2.   Only the manufacturing-cost category is relevant to considering this special order; no additional marketing costs will be incurred. The relevant manufacturing costs for the 200-crate special order are:

Variable manufacturing cost per unit	
$40 × 200 crates	$ 8,000
Special packaging	2,000
	$10,000

Any price above $50 per crate ($10,000 ÷ 200) will make a positive contribution to operating income.

The reasoning based on a comparison of $55 per crate price with the $60 per crate absorption cost ignores monthly cost-volume-profit relationships. The $60 per crate absorption cost includes a $20 per crate cost component that is irrelevant to the special order. The relevant range for the fixed manufacturing costs is from 500 to 1,500 crates per month; the special order will increase production from 1,000 to 1,200 crates per month. Furthermore, the special order requires no incremental marketing costs.

3.   If the new customer is likely to remain in business, Stardom should consider whether a strictly short-run focus is appropriate. For example, what is the likelihood of demand from other customers increasing over time? If Stardom accepts the 200-crate special offer for more than one month, it may preclude accepting other customers at prices exceeding $55 per crate. Moreover, the existing customers may learn about Stardom's willingness to set a price based on variable cost plus a small contribution margin. The longer time frame over which Stardom keeps selling 200 crates of canned peaches at $55 a crate, the more likely that the existing customers will approach Stardom for their own special price reductions.

12-30 (20–25 min.) **Product costs, activity-based costing systems.**

This problem assumes knowledge of activity-based costing systems as described in Chapters 4 and 5. The problem illustrates how both product designers and manufacturing personnel can play key roles in a company manufacturing competitively priced products. Solution Exhibit 12-30 presents an overview of the product costing system at Executive Power. The following table presents the manufacturing cost per unit for different cost categories for P-41 and P-63.

Cost Categories	P-41	P-63
Direct manufacturing product costs		
Direct materials	$407.50	$292.10
Indirect manufacturing product costs		
Materials handling		
(85 × $1.20; 46 × $1.20)	102.00	55.20
Assembly management		
(3.2 × $40; 1.9 × $40)	128.00	76.00
Machine insertion of parts		
(49 × $0.70; 31 × $0.70)	34.30	21.70
Manual insertion of parts		
(36 × $2.10; 15 × $2.10)	75.60	31.50
Quality testing		
(1.4 × $25; 1.1 × $25)	35.00	27.50
Total indirect manufacturing product costs	$374.90	$211.90
Total manufacturing product costs	$782.40	$504.00

12-30 (Cont'd.)

SOLUTION EXHIBIT 12-30
Overview of Product Costing at Executive Power

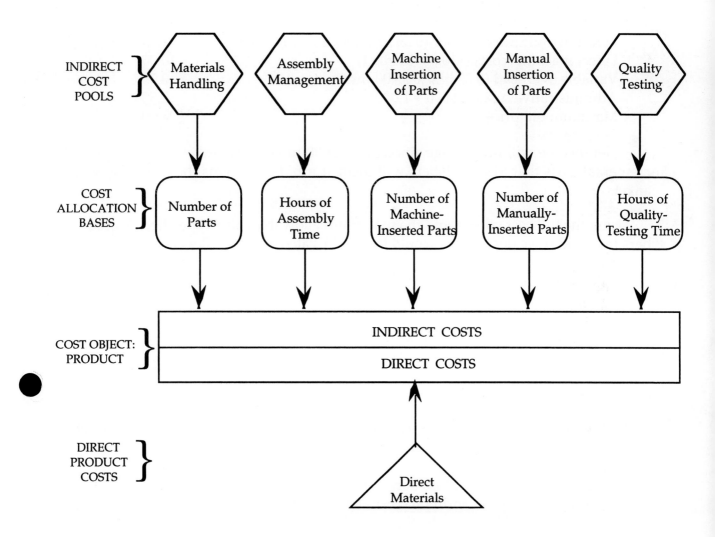

12-32 (30 min.) Cost-plus pricing.

1. The minimum price per blanket that Marcus Fibers Inc. could bid without reducing the company's net income is $24.00. The incremental costs that Marcus Fibers will incur if it bids on the 800,000 order for blankets follows:

Direct materials (6 lb × $1.50/lb)	$ 9.00
Direct manufacturing labor (0.25 hrs. × $7.00/hr.)	1.75
Direct machine costs ($10.00/blanket)	10.00
Variable overhead (0.25 hrs. × $3.00/hr.)	0.75
Administrative costs ($2,500 ÷ 1,000)	2.50
Minimum bid price	$24.00

Net income will not change since the $24.00 price per blanket exactly equals the incremental costs that Marcus Fibers will incur if it bids and wins the order for 800,000 blankets.

2. Using the full cost criteria and the maximum allowable return specified, Marcus Fibers Inc.'s bid price per blanket would be $29.90, calculated as follows:

Relevant costs from requirement 1	$24.00
Fixed overhead (0.25 hrs. × $8.00/hr.)	2.00
Subtotal	26.00
Allowable return (0.15* × $26.00)	3.90
Bid price	$29.90

*9% ÷ (1 − tax rate of 40%)

3. Factors that Marcus Fibers Inc. should consider before deciding whether or not to submit a bid at the maximum acceptable price of $25.00 per blanket include the following:
   (a) The company should be sure there is sufficient excess capacity to fulfill the order and that no additional investment is necessary in facilities or equipment which would increase the fixed cost.
   (b) If the order is accepted at $25.00 per blanket, there will be a $1.00 contribution per blanket to fixed costs. However, the company should consider whether or not there are other jobs that would make a greater contribution.
   (c) Acceptance of the order at a low price could cause problems with current customers who might demand a similar pricing arrangement.

12-34 (30 min.) **Airline pricing , considerations other than cost in pricing.**

1. If the fare is $2,000,
    (a) Air Americo would expect to have 190 business and 20 pleasure travelers.
    (b) Variable costs per passenger would be: food and beverages, $40; and ticket commissions of 8% × $2,000 = $160.
    (c) Contribution margin per passenger = $2,000 – $40 – $160 = $1,800.

    If the fare is $500,
    (a) Air Americo would expect to have 200 business and 100 pleasure travelers.
    (b) Variable costs per passenger would be: food and beverages, $40; and ticket commissions of 8% × $500 = $40.
    (c) Contribution margin per passenger = $500 – $40 – $40 = $420

    Contribution margin from business travelers at prices of $500 and $2,000, respectively, follow:

At a price of $500 : $420 × 200 passengers	=	$84,000
At a price of $2,000 : $1,800 × 190 passengers	=	$342,000

    Air Americo would maximize contribution margin and operating income by charging business travelers a fare of $2,000. The reason is that the demand for business travel drops only slightly (from 200 passengers per flight to 190 passengers per flight) despite the large increase in fare. Also note that, in deciding between the alternative prices, all other costs such as fuel costs, allocated annual lease costs, allocated ground services costs, and allocated flight crew salaries are irrelevant. Why? Because these costs will not change whatever price Air America chooses to charge.

    Contribution margin from pleasure travelers at prices of $500 and $2,000, respectively, follow:

At a price of $500 : $420 × 100 passengers	=	$42,000
At a price of $2,000 : $1,800 × 20 passengers	=	$36,000

    Air Americo would maximize contribution margin and operating income by charging pleasure travelers a fare of $500. The reason is that the demand for pleasure travel drops significantly (from 100 passengers per flight to 20 passengers per flight) as a result of increasing the fare. Once again, in deciding between the alternative prices to charge pleasure travelers, all other costs such as fuel costs, allocated annual lease costs, allocated ground services costs, and allocated flight crew salaries are irrelevant.

    Air Americo would maximize contribution margin and operating income by a price differentiation strategy, where business travelers are charged $2,000 and pleasure travelers $500.

2.   The elasticity of demand of the two classes of passengers drives the different demands of the travelers. Business travelers are relatively price insensitive because they must get to their destination during the week (exclusive of weekends) and their fares are paid by their companies. A 300% increase in fares from $500 to $2,000 will only deter 5% of the business passengers from flying with Air Americo.

In contrast, a similar fare increase will lead to an 80% drop in pleasure travelers who are paying for their own travels, unlike business travelers, and who may have alternative vacation plans they could pursue instead.

3.   Since business travelers often want to return within the same week, while pleasure travelers often stay over weekends, a requirement that a Saturday night stay is needed to qualify for the $500 discount fare would discriminate between the passenger categories. This price discrimination is legal because airlines are service companies rather than manufacturing companies and because these practices do not, nor are they intended to, destroy competition.

12-36 (25 min.) **Ethics and pricing.**

1. Full product costs for the new ball-bearings order are as follows:

Direct materials		$40,000
Direct manufacturing labor		10,000
Overhead costs		
Design and parts administration overhead	$4,000	
Production-order overhead	5,000	
Setup overhead	5,500	
Materials handling overhead	6,500	
General and administration overhead	9,000	
Total overhead costs		30,000
Full product costs		$80,000

Baker prices at full product costs plus a mark-up of 10% = $80,000 + 10% of $80,000 = $80,000 + $8,000 = $88,000.

2. The incremental costs of the order are as follows:

Direct materials	$40,000
Direct manufacturing labor	10,000
30% of overhead costs 30% x $30,000	9,000
Incremental costs	$59,000

Any bid above $59,000 will generate positive contribution margin for Baker. Baker may prefer to use full product costs because it regards the new ball-bearings order as a long-term business relationship rather than a special order. For long-run pricing decisions, managers prefer to use full product costs because it indicates the bare minimum costs they need to recover to continue in business rather than shut down. For a business to be profitable in the long run, it needs to recover *both* its variable and its fixed product costs. Using only variable costs may tempt the manager to engage in excessive long-run price cutting as long as prices give a positive contribution margin. Using full product costs for pricing thereby prompts price stability.

     If Baker had regarded the ball-bearings order as a one-time-only special order and if Baker had excess capacity, it may have bid on the basis of its incremental costs with the goal of earning some contribution margin. On the other hand, if this were a special order and Baker was already operating at capacity, it would need to consider *both* the incremental costs and the opportunity costs of using limited capacity to satisfy the ball-bearings order, once again driving the price up toward its full product costs.

3. Not using full product costs (including an allocation of fixed overhead) to price the order, particularly if it is in direct contradiction of company policy, may be unethical. In assessing the situation, the specific "Standards of Ethical Conduct for Management Accountants," described in Chapter 1 (p. 10), that the management accountant should consider are listed below.

12-36 (Cont'd.)

Competence

Clear reports using relevant and reliable information should be prepared. Reports prepared on the basis of excluding certain fixed costs that should be included would violate the management accountant's responsibility for competence. It is unethical for Lazarus to suggest that Decker change the cost numbers that were prepared for the bearings order and for Decker to change the numbers in order to make Lazarus's performance look good.

Integrity

The management accountant has a responsibility to avoid actual or apparent conflicts of interest and advise all appropriate parties of any potential conflict. Lazarus's motivation for wanting Decker to reduce costs was precisely to earn a larger bonus. This action could be viewed as violating the responsibility for integrity. The Standards of Ethical Conduct require the management accountant to communicate favorable as well as unfavorable information. In this regard, both Lazarus's and Decker's behavior (if Decker agrees to reduce the cost of the order) could be viewed as unethical.

Objectivity

The Standards of Ethical Conduct for Management Accountants require that information should be fairly and objectively communicated and that all relevant information should be disclosed. From a management accountant's standpoint, reducing fixed overhead costs in deciding on the price to bid are clearly violating both of these precepts. For the various reasons cited above, we should take the position that the behavior described by Lazarus and Decker (if he goes along with Lazarus's wishes) is unethical.

Decker should indicate to Lazarus that the costs were correctly computed given the long-term nature of the ball-bearings contract, and that determining prices on the basis of full product costs plus a mark-up of 10% are also required by company policy. If Lazarus still insists on making the changes and reducing the costs of the order, Decker should raise the matter with Lazarus's superior. If, after taking all these steps, there is continued pressure to understate the costs, Decker should consider resigning from the company, rather than engaging in unethical behavior.

CHAPTER 13
COST ALLOCATION: I

13-2 The salary of a plant security guard would be a direct cost when the cost object is the security department or the plant. It would be an indirect cost when the cost object is a product.

13-4 Exhibit 13-2 lists four criteria used to guide cost allocation decisions:
1. Cause and effect.
2. Benefits received.
3. Fairness or equity.
4. Ability to bear.

Either the cause-and-effect criterion or the benefits received criterion is the dominant one when the purpose of the allocation is related to the economic decision purpose or the motivation purpose.

13-6 Cost-benefit considerations can affect costing choices in several ways:

(a) Classifying some immaterial costs as indirect when they could, at high cost, be traced to products, services, or customers as direct costs.

(b) Using a small number of indirect cost pools when, at high cost, an increased number of indirect cost pools would provide more homogeneous cost pools.

(c) Using allocation bases that are readily available (or can be collected at low cost) when, at high cost, more appropriate cost allocation bases could be developed.

13-8 Three decisions managers face when designing the cost allocation component of an accounting system are:
    a. Which cost items should be included in the indirect cost pools?
    b. How many indirect cost pools should be used?
    c. Which allocation base should be used for each indirect cost pool?

13-10 Examples of bases used to allocate corporate cost pools to operating divisions are:

Corporate Cost Pools	Possible Allocation Bases
Corporate executive dept.	Sales; assets employed; operating income
Treasury department	Sales; assets employed; estimated time or usage
Legal department	Estimated time or usage; sales; assets employed
Marketing department	Sales; number of sales personnel
Payroll department	Number of employees; payroll dollars
Personnel department	Number of employees; payroll dollars; number of new hires

13-12 Disagree. Allocating costs on "the basis of estimated long-run use by user department managers" means department managers can lower their cost allocations by deliberately underestimating their long-run use.

13-14 The *reciprocal method* is theoretically the most defensible method because it explicitly recognizes the mutual services rendered among all departments, irrespective of whether those departments are operating or support departments.

13-16 (15-20 min.) **Cost allocation in hospitals, alternative allocation criteria.**

This problem relates to the Chapter 14 Concepts in Action box on "How a Quart of Distilled Water Cost Cindy Chase $17."

1. Direct costs   = $2.40
    Indirect costs   = $11.52 − $2.40 = $9.12
    Overhead rate   = $\dfrac{\$9.12}{\$2.40}$ = 380%

2. The answers here are less than clear-cut in some cases.

Overhead Cost Item	Allocation Criteria
Processing of paperwork for purchase	Cause and effect
Supplies room-management fee	Benefits received
Operating room and patient room-handling charge	Cause and effect
Administrative hospital costs	Benefits received
University teaching-related recoupment	Ability to bear
Malpractice insurance costs	Ability to bear or benefits received
Costing of treating uninsured patients	Ability to bear
Profit component	None. This is not a cost.

3. Assuming that Meltzer's insurance company is responsible for paying the $4,800 bill, Meltzer probably can only express outrage at the amount of the bill. The point of this question is to note that even if Meltzer objects strongly to one or more overhead items, it is his insurance company that likely has the greater incentive to challenge the bill. Individual patients have very little power in the medical arena. In contrast, insurance companies have considerable power and may decide that certain costs are not reimbursable--for example, the costs of treating uninsured patients.

One student commented that Meltzer is best advised to avoid subsequent visits to Sierra University Hospital by becoming a better skier.

13-18 (20 min.) **Single-rate versus dual-rate allocation methods, support department.**

Bases available (kilowatt hours):

	Rockford	Peoria	Hammond	Kankakee	Total
Practical capacity	10,000	20,000	12,000	8,000	50,000
Expected monthly usage	8,000	9,000	7,000	6,000	30,000

1. a. Single-rate method based on practical capacity:

Total costs in pool = $6,000 + $9,000 = $15,000
Practical capacity = 50,000 kilowatt hours
Allocation rate = $15,000 ÷ 50,000 = $0.30 per hour of capacity

	Rockford	Peoria	Hammond	Kankakee	Total
Practical capacity in hours	10,000	20,000	12,000	8,000	50,000
Costs allocated at $0.30 per hour	$3,000	$6,000	$3,600	$2,400	$15,000

b. Single-rate method based on expected monthly usage:

Total costs in pool = $6,000 + $9,000 = $15,000
Expected usage = 30,000 kilowatt hours
Allocation rate = $15,000 ÷ 30,000 =$0.50 per hour of expected usage

	Rockford	Peoria	Hammond	Kankakee	Total
Expected monthly usage in hours	8,000	9,000	7,000	6,000	30,000
Costs allocated at $0.50 per hour	$4,000	$4,500	$3,500	$3,000	$15,000

2. Variable Cost Pool:

Total costs in pool	=	$6,000
Expected usage	=	30,000 kilowatt hours
Allocation rate	=	$0.20 per hour of expected usage

Fixed Cost Pool:

Total costs in pool	=	$9,000
Practical capacity	=	50,000 kilowatt hours
Allocation rate	=	$0.18 per hour of capacity

13-18 (Cont'd.)

	Rockford	Peoria	Hammond	Kankakee	Total
Variable cost pool	$1,600	$1,800	$1,400	$1,200	$ 6,000
Fixed cost pool	1,800	3,600	2,160	1,440	9,000
Total	$3,400	$5,400	$3,560	$2,640	$15,000

The dual-rate method permits a more refined allocation of the power department costs; it permits the use of different allocation bases for different cost pools. The fixed costs result from decisions most likely associated with the practical capacity level. The variable costs result from decisions most likely associated with monthly usage.

13-20 (20 min.) **Dual-rate cost allocation method, budgeted versus actual costs an quantities.** (continuation of 13-19)

1.   Charges with Dual Rate Method

Variable indirect cost rate   = $1,500 per trip

Fixed indirect cost rate   = $\dfrac{\$200,000 \text{ budgeted costs}}{250 \text{ budgeted trips}}$

                                      = $800 per budgeted trip

Orange Juice Division
    Variable indirect costs, $1,500 × 200 $300,000
    Fixed indirect costs, $800 × 150   120,000
                                     $420,000

Grapefruit Division
    Variable indirect costs, $1,500 × 100 $150,000
    Fixed indirect costs, $800 × 100   80,000
                                     $230,000

2.

	Orange Juice Division	Grapefruit Juice Division
Single Rate I (budgeted rate × actual use)	$460,000	$230,000
Single Rate II (Actual rate × actual use)	430,000	215,000
Dual rate	420,000	230,000

If the dual-rate method used actual trips made as the allocation base, it would give the same answer as Single Rate I. The dual rate changes how the fixed indirect cost component is treated. By using budgeted trips made, the Orange Juice Division is unaffected by changes from its own budgeted usage or that of other divisions.

13-22 (20 min.) **Allocation of travel costs.**

1. Allocation of the $1,800 airfare: Alternative approaches include:

a. The stand-alone cost allocation method. This method would allocate the air fare on the basis of each user's percentage of the total of the individual stand-alone costs:

New York employer $\dfrac{\$1,400}{(\$1,400 + \$1,100)} \times \$1,800 =$ $1,008

Chicago employer $\dfrac{\$1,100}{(\$1,400 + \$1,100)} \times \$1,800 =$ $\underline{\quad 792}$

$\underline{\$1,800}$

Advocates of this method often emphasize an equity or fairness rationale.

b. The incremental cost allocation method. This requires the choice of a primary party and an incremental party.

If the New York employer is the primary party, the allocation would be:

New York employer	$1,400
Chicago employer	$\underline{\quad 400}$
	$\underline{\$1,800}$

One rationale is Ernst was planning to make the New York trip and the Chicago stop was added subsequently. Some students have suggested allocating as much as possible to the New York employer since Ernst was not joining them.

If the Chicago employer is the primary party, the allocation would be:

Chicago employer	$1,100
New York employer	$\underline{\quad 700}$
	$\underline{\$1,800}$

One rationale is that the Chicago employer is the successful recruiter and presumably receives more benefits from the recruiting expenditures.

2. A simple approach is to split the $60 equally between the two employers. The limousine costs at the San Francisco end are not a function of distance traveled on the plane.

13-22 (Cont'd.)

An alternative approach is to add the $60 to the $1,800 and repeat requirement 1:

a. Stand-alone cost allocation method:

New York employer
$$\frac{\$1,460}{(\$1,460 + \$1,160)} \times \$1,860 = \$1,036$$

Chicago employer
$$\frac{\$1,160}{(\$1,460 + \$1,160)} \times \$1,860 = \$824$$

b. Incremental cost allocation method. With New York employer as the primary party:

New York employer	$1,460
Chicago employer	400
	$1,860

With Chicago employer as the primary party:

Chicago employer	$1,160
New York employer	700
	$1,860

Note: Ask any students in the class how they handled this situation if they have faced it.

13-24 (30 min.) **Support department cost allocation, reciprocal method.** (continuation of 13-23)

1.

	A/HR	IS	GOVT	CORP
Costs	$600,000	$2,400,000		
Alloc. of A/HR				
(0.25, 0.40, 0.35))	(861,538)	215,385	$ 344,615	$ 301,538
Alloc. of I.S.				
(0.10, 0.30, 0.60)	261,538	(2,615,385)	784,615	1,569,231
			$1,129,230	$1,870,769

Reciprocal Method Computation

$$A = \$600,000 + 0.10 \text{ IS}$$
$$IS = \$2,400,000 + 0.25 \text{ A}$$

$$IS = \$2,400,000 + 0.25 (\$600,000 + 0.10 \text{ IS})$$
$$= \$2,400,000 + \$150,000 + 0.025 \text{IS}$$
$$0.975 \text{IS} = \$2,550,000$$
$$IS = \$2,550,000 \div 0.975$$
$$= \$2,615,385$$

$$A = \$600,000 + 0.10 (\$2,615,385)$$
$$= \$600,000 + \$261,538$$
$$= \$861,538$$

2.

		Govt. Consulting	Corp Consulting
(a)	Direct	$1,120,000	$1,880,000
(b)	Step-Down (Ad/HR first)	1,090,000	1,910,000
(c)	Step-Down (IS first)	1,168,000	1,832,080
(d)	Reciprocal	1,129,230	1,870,769

The four methods differ in the level of service department cost allocation across service departments. The level of reciprocal service department is material. Administrative/HR supplies 25% of its services to Information Systems. Information Systems supplies 10% of its services to Administrative/HR. The Information Department has a budget of $2,400,000 which is 400% higher than Administrative/HR.

The reciprocal method recognizes all the interactions and is thus the most accurate.

13-26 (40 min.) **Allocation of central corporate costs to divisions.**

1.   The purposes for allocating central corporate costs to each division include:

a.   **To provide information for economic decisions.** Allocations can signal to division managers that decisions to expand (contract) activities will likely require increases (decreases) in corporate costs that should be considered in the initial decision about expansion (contraction). When top management is allocating resources to divisions, analysis of relative division profitability should consider differential use of corporate services by divisions. Some allocation schemes can encourage the use of central services that would otherwise be underutilized. A common rationale related to this purpose is "to remind profit center managers that central corporate costs exist and that division earnings must be adequate to cover some share of those costs."

b.   **Motivation.** Creates an incentive for division managers to control costs; for example, by reducing the number of employees at a division, a manager will save direct labor costs as well as central personnel and payroll costs allocated on the basis of number of employees. Allocation also creates incentives for division managers to monitor the effectiveness and efficiency with which central corporate costs are spent.

c.   **Cost justification or reimbursement.** Some lines of business of Richfield Oil may be regulated with cost data used in determining "fair prices"; allocations of central corporate costs will result in higher prices being set by a regulator.

d.   **Income measurement for external parties.** Richfield Oil may include allocations of central corporate costs in its external line-of-business reporting.

    Instructors may wish to discuss the "Surveys of Company Practice" evidence from the U.S., Canada, Australia, and the United Kingdom in Chapter 13 (p. 474).

2. Total costs in single pool = $3,000
    Allocation base = $30,000 revenue
    Allocation rate = $3,000 ÷ $30,000 = $0.10 per $1 of revenue

See Solution Exhibit 13-26 for additional answers.

3. See Solution Exhibit 13-26 for answer.

13-26 (Cont'd.)

SOLUTION EXHIBIT 13-26
(in millions)

	Oil & Gas Upstream	Oil & Gas Downstream	Chemical Products	Copper Mining	Total
Revenues	$7,000	$16,000	$4,000	$3,000	$30,000
Operating costs	3,000	15,000	3,800	3,200	25,000
Allocated costs, $0.10 per $1 revenue	700	1,600	400	300	3,000
Division income	$3,300	$ (600)	$ (200)	$ (500)	$ 2,000

Allocation Base	Oil & Gas Upstream	Oil & Gas Downstream	Chemical Products	Copper Mining
1. Allocated on basis of identifiable assets	14/25	6/25	3/25	2/25
Total costs = $2,000	$1,120	$480	$240	$160
2. Allocated on basis of revenues	7/30	16/30	4/30	3/30
Total costs = $600	$140	$320	$ 80	$ 60
3. Allocated on basis of operating income (if positive)	40/52	10/52	2/52	--
Total costs = $208	$160	$ 40	$ 8	$ 0
4. Allocated on basis of number of employees	9/30	12/30	6/30	3/30
Total costs = $192	$ 57.6	$ 76.8	$ 38.4	$ 19.2

	Oil & Gas Upstream	Oil & Gas Downstream	Chemical Products	Copper Mining	Total
Revenues	$7,000	$16,000	$4,000	$3,000	$30,000
Operating costs	3,000	15,000	3,800	3,200	25,000
Cost Pool 1 Allocation	1,120	480	240	160	2,000
Cost Pool 2 Allocation	140	320	80	60	600
Cost Pool 3 Allocation	160	40	8	0	208
Cost Pool 4 Allocation	57.6	76.8	38.4	19.2	192
Division income	$2,522.4	$ 83.2	$ (166.4)	$ (439.2)	$ 2,000

4. Strengths of Rhodes' proposal relative to existing single-cost pool method:
a. Better able to capture cause-and-effect relationships. Interest on debt is more likely caused by the financing of assets than by revenues. Personnel and payroll costs are more likely caused by the number of employees than by revenues.

b. Relatively simple. No extra information need be collected beyond that already available. (Some students will list the extra costs of Rhodes' proposal as a weakness. However, for a company with $30 billion in revenues, those extra costs are minimal.)

Weaknesses of Rhodes' proposal relative to existing single-cost pool method:

a. May promote dysfunctional decision making. May encourage division managers to lease or rent assets rather than to purchase assets, even where it is economical for Richfield Oil to purchase them. This off-balance sheet financing will reduce the "identifiable assets" of the division and thus will reduce the interest on debt costs allocated to the division. (Richfield Oil could counteract this problem by incorporating leased and rented assets in the "identifiable assets" base.)

Note: Some students criticized Rhodes' proposal, even though agreeing that it is preferable to the existing single-cost pool method. These criticisms include:

a. Proposal does not adequately capture cause-and-effect relationships for the legal and research and development cost pools. For these cost pools, specific identification of individual projects with an individual division can better capture cause-and-effect relationships.

b. Proposal may give rise to disputes over the definition and valuation of "identifiable assets."

c. Use of actual rather than budgeted amounts in the allocation bases creates interdependencies between divisions. Moreover, use of actual amounts means that division managers do not know cost allocation consequences of their decisions until the end of each reporting period.

d. Separate allocation of fixed and variable costs would result in more refined cost allocations.

e. Questionable that 100% of central corporate costs should be allocated. Many students argue that public affairs should not be allocated to any division, based on the notion that division managers may not control many of the individual expenditures in this cost pool.

13-28 (20-30 min.) **Departmental cost allocation, university computer-service center.**

1.   Each school would be allocated half the $100,000:

         H&S: $(100/200) \times \$100{,}000 = \$50{,}000$
         Engineering: $(100/200) \times \$100{,}000 = \$50{,}000$

The allocation of the $10,000 costs of inefficiency seems unjustified because the "consuming departments" have to bear another department's cost of inefficiency. The system provides no incentive to the service department manager to control operating costs. An improvement would be to use budgeted unit prices (at least) and, where feasible, budgeted total prices for various kinds of work based on flexible budgets and standards. In this way, the consuming department managers will know in advance that inefficiencies will be borne by the supplier, not the consumer.

2.   Total costs incurred: $80,000 + 150($100) = $95,000

         H&S: $(50/150) \times \$95{,}000 = \$31{,}667$
         Engineering: $(100/150) \times \$95{,}000 = \$63{,}333$

Note that the unit cost per hour has risen from $100,000 ÷ 200 = $500 in requirement 1 to $95,000 ÷ 150 = $633 in requirement 2. Engineering's total cost rose from $50,000 to $63,333, an increase of 26.7% solely because H&S's usage declined.

3.   Planned long-run usage: 180 + 120 = 300 hours

		H&S	Engineering
Fixed Costs:	$(180/300) \times \$80{,}000$	$48,000	
	$(120/300) \times \$80{,}000$		$32,000
Variable costs:	$50 \times \$100$	5,000	
	$100 \times \$100$		10,000
		$53,000	$42,000

The advantages were described above:
a.   Use of a budgeted unit rate for variable costs helps planning by consumers and insulates them from intervening price changes and some inefficiencies.
b.   Use of the lump-sum approach for fixed costs prevents the total charges from being affected by the short-run usage of the service department by other consuming departments.

13-28 (Cont'd.)

4. Consumers would tend to understate their predictions of long-run usage. Conceivably, if all played the same game, the lump-sum allocations may be unchanged--although that result is unlikely. Top management copes with these tendencies by monitoring these predictions, following up, and using feedback to keep future predictions more reliable. Also, in some organizations there are definite rewards in the form of salary increases for managers who demonstrate skills in making accurate predictions. In addition, some organizations charge a high price for usage that exceeds a budgeted commitment.

13-30 (40-60 min.) **Support department cost allocations; single-department cost pools; direct, step-down, and reciprocal methods.**

All the following computations are in dollars.

1.

Direct method:

	To X	To Y
A	250/400 × $100,000 = $62,500	150/400 × $100,000 = $37,500
B	100/500 × $40,000 = $8,000	400/500 × $40,000 = $32,000
Total	$70,500	$69,500

Step-down method, allocating B first:

	A	B	X	Y
Costs to be allocated	$100,000	$40,000	—	—
Allocate B: (0.5, 0.1, 0.4)	20,000	(40,000)	$ 4,000	$16,000
Allocate A: (250/400, 150/400)	(120,000)	—	75,000	45,000
Total	$ 0	$ 0	$79,000	$61,000

Step-down method, allocating A first:

	A	B	X	Y
Costs to be allocated	$100,000	$40,000	—	—
Allocate A: (0.2, 0.5, 0.3)	(100,000)	20,000	$50,000	$30,000
Allocate B: (0.2, 0.8)	—	(60,000)	12,000	48,000
Total	$ 0	$ 0	$62,000	$78,000

Note that these methods produce significantly different results, so the choice of method may frequently make a difference in the budgeted department overhead rates.

Reciprocal method:

Stage 1: Let A = total costs of materials-handling department
B = total costs of power-generating department
(1) A = $100,000 + 0.5B
(2) B = $ 40,000 + 0.2A

Stage 2: Substituting in (1): A = $100,000 + 0.5($40,000 + 0.2A)
A = $100,000 + $20,000 + 0.1A
0.9A = $120,000
A = $133,333

Substituting in (2): B = $40,000 + 0.2($133,333)
B = $66,666

13-30 (Cont'd.)

Stage 3:

	A	B	X	Y
Original amounts	100,000	40,000	—	—
Allocation of A	(133,333)	26,666(20%)	66,667(50%)	40,000(30%)
Allocation of B	33,333(50%)	(66,666)	6,666(10%)	26,667(40%)
Totals accounted for	—	—	73,333	66,667

Comparison of methods:

Method of Allocation	X	Y
Direct method	$70,500	$69,500
Step-down: B first	79,000	61,000
Step-down: A first	62,000	78,000
Reciprocal method	73,333	66,667

Note that in this case the direct method produces answers that are the closest to the "correct" answers (that is, those from the reciprocal method), step-down allocating B first is next, and step-down allocating A first is least accurate.

2. At first glance, it appears that the cost of power is $40 per unit plus the material handling costs. If so, Manes would be better off by purchasing from the power company. However, the decision should be influenced by the effects of the interdependencies and the fixed costs. Note that the power needs would be less (students miss this) if they were purchased from the outside:

	Outside Power Units Needed
X	100
Y	400
A (500 units minus 20% of 500 units, because there is no need to service the nonexistent power department)	400
Total units	900

Total costs, 900 × $40 = $36,000

13-30 (Cont'd)

In contrast, the total costs that would be saved by not producing the power inside would depend on the effects of the decision on various costs:

	Avoidable Costs of 100 Units of Power Produced Inside
Variable indirect labor and indirect material costs	$10,000
Supervision in power department	10,000
Materials handling, 20% of $70,000*	14,000
Probable minimum cost savings	$34,000
Possible additional savings:	
a. Can any supervision in materials handling be saved because of overseeing less volume? Minimum savings is probably zero; the maximum is probably 20% of $10,000 or $2,000.	?
b. Is any depreciation a truly variable, wear-and-tear type of cost?	?
Total savings by not producing 100 units of power	$34,000 + ?

* Materials handling costs are higher because the power department uses 20% of materials handling. Therefore, materials-handling costs will decrease by 20%.

In the short run (at least until a capital investment in equipment is necessary), the data suggest continuing to produce internally because the costs eliminated would probably be less than the comparable purchase costs.

13-32 (60 min.) **Allocating costs of support departments; dual rates; direct, step-down, and reciprocal methods.**

This problem is similar to the Problem for Self Study.

1.   Solution Exhibit 13-32 presents the costs allocated to each assembly department under the four service department cost allocation methods. The linear equations underlying the complete reciprocated costs reported in Solution Exhibit 13-35 are:

Fixed-Cost Pool:

$$ES = \$2,700 + 0.20IS$$
$$IS = \$8,000 + 0.10ES$$

$$ES = \$2,700 + 0.20(\$8,000 + 0.10ES)$$
$$ES = \$4,300 + 0.02ES$$
$$0.98ES = \$4,300$$
$$ES = \$4,300 \div 0.98 = \$4,387.76$$

$$IS = \$8,000 + 0.10(\$4,387.76)$$
$$= \$8,438.78$$

Variable-Cost Pool:

$$ES = \$8,500 + 0.25IS$$
$$IS = \$3,750 + 0.15ES$$

$$ES = \$8,500 + 0.25 (\$3,750 + 0.15ES)$$
$$ES = \$9,437.5 + 0.0375ES$$
$$0.9625\,ES = \$9,437.5$$
$$ES = \$9,437.5 \div 0.9625 = \$9,805.19$$

$$IS = \$3,750 + 0.15(\$9,805.19)$$
$$= \$3,750 + \$1,470.78 = \$5,220.78$$

13-32 (Cont'd.)

A summary of the costs allocated under each method is:

		Home Security Systems	Business Security Systems
a.	Direct Method:		
	Fixed-cost pool	$4,200.00	$ 6,500.00
	Variable-cost pool	3,750.00	8,500.00
		$7,950.00	$15,000.00
b.	Step-Down (Information First):		
	Fixed-cost pool	$4,311.11	$ 6,388.89
	Variable-cost pool	3,893.38	8,356.62
		$8,204.49	$14,745.51
c.	Step-down (Engineering First):		
	Fixed-cost pool	$4,181.25	$ 6,518.75
	Variable- cost pool	3,555.00	8,695.00
		$7,736.25	$15,213.75
d.	Reciprocal Method:		
	Fixed-cost pool	$4,286.73	$ 6,413.27
	Variable-cost pool	3,724.68	8,525.32
		$8,011.41	$14,938.59

2. Support department costs allocated per unit:

		Home Security Systems	Business Security Systems
a.	Direct method	$1.00	$4.00
b.	Step-down (Information first)	$1.03	$3.93
c.	Step-down (Engineering first)	$0.97	$4.06
d.	Reciprocal method	$1.01	$3.98

13-32 (Cont'd.)

3. Factors that might explain the very limited adoption of the reciprocal method include:

a.   Managers find the reciprocal method difficult to understand, especially where there are many support departments.
b.   The final cost allocations yielded by using the reciprocal method differ little in some cases from those yielded by using the direct or step-down methods. As illustrated in requirement 2, the differences among the four methods in this problem appear small.
c.   It is costly to maintain records of the use of the support departments by other support departments.

SOLUTION EXHIBIT 13-32
(in thousands)

	Engineering Support	Information Systems Support	Home Security Systems	Business Security Systems
a. Direct Method				
Fixed- Cost Pool	$ 2,700	$ 8,000		
Eng. Support (4/9, 5/9)	(2,700)		$1,200.00	$1,500.00
Info. Support (3/8, 5/8)		(8,000)	3,000.00	5,000.00
			$4,200.00	$6,500.00
Variable-Cost Pool:	$ 8,500	$ 3,750		
Eng. Support (30/85, 55/85)	(8,500)		$3,000.00	$5,500.00
Info. Support 15/75,60/75)		(3,750)	750.00	3,000.00
			$3,750.00	$8,500.00
b. Step-down (Information First)				
Fixed-Cost Pool:	$ 2,700	$ 8,000		
Info. Support (.2, .3, .5)	1,600	(8,000)	$2,400.00	$4,000.00
Eng. Support (4/9, 5/9)	(4,300)	—	1,911.11	2,388.89
			$4,311.11	$6,388.89
Variable-Cost Pool:	$ 8,500	$ 3,750		
Info. Support (.25, .15, .60)	937.5	(3,750)	$ 562.50	$2,250.00
Eng. Support (30/85, 55/85)	(9,437.5)	—	3,330.88	6,106.62
			$3,893.38	$8,356.62
c. Step-down (Engineering First):				
Fixed-Cost Pool:				
Eng. Support (.1, .4, .5)	$ 2,700	$ 8,000		
Info. Support (3/8, 5/8)	(2,700)	270	$1,080.00	$1,350.00
		(8,270)	3,101.25	5,168.75
			$4,181.25	$6,518.75
Variable-Cost Pool:				
Eng. Support (.15, .30, .55)	$ 8,500	$ 3,750		
Info. Support (.2, .8)	(8,500)	1,275	$ 2,550.00	$4,675.00
		(5,025)	1,005.00	4,020.00
			$3,555.00	$8,695.00
d. Reciprocal Method				
Fixed-Cost Pool:	$ 2,700	$ 8,000.00		
Eng. Support (.1, .4, .5)	(4,387.76)	438.78	$1,755.10	$2,193.88
Info. Support (.2, .3, .5)	1,687.76	(8,438.78)	2,531.63	4,219.39
			$4,286.73	$6,413.27
Variable-Cost Pool:	$ 8,500.00	$ 3,750.00		
Eng. Support (.15, .30, .55)	(9,805.19)	1,470.78	$ 2,941.56	$5,392.85
Info. Support (.25, .15, .60)	1,305.19	(5,220.78)	783.12	3,132.47
			$3,724.68	$8,525.32

13-21

13-34 (20 min.) **Division cost allocation, R&D, ethics.**

1.   The overhead cost charged to each division for use of the San Diego facility is:

$$\begin{bmatrix} \text{Budgeted \% use} \\ \text{by division of} \\ \text{San Diego facility} \end{bmatrix} \times \begin{bmatrix} \text{Budgeted overhead costs} \\ \text{at San Diego facility} \end{bmatrix}$$

If the ASD division understates its budgeted use of the San Diego facility and all other divisions provide unbiased estimates of their budgeted use, the ASD division will have a lower budgeted % use factor for the San Diego facility, and thus a lower overhead cost charge.   If all divisions understate their budgeted use, those division(s) providing the greatest understatements will be those benefiting by their understatement.

2.   Alternative approaches San Diego might take include:
   a.   Charging a division a penalty rate when it uses a higher number of hours than it submitted as its budgeted amount.
   b.   Change the charge structure so that each hour of research scientist time used has a budgeted overhead charge component. (This approach only partially reduces the problem because the fixed overhead rate per hour must be determined.)
   c.   Use actual costs per hour rather than budgeted costs per hour as the charge to each using division.

3.   Under the "Standards of Ethical Conduct for Management Accountants," Goodwin has an objectivity responsibility—to communicate information fairly and objectively and to disclose all relevant information that could be reasonably expected to influence an intended user's understanding of the reports, comments, and recommendations presented. Goodwin's first response should be to develop a well-constructed argument to present to Roy Masters for using the 30,000 number. Masters should be given at least one more chance to respond to Goodwin's concerns. Ideally, Goodwin should give Masters a short time period (say one week) to think about her concerns.   This is especially the case if there is already documentation at ASD for the 30,000 number. Goodwin might note that if internal control people at WS are called in to consider any allegations by other divisions that ASD is deliberately understating budgeted usage, the 30,000 figure likely will be observable.

   If Masters continues with his threats about dropping Goodwin from "the ASD team," she should contact the corporate controller at WS to seek guidance on how to handle the situation.

CHAPTER 14
COST ALLOCATION: II

14-2 Factors that affect the indirect costs allocated to individual products or services are:
- The aggregate costs in each indirect cost pool.
- The allocation base used for each indirect cost pool.
- The allocation rate used for each indirect cost pool.

14-4 Agree. More cost pools ordinarily increase homogeneity. Individual cost items typically have different cause-and-effect or benefits-received relationships between cost incurrence and variables such as direct manufacturing labor-hours, direct manufacturing labor costs, machine-hours, or direct materials cost or weight.

14-6 The distinction between labor-paced and machine-paced operations is important when examining the possible cost allocation bases to use in a costing system. In labor-paced operations, it is likely that labor-hours will capture cause-and-effect relationships. In machine-paced operations, however, there is a greater likelihood that machine-related variables (such as machine-hours) will capture cause-and-effect relationships. These are general guidelines whose validity needs to examined in specific cases.

14-8 The consequences of using direct manufacturing labor-hours as an allocation base in a machine-paced manufacturing environment are:

(a)   Product managers make excessive use of external vendors to obtain parts with a high direct labor content.
(b)   Excessive attention is paid by manufacturing managers to controlling direct manufacturing labor-hours relative to the attention paid to controlling the more costly categories of materials and machining.
(c)   Managers attempt to classify shop-floor personnel as indirect manufacturing labor rather than as direct manufacturing labor.

14-10 Two ways firms are reimbursed under government contracts are:
(a)   Contractor is paid a preset price without analysis of actual contract cost data.
(b)   The contractor is paid after analysis of actual contract cost data. This includes cost-plus contracts.

14-12 Unused capacity is the difference between the productive capacity available and the productive capacity required to meet consumer demand in the current period. The role that unused capacity plays in the setting of indirect-cost rates depends on the chosen denominator level. If productive capacity available is used as the denominator volume, unused capacity potentially will be one explanation for a production-volume variance. In contrast, if budgeted usage is used as the denominator volume, there will be less visible signals about unused capacity.

14-14 The downward demand spiral can arise when a company attempts to recover fixed costs by increasing selling prices but suffers a decline in demand; it then increases selling prices again and suffers a further decline in demand; and so on.

14-16 (15 min.) **Alternative allocation bases for a professional-services firm.**

1.

Client	Direct Professional Time			Support Services		Amount
	Rate per Hour	Number of Hours	Total	Rate	Total	Billed to Client
(1)	(2)	(3)	(4) = (2) × (3)	(5)	(6) = (4) × (5)	(7) = (4) + (6)
SEATTLE DOMINION						
Wolfson	$500	15	$7,500	30% of (4)	$2,250	$ 9,750
Brown	120	3	360	30% of (4)	108	468
Anderson	80	22	1,760	30% of (4)	528	2,288
						$12,506
TOKYO ENTERPRISES						
Wolfson	$500	2	$1,000	30% of (4)	$300	$1,300
Brown	120	8	960	30% of (4)	288	1,248
Anderson	80	30	2,400	30% of (4)	720	3,120
						$5,668

2.

Client	Direct Professional Time			Support Services		Amount
	Rate per Hour	Number of Hours	Total	Rate	Total	Billed to Client
(1)	(2)	(3)	(4) = (2) × (3)	(5)	(6) = (3) × (5)	(7) = (4)+(6)
SEATTLE DOMINION						
Wolfson	$500	15	$7,500	$50 per hr.	$ 750	$ 8,250
Brown	120	3	360	$50 per hr.	150	510
Anderson	80	22	1,760	$50 per hr.	1,100	2,860
						$11,620
TOKYO ENTERPRISES						$1,100
Wolfson	$500	2	$1,000	$50 per hr.	$ 100	1,360
Brown	120	8	960	$50 per hr.	400	3,900
Anderson	80	30	2,400	$50 per hr.	1,500	$6,360

14-2

14-16 (Cont'd.)

	Requirement 1	**Requirement 2**
Seattle Dominion	$12,506	$11,620
Tokyo Enterprises	5,668	6,360
	$18,174	$17,980

Both clients use 40 hours of professional labor time. However, Seattle Dominion uses a higher proportion of Wolfson's time (15 hours), which attracts the highest support-services charge.

3.   Assume that the Wolfson Group uses a cause-and-effect criterion when choosing the allocation base for support services. You could use several pieces of evidence to determine whether professional labor costs or hours is the driver of support-service costs:

a.   *Interviews with personnel.* For example, staff in the major cost categories in support services could be interviewed to determine whether Wolfson requires more support per hour than, say, Anderson. The professional labor costs allocation base implies that an hour of Wolfson's time requires 6.25 ($500 ÷ $80) times more support-service dollars than does an hour of Anderson's time.

b.   *Analysis of tasks undertaken for selected clients.* For example, if computer-related costs are a sizable part of support costs, you could determine if there was a systematic relationship between the percentage involvement of professionals with high billing rates on cases and the computer resources consumed for those cases.

14-18   (30 min.)   **Department indirect cost rates** . (continuation of 14-17)

1.

	19_7 Variable MOH Costs	Total Driver Units	Rate
Design-CAD	$ 39,000	390	$100 per design-hour
Engineering	29,600	370	$ 80 per engineer-hour
Production	240,000	4,000	$ 60 per machine

2.

	United Motors	Holden Motors	Leland Vehicle
Design			
$100 × 110; 200; 80	$11,000	$ 20,000	$ 8,000
Engineering			
$80 × 70; 60; 240	5,600	4,800	19,200
Production			
$60 × 120; 2,800; 1,080	7,200	168,000	64,800
Total	$23,800	$192,800	$92,000

3.

	United Motors	Holden Motors	Leland Vehicle
(a) Department rate			
(Question 14-18)	$23,800	$192,800	$92,000
(b) Plantwide rate			
(Question 14-17)	9,258	216,020	83,322
Ratio of (a) ÷ (b)	2.57	0.89	1.10

The three contracts differ sizably in the way they use the resources of the three departments. The percentage of total driver units in each department is:

Department	United Motors	Holden Motors	Leland Vehicle
Design	28%	51%	21%
Engineering	19	16	65
Production	3	70	27

The United Motors contract uses only 3% of total machines-hours in 19_7, yet uses 28% of CAD design-hours and 19% of engineering hours. The result is that the plantwide rate, based on machine-hours, will greatly underestimate the cost of resources used on the United Motors contract. Hence, the 257% increase in indirect costs assigned to the United Motors contract when department rates are used.

In contrast, the Holden Motors contract uses less of design (51%) and engineering (16%) than of machine-hours (70%). Hence, department rates will report lower indirect costs than does a plantwide rate.

14-20 (14-20 min.) **Cost allocation with a nonfinancial variable, retailing.**

1. and 2.

	Breakfast cereal	Cheese product	Paper towels	Toothpaste
Revenue	$82	$64	$36	$100
Cost of goods sold	56	52	26	74
Gross margin	26	12	10	26
Goods-handling cost	12	6	12	6
Product contribution	$14	$ 6	$(2)	$ 20

Rankings on gross margin % and a product contribution to revenue % are:

Gross-margin percentage		Product contribution to revenue %	
1. Breakfast cereal	31.7%	1. Toothpaste	20%
2. Paper towels	27.8%	2. Breakfast cereal	17.1%
3. Toothpaste	26.0%	3. Cheese product	9.4%
4. Cheese product	18.7%	4. Paper towels	–5.5%

3. Assigning the goods-handling costs to each product:
    a. Changes the rankings in terms of profitability.
    b. Makes high-volume (cubic feet) products relatively less profitable than low-volume products.
    This information is useful in product-emphasis decisions.

14-22 (30–40 min.) **Overhead disputes.**

1.   This problem, which is based on an actual case, shows how overhead cost allocation can affect contract pricing. The Navy would claim a refund of $689,658.

The overhead cost would be allocated differently:

$$\text{Previous overhead allocation rate} \quad = \frac{\$30}{\$50 + \$100} = 20\%$$

$$\text{Revised overhead allocation rate} \quad = \frac{\$30}{\$45 + \$100} = 20.68965\%$$

	Navy Costs	Commercial Costs
Original cost assignment:		
Direct materials	$ –	$ –
Direct labor	45,000,000	100,000,000
SE group	5,000,000	–
Allocated overhead (20% × DL$)	10,000,000(a)	20,000,000(b)
Total	$60,000,000	$120,000,000
Revised cost assignment:		
Direct materials	$ —	$ –
Direct labor	45,000,000	100,000,000
SE group	5,000,000	–
Allocated overhead (20.68965% × DL$)	9,310,342(c)	20,689,650(d)
Total	$59,310,342	$120,689,650

(a) 20% × ($45,000,000 direct labor + $5,000,000 SE group classified as direct labor) = $10,000,000

(b) 20% × $100,000,000 = $20,000,000

(c) 20.68965% × $45,000,000 = $9,310,342

(d) 20.68965% × $100,000,000 = $20,689,650

14-22 (Cont'd.)

The Navy claim would be:

Remove the original overhead allocation of $50 million × 0.20	$10,000,000

This means that the overhead pool, which has been totally
  allocated to products, is now underallocated by $10 million. This
  overhead must be reallocated in proportion to the "corrected"
  direct labor in nuclear work and commercial work. In short,
  if the overhead allocation base shrinks from $150 to $145
  million, the overhead rate increases from 20% to 20.68965%.

The revised allocation is $45 million × .2068965.	9,310,342
	$ 689,658

2.   Revised overhead allocation rate $= \dfrac{\$26}{\$45 + \$100} = 17.93103\%$

	Navy Costs	Commercial Costs
Revised cost assignment:		
Direct materials	$ –	$ –
Direct labor	45,000,000	100,000,000
SE group	5,000,000	–
Commercial purchasing	–	4,000,000
Allocated overhead (17.93103% × DL$)	8,068,964	17,931,030
	$58,068,964	$121,931,030

Given that the original Navy cost is $60,000,000, and the revised cost is $58,068,964, the Navy would claim a total refund of $1,931,036.

14-24 (20-30 min.) **Downward demand spiral, pricing, cost hierarchy.**

1.

Revenues (15,000 passenger round trips × $150)	$2,250,000
Passenger level costs (15,000 × $20)	300,000
Passenger-related contribution	1,950,000
Flight level costs (150 × $6,000)	900,000
Passenger-and flight-related contribution	1,050,000
Fixed costs	1,200,000
Operating income	$ (150,000)

This hierarchy highlights how costs at Sky Shuttle are driven by different factors. For example, LeMay could observe that a 20% reduction in costs per passenger will have a limited effect on bottom-line operating income. In contrast, a 20% reduction in flight level cost has a more sizable effect. The high level of fixed costs highlights how critical decisions pertaining to acquisitions of planes and other infrastructure items are to an airline. Using the terminology of Chapter 12, many costs of an airline are locked in at a very early stage in cost planning.

2.

	$180 Pricing Strategy		$200 Pricing Strategy	
Revenues	$2,430,000	(150 × 90 × $180)	$2,250,000	(150 × 75 × $200)
Passenger level costs	270,000	(150 × 90 × $20)	225,000	(150 × 75 × $20)
Passenger-related contribution	2,160,000		2,025,000	
Flight level costs	900,000	(150 × $6,000)	900,000	(150 × $6,000)
P&F-related contribution	1,260,000		1,125,000	
Fixed costs	1,200,000		1,200,000	
Operating income	$ 60,000		$ (75,000)	

Either pricing strategy has a positive effect on operating income relative to the $150 price. However, Sky Shuttle faces the issue of declining passenger loads when they raise prices. Thus, the increase in round-trip fare from $180 to $200 reduces operating income.

Note, however, that Sky Shuttle can gain much by reducing the number of round-trip flights or by reducing the cost per round trip.

3. LeMay may have few options other than matching the price promotion if she wants to keep reasonable traffic on the route. One approach may be to place very specific restrictions on the $120 tickets so that key customers (such as business travelers) who are not as price sensitive are willing to pay the higher prices.

Airline pricing in the short run appears to have little relationship to long-run average costs. It is an industry with high fixed costs in which "kamikaze pricing policies" have resulted in numerous bankruptcies.

14-26 (40–50 min.) **Cost allocation for financial institution.**

1.   See Solution Exhibit 14-26.

2.   (a)   Cost of money

A key issue is whether there is a traceable link between individual sources of funds and individual uses of funds. There is no attempt at FPFCU to keep separate pools of cash such that (say) all deposit funds go to consumer loans. The funds in each source and each use show that for FPFCU it is not valid to assume (say) consumer loans are always sourced from deposits:

	SOURCES		USES	
	Deposits	**Borrowings**	**Consumer Loans**	**Investments**
19_4	$10.5 (96.33%)	$0.4 (3.67%)	$9.1 (83.49%)	$1.8 (16.51%)
19_5	11.6 (85.93)	1.9 (14.07)	12.6 (93.33)	0.9 (6.67)
19_6	12.8 (95.52)	0.6 (4.48)	10.7 (79.85)	2.7 (20.15)

The relatively high percentage of funds sourced from deposits means that the weighted average cost of funds will often be similar to the cost of deposits.

(b)   Trace as many costs directly to each product line. This assumption will result in more accurate product-line costs. If a cost can be traced to a single product line, it is more accurate to do so than allocating it among two or more product lines. Examples of costs traceable to loans would be credit checks by a third party and loan contract fees. Examples of costs traceable to investments would be brokerage charges and investment information services subscribed to.

(c)   Allocate non-specific costs on the basis of percentage of total earning assets. A key issue here is the line items included in this "other costs" pool. Many students will correctly argue that consumer loans are sizably more resource-intensive than investments. However, many of the costs of consumer loan activities are already included in the costs traceable to loans.

The "other costs" item line items (such as building occupancy costs and administrative costs) could be individually examined and their cost drivers determined; e.g., head count in the consumer loans and investments areas could be used to allocate building occupancy costs across the product lines.

Some students will suggest other allocation bases. Examples include:

(i)   Number of loans/number of investments. The argument is that the size of the loan does not drive costs. It takes the same resources to make a $20,000 loan and a $40,000 loan.

(ii)   Relative magnitude of traceable costs. The assumption here is that overhead has a relatively constant relationship per dollar of traceable costs. It would be important to empirically examine the validity of this assumption.

3.   (a)   *Product-line emphasis.* Product-line profitability reports provide signals as to which product line is contributing most to overall profitability. Consumer loans are profitable for FPFCU, while investments are unprofitable. At the margin, FPFCU should continue to make additional consumer loans, subject to their having acceptable credit risk. Relative to investments, they are a high margin business.

(b)   *Pricing.*   Product-line profitability statements can assist in pricing decisions. FPFCU has some discretion on the pricing and conditions associated with consumer loans. If it finds the spread between its lending rate and its average cost of funds narrowing, there would be pressure on it to raise its prices (charge a higher lending rate for consumer loans).

(c)   *Cost Management.* FPFCU may use external data on line of business margins in other financial institutions to benchmark its cost management activities. Line of business statements assist in the comparison of FPFCU with other institutions that have different mixes of business.

SOLUTION EXHIBIT 14-26
Product-line Income Statements

	19_4	19_5	19_6
Consumer Loans			
Interest earned	937,300	932,400	920,200
Interest costs	711,620	631,260	659,120
Net interest margin	225,680	301,140	261,080
Non-cost of money costs			
Traceable costs	82,700	91,500	86,700
Allocated costs	81,653	124,596	109,874
	164,353	216,096	196,574
Operating income	$ 61,327	$ 85,044	$ 64,506
Investments			
Interest earned	145,800	50,400	194,400
Interest costs	140,760	45,090	166,320
Net interest margin	5,040	5,310	28,080
Non-cost of money costs			
Traceable costs	6,100	4,500	8,900
Allocated costs	16,147	8,904	27,726
	22,247	13,404	36,626
Operating income	$(17,207)	$(8,094)	$ (8,546)

Average Balance of Earning Assets

	19_4		19_5		19_6	
	Amount	**%**	**Amount**	**%**	**Amount**	**%**
Consumer Loans	9,100,000	83.49%	12,600,000	93.33%	10,700,000	79.85%
Investments	1,800,000	16.51%	900,000	6.67%	2,700,000	21.15%
Total	$10,900,000		$13,500,000		$13,400,000	

Average Balance of Earning Assets

	19_4	19_5	19_6
Consumer Loans	10.30%	7.40%	8.60%
Investments	8.10%	5.60%	7.20%

Average Interest Earned on Assets

Consumer Loans[a]	$937,300	$932,400	$920,200
Investments[b]	145,800	50,400	194,400

[a]$9.1 million × 10.30% = $937,300
$12.6 million × 7.40% = $932,400
$10.7 million × 8.60% = $920,200

[b]$1.8 million × 8.10% =$145,800
$0.9 million × 5.60% = $50,400
$2.7 million × 7.20% =$194,400

Sources of Funds ($ millions)

	19_4		19_5		19_6	
	Amount	**%**	**Amount**	**%**	**Amount**	**%**
Deposits	$10.5	96.33%	$11.6	85.93%	$12.8	95.52%
Borrowings	0.4	3.67%	1.9	14.07%	0.6	4.48%
	$10.9		$13.5		$13.4	

Weighted Average Cost of Money

	19_4		19_5		19_6	
	Cost	**W. Avg.**	**Cost**	**W. Avg.**	**Cost**	**W. Avg.**
Deposits	7.80%	7.51%	4.90%	4.21%	6.10%	5.83%
Borrowings	8.30%	0.30%	5.70%	0.80%	7.40%	0.33%
Weighted Average		7.82%[a]		5.01%[b]		6.16%[c]

[a] $(7.80\% \times 0.9633) + (8.30\% \times 0.0367) = 7.82\%$
[b] $(4.90\% \times 0.8593) + (5.70\% \times 0.1407) = 5.01\%$
[c] $(6.10\% \times 0.9552) + (7.40\% \times 0.0448) = 6.16\%$

Interest Cost Using Weighted Average Cost of Money

	19_4	19_5	19_6
Consumer Loans[a]	$711,620	631,260	659,120
Investements[b]	140,760	45,090	166,320

[a] $\$ 9.1$ mil $\times 7.82\% = \$711,620$
$\$12.6$ mil $\times 5.01\% = \$631,260$
$\$10.7$ mil $\times 6.16\% = \$659,120$

[b] $\$1.8$ mil $\times 7.82\% = \$140,760$
$\$0.9$ mil $\times 5.01\% = \$ 45,090$
$\$2.7$ mil $\times 6.16\% = \$166,320$

Allocation of "Other Costs" Using Average Balance of Earning Assets

	Consumer Loans	Investments	Total
19_7 ($97,800 × 0.8349; 0.1651)	$81,653	$16,147	$ 97,800
19_8 ($133,500 × 0.9333; 0.0667)	124,596	8,904	133,500
19_9 ($137,600 × 0.7985; 0.2015)	109,874	27,726	137,600

14-28 (30 min.) **Plantwide versus department overhead cost rates.**

1.

| | Amounts (in thousands) | | | |
	Molding	Component	Assembly	Total
Manufacturing departments:				
Variable overhead	$ 3,500	$10,000	$16,500	$30,000
Fixed overhead	17,500	6,200	6,100	29,800
Total manufacturing				
department overhead	$21,000	$16,200	$22,600	$59,800
Service departments:				
Power				18,400
Maintenance				4,000
Total estimated plantwide overhead				$82,200

Estimated direct manufacturing labor hours (DLH):

Molding	500
Component	2,000
Assembly	1,500
Total estimated DLH	4,000

$$\text{Plantwide overhead rate} = \frac{\text{Estimated plantwide overhead}}{\text{Estimated DLH}}$$

$$= \frac{\$82,200}{4,000} = \$20.55 \text{ per DLH}$$

2.   The department overhead cost rates are in Solution Exhibit 14-28

3.   MumsDay Corporation should use department rates to allocate plant overhead to its products. A plantwide rate is appropriate when all products pass through the same processes, and all departments are similar. Departmental rates are appropriate when the converse is true. MumsDay's departments are dissimilar in that the Molding Department is machine-intensive and the other two departments are labor-intensive. Department rates better capture cause-and-effect relationships at MumsDay than does a plantwide rate.

SOLUTION EXHIBIT 14-28

| | Departments (in thousands) | | | | |
| | Service | | Manufacturing | | |
	Power	Maintenance	Molding	Component	Assembly
Departmental overhead costs	$18,400	$ 4,000	$21,000	$16,200	$22,600
Allocation of maintenance costs (direct method) $4,000 × 90/125, 25/125, 10/125		(4,000)	2,880	800	320
Allocation of fixed power costs (dual method) Fixed: $12,000 × 500/1000, 350/1000, 150/1000	(12,000)		6,000	4,200	1,800
Variable: ($5,000 + $1,400) × 360/800, 320/800, 120/800	(6,400)		2,880	2,560	960
Total budgeted overhead of manufacturing departments	$ 0	$ 0	$32,760	$23,760	$25,680
Allocation Base			875 MH	2,000 DLH	1,500 DLH
Budgeted Rate (Budgeted overhead ÷ Base)			$37.44/MH	$11.88/DLH	$17.12/DLH

14-30 (15 min.) **Single versus multiple indirect cost pools, behavior change or accuracy in product costing.** (continuation of 14-29)

There are two aspects to the manufacturing manager's rationale:

i.   Reducing manufacturing lead time is of key strategic importance to Medical Instruments.

ii. Having a product-costing system with six or eight production overhead cost pools would be "overly complex and complete overkill."

These two aspects need not be linked.

A straightforward way to signal the importance of manufacturing lead time is to develop manufacturing lead time as a performance measure. For example, monthly bonuses could be paid on reductions in manufacturing lead time. Signaling the importance of manufacturing lead time through the accounting system is a less straightforward way of highlighting its importance. Accounting systems serve multiple purposes, and it may be ambiguous which purpose is being promoted by a specific aspect of the system design, such as the number of cost pools or the chosen application bases.

Whether six or eight production overhead cost pools are overly complex is a function of:

a. How heterogeneous the different activity areas of the production floor are.

b. How heterogeneous the products are in the way they use each of the different activity areas.

The general concern of the manufacturing manager is well worth considering. However, it might be useful to gather evidence on a. and b. before making decisions on the number of overhead cost pools.

14-32 (20 min.)   **Cost allocation, brand-cost hierarchies.**

1.   Many costs of Heinz are not driven by output-unit related variables. For example, television advertising costs are based on the number of times an advertisement is run (and the time when it is run).

Allocating non-output-unit driven costs to individual product units results in the cost numbers not matching the levels at which decisions pertaining to them are made. Some of the purposes for allocating costs to individual products do not apply to many brand-related costs. For example, under GAAP, marketing costs are not inventoriable costs.

2.   a.   Individual product-level costs for the Heinz ketchup 28-ounce plastic bottle:
- tomatoes and other ingredients.
- packaging costs.

b.   Related product-line costs for the Heinz ketchup product line:
- television advertisement for Heinz ketchup.
- point of sale promotion at supermarkets for Heinz ketchup.

c.   Brand-level costs for the Heinz brand name:
- balloon at a hot-air contest with only the Heinz name.
- cost of hats with Heinz printed on them for distribution at a trade fair.

3.   Planning and budgeting of costs is facilitated by collecting costs at the level at which they are driven. A budgeted doubling of output units will only double individual product-level costs but not product-line or brand-level costs.

Performance evaluation is also facilitated by flexible budgeting based on the appropriate variables to "flex" on.

14-34 (20 min.) **Cost allocation, budgeted rates, ethics.**

1.   Hospitals are charged a budgeted variable cost rate and an allocation of budgeted fixed costs. By overestimating budgeted meal counts, the denominator of the budgeted fixed cost rate is larger, and hence the amount charged to individual hospitals is lower. Consider 19_7 where the budgeted fixed cost rate of $1.50 is computed as follows:

$$\frac{\$4,380,000}{2,920,000 \text{ meals}} = \$1.50 \text{ per meal}$$

Suppose in 19_7, hospital administrators "inflated" their budgeted meal count by 20%: The budgeted 19_7 rate would have been

$$\frac{\$4,380,000}{3,504,000 \text{ meals}} = \$1.25 \text{ per meal}$$

Hence, by deliberately overstating budgeted meal count demand, they could reduce the costs charged per meal in 19_7. The use of budgeted meals as the denominator means the central food-catering facility bears the risk of demand overestimates.

2.   Evidence that could be collected include:

(a)   Budgeted meal-count estimates and actual meal-count figures each year for each hospital controller. Over an extended time period, there should be a sizable number of both underestimates and overestimates. Controllers could be ranked on both their percentage of overestimation and the frequency of their overestimation.

(b)   Look at the underlying demand estimates by patients at individual hospitals. Each hospital controller has other factors (such as hiring of nurses) that give insight into their expectations of future meal-count demands. If these factors are inconsistent with the meal-count demand figures provided to the central food-catering facility, explanations should be sought.

3.   (a)   Highlight the importance of a corporate culture of honesty and openness. WHM could institute a Code of Ethics that highlights the upside of individual hospitals providing honest estimates of demand (and the penalties for those who do not).

(b)   Have individual hospitals contract in advance for their budgeted meal count. Unused amounts would be charged to each hospital at the end of the accounting period. This approach puts a penalty on hospital administrators who overestimate demand.

(c)   Use an incentive scheme that has an explicit component for meal-count forecasting accuracy. For example, a bonus of $20,000 could be set aside for each hospital that is approximately $0.05 per meal times last year's actual demand. Assume this amount is $14,600 for 19_8. Each meal-count "forecasting error" would reduce the bonus by $0.05. Thus, if a hospital bids for 292,000 meals and actually uses 200,000 meals, its bonus would be $10,000 (200,000 × $0.05) rather than $14,600.

14-17

CHAPTER 15
COST ALLOCATION: JOINT PRODUCTS AND BYPRODUCTS

15-2 *Separable costs* are costs incurred beyond the splitoff point that are assignable to one or more individual products.

15-4 The distinction between a joint product and a byproduct is based on relative sales value. A *joint product* is a product that has a relatively high sales value. A *byproduct* is a product that has low sales value compared to the sales value of the joint (or main) products.

15-6 The chapter lists the following six reasons for allocating joint costs:

1. Inventory cost and cost-of-goods-sold computations for external financial statements and reports for income tax authorities.
2. Inventory cost and cost-of-goods-sold computations for internal financial reporting.
3. Cost reimbursement under contracts when only a portion of a business' products or services is sold or delivered to a single customer.
4. Customer-profitability analysis where individual customers purchase varying combinations of joint products or byproducts as well as other products of the company.
5. Insurance settlement computations.
6. Rate regulation when one or more of the jointly-produced products or services are subject to price regulation.

15-8 The joint production process yields individual products that are either sold this period or held as inventory to be sold in subsequent periods. Hence, the joint costs need to be allocated between total production rather than just those sold this period.

15-10 Limitations of the physical measure method of joint-cost allocation include:
   a. The physical weights used for allocating joint costs may have no relationship to the revenue-producing power of the individual products.
   b. The joint products may not have a common physical denominator—for example, one may be a liquid while another a solid with no readily available conversion factor.

15-12 No. Any method used to allocate joint costs to individual products that is applicable to the problem of joint product-cost allocation should not be used for management decisions regarding whether a product should be sold or processed further. When a product is an inherent result of a joint process, the decision to process further should not be influenced by either the size of the total joint costs or by the portion of the joint costs assigned to particular products. Joint costs are irrelevant for these decisions. The only relevant items for these decisions are the incremental revenue and the incremental costs beyond the splitoff point.

15-14 Two main questions addressed by the methods of accounting for byproducts are:

a.   When are byproducts first recognized in the general ledger? The two main answers are (i) at the time of production, and (ii) at the time of sale.

b.   Where do byproducts appear in the income statement? The two main answers are (i) as a cost reduction of the main (or joint) products, and (ii) as a separate item of revenue or other income.

15-16 (10 min.)   **Matching terms with definitions.**

a. 3	b. 4	c. 5
d. 1	e. 6	f. 2

15-18 (10 min.) Estimated net realizable value method.

A diagram of the situation is in Solution Exhibit 15-18 (all numbers are in thousands).

	Cooking Oil	Soap Oil	Total
Expected final sales value of production, CO, 1,000 × $50; SO, 500 × $25	$50,000	$12,500	$62,500
Deduct expected separable costs to complete and sell	30,000	7,500	37,500
Estimated net realizable value at splitoff point	$20,000	$ 5,000	$25,000
Weighting	$\frac{\$20,000}{\$25,000} = 0.8$	$\frac{\$5,000}{\$25,000} = 0.2$	
Joint costs allocated, CO, 0.8 × $24,000; SO, 0.2 × $24,000	$19,200	$ 4,800	$24,000

SOLUTION EXHIBIT 15-18

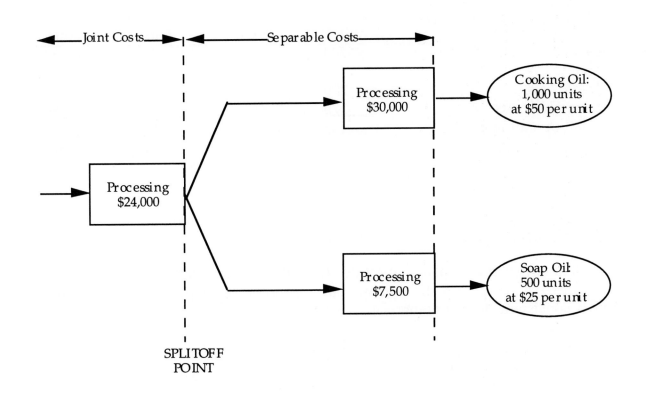

15-20 (20 min.) **Joint-cost allocation, physical measures method.**
(continuation of 15-19)

	Crude Oil	NGL	Total
1. Expected final sales value of production	$2,700	$ 750	$ 3,450
2. Deduct expected separable costs	175	105	280
3. Estimated NRV at splitoff	$2,525	$ 645	$3,170
4. Weighting	0.7965	0.2035	1.000
5. Joint costs allocated (Weights × $1,800)	$1,433.70	$366.30	$1,800

	Crude Oil	NGL	Total
Sales	$2,700.00	$750.00	$3,450
Operating Costs			
Joint costs	1,433.70	366.30	1,800
Separable costs	175.00	105.00	280
Total operating costs	1,608.70	471.30	2,080
Operating margin	$1,091.30	$278.70	$1,370

2. The State's proposed method results in large profits on crude oil and large losses on gas:

	Crude Oil	NGL	Gas	Total
Sales	$2,700	$750	$ 0	$3,450
Operating Costs				
Joint costs	270	90	1,440	1,800
Separable costs	175	105	0	280
Total operating costs	445	195	1,440	2,080
Operating margin	$2,255	$555	$(1,440)	$1,370

The main points to note are:

(a) Gas is not a salable product. It is simply a recycled output that adds no revenues. Indeed, costs are incurred to recycle the gas.

(b) The physical measure method has all the problems alluded to in the literature—e.g., it ignores the revenue earning potential of products, and it may not have a consistent denominator.

15-22 (20-30 min.) **Net realizable value cost-allocation method, further process decision.**

A diagram of the situation is in Solution Exhibit 15-22.

1.

	Quantity in Pounds	Sales Price per Pound	Final Sales Value	Separable Processing Costs	Estimated Net Realizable Value at Splitoff	Weighting
Alco	20,000	$20	$400,000	$100,000	$300,000	30/56
Devo	60,000	6	360,000	200,000	160,000	16/56
Holo	100,000	1	100,000	0	100,000	10/56
Totals			$860,000	$300,000	$560,000	

Allocation of $420,000 joint costs:

Alco	30/56 × $420,000	= $225,000	
Devo	16/56 × 420,000	= 120,000	
Holo	10/56 × 420,000	= 75,000	
		$420,000	

	Joint Costs Allocated	Separable Processing Costs	Total Costs	Units	Unit Cost
Alco	$225,000	$100,000	$325,000	20,000	$16.25
Devo	120,000	200,000	320,000	60,000	5.33
Holo	75,000	0	75,000	100,000	0.75
Totals	$420,000	$300,000	$720,000	180,000	

The ending inventory is:

Alco	1,000 × $16.25	= $16,250
Devo	1,000 × $ 5.33	= 5,330
Holo	1,000 × $ 0.75	= 750
		$22,330

15-22 (Cont'd.)

2.

	Unit sales price	Unit cost	Gross margin	Gross-margin Percentage
Alco	$20	$16.25	$3.75	18.75%
Devo	6	5.33	0.67	11.17
Holo	1	0.75	0.25	25.00

3. Further processing of Devo yields incremental income of $40,000:

Incremental revenue of further processing Devo, ($6 – $2) × 60,000	$240,000
Incremental processing costs	200,000
Incremental operating income from further processing	$ 40,000

Tuscania should process Devo further. Note that joint costs are irrelevant to this decision; they remain the same, whichever alternative (sell at splitoff or process further) is selected.

SOLUTION EXHIBIT 15-22

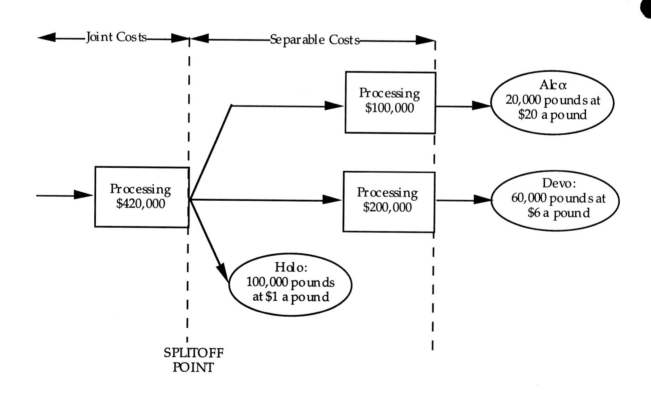

15-24 (35-45 min.) **Joint costs and byproducts.**

A diagram of the situation is in Solution Exhibit 15-24.

1. Computing byproduct deduction to joint costs:

Marketing price of X, 100,000 × $3	$300,000
Deduct: Gross margin, 10% of sales	30,000
Marketing costs, 25% of sales	75,000
Department 3 separable costs	50,000
Estimated net realizable value of X	$145,000
Joint costs	$800,000
Deduct byproduct contribution	145,000
Net joint costs to be allocated	$655,000

	Quantity	Unit Sales Price	Final Sales Value	Deduct Separable Processing Cost	Est. Net Realizable Value at Splitoff	Weighting	Allocation of $655,000 Joint Costs
L	50,000	$10	$ 500,000	$100,000	$ 400,000	40%	$262,000
W	300,000	2	600,000	-	600,000	60%	393,000
Totals			$1,100,000	$100,000	$1,000,000		$655,000

	Joint Costs Allocation	Add Separable Processing Costs	Total Costs	Units	Unit Cost
L	$262,000	$100,000	$362,000	50,000	$7.24
W	393,000	-	393,000	300,000	1.31
Totals	$655,000	$100,000	$755,000	350,000	

Unit cost for X: $1.45 + $0.50   = $1.95,
or $3.00 − $0.30 − $0.75 = $1.95.

15-24 (Cont'd.)

2. If all three products are treated as joint products:

	Quantity	Unit Sales Price	Final Sales Value	Deduct Separable Processing Cost	Est. Net Realizable Value at Splitoff	Weighting	Allocation of $800,000 Joint Costs
L	50,000	$10	$ 500,000	$100,000	$ 400,000	40/125	$256,000
W	300,000	2	600,000	-	600,000	60/125	384,000
X	100,000	3	300,000	50,000	250,000	25/125	160,000
Totals			$1,400,000	$150,000	$1,250,000		$800,000

	Joint Costs Allocation	Add Separable Processing Costs	Total Costs	Units	Unit Cost
L	$256,000	$100,000	$356,000	50,000	$7.12
W	384,000	-	384,000	300,000	1.28
X	160,000	50,000	210,000	100,000	2.10
Totals	$800,000	$150,000	$950,000	450,000	

Call the attention of students to the differing unit "costs" between the two assumptions regarding the relative importance of Product X. The point is that costs of individual products depend heavily on which assumptions are made and which accounting methods and techniques are used.

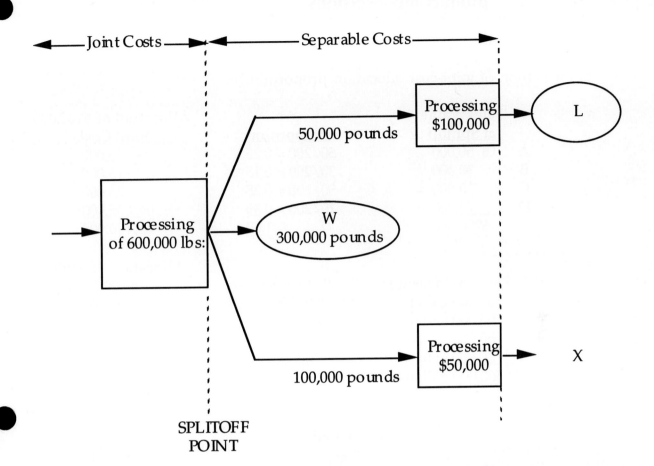

15-26 (40 min.) **Alternative methods of joint-cost allocation, product-mix decisions.**

A diagram of the situation is in Solution Exhibit 15-26.

1. Computation of joint-cost allocation proportions:

a.

	Sales Value at Splitoff	Proportions	Allocation of $100,000 Joint Costs
A	$ 50,000	50/200 = 0.25	$ 25,000
B	30,000	30/200 = 0.15	15,000
C	50,000	50/200 = 0.25	25,000
D	70,000	70/200 = 0.35	35,000
	$200,000	1.00	$100,000

b.

	Physical Measure	Proportions	Allocation of $100,000 Joint Costs
A	300,000 gallons	300/500 = 0.60	$ 60,000
B	100,000 gallons	100/500 = 0.20	20,000
C	50,000 gallons	50/500 = 0.10	10,000
D	50,000 gallons	50/500 = 0.10	10,000
	500,000 gallons	1.00	$100,000

c.

	Final Sales Value	Separable Costs	Estimated Net Realizable Value	Proportions	Allocation of $100,000 Joint Costs
A	$300,000	$200,000	$100,000	100/200 =0.50	$ 50,000
B	100,000	80,000	20,000	20/200 = 0.10	10,000
C	50,000	–	50,000	50/200 = 0.25	25,000
D	120,000	90,000	30,000	30/200 = 0.15	15,000
			$200,000	1.00	$100,000

Computation of gross-margin percentages:

a. Sales value at splitoff method:

	Super A	Super B	C	Super D	Total
Sales	$300,000	$100,000	$50,000	$120,000	$570,000
Joint costs	25,000	15,000	25,000	35,000	100,000
Separable costs	200,000	80,000	0	90,000	370,000
Total costs	225,000	95,000	25,000	125,000	470,000
Gross margin	$ 75,000	$ 5,000	$25,000	$ (5,000)	$100,000
Gross-margin percentage	25%	5%	50%	(4.17%)	17.54%

15-26 (Cont'd.)

b. Physical measure method:

	Super A	Super B	C	Super D	Total
Sales	$300,000	$100,000	$50,000	$120,000	$570,000
Joint costs	60,000	20,000	10,000	10,000	100,000
Separable costs	200,000	80,000	0	90,000	370,000
Total costs	260,000	100,000	10,000	100,000	470,000
Gross margin	$ 40,000	$ 0	$40,000	$ 20,000	$100,000
Gross-margin percentage	13.33%	0%	80%	16.67%	17.54%

c. Estimated net realizable value method:

	Super A	Super B	C	Super D	Total
Sales	$300,000	$100,000	$50,000	$120,000	$570,000
Joint costs	50,000	10,000	25,000	15,000	100,000
Separable costs	200,000	80,000	0	90,000	370,000
Total costs	250,000	90,000	25,000	105,000	470,000
Gross margin	$ 50,000	$ 10,000	$25,000	$ 15,000	$100,000
Gross-margin percentage	16.67%	10%	50%	12.5%	17.54%

Summary of gross-margin percentages:

Joint-Cost Allocation Method	Super A	Super B	C	Super D
Sales value at splitoff	25.00%	5%	50%	(4.17%)
Physical measure	13.33%	0%	80%	16.67%
Estimated net realizable value	16.67%	10%	50%	12.50%

15-26 (Cont'd.)

2.   Further Processing of A into Super A:

Incremental revenue, $300,000 – $50,000	$250,000
Incremental costs	200,000
Incremental operating income from further processing	$ 50,000

Further Processing of B into Super B:

Incremental revenue, $100,000 – $30,000	$ 70,000
Incremental costs	80,000
Incremental operating income from further processing	($ 10,000)

Further Processing of D into Super D:

Incremental revenue, $120,000 – $70,000	$ 50,000
Incremental costs	90,000
Incremental operating income from further processing	$ (40,000)

Operating income can be increased by $50,000 if both B and D are sold at their splitoff point.

SOLUTION EXHIBIT 15-26

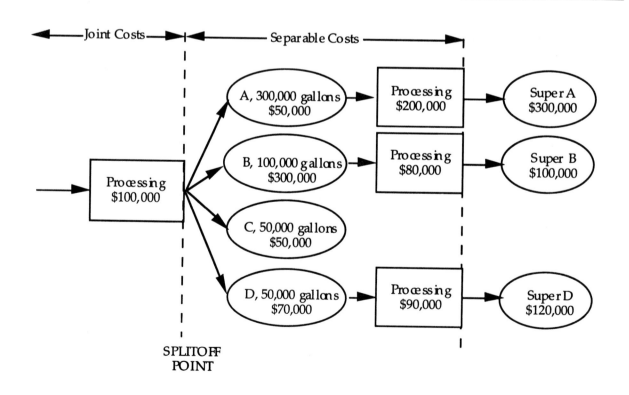

15-28 (40-50 min.) **Alternative methods of joint-cost allocation, further process decision, memory chips.**

A diagram of the situation is in Solution Exhibit 15-28.

1. a.   Sales value at splitoff method:

	High-Density (HD) Chips	Low-Density (LD) Chips	Total
Sales value at splitoff, HD, 300 × $10; LD, 900 × $5	$3,000	$4,500	$7,500
Weighting	$\frac{30}{75} = 0.40$	$\frac{45}{75} = 0.60$	1.00
Joint costs allocated, HD, 0.4 × $5,000; LD, 0.6 × $5,000	$2,000	$3,000	$5,000

b.   Physical measure method:

	High-Density (HD) Chips	Low-Density (LD) Chips	Total
Physical measure (number of good chips)	300	900	1,200
Weighting	$\frac{300}{1,200} = 0.25$	$\frac{900}{1,200} = 0.75$	1.00
Joint costs allocated, HD, 0.25 × $5,000; LD, 0.75 × $5,000	$1,250	$3,750	$5,000

c. Estimated net realizable value method:

	High-Density (HD) Chips	Low-Density (LD) Chips	Total
Expected final sales value of production, EL-HD, 200 × $30; EL-LD, 500 × $18	$6,000	$9,000	$15,000
Expected separable costs	1,000	3,000	4,000
Estimated net realizable value at splitoff point	$5,000	$6,000	$11,000
Weighting	5/11	6/11	
Joint costs allocated, HD, 5/11 × $5,000; LD, 6/11 × $5,000	$2,273	$2,727	5,000

d. Constant gross-margin percentage net realizable value method:

Step 1:

Total final sales value: (200 × $30) + (500 × $18)	$15,000
Joint and separable costs: ($5,000 + $1,000 + $3,000)	9,000
Gross margin	$ 6,000
Gross-margin percentage ($6,000 ÷ $15,000)	40%

	High-Density (HD) Chips	Low-Density (LD) Chips	Total
Expected final sales value of production, EL-HD, 200 × $30; EL-LD, 500 × $18	$6,000	$9,000	$15,000
Step 2: Deduct gross margin, using overall gross-margin percentage of sales, 40%	2,400	3,600	6,000
Cost of goods sold	3,600	5,400	9,000
Step 3: Deduct separable costs	1,000	3,000	4,000
Joint costs allocated	$2,600	$2,400	$ 5,000

2.   Comparison of gross-margin percentages:

	Sales Value at Splitoff	Physical Measure	Estim. NRV	Constant Gross-Margin % NRV
Extended Life High-Density (EL-HD) Chips:				
Sales	$6,000	$6,000	$6,000	$6,000
Joint costs allocated	2,000	1,250	2,273	2,600
Separable costs	1,000	1,000	1,000	1,000
Total costs	3,000	2,250	3,273	3,600
Gross margin	$3,000	$3,750	$2,727	$2,400
Gross-margin percentage	50%	62.50%	45.45%	40%
Extended Life Low-Density (EL-LD) Chips:				
Sales	$9,000	$9,000	$9,000	$9,000
Joint costs allocated	3,000	3,750	2,727	2,400
Separable costs	3,000	3,000	3,000	3,000
Total costs	6,000	6,750	5,727	5,400
Gross margin	$3,000	$2,250	$3,273	$3,600
Gross-margin percentage	33.33%	25%	36.37%	40%

3.   Incremental revenue from further
        processing, $(500 \times \$18) - (900 \times \$5)$ $4,500
     Incremental cost of further processing 3,000
     Incremental operating income from further processing $1,500

The operating income of AMC would decline by $1,500 if it sold 900 LD chips to Peach Computer Systems rather than processing them further to EL-LD chips.

15-28 (Cont'd.)

SOLUTION EXHIBIT 15-28

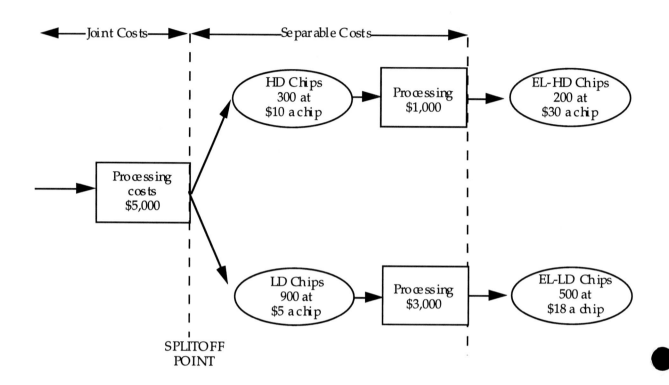

15-30 (30 min.) Estimated net realizable value method, byproducts.

1. a. For the month of November, 19_7, Princess Corporation's output was:
   - apple slices   89,100
   - applesauce   81,000
   - apple juice   67,500
   - animal feed   27,000

These amounts were calculated as follows:

Product	Input	Proportion	Total Pounds	Pounds Lost	Net Pounds
Slices	270,000 lbs.	0.33	89,100	–	89,100
Sauce	270,000	0.30	81,000	–	81,000
Juice	270,000	0.27	72,900	5,400	67,500*
Feed	270,000	0.10	27,000	–	27,000
		1.00	270,000	5,400	264,600

*Net pounds: = 72,900 – (0.08 × net pounds)
1.08 net pounds = 72,900
Net pounds   = 67,500

b. The estimated net realizable value for each of the three main products is calculated below:

Product	Net Pounds	Price	Revenue	Separable Costs	Estimated Net Realizable Value
Slices	89,100	$0.80	$ 71,280	$11,280	$ 60,000
Sauce	81,000	0.55	44,550	8,550	36,000
Juice	67,500	0.40	27,000	3,000	24,000
			$142,830	$22,830	$120,000

15-30 (Cont'd.)

c. and d.

The estimated net realizable value of the byproduct is deducted from the production costs prior to allocation to the joint products, as presented below:

Allocation of Cutting Department Costs
To Joint Products and Byproducts

Net realizable value
(NRV) of byproduct

= Byproduct revenue – Separable costs
= $0.10 (270,000 × 10%) – $700
= $2,700 – $700
= $2,000

Costs to be allocated

= Joint costs – NRV of byproduct
= $60,000 – $2,000
= $58,000

Product	Revenue	Separable Costs	Joint Costs	Gross Margin
Slices	$ 71,280	$11,280	$29,000	$31,000
Sauce	44,550	8,550	17,400	18,600
Juice	27,000	3,000	11,600	12,400
	$142,830	$22,830	$58,000	$62,000

2. The gross-margin dollar information by main product is determined by the arbitrary allocation of joint production costs. As a result, these cost figures and the resulting gross-margin information are of little significance for planning and control purposes. The allocation is made only for purposes of inventory costing and income determination.

15-32   (60 min.)   **Joint-cost allocation, process further or sell byproducts**

1.

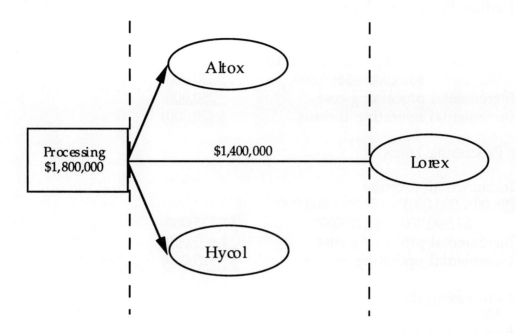

	Altox	**Lorex**	**Hycol**	**Total**
Expected final sales value of production[a]	$595,000	$2,500,000	$660,000	$3,755,000
Deduct expected separable costs to complete and sell	–	1,400,000	–	1,400,000
Estimated net realizable value at splitoff point	$595,000	$1,100,000	$660,000	$2,355,000
Weighting[b]	0.253	0.467	0.280	1.000
Joint costs allocated[c]	$455,400	$840,600	$504,000	$1,800,000

[a]($3.50 × 170,000); ($5.00 × 500,000); ($2 × 330,000)
[b]($595,000 ÷ 2,355,000); ($1,100,000 ÷ $2,355,000); ($660,000 ÷ $2,355,000)
[c]$1,800,000 × 0.253; 0.467; 0.280

2. Further Processing Altox

Incremental revenue
($5.50 × 150,000) – ($3.50 × 170,000)
$825,000 – $595,000 $230,000
Incremental processing cost   250,000
Incremental operating income $ (20,000)

Further Processing Lorex

Incremental revenue
($5.00 × 500,000) – ($2.25 × 500,000)
$2,500,000 – $1,125,000 $1,375,000
Incremental processing cost   1,400,000
Incremental operating income $ (25,000)

Further Processing Hycol

Incremental revenue
($1.80 × (330,000 × 1.25)) – ($2 × 330,000)
$742,500 – $660,000 $82,500
Incremental processing cost   75,000
Incremental operating income $ 7,500

Current Policy

Sell Altox at splitoff	$ 595,000
Process Lorex further	1,100,000
Sell Hycol at splitoff	660,000
	2,355,000
Joint costs	1,800,000
Operating income	$ 555,000

Preferred Options

Sell Altox at splitoff	$ 595,000
Sell Lorex at splitoff	1,125,000
Process Hycol further	667,500
	2,387,500
Joint costs	1,800,000
Operating income	$ 587,500

Goodson is $32,500 better off by changing two of its current policies—it should sell Lorex at splitoff ($25,000 improvement) and process Hycol further ($7,500 improvement).

15-32 (Cont'd.)

3.   (a)   Goodson would be better off by $12,000 by selling Dorzine to Dietriech Mills.

Further Processing Dorzine

Incremental revenue	
($0.75 × 50,000) + $17,500[a]	$55,000
$37,500 + $17,500	
Incremental processing cost	43,000
Incremental operating income	$12,000

[a]Disposal costs avoided by processing further $0.35 × 50,000 = $17,500

(b)   The decision to treat Dorzine should not affect decisions as to whether to process further or sell at the splitoff point.   Accounting decisions about joint product/byproduct distinctions do not affect total revenues or total costs.

CHAPTER 16
REVENUES, REVENUE VARIANCES, AND
CUSTOMER-PROFITABILITY ANALYSIS

16-2 To avoid overstating sales, because it is known that sales returns are an inevitable part of most businesses. It is unclear at the time of sale which specific customers will return a product. Past sales return experience, or the return experience of companies with similar products, can guide the specific sales-return amounts assumed.

16-4 An increasing number of individual products or services are being bundled together and sold as a package for a single price. Companies who sell such bundles need to allocate this single price (revenue amount) across the individual items included therein if they wish to conduct individual product profitability studies.

16-6 Using the levels approach introduced in Chapter 7, the sales-volume variance is a Level 2 variance. By sequencing through Level 3 (sales-mix and sales-quantity variances) and then Level 4 (market-size and market-share variances), managers can gain insight into the causes of a specific sales-volume variance.

16-8 A favorable sales-quantity variance arises because the actual units of product sold exceed the budgeted units of product sold.

16-10 Some companies who believe that reliable information on total market size is not available, choose not to compute market-size and market-share variances.

16-12 Companies that separately record (a) the list price and (b) the discount have sufficient information to subsequently examine the level of discounting by each individual customer and by each individual salesperson.

16-14 No. A customer-profitability profile highlights differences in current period's profitability across customers. Dropping customers should be the last resort. An unprofitable customer in one period may be highly profitable in subsequent future periods. Moreover, costs assigned to individual customers need not be purely variable with respect to short-run elimination of sales to those customers. Thus, when customers are dropped, costs assigned to those customers may not disappear in the short run.

16-16 (20-30 min.) Revenue tracing, sales returns.

1.

	Intro. to Marketing	Principles of Economics	Corporate Finance	Total
Actual units sold	22,000	17,000	11,000	
Actual selling price	$ 20	$ 20	$ 20	
Gross revenues	$440,000	$340,000	$220,000	$1,000,000
Deduct sales-return provision				
(3%, 22%, 12%)	13,200	74,800	26,400	114,400
Net revenues	$426,800	$265,200	$193,600	$ 885,600

The actual average return percentage of gross revenues in 19_7 was 11.44%:

$$\frac{\$114{,}400}{\$1{,}000{,}000} = 11.44\%$$

2.   The three study guides differ markedly in their return percentage—from a low of 3% for Marketing to a high of 22% of Economics. By using the 11.44% average percentage, differences across books will be smoothed over (peanut-buttered).

Companies may use actual average return percentages for several reasons:

(a)   Reliable information about actual returns for individual books may not be available. It is noted that "up to 19_6, SB did not have reliable information on individual title sales returns. Books could be returned to any university book store, not all of whom kept detailed records on the titles of returns."

(b)   Differences across books in their returns may not be large. A company might sample data on returns and conclude that it is not cost-effective to collect detailed return data at the individual book level.

3.

	Intro to Marketing	Principles of Economics	Corporate Finance
(a) Actual average sales returns:			
Gross revenues	$440,000	$340,000	$220,000
Actual average returns —11.44%	50,336	38,896	25,168
Net revenues	389,664	301,104	194,832
Author royalty—17%, 15%, 15%	$ 66,243	$ 45,166	$ 29,225
(b) Actual sales returns			
Net revenues			
(Requirement 1)	$426,800	$265,200	$193,600
Author royalty—			
17%, 15%, 15%	$ 72,556	$ 39,780	$ 29,040
Difference between (a) and (b)	$ 6,313	$ (5,386)	$ (185)

Introduction to Marketing has a much lower return % than the 11.44% average rate. The result is that the net revenues are understated with the 11.44% average return rate which means that the royalties paid to the author are also understated. The opposite case holds for *Principles of Economics* where the author receives an overpayment of $5,386 when the average return percentage of 11.44% is used rather than the actual 22% rate.

16-18 (10–15 min.) Revenue allocation, bundled products, additional complexities.

Alternatives include:

(a)   Use information about how each individual package is used to make the revenue allocations. Thus, if one party uses only lodging and food, the $700 is allocated among those two groups. This would be the most accurate approach, as it captures actual usage and non-usage of the facilities.

(b)   Use the average non-usage information to compute an "adjusted unit selling price:"

Lodging: $640 × 1.00 =	$ 640
Food: $160 × 0.95	152
Recreation: $300 × 0.90	270
	$1,062

These adjusted revenues can be used in either the stand-alone or incremental methods. For example, the stand-alone allocations are:

Lodging: $\dfrac{640}{\$1,062} \times \$700$ = $422

Food: $\dfrac{152}{\$1,062} \times \$700$ = $100

Recreation: $\dfrac{270}{\$1,062} \times \$700$ = $178

$700

16-20 (30 min.)   **Variance analysis of contribution margin, multiple products, working backward.**

1, and 2.   Solution Exhibit 16-20 presents the sales-volume, sales-quantity and sales-mix variances for the Plain and Chic wine glasses and in total for Jinwa Corporation in June 19_7. The steps to fill in the numbers in Solution Exhibit 16-20 follow:

Step 1:

    Consider the static budget column (Column 3):

Static budget total contribution margin	$5,600
Budgeted units of all glasses to be sold	2,000
Budgeted contribution margin per unit of Plain	$ 2
Budgeted contribution margin per unit of Chic	$ 6

    Suppose that the budgeted sales-mix percentage of Plain is y. Then the budgeted sales-mix percentage of Chic is $(1-y)$. Hence,

$$
\begin{aligned}
(2{,}000 \times y \times \$2) + (2{,}000 \times (1-y) \times \$6) &= \$5{,}600 \\
4000y + 12{,}000 - 12{,}000y &= 5{,}600 \\
8000y &= 6{,}400 \\
y &= 0.8 \text{ or } 80\%
\end{aligned}
$$

$$1 - y = 1 - 0.8 = 0.2 \text{ or } 20\%$$

Jinwa's budgeted sales mix is 80% of Plain and 20% of Chic. We can then fill in all the numbers in Column 3.

Step 2:

    Consider next Column 2 of Solution Exhibit 16-20.

    The total of Column 2 in Panel C is $4,200 (the static budget total contribution margin of $5,600—the total sales-quantity variance of $1,400 U which was given in the problem).

We need to find the actual units sold of all glasses, which we denote by q. From Column 2, we know that

$$
\begin{aligned}
(q \times 0.8 \times \$2) + (q \times 0.2 \times \$6) &= \$4{,}200 \\
\$1.6q + \$1.2q &= \$4{,}200 \\
\$2.8q &= \$4{,}200 \\
q &= 1{,}500 \text{ units}
\end{aligned}
$$

Hence, the total quantity of all glasses sold is 1,500 units. This computation allows us to fill in all the numbers in Column 2.

16-20 (Cont'd.)

Step 3:

Consider next Column 1 of Solution Exhibit 16-20. We know actual units sold of all glasses (1,500 units), the actual sales-mix percentage (given in the problem information as Plain, 60%; and Chic, 40%), and the budgeted unit contribution margin of each product (Plain, $2; Chic, $6). We can therefore determine all the numbers in Column 1.

Solution Exhibit 16-20 displays the following sales-quantity, sales-mix, and sales-volume variances:

<u>Sales-Volume Variance</u>

Plain	$1,400 U
Chic	1,200 F
All Glasses	$ 200 U

<u>Sales-Mix Variances</u>		<u>Sales-Quantity Variances</u>	
Plain	$ 600 U	Plain	$ 800 U
Chic	1,800 F	Chic	600 U
All Glasses	$1,200 F	All Glasses	$1,400 U

3.   Jinwa Corporation shows an unfavorable sales-quantity variance because it sold fewer wine glasses in total than was budgeted. This unfavorable sales-quantity variance is partially offset by a favorable sales-mix variance because the actual mix of wine glasses sold has shifted in favor of the higher contribution margin Chic wine glasses. The problem illustrates how failure to achieve the budgeted market penetration can have negative effects on operating income.

16-20 (Cont'd.)

SOLUTION EXHIBIT 16-20
Columnar Presentation of Sales-Volume, Sales-Quantity and Sales-Mix Variances for Jinwa Corporation

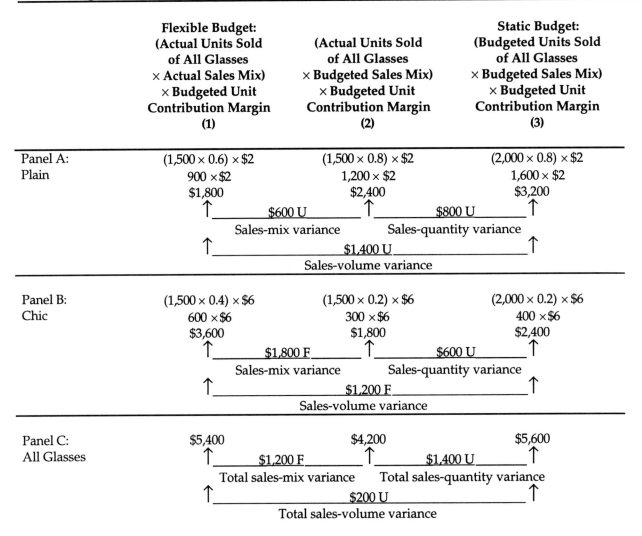

	Flexible Budget: (Actual Units Sold of All Glasses × Actual Sales Mix) × Budgeted Unit Contribution Margin (1)	(Actual Units Sold of All Glasses × Budgeted Sales Mix) × Budgeted Unit Contribution Margin (2)	Static Budget: (Budgeted Units Sold of All Glasses × Budgeted Sales Mix) × Budgeted Unit Contribution Margin (3)
Panel A: Plain	(1,500 × 0.6) × $2 900 × $2 $1,800	(1,500 × 0.8) × $2 1,200 × $2 $2,400	(2,000 × 0.8) × $2 1,600 × $2 $3,200

$600 U
Sales-mix variance

$800 U
Sales-quantity variance

$1,400 U
Sales-volume variance

| Panel B: Chic | (1,500 × 0.4) × $6 600 × $6 $3,600 | (1,500 × 0.2) × $6 300 × $6 $1,800 | (2,000 × 0.2) × $6 400 × $6 $2,400 |

$1,800 F
Sales-mix variance

$600 U
Sales-quantity variance

$1,200 F
Sales-volume variance

| Panel C: All Glasses | $5,400 | $4,200 | $5,600 |

$1,200 F
Total sales-mix variance

$1,400 U
Total sales-quantity variance

$200 U
Total sales-volume variance

F = favorable effect on operating income; U = unfavorable effect on operating income.

16-22 (30-40 min.) **Variance analysis of contribution margin, multiple countries.** (continuation of 16-21)

Note: Instructors who cover both 16-21 and 16-22 may want to hand out the solution to 16-22 rather than have students spend time on the mechanics of both questions.

1.   All amounts are in thousands.

Budget for 19_8

	Selling Price per Unit (1)	Variable Cost per Unit (2)	Contrib. Margin per Unit (3) = (1) – (2)	Units Sold (4)	Sales Mix (5)	Contribution Margin (6) = (3) × (4)
Canada	$6.00	$4.00	$2.00	400,000	16%	$ 800,000
Mexico	$4.00	$2.80	$1.20	600,000	24	720,000
United States	$7.00	$4.50	$2.50	1,500,000	60	3,750,000
Total				2,500,000	100%	$5,270,000

Actual for 19_8

	Selling Price per Unit (1)	Variable Cost per Unit (2)	Contrib. Margin per Unit (3) = (1) – (2)	Units Sold (4)	Sales Mix (5)	Contribution Margin (6) = (3) × (4)
Canada	$6.20	$4.50	$1.70	480,000	16%	$ 816,000
Mexico	$4.25	$2.75	$1.50	900,000	30	1,350,000
United States	$6.80	$4.60	$2.20	1,620,000	54	3,564,000
Total				3,000,000	100%	$5,730,000

$$\begin{array}{c} \text{Static-budget variance} \\ \text{of contribution margin} \end{array} = \begin{array}{c} \text{Actual} \\ \text{results} \end{array} - \begin{array}{c} \text{Static-budget} \\ \text{amount} \end{array}$$

Canada	= $ 816,000 – $ 800,000 = $ 16,000 F
Mexico	= $1,350,000 – $ 720,000 = 630,000 F
United States	= $3,564,000 – $3,750,000 = 186,000 U
Total	$460,000 F

$$\begin{array}{c} \text{Flexible-budget variance} \\ \text{of contribution margin} \end{array} = \begin{array}{c} \text{Actual} \\ \text{results} \end{array} - \begin{array}{c} \text{Flexible-budget} \\ \text{amount} \end{array}$$

Canada	= $ 816,000 – ($2.00 × 480,000) = $144,000 U
Mexico	= $1,350,000 – ($1.20 × 900,000) = 270,000 F
United States	= $3,564,000 – ($2.50 × 1,620,000 = 486,000 U
Total	$360,000 U

$$\text{Sales-volume variance of contribution margin} = \left(\begin{array}{cc}\text{Actual sales} & \text{Budgeted sales}\\ \text{quantity} & - \quad \text{quantity}\\ \text{in units} & \text{in units}\end{array}\right) \times \begin{array}{c}\text{Budgeted}\\ \text{contrib. margin}\\ \text{per unit}\end{array}$$

Canada	= (	480,000 –	400,000) × $2.00	=	$ 160,000 F
Mexico	= (	900,000 –	600,000) × $1.20	=	360,000 F
United States	= (1,620,000 –	1,500,000) × $2.50		=	300,000 F
Total					$820,000 F

$$\begin{array}{c}\text{Sales-quantity}\\ \text{variance of}\\ \text{contribution margin}\end{array} = \left(\begin{array}{cc}\text{Actual units} & \text{Budgeted units}\\ \text{of all products} & - \text{ of all products}\\ \text{sold} & \text{sold}\end{array}\right) \times \begin{array}{c}\text{Budgeted}\\ \text{sales-mix}\\ \text{percentage}\end{array} \times \begin{array}{c}\text{Budgeted}\\ \text{contrib. margin}\\ \text{per unit}\end{array}$$

Canada	= (3,000,000 – 2,500,000) × 0.16 × $2.00	=	$ 160,000 F
Mexico	= (3,000,000 – 2,500,000) × 0.24 × $1.20	=	144,000 F
United States	= (3,000,000 – 2,500,000) × 0.60 × $2.50	=	750,000 F
Total			$1,054,000 F

$$\begin{array}{c}\text{Sales-mix}\\ \text{variance of}\\ \text{contribution margin}\end{array} = \begin{array}{c}\text{Actual units}\\ \text{of all}\\ \text{products sold}\end{array} \times \left(\begin{array}{cc}\text{Actual} & \text{Budgeted}\\ \text{sales-mix} & - \text{ sales-mix}\\ \text{percentage} & \text{percentage}\end{array}\right) \times \begin{array}{c}\text{Budgeted}\\ \text{contrib. margin}\\ \text{per unit}\end{array}$$

Canada	= 3,000,000 × (0.16 – 0.16) × $2.00	=	$ 0
Mexico	= 3,000,000 × (0.30 – 0.24) × $1.20	=	216,000 F
United States	= 3,000,000 × (0.54 – 0.60) × $2.50	=	450,000 U
Total			$ 234,000 U

2.   There is a favorable static-budget variance (Level 1) of contribution margin of $460,000. This is the result of two offsetting variances—an unfavorable flexible-budget variance of $360,000 (due to the average actual contribution margin being below the budgeted margin), and a favorable sales-volume variance of $820,000 (due to actual sales being 500,000 units above that budgeted).

The Level 3 breakdown of the favorable sales-volume variance of $820,000 shows that the biggest contributor is the 500,000 unit increase in sales. There is a partially offsetting unfavorable sales-mix variance of $234,000 in contribution margin.

SOLUTION EXHIBIT 16-22
Contribution-Margin Variance Analysis for Cola-King

<u>Static-Budget Variance of C.M.</u>

Canada	$ 16,000 F
Mexico	630,000 F
United States	186,000 U
Total	$460,000 F

<u>Flexible-Budget Variance of C.M.</u>		<u>Sales-Volume Variance of Revenues</u>	
Canada	$144,000 U	Canada	$160,000 F
Mexico	270,000 F	Mexico	360,000 F
United States	486,000 U	United States	300,000 F
Total	$360,000 U	Total	$820,000 F

<u>Sales-Mix Variance of C.M.</u>		<u>Sales-Quantity Variance of C.M.</u>	
Canada	$ 0	Canada	$ 160,000 F
Mexico	216,000 F	Mexico	144,000 F
United States	450,000 U	United States	750,000 F
Total	$234,000 U	Total	$1,054,000 F

16-24 (20-25 min.) **Customer profitability, distribution.**

1.   The activity-based costing for each customer is:

		Charleston Pharmacy	Chapel Hill Pharmacy
1.	Order processing, $40 × 12; 10	$ 480	$ 400
2.	Line-item ordering, $3 × (12 × 10; 10 × 18)	360	540
3.	Store deliveries, $50 × 6; 10	300	500
4.	Carton deliveries, $1 × (6 × 24; 10 × 20)	144	200
5.	Shelf-stocking, $16 × (6 × 0; 10 × 0.5)	0	80
	Operating costs	$1,284	$1,720

The operating income of each customer is:

	Charleston Pharmacy	Chapel Hill Pharmacy
Revenues, $2,400 × 6; 1,800 × 10	$14,400	$18,000
Cost of goods sold, $2,100 × 6; $1,650 × 10	12,600	16,500
Gross margin	1,800	1,500
Operating costs	1,284	1,720
Operating income	$ 516	$ (220)

2.   Ways Figure Four could use this information include:

(a) Pay increased attention to the top 20% of the customers. This could entail asking them for ways you can improve service. Alternatively, you may want to highlight to your own personnel the importance of these customers, e.g., it could entail stressing to delivery people the importance of never missing delivery dates for these customers.

(b) Work out ways internally at Figure Four to reduce the rate per cost driver, e.g., reduce the cost per order by having better order placement linkages with customers. This cost reduction by Figure Four will improve the profitability of all customers.

(c) Work with customers so that their behavior reduces the total "system-wide" costs. At a minimum, this approach could entail having customers make fewer orders and fewer line items. This latter point is controversial with students; the rationale is that a reduction in the number of line items (diversity of products) carried by Ma and Pa stores may reduce the diversity of products Figure Four carries.

There are several options here:
- Simple verbal persuasion by showing customers cost drivers at Figure Four
- Explicitly pricing out activities like cartons delivered and shelf-stocking so that customers pay for the costs they cause.
- Restricting options available to certain customers, e.g., customers with low revenues could be restricted to one free delivery per week.

An even more extreme example is working with customers so that deliveries are easier to make and shelf-stocking can be done faster.

(d)   Offer salespeople bonuses based on the operating income of each customer rather than the gross margin of each customer.

Some students will argue that the bottom 40% of the customers should be dropped. This action should be only a last resort after all other avenues have been explored. Moreover, an unprofitable customer today may well be a profitable customer tomorrow, and it is myopic to focus on only a 1-month customer-profitability analysis to classify a customer as unprofitable.

16-26 (30-40 min.)   **Revenue allocation, bundled products.**

1. Royalties on individual sales

   SuperAbs ($40 × 27,000 × 0.15) $162,000

   SuperArms ($35 × 53,000 × 0.25)   463,750

   SuperLegs ($25 × 20,000 × 0.18)   90,000

2. (a)   Stand-alone revenue allocation method.

	SuperAbs	**SuperArms**	**SuperLegs**
SuperAbs + SuperArms			
31.80^a × 18,000 × 0.15	$85,860		
28.20^b × 18,000 × 0.25		$126,900	
SuperAbs + SuperLegs			
32.24^c × 6,000 × 0.15	29,016		
19.76^d × 6,000 × 0.18			$21,341
SuperArms + SuperLegs			
24.36^e × 11,000 × 0.25		66,990	
17.64^f × 11,000 × 0.18			34,927
SuperAbs + SuperArms + SuperLegs			
26.00^g × 22,000 × 0.15	85,800		
22.75^h × 22,000 × 0.25		125,125	
16.25^i × 22,000 × 0.18			64,350
	$200,676	$319,015	$120,618

$^a(40/(40 + 35)) \times \$60 = 0.53 \times \$60$ = $31.80
$^b(35/(40 + 35)) \times \$60 = 0.47 \times \$60$ =   28.20
$^c(40/(40 + 25)) \times \$52 = 0.62 \times \$52$ =   32.24
$^d(25/(40 + 25)) \times \$52 = 0.38 \times \$52$ =   19.76
$^e(35/(35 + 25)) \times \$42 = 0.58 \times \$42$ =   24.36
$^f (25/(35 + 25)) \times \$42 = 0.42 \times \$42$ =   17.64
$^g(40/(40 + 35 + 25)) \times \$65 = 0.40 \times \$65$ =   26.00
$^h(35/(40 + 35 + 25)) \times \$65 = 0.35 \times \$65$ =   22.75
$^i (25/(40 + 35 + 25)) \times \$65 = 0.25 \times \$65$ =   16.25

(b)   Incremental revenue allocation method

	SuperAbs	SuperArms	SuperLegs
SuperAbs + SuperArms			
$25[a] × 18,000 × 0.15	67,500		
$35[a] × 18,000 × 0.25		157,500	
SuperAbs + SuperLegs			
$40 × 6,000 × 0.15	36,000		
$12 × 6,000 × 0.18			12,960
SuperArms + SuperLegs			
$35 × 11,000 × 0.25		96,250	
$ 7 × 11,000 × 0.18			13,860
SuperAbs + SuperArms + SuperLegs			
$30 × 22,000 × 0.15	99,000		
$35 × 22,000 × 0.25		192,500	
$ 0 × 22,000 × 0.18			0
	$202,500	$446,250	$26,820

a.   SuperArms $35
       SuperAbs $25 ($60 – $35)

b.   SuperAbs $40
       SuperLegs $12 ($52 –$40)

c.   SuperArms $35
       SuperLegs $ 7 ($42 – $35)

d.   SuperArms $35
       SuperAbs $30 ($65 – $35)
       SuperLegs $ 0

3.   The pros of the stand-alone revenue allocation method include:

(a)   Each item in the bundle receives a positive weight, which means the resulting allocations are more likely to be accepted by all parties than a method allocating zero revenues to one or more products.

(b)   Uses market-based evidence (unit selling prices) to decide the revenue allocations —unit prices are one indicator of benefits received.

(c)   Simple to implement.

The cons of the stand-alone revenue allocation method include:

(a)   Ignores the relative importance of the individual components in attracting consumers to purchase the bundle.

16-26 (Cont'd.)

(b) Ignores the opportunity cost of the individual components in the bundle. If there was a shortage of (say) SuperArms tapes, the manager of SuperArms is better off by selling the tape on its own.

The pros of the incremental method include:

(a) It has the potential to reflect that some products in the bundle are more highly valued than others. Not all products in the bundle have a similar "write-down " from unit list prices. Ensuring this "potential pro" becomes an "actual pro" that requires that the choice of the primary product be guided by reliable evidence on consumer preferences. This is not an easy task.

(b) Once the sequence is chosen, it is straight forward to implement.

The cons of the incremental method include:

(a) Obtaining the rankings can be highly contentious and place managers in a "no-win" acrimonious debate. The revenue allocations can be highly sensitive to the chosen rankings.

(b) Some products will have zero revenues assigned to them. The SuperLegs tape in the three-tape package illustrates this con.

4. (a) Rank on consumer preferences.

(b) Rank on total stand-alone revenues of products included in the bundle.

(c) Rank on age of the products where the newest product receives the first (primary) rank. The assumption here is that older products are likely to be already purchased and what the new bundled package provides is an updated version of these older products as opposed to a new separate product.

16-28 (15 min.) **Market-size and market-share variances.** (continuation of 16-27).

1.

	Actual	Budgeted
Chicago Market	960,000	1,000,000
Debbie's Delight	120,000	100,000
Market share	0.125	0.100

The budgeted average contribution margin per unit is $2.35:

	Budgeted Contribution Margin per Pound	Budgeted Sale Volume in Pounds	Budgeted Contribution Margin
Chocolate chip	$2.00	45,000	$90,000
Oatmeal raisin	2.30	25,000	57,500
Coconut	2.60	10,000	26,000
White chocolate	3.00	5,000	15,000
Macadamia nut	3.10	15,000	46,500
All cookies		100,000	$235,000

$$\text{Budgeted average contribution margin per unit} = \frac{\$235,000}{100,000} = \$2.35$$

$$\begin{array}{l}\text{Market-size} \\ \text{variance in} \\ \text{contribution margin}\end{array} = \left(\begin{array}{c}\text{Actual} \\ \text{market size} \\ \text{in units}\end{array} - \begin{array}{c}\text{Budgeted} \\ \text{market size} \\ \text{in units}\end{array}\right) \times \begin{array}{c}\text{Budgeted} \\ \text{market} \\ \text{share}\end{array} \times \begin{array}{c}\text{Budgeted} \\ \text{average} \\ \text{contrib. margin} \\ \text{per unit}\end{array}$$

$$= (960,000 - 1,000,000) \times 0.100 \times \$2.35$$

$$= \$9,400 \text{ U}$$

$$\begin{array}{l}\text{Market-share} \\ \text{variance in} \\ \text{contribution margin}\end{array} = \begin{array}{c}\text{Actual} \\ \text{market size} \\ \text{in units}\end{array} \times \left(\begin{array}{c}\text{Actual} \\ \text{market} \\ \text{share}\end{array} - \begin{array}{c}\text{Budgeted} \\ \text{market} \\ \text{share}\end{array}\right) \times \begin{array}{c}\text{Budgeted} \\ \text{average} \\ \text{contrib. margin} \\ \text{per unit}\end{array}$$

$$= 960,000 \times (0.125 - 0.100) \times \$2.35$$

$$= \$56,400 \text{ F}$$

By increasing its actual market share from the 10% budgeted to the actual 12.50%, Debbie's Delight has a favorable market-share variance of $56,400. There is a smaller offsetting unfavorable market-size variance of $9,400 due to the 40,000 unit decline in the Chicago market (from 1,000,000 budgeted to an actual of 960,000).

16-28 (Cont'd.)

An overview of Problems 16-27 and 16-28 is:

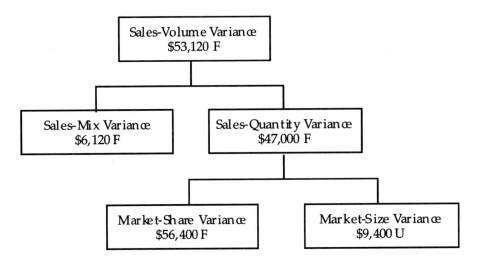

16-30 (20 min.) **Market-size and market-share variances.**
(continuation of 16-29)

Solution Exhibit 16-30 presents the market-size and market-share variances for Computer Horizons for 19_7.

The market-size variance can also be computed as:

$$\begin{array}{c}\text{Market-size} \\ \text{variance of} \\ \text{contribution margin}\end{array} = \left(\begin{array}{c}\text{Actual} \\ \text{market size} \\ \text{in units}\end{array} - \begin{array}{c}\text{Budgeted} \\ \text{market size} \\ \text{in units}\end{array}\right) \times \begin{array}{c}\text{Budgeted} \\ \text{market} \\ \text{share}\end{array} \times \begin{array}{c}\text{Budgeted average} \\ \text{contribution margin} \\ \text{per unit}\end{array}$$

$$= \ (6{,}875{,}000 - 5{,}000{,}000) \times 0.20 \times \$780$$
$$= \ \$292{,}500{,}000 \ F$$

The market-share variance can also be computed as:

$$\begin{array}{c}\text{Market-share} \\ \text{variance of} \\ \text{contribution margin}\end{array} = \begin{array}{c}\text{Actual} \\ \text{market size} \\ \text{in units}\end{array} \times \left(\begin{array}{c}\text{Actual} \\ \text{market} \\ \text{share}\end{array} - \begin{array}{c}\text{Budgeted} \\ \text{market} \\ \text{share}\end{array}\right) \times \begin{array}{c}\text{Budgeted average} \\ \text{contribution margin} \\ \text{per unit}\end{array}$$

$$= \ 6{,}875{,}000 \times (0.16 - 0.20) \times \$780$$
$$= \ \$214{,}500{,}000 \ U$$

The market-size variance measures the additional contribution margin, $292.5 million, that would be expected as a result of the 37.5% increase in the market, provided Computer Horizons maintained a market share of 20%. Unfortunately, the company's market share dropped to 16%. This failure to maintain the budgeted market share—the drop from 20% to 16%—created an offsetting unfavorable market-share variance of $214.5 million. The lower market share means that Computer Horizons did not take advantage of the growing market.

16-30 (Cont'd.)

SOLUTION EXHIBIT 16-30
Columnar Presentation of Market-Size and Market-Share Variance Analysis
for Computer Horizons

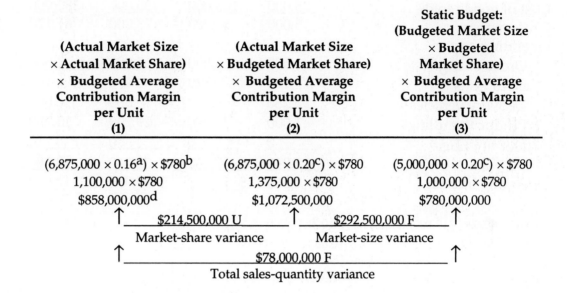

(Actual Market Size × Actual Market Share) × Budgeted Average Contribution Margin per Unit (1)	(Actual Market Size × Budgeted Market Share) × Budgeted Average Contribution Margin per Unit (2)	Static Budget: (Budgeted Market Size × Budgeted Market Share) × Budgeted Average Contribution Margin per Unit (3)
$(6{,}875{,}000 \times 0.16^a) \times \$780^b$	$(6{,}875{,}000 \times 0.20^c) \times \$780$	$(5{,}000{,}000 \times 0.20^c) \times \$780$
$1{,}100{,}000 \times \$780$	$1{,}375{,}000 \times \$780$	$1{,}000{,}000 \times \$780$
$\$858{,}000{,}000^d$	$\$1{,}072{,}500{,}000$	$\$780{,}000{,}000$

↑_____$214,500,000 U_____↑_____$292,500,000 F_____↑
      Market-share variance   Market-size variance

↑_____$78,000,000 F_____↑
           Total sales-quantity variance

F = favorable effect on operating income; U = unfavorable effect on operating income.

[a]Actual Market Share: $1{,}100{,}000 \div 6{,}875{,}000 = 16\%$

[b]Budgeted Average Contribution Margin per Unit:

$$\frac{[(700{,}000 \times \$500) + (100{,}000 \times \$300) + (200{,}000 \times \$2{,}000)]}{(700{,}000 + 100{,}000 + 200{,}000)}$$

$$= \frac{\$350{,}000{,}000 + \$30{,}000{,}000 + \$400{,}000{,}000}{1{,}000{,}000} = \$780 \text{ per unit}$$

[c]Budgeted Market Share: $1{,}000{,}000 \div 5{,}000{,}000 = 20\%$

[d]Although expressed and calculated differently, this $858,000,000 number is the same $858,000,000 number shown in Problem 16-29, Panel D, Column 2.

16-32 (40 min.) **Customer profitability, distribution.**

1.

	Customer				
	P	Q	R	S	T
Revenues at list prices[a]	$30,000	$126,000	$876,000	$458,400	$56,400
Discount[b]	0	2,100	73,000	15,280	5,640
Net revenues	30,000	123,900	803,000	443,120	50,760
Cost of goods sold[c]	25,000	105,000	730,000	382,000	47,000
Gross margin	5,000	18,900	73,000	61,120	3,760
Operating costs					
Order taking[d]	1,500	2,500	3,000	2,500	3,000
Sales visits[e]	160	320	480	160	240
Delivery vehicles[f]	280	240	360	640	1,600
Product handling[g]	1,000	4,200	29,200	15,280	1,880
Hot-hot runs[h]	0	0	0	0	300
Total	2,940	7,260	33,040	18,580	7,020
Operating income	$ 2,060	$ 11,640	$ 39,960	$ 42,540	$ (3,260)

[a] $0.60 × 50,000; 210,000; 1,460,000; 764,000; 94,000

[b] ($0.00 × 50,000); ($0.01 × 210,000); ($0.05 × 1,460,000);
      ($0.02 × 764,000); ($0.06 × 94,000)

[c] $0.50 × 50,000; 210,000; 1,460,000; 764,000; 94,000

[d] $100 × 15; 25; 30; 25; 30

[e] $80 × 2; 4; 6; 2; 3

[f] $2 × (10 × 14); (30 × 4); (60 × 3); (40 × 8); (20 × 40)

[g] $0.02 × 50,000; 210,000; 1,460,000; 764,000; 94,000

[h] $300 × 0; 0; 0; 0; 1

Customer S is the most profitable customer, despite having only 52% of the unit volume of Customer R. A major explanation is that Customer R receives a $0.05 discount per bottle while Customer S receives only a $0.02 discount per bottle.

    Customer T is unprofitable, despite the smaller customer P being profitable. Customer T receives a $0.06 discount per bottle, makes more frequent orders, requires more deliveries, and requires more delivery miles than Customer P.

16-32 (Cont'd.)

2.　　Separate reporting of both the list selling price and the actual selling price enables Spring Distribution to examine which customers receive different discounts and how salespeople may differ in the discounts they grant. There is size pattern in the discounts across the 5 customers; except for Customer T:

Gross Revenues	Discount
R (1,460,000 units)	$0.05
S (764,000 units)	$0.02
Q (210,000 units)	$0.01
T (94,000 units)	$0.06
P (50,000 units)	$0.00

The reasons for the $0.06 discount for T should be expired.

3.　　Dropping customers should be the last resort taken by Spring Distribution. Factors to consider include:

(a)　　What is the expected future profitability of each customer? Are the currently unprofitable (T) or low-profit (P) customers likely to be highly profitable in the future?

(b)　　Are there externalities from having some customers, even if they are unprofitable in the short run? For example, some customers have a marque-value that is "in effect" advertising that benefits the business.

(c)　　What costs are avoidable if one or more customers are dropped?

(d)　　Can the relationship with the "problem" customers be restructured so that there is a "win-win" situation? For example, could Customer T get by with fewer deliveries per month?

16-34 (40–60 min.) **Customer profitability, credit card operations.**

1.

	Customer			
	A	**B**	**C**	**D**
Customer revenues				
Annual fee	$ 50	$ 0	$ 50	$ 0
Merchant payments[a]	1,600	520	680	160
Interest spread[b]	540	0	180	9
Total	2,190	520	910	169
Customer costs				
Annual maintenance costs	108	108	108	108
Bad debt provision[c]	400	130	170	40
Transaction costs[d]	400	260	136	100
Customer inquiries[e]	30	60	40	10
Card replacements[f]	0	240	120	0
Total	938	798	574	258
Customer operating income	$1,252	$(278)	$336	$(89)

[a] 2% × $80,000; $26,000; $34,000; $8,000
[b] 9% × $6,000; $0; $2,000; $100
[c] 0.5% × $80,000; $26,000; $34,000; $8,000
[d] $0.50 × 800; 520; 272; 200
[e] $5 × 6; 12; 8; 2
[f] $120 × 0; 2; 1; 0

Note: The above analysis uses the average 0.5% bad debt provision. Bay Bank may want to adjust individual customer-profitability reports at a subsequent date to reflect actual bad debt experience.

2.

	Profitable Customers	**Unprofitable Customers**
Revenues		
Fees	Pays fee	Fee waived
Merchant payments	High billings and high billings per transaction	Low billings and low billings per transaction
Interest spread	High outstanding balance	Pays on time and has no outstanding balance
Costs		
Bad debt "provision"	Pays account	Defaults on account
Transaction costs	Low number of transactions & high billings per transaction	High number of transactions & low billings per transaction
Customer inquiries	Zero or few inquiries	Many inquiries
Card replacement	No replacements	Multiple replacements

16-34 (Cont'd.)

3. <u>The pros of charging for individual services include</u>:

(a)   Additional source of revenues. If Bay Bank is able to charge more than the cost of each service, it may prefer that customers be prolific users of its services.
(b)   If Bay Bank is not able to charge the "full cost" for each services, the charge may reduce customer usage. For example, Customer B may make fewer inquiries about his or her balance.

<u>The cons of charging for individual services include</u>:

(a)   May cause customers to drop card or decrease its usage vis-a-vis competitions with zero or minimal charges.
(b)   May attract much negative publicity from consumer groups who target companies such as banks and credit card companies.

4. <u>Factors to consider include</u>:

(a)   The potential growth potential of individual customers. Some low-volume credit customers (such as students) may be high-volume users in the medium run.
(b)   The costs saved by discontinuing low-volume credit card customers. Many costs may be relatively "fixed" and may not be eliminated by dropping customers.
(c)   The publicity Bay Bank may attract from discontinuing these customers. There is the potential for much negative publicity from such decisions.
(d)   Alternatives available to discontinuance, e.g., adopt individual service charges.

5. <u>The pros of providing the service at Lucky Roller include</u>:

(a)   Potential increased profitability due to higher usage by Freedom Card holders at Lucky Roller.
(b)   Potential increased attraction to current and future Freedom Card holders. As a general rule, the more services available, the more attractive the card.

<u>Possible cons include</u>:

(a)   Potential bad debts. While money advances in general may have been profitable in 19_7, it is possible that some specific money advance outlets may be unprofitable. Verdolini should examine this issue in more detail to determine if the Bay Bank has made money advances at other gambling venues.
(b)   Potential negative publicity from media stories arguing that the Bay Bank is helping gamblers to lose money. These stories often focus on individuals with gambling addictions.
(c)   Ethical position of the Bay Bank as regards gambling. Providing a money advance service at the casino may conflict with the ethical beliefs of senior management or the Board of Directors.

CHAPTER 17
PROCESS-COSTING SYSTEMS

17-2   Process costing systems separate costs into cost categories according to the timing of when costs are introduced into the process. Often, only two cost classifications, direct materials and conversion costs, are necessary. Direct materials are frequently added at one point in time, often the start or the end of the process, and all conversion costs are added at about the same time, but in a pattern different from direct materials costs.

17-4   The accuracy of the estimates of completion depend on the care and skill of the estimator and the nature of the process. Aircraft blades may differ substantially in the finishing necessary to obtain a final product. The amount of work may not always be easy to ascertain in advance.

17-6   Three inventory methods associated with process costing are:
- Weighted average.
- First-in, first-out.
- Standard costing.

17-8   FIFO computations are distinctive because they assign the cost of the earliest equivalent units available (starting with equivalent units in beginning work-in-process inventory) to units completed and transferred out, and the cost of the most recent equivalent units worked on during the period to ending work-in-process inventory. In contrast, the weighted average method costs units completed and transferred out and in ending work in process at the same average cost.

17-10   A major advantage of FIFO is that managers can judge the performance in the current period independently from the performance in the preceding period.

17-12   Standard-cost procedures are particularly appropriate to process-costing systems where there are various combinations of materials and operations. Standard-cost procedures avoid the intricacies involved in detailed tracking with weighted-average or FIFO methods when there are frequent price variations over time.

17-14   No. Previous department costs (also called transferred-in costs) are costs incurred in a previous department that have been charged to a subsequent department. These costs may be costs incurred in that previous department during this accounting period or a preceding accounting period.

17-16 (25 min.) **No beginning inventory.**

1. Direct materials cost per unit ($720,000 ÷ 10,000) $ 72
    Conversion cost per unit ($760,000 ÷ 10,000)   76
    Assembly Department cost per unit $148

2.   Solution Exhibit 17-16A calculates the equivalent units of direct materials and conversion costs in the Assembly Department of International Electronics in February 19_7.

Solution Exhibit 17-16B computes equivalent units costs

    Direct materials cost per unit $ 72
    Conversion cost per unit   80
    Assembly Department cost per unit $152

3.   The difference in the Assembly Department cost per unit calculated in requirements 1 and 2 arises because the costs incurred in January and February are the same but fewer equivalent units of work are done in February relative to January. In January, all 10,000 units introduced are fully completed resulting in 10,000 equivalent units of work done with respect to direct materials and conversion costs. In February, of the 10,000 units introduced, 10,000 equivalent units of work is done with respect to direct materials but only 9,500 equivalent units of work is done with respect to conversion costs. The Assembly Department cost per unit is, therefore, higher.

SOLUTION EXHIBIT 17-16A
Steps 1 and 2: Summarize Output in Physical Units and Compute Equivalent Units
Assembly Department of International Electronics for February 19_7

| | (Step 1) | (Step 2) Equivalent Units | |
| | Physical | Direct | Conversion |
Flow of Production	Units	Materials	Costs
Completed and transferred out during current period	9,000	9,000	9,000
Add work in process, ending*	1,000		
1,000 × 100%; 1,000 × 50%		1,000	500
Total accounted for	10,000	10,000	9,500
Deduct work in process, beginning	0	0	0
Started during current period	10,000		
Work done in current period only		10,000	9,500

*Degree of completion in this department: direct materials, 100%; conversion costs, 50%.

SOLUTION EXHIBIT 17-16B
Step 3 : Compute Equivalent Unit Costs
Assembly Department of International Electronics for February 19_7

	Direct Materials	Conversion Costs
Costs added during February (given)	$720,000	$760,000
Divide by equivalent units of work done in February 19_7 (from Soln. Exh. 17-16A)	÷ 10,000	÷ 9,500
Cost per equivalent unit of work done in February 19_7	$ 72	$ 80

17-18 (25 min.) **No beginning inventory, materials introduced in middle of process.**

1.   Solution Exhibit 17-18A shows equivalent units of work done in the current period of Chemical P, 50,000; Chemical Q, 35,000; Conversion costs, 45,000.

2.   Solution Exhibit 17-18B calculates cost per equivalent unit of work done in the current period for Chemical P, Chemical Q, and Conversion costs.
        Solution Exhibit 17-18C summarizes the total Mixing Department costs for July 19_7, and assigns these costs to units completed (and transferred out) and to units in ending work in process.

SOLUTION EXHIBIT 17-18A
Steps 1 and 2: Summarize Output in Physical Units and Compute Equivalent Units
Mixing Department of Vaasa Chemicals for July 19_7

| | (Step 1) | (Step 2) Equivalent Units | | |
| | Physical | | | Conversion |
Flow of Production	Units	Chemical P	Chemical Q	Costs
Completed and transferred out				
during current period	35,000	35,000	35,000	35,000
Add work in process, ending*	15,000†			
15,000 × 100%; 15,000 × 0%;				
15,000 × 66 2/3%		15,000	0	10,000
Total accounted for	50,000	50,000	35,000	45,000
Deduct work in process, beginning	0	0	0	0
Started during current period	50,000			
Work done in current period only		50,000	35,000	45,000

*Degree of completion in this department: Chemical P, 100%; Chemical Q, 0%; Conversion costs, 66 2/3%.
Note that Chemical Q has not been included in the ending work in process, since the ending WIP is 66 2/3% complete and Chemical Q is only added when the units are 75% or three-fourths complete.
† Ending work in process   = Beginning work in process + Units started – Units completed
                            = 0 + 50,000 – 35,000 = 15,000 units

SOLUTION EXHIBIT 17-18B
Step 3 : Compute Equivalent Unit Costs
Mixing Department of Vaasa Chemicals for July 19_7

	Chemical P	Chemical Q	Conversion Costs
Costs added during July (given)	$250,000	$70,000	$135,000
Divide by equivalent units of work done in			
July 19_7 (from Solution Exhibit 17-18A)	÷ 50,000	÷35,000	÷45,000
Cost per equivalent unit of work done in			
July 19_7	$ 5	$ 2	$ 3

SOLUTION EXHIBIT 17-18C

Step 4: Summarize Total Costs to Account For and Assign These Costs to Units Completed, and Units in Ending Work in Process Mixing Department of Vaasa Chemicals for July 19_7

	Chemical P			Chemical Q			Conversion Costs			Total Production Costs
	Equivalent Units (1)	Cost per Equivalent Unit (2)	Total Costs (3)=(1)×(2)	Equivalent Units (4)	Cost per Equivalent Unit (5)	Total Costs (6)=(4)×(5)	Equivalent Units (7)	Cost per Equivalent Unit (8)	Total Costs (9)=(7)×(8)	(10)= (3)+(6)+(9)
Panel A: Total Costs to Account For Work done in July										
(from Solution Exhibit 17-18B)	50,000	$5	$250,000	35,000	$2	$70,000	45,000	$3	$135,000	$455,000
Panel B: Assignment of Costs										
Completed and transferred out:										
(35,000 physical units)	35,000[1]	$5	$175,000	35,000[1]	$2	$70,000	35,000[1]	$3	$105,000	$350,000
Work in process, ending										
(15,000 physical units)	15,000[1]	$5	75,000	0[1]	$2	0	10,000[1]	$3	30,000	105,000
Accounted for	50,000		$250,000	35,000		$70,000	45,000		$135,000	$455,000

[1]From Solution Exhibit 17-18A.

17-20 (20 min.) Equivalent units and equivalent unit costs.

1&2. Solution Exhibit 17-20A shows equivalent units of work done in the current period. Solution Exhibit 17-20B calculates cost per equivalent unit of beginning work in process and of work done in the current period.

SOLUTION EXHIBIT 17-20A
Steps 1 and 2: Summarize Output in Physical Units and Compute Equivalent Units
Assembly Division of Aerospatiale for May 19-7

| | (Step 1) Physical Units | (Step 2) Equivalent Units | |
Flow of Production		Direct Materials	Conversion Costs
Completed and transferred out during current period	46	46.0	46.0
Add work in process, ending*	12		
12 × 60%; 12 × 30%	__	7.2	3.6
Total accounted for	58	53.2	49.6
Deduct work in process, beginning§	8		
8 × 90%; 8 × 40%	__	7.2	3.2
Started during current period	50	___	___
Work done in current period only		46.0	46.4

* Degree of completion in this department: direct materials, 60%; conversion costs, 30%.
§ Degree of completion in this department: direct materials, 90%; conversion costs, 40%.

SOLUTION EXHIBIT 17-20B
Step 3: Compute Equivalent Unit Costs
Assembly Division of Aerospatiale for May 19_7

	Direct Materials	Conversion Costs
Equivalent unit costs of beginning work in process		
Work in process, beginning (given)	$ 4,968,000	$ 928,000
Divide by equivalent units of beginning work in process (from Solution Exhibit 17-20A)	÷7.2	÷3.2
Cost per equivalent unit of beginning work in process	$ 690,000	$ 290,000
Equivalent unit costs of work done in current period only		
Costs added in current period (given)	$32,200,000	$13,920,000
Divide by equivalent units of work done in current period (from Solution Exhibit 17-20A)	÷ 46	÷ 46.4
Cost per equivalent unit of work done in current period only	$ 700,000	$ 300,000

17-22 (25 min.) **FIFO method.** See Solution Exhibit 17-22 below.

SOLUTION EXHIBIT 17-22
Step 4: Summarize Total Costs to Account For and Assign These Costs to Units Completed, and Units in Ending Work in Process Using the FIFO Method
Chatham Company for July 19_7

	Direct Materials			Conversion Costs			Total Production Costs
	Equivalent Units (1)	Cost per Equivalent Unit (2)	Total Costs (3)=(1)×(2)	Equivalent Units (4)	Cost per Equivalent Unit (5)	Total Costs (6)=(4)×(5)	(7)=(3)+(6)
Panel A: Total Costs to Account For							
Work in process, beginning	20,000	$6.00	$120,000	14,000	$10.00	$140,000	$260,000
Work done in current period only	30,000	$7.00	210,000	28,000	$10.75	301,000	511,000
To account for	50,000		$330,000	42,000		$441,000	$771,000
Panel B: Assignment of Costs							
Completed and transferred out:							
Work in process, beginning	20,000	$6.00	$120,000	14,000	$10.00	$140,000	$260,000
Work done in current period to complete beginning work in process	0*	$7.00	0	6,000†	$10.75	64,500	64,500
Total from beginning inventory	20,000		120,000	20,000		204,500	324,500
Started and completed	14,000‡	$7.00	98,000	14,000‡	$10.75	150,500	248,500
Total completed and transferred out	34,000		218,000	34,000		355,000	573,000
Work in process, ending	16,000	$7.00	112,000	8,000	$10.75	86,000	198,000
Accounted for	50,000		$330,000	42,000		$441,000	$771,000

*Beginning work in process is 100% complete as to direct materials so zero equivalent units of direct materials need to be added to complete beginning work in process.
†Beginning work in process is 70% complete, which equals 14,000 equivalent units of conversion costs. To complete the 20,000 physical units of beginning work in process, 6,000 (20,000 – 14,000) equivalent units of conversion costs need to be added.
‡34,000 total equivalent units completed and transferred out minus 20,000 equivalent units completed and transferred from beginning inventory equals 14,000 equivalent units.

17-24 (30 min.) **Transferred-in costs, equivalent unit costs, working backwards.**

1.   Solution Exhibit 17-24A calculates equivalent units of (a) beginning work in process, and (b) work done in the current period for each cost element. To calculate equivalent units of beginning work in process, divide the value of beginning work in process by the cost per equivalent unit of beginning work in process. Similarly, to calculate equivalent units of work done in the current period, divide total costs added in the current period by the cost per equivalent unit of work done in the current period.

2 & 3. See Solution Exhibit 17-24B.

Using information about physical units given in the exercise,

Physical units completed and transferred out	=	Physical units in beginning work in process	+	Physical units transferred in during period	−	Physical units in ending work in process
	=	15,000	+	9,000	−	5,000
	=	19,000				

Equivalent units of beginning work in process and equivalent units of work done in current period (rows 4 and 5 of Solution Exhibit 17-24B) have been calculated in Solution Exhibit 17-24A. Equivalent units of units completed and transferred out for each cost element equal the 19,000 physical units completed and transferred out. Equivalent units of ending work in process for each cost element are then given by:

Equivalent units in ending work in process	=	Equivalent units in beginning work in process	+	Equivalent units of work done in current period	−	Equivalent units completed and transferred out during current period

Equivalent units of transferred-in costs in ending work in process
$$= 15,000 + 9,000 - 19,000 = 5,000 \text{ units}$$

Equivalent units of direct materials in ending work in process
$$= 0 + 19,000 - 19,000 = 0 \text{ units}$$

Equivalent units of conversion costs in ending work in process
$$= 9,000 + 11,000 - 19,000 = 1,000 \text{ units}$$

3a.   Percentage of completion of beginning work-in-process inventory

Transferred-in costs: 15,000 equivalent units ÷ 15,000 physical units = 100%
Direct materials: 0 equivalent units ÷ 15,000 physical units =   0%
Conversion costs: 9,000 equivalent units ÷ 15,000 physical units =   60%

17-24 (Cont'd.)

3b. Percentage of completion of ending work-in-process inventory

Transferred-in costs: 5,000 equivalent units ÷ 5,000 physical units = 100%
Direct materials: 0 equivalent units ÷ 5,000 physical units = 0%
Conversion costs: 1,000 equivalent units ÷ 5,000 physical units = 20%

SOLUTION EXHIBIT 17-24A
Step 3: Compute Equivalent Units Under the Weighted-Average Method
Thermoassembly Process of Bangkok Plastics for June 19_7

	Transferred-in Costs	Direct Materials	Conversion Costs
Equivalent unit costs of beginning work in process			
Work in process, beginning (given)	$90,000	—	$45,000
Divide by cost per equivalent unit of beginning work in process	÷ $6	—	÷ $5
Equivalent units of beginning work in process	15,000	—	9,000
Equivalent unit costs of work done in current period only			
Costs added in current period (given)	$58,500	$57,000	$57,200
Divide by cost per equivalent unit of work done in current period	÷ $6.50	÷ $3	÷ $5.20
Equivalent units of work done in current period only	9,000	19,000	11,000

SOLUTION EXHIBIT 17-24B
Step 1 and 2: Summarize Output in Physical Units and Compute Equivalent Units
Thermoassembly Process of Bangkok Plastics for June 19_7

	(Step 1)	(Step 2) Equivalent Units		
Flow of Production	Physical Units	Transferred-in Costs	Direct Materials	Conversion Costs
Completed and transferred out during current period	19,000	19,000	19,000	19,000
Add work in process, ending	5,000			
(5,000 × 100%; 5,000 × 0%; 5,000 × 20%)		5,000	0	1,000
Total accounted for	24,000	24,000	19,000	20,000
Deduct work in process, beginning	15,000			
(15,000 × 100%; 15,000 × 0%; 15,000 × 60%)		15,000	0	9,000
Transferred in during current period	9,000			
Work done in current period only		9,000	19,000	11,000

17-26 (35–40 min.) **Transferred-in costs, FIFO method.**

1. The calculations for equivalent tons of solvent completed and ending work in process for each cost element are exactly as in requirement 1 of Exercise 17-25 shown in Solution Exhibit 17-25A.

2. Solution Exhibit 17-26A presents computations of equivalent unit costs under the FIFO method.

3. Solution Exhibit 17-26B presents a summary of total costs to account for and assigns these costs to tons completed and to tons in ending work in process using the FIFO method.

SOLUTION EXHIBIT 17-25A
Step 1 and 2: Summarize Output in Physical Units and Compute Equivalent Units
Cooking Department of Hideo Chemicals for June 19_7

| | (Step 1) | (Step 2) Equivalent Units | | |
| | Physical | Transferred- | Direct | Conversion |
Flow of Production	Units	in Costs	Materials	Costs
Completed and transferred out during current period	90	90	90	90
Add work in process, ending*	30			
(30 × 100%; 30 × 0%; 30 × 50%)		30	0	15
Total accounted for	120	120	90	105
Deduct work in process, beginning‖	40			
(40 × 100%; 40 × 0%; 40 × 75%)		40	0	30
Transferred in during current period	80			
Work done in current period only		80	90	75

* Degree of completion in this department: transferred-in costs, 100%; direct materials, 0%; conversion costs, 50%; calculated by dividing equivalent units for each cost element by the physical units.

‖ Degree of completion in this department: transferred-in costs, 100%; direct materials, 0%; conversion costs, 75%; calculated by dividing equivalent units for each cost element by the physical units.

SOLUTION EXHIBIT 17-26A
Step 3: Compute Equivalent Unit Costs Under the FIFO Method
Cooking Department of Hideo Chemicals for June 19_7

	Transferred-in Costs	Direct Materials	Conversion Costs
Equivalent unit costs of beginning work in process			
Work in process, beginning (given)	$39,200	—	$18,000
Divide by equivalent units of beginning work in process (from Solution Exhibit 17-25A)	÷ 40	—	÷ 30
Cost per equivalent unit of beginning work in process	$ 980	—	$ 600
Equivalent unit costs of work done in current period only			
Costs added in current period (given)	$85,600	$36,000	$49,725
Divide by equivalent units of work done in current period (from Solution Exhibit 17-25A)	÷ 80	÷ 90	÷ 75
Cost per equivalent unit of work done in current period only	$ 1,070	$ 400	$ 663

SOLUTION EXHIBIT 17-26B

Step 4: Summarize Total Costs to Account For and Assign These Costs to Units Completed, and Units in Ending Work in Process Using the FIFO Method Cooking Department of Hideo Chemicals for June 19_7

	Transferred-in Costs			Direct Materials			Conversion Costs			Total Production Costs
	Equivalent Units (1)	Cost per Equivalent Unit (2)	Total Costs (3)=(1)×(2)	Equivalent Units (4)	Cost per Equivalent Unit (5)	Total Costs (6)=(4)×(5)	Equivalent Units (7)	Cost per Equivalent Unit (8)	Total Costs (9)=(7)×(8)	(10)= (3)+(6)+(9)
Panel A: Total Costs to Account For										
Work in process, beginning (from Solution Exhibit 17-26A)	40	$ 980	$ 39,200	0	—	$ 0	30	$600	$18,000	$ 57,200
Work done in current period only (from Solution Exhibit 17-26A)	80	$1,070	85,600	90	$400	36,000	75	$663	49,725	171,325
To account for	120		$124,800	90		$36,000	105		$67,725	$228,525
Panel B: Assignment of Costs										
Completed and transferred out (90 physical tons)										
Work in process, beginning (40 physical tons)	40	$ 980	$ 39,200	0	—	$ 0	30	$600	$18,000	$ 57,200
Work done in current period to complete beginning work in process	0*		0	40†	$400	16,000	10†	$663	6,630	22,630
Total from beginning inventory	40		39,200	40		16,000	40		24,630	79,830
Started and completed (50 physical tons)	50 ||	$1,070	53,500	50 ||	$400	20,000	50 ||	$663	33,150	106,650
Total completed and transferred out (90 physical tons)	90§		92,700	90§		36,000	90§		57,780	186,480
Work in process, ending (30 physical tons)	30§	$1,070	32,100	0§	$400	0	15§	$663	9,945	42,045
Accounted for	120		$124,800	90		$36,000	105		$67,725	$228,525

*Beginning work in process is 100% complete as to transferred-in costs so zero equivalent tons of transferred-in costs need to be added to complete beginning work in process.

†Beginning work in process is 0% complete as to direct materials, which equals 0 equivalent tons of direct materials need to be added. To complete the 40 physical tons of beginning work in process, 40 equivalent tons of direct materials need to be added.

‡Beginning work in process is 75% complete as to conversion costs, which equals 30 equivalent tons of conversion costs. To complete the 40 physical tons of beginning work in process, 10 (40 – 30) equivalent tons of conversion costs need to be added.

|| 90 total equivalent tons completed and transferred out (Solution Exhibit 17-25A) minus 40 equivalent tons completed and transferred from beginning inventory equals 50 equivalent tons.

§From Solution Exhibit 17-25A

17-28 (25 min.) **Weighted-average method.**

1. Solution Exhibit 17-28A shows equivalent units of work done in the current period of

Direct materials	80 equivalent units
Conversion costs	85 equivalent units

2. Solution Exhibit 17-28B calculates cost per equivalent unit of beginning work in process and of work done in the current period for direct materials and conversion costs.

3. Solution Exhibit 17-28C summarizes the total Assembly Department costs for October 19_7, and assigns these costs to units completed (and transferred out) and to units in ending work in process using the weighted-average method.

SOLUTION EXHIBIT 17-28A
Steps 1 and 2: Summarize Output in Physical Units and Compute Equivalent Units
Assembly Department of Global Defense Inc. for October 19_7

	(Step 1)	(Step 2) Equivalent Units	
Flow of Production	**Physical Units**	**Direct Materials**	**Conversion Costs**
Completed and transferred out during current period	90	90	90
Add work in process, ending*	10		
10 × 100[†]%; 10 × 70%		10	7
Total accounted for	100	100	97
Deduct work in process, beginning[§]	20		
20 × 100[†]%; 20 × 60%		20	12
Started during current period	80		
Work done in current period only		80	85

* Degree of completion in this department: direct materials, 100%; conversion costs, 70%.

[†] Direct materials are 100% complete in work in process inventories since all direct materials are introduced at the beginning of the Assembly Process.

[§] Degree of completion in this department: direct materials, 100%; conversion costs, 60%.

17-28 (Cont'd.)

SOLUTION EXHIBIT 17-28B
Step 3: Compute Equivalent Unit Costs
Assembly Department of Global Defense Inc. for October 19_7

	Direct Materials	Conversion Costs
Equivalent unit costs of beginning work in process		
Work in process, beginning (given)	$ 460,000	$120,000
Divide by equivalent units of beginning work in process (from Solution Exhibit 17-25A)	÷ 20	÷ 12
Cost per equivalent unit of beginning work in process	$ 23,000	$ 10,000
Equivalent unit costs of work done in current period only		
Costs added in current period (given)	$2,000,000	$935,000
Divide by equivalent units of work done in current period (from Solution Exhibit 17-28A)	÷ 80	÷ 85
Cost per equivalent unit of work done in current period only	$ 25,000	$ 11,000

17-28 (Cont'd.)

SOLUTION EXHIBIT 17-28C

Step 4: Summarize Total Costs to Account For and Assign These Costs to
Units Completed, and Units in Ending Work in Process Using the Weighted-Average Method
Assembly Department of Global Defense Inc. for October 19_7

	Direct Materials			Conversion Costs			Total Production Costs
	Equivalent Units (1)	Cost per Equivalent Unit (2)	Total Costs (3)=(1)×(2)	Equivalent Units (4)	Cost per Equivalent Unit (5)	Total Costs (6)=(4)×(5)	(7) = (3) + (6)
Panel A: Total Costs to Account For							
Work in process, beginning (from Solution Exhibit 17-28B)	20	$23,000	$ 460,000	12	$10,000.00	$ 120,000	$ 580,000
Work done in current period only (from Solution Exhibit 17-28B)	80	$25,000*	2,000,000	85	$11,000.00	935,000	2,935,000
To account for	100	$24,600*	$2,460,000	97	$10,876.29+	$1,055,000	$3,515,000
Panel B: Assignment of Costs							
Completed and transferred out: (90 physical units)	90‡	$24,600	$2,214,000	90‡	$10,876.29	$978,866	$3,192,866
Work in process, ending (10 physical units)	10+	$24,600	246,000	7‡	$10,876.29	76,134	322,134
Accounted for	100		$2,460,000	97		$1,055,000	$3,515,000

*Weighted-average cost per equivalent unit of direct materials = Total direct materials costs divided by total equivalent units of direct materials
= $2,460,000 ÷ 100 = $24,600.
+Weighted-average cost per equivalent unit of conversion costs = Total conversion costs divided by total equivalent units of conversion costs
= $1,035,000 ÷ 97 = $10,876.29.
‡From Solution Exhibit 17-28A.

17-30 (20 min.) **FIFO method.**

1.   The equivalent units of work done in the Assembly Department in October 19_7 for direct materials and conversion costs are the same as in problem 17-28 and are shown in Solution Exhibit 17-28A.

2.   The cost per equivalent unit of work done in the Assembly Department in October 19_7 for direct materials and conversion costs are calculated in problem 17-28 in Solution Exhibit 17-28B.

3.   Solution Exhibit 17-30 summarizes the total Assembly Department costs for October 19_7, and assigns these costs to units completed (and transferred out) and units in ending work in process under the FIFO method.

The cost per equivalent unit of beginning inventory and of work done in the current period differ:

	Beginning Inventory	Work Done in Current Period
Direct materials	$23,000	$25,000
Conversion costs	$10,000	$11,000

The following table summarizes the costs assigned to units completed and those still in process under the weighted-average and FIFO process-costing methods for our example.

	Weighted Average (Solution Exhibit 17-28C)	FIFO (Solution Exhibit 17-30)	Difference
Cost of units completed and transferred out	$3,192,866	$3,188,000	−$4,866
Work in process, ending	322,134	327,000	+$4,866
Total costs accounted for	$3,515,000	$3,515,000	

The FIFO ending inventory is higher than the weighted-average ending inventory by $4,866. This is because FIFO assumes that all the lower-cost prior-period units in work in process are the first to be completed and transferred out while ending work in process consists of only the higher-cost current-period units. The weighted-average method, however, smoothes out cost per equivalent unit by assuming that more of the higher-cost units are completed and transferred out, while some of the lower-cost units in beginning work in process are placed in ending work in process. Hence, in this case, the weighted-average method results in a higher cost of units completed and transferred out and a lower ending work-in-process inventory relative to FIFO.

17-30 (Cont'd.)

SOLUTION EXHIBIT 17-30

Step 4: Summarize Total Costs to Account For and Assign These Costs to Units Completed, and Units in Ending Work in Process Using the FIFO Method Testing Department of Global Defense Inc. for October 19_7

	Direct Materials			Conversion Costs			Total Production Costs
	Equivalent Units (1)	Cost per Equivalent Unit (2)	Total Costs (3)=(1)×(2)	Equivalent Units (4)	Cost per Equivalent Unit (5)	Total Costs (6)=(4)×(5)	(7) = (3) + (6)
Panel A: Total Costs to Account For							
Work in process, beginning (from Solution Exhibit 17-28B)	20	$23,000	$ 460,000	12	$10,000	$ 120,000	$ 580,000
Work done in current period only (from Solution Exhibit 17-28B)	80	$25,000	2,000,000	85	$11,000	935,000	2,935,000
To account for	100		$2,460,000	97		$1,055,000	$3,515,000
Panel B: Assignment of Costs							
Completed and transferred out: (90 physical units)							
Work in process, beginning (20 physical units)	20	$23,000	$ 460,000	12	$10,000	$ 120,000	$ 580,000
Work done in current period to complete beginning work in process	0*	$25,000	0	8†	$11,000	88,000	88,000
Total from beginning inventory	20		460,000	20		208,000	668,000
Started and completed (70 physical units)	70‡	$25,000	1,750,000	70‡	$11,000	770,000	2,520,000
Total completed and transferred out (90 physical units)	90		2,210,000	90		978,000	3,188,000
Work in process, ending (10 physical units)	10§	$25,000	250,000	7§	$11,000	77,000	327,000
Accounted for	100		$2,460,000	97		$1,055,000	$3,515,000

*Beginning work in process is 100% complete as to direct materials so zero equivalent units of direct materials need to be added to complete beginning work in process.

†Beginning work in process is 60% complete as to conversion costs, which equals 12 equivalent units of conversion costs. To complete the 20 physical units of beginning work in process, 8 (20 − 12) equivalent units of conversion costs need to be added.

‡90 total equivalent units completed and transferred out (Solution Exhibit 17-28A) minus 20 equivalent units completed and transferred from beginning inventory equals 70 equivalent units.

§From Solution Exhibit 17-28A.

17-32 (30 min.) Transferred-in costs, FIFO costing.

1. As explained in Problem 17-31, requirement 1, transferred-in costs are 100% complete and direct materials are 0% complete in both beginning and ending work-in-process inventory.

2. The equivalent units of work done in October 19_7 in the Testing Department for transferred-in costs, direct materials and conversion costs are exactly as in Solution Exhibit 17-31A.

3. Solution Exhibit 17-32A calculates the cost per equivalent unit of beginning work in process and of work done in October 19_7 in the Testing Department for transferred-in costs, direct materials, and conversion costs.

4. Solution Exhibit 17-32B summarizes total Testing Department costs for October 19_7, and assigns these costs to units completed and transferred out and to units in ending work in process using the FIFO method.

5. Journal entries:
   a. Work in Process—Testing Department   3,188,000
        Work in Process—Assembly Department   3,188,000
      Cost of goods completed and transferred out
        during October from the Assembly Dept. to
        the Testing Dept.

   b. Finished Goods   9,281,527
        Work in Process—Testing Department   9,281,527
      Cost of goods completed and transferred out
        during October from the Testing Department
        to Finished Goods inventory.

17-32 (Cont'd.)

SOLUTION EXHIBIT 17-31A
Steps 1 and 2: Summarize Output in Physical Units and Compute Equivalent Units
Testing Department of Global Defense Inc. for October 19_7

Flow of Production	(Step 1) Physical Units	(Step 2) Equivalent Units		
		Transferred-in Costs	Direct Materials	Conversion Costs
Completed and transferred out during current period	105	105	105	105
Add work in process, ending* (15 × 100%; 15 × 0%; 15 × 60%)	15	15	0	9
Total accounted for	120	120	105	114
Deduct work in process, beginning‖ (30 × 100%; 30 × 0%; 30 × 70%)	30	30	0	21
Transferred in during current period	90			
Work done in current period only		90	105	93

* Degree of completion in this department: transferred-in costs, 100%; direct materials, 0%; conversion costs, 60%.

‖Degree of completion in this department: transferred-in costs, 100%; direct materials, 0%; conversion costs, 70%.

SOLUTION EXHIBIT 17-32A
Step 3: Compute Equivalent Unit Costs Under the FIFO Method
Testing Department of Global Defense Inc. for October 19_7

	Transferred-in Costs	Direct Materials	Conversion Costs
Equivalent unit costs of beginning work in process			
Work in process, beginning (given)	$ 980,060	—	$ 331,800
Divide by equivalent units of beginning work in process (from Solution Exhibit 17-31A)	÷ 30	—	÷ 21
Cost per equivalent unit of beginning work in process	$ 32,668.67	—	$ 15,800

SOLUTION EXHIBIT 17-32B

Step 4: Summarize Total Costs to Account For and Assign These Costs to
Units Completed, and Units in Ending Work in Process Using the FIFO Method
Testing Department of Global Defense Inc. for October 19_7

	Transferred-in Costs			Direct Materials			Conversion Costs			Total Production Costs
	Equivalent Units (1)	Cost per Equivalent Unit (2)	Total Costs (3)=(1)×(2)	Equivalent Units (4)	Cost per Equivalent Unit (5)	Total Costs (6)=(4)×(5)	Equivalent Units (7)	Cost per Equivalent Unit (8)	Total Costs (9)=(7)×(8)	(10)=(3)+(6)+(9)
Panel A: Total Costs to Account For										
Work in process, beginning (from Solution Exhibit 17-32A)	30	$32,668.67	$ 980,060	0	—	$ 0	21	$15,800	$ 331,800	$1,311,860
Work done in current period only (from Solution Exhibit 17-32A)	90	$35,422.22	3,188,000	105	$37,000	3,885,000	93	$17,000	1,581,000	8,654,000
To account for	120		$4,168,060	105		$3,885,000	114		$1,912,800	$9,965,860
Panel B: Assignment of Costs										
Completed and transferred out:										
Work in process, beginning (105 physical units)	30	$32,668.67	$ 980,060	0	—	$ 0	21	$15,800	$ 331,800	$1,311,860
Work done in current period to complete beginning work in process (30 physical units)	0*		0	30†	$37,000	1,110,000	9‡	$17,000	153,000	1,263,000
Total from beginning inventory (30 physical units)	30		980,060	30		1,110,000	30		484,800	2,574,860
Started and completed (75 physical units)	75∥	$35,422.22	2,656,667	75∥	$37,000	2,775,000	75∥	$17,000	1,275,000	6,706,667
Total completed and transferred out (105 physical units)	105§		3,636,727	105§		3,885,000	105§		1,759,800	9,281,527
Work in process, ending (15 physical units)	15§	$35,422.22	531,333	0§		0	9§	$17,000	153,000	684,333
Accounted for	120		$4,168,060	105		$3,885,000	114		$1,912,800	$9,965,860

* Beginning work in process is 100% complete as to transferred-in costs so zero equivalent units of transferred-in costs need to be added to complete beginning work in proceess.
† Beginning work in process is 0% complete as to direct materials, which equals 0 equivalent units of direct materials. To complete the 30 physical units of beginning work in process, 30 equivalent units of direct materials need to be added.
‡ Beginning work in process is 70% complete as to conversion costs, which equals 21 equivalent units of conversion costs. To complete the 30 physical units of beginning work in process, 9 (30-21) equivalent units of conversion costs need to be added.
∥ 105 total equivalent units completed and transferred out (Solution Exhibit 17-31A) minus 30 equivalent units completed and transferred from beginning inventory equals 75 equivalent units.
§ From Solution Exhibit 17-31A.

17-34 (5–10 min.) **Journal entries.**

1. Work in Process—Forming Department   70,000
        Accounts Payable   70,000
        To record direct materials purchased and
        used in production during April

2. Work in Process—Forming Department   42,500
        Various Accounts   42,500
        To record Forming Department conversion
        costs for April

3. Work in Process—Finishing Department   104,000
        Work in Process—Forming Department   104,000
        To record cost of goods completed and transferred
        out in April from the Forming Department
        to the Finishing Department

Work in Process—Forming Department			
Beginning inventory, April 1	9,625	3. Transferred out to	
1. Direct materials	70,000	Work in Process—Finishing	104,000
2. Conversion costs	42,500		
Ending inventory, April 30	18,125		

17-36 (30 min.) Transferred-in costs, weighted average.

1. Solution Exhibit 17-36A computes the equivalent units of work done in April 19_7 in the Finishing Department for transferred-in costs, direct materials, and conversion costs.

Solution Exhibit 17-36B calculates the cost per equivalent unit of beginning work in process and of work done in April 19_7 in the Finishing Department for transferred-in costs, direct materials, and conversion costs.

Solution Exhibit 17-36C summarizes total Finishing Department costs for April 19_7, and assigns these costs to units completed and transferred out and to units in ending work in process using the weighted-average method.

2.   Journal entries:

a.   Work in Process—Finishing Department   104,000
      Work in Process—Forming Department   104,000
     Cost of goods completed and transferred out
       during April from the Forming Department
       to the Finishing Department

b.   Finished Goods   168,552
      Work in Process—Finishing Department   168,552
     Cost of goods completed and transferred out
       during April from the Finishing Department
       to Finished Goods inventory

17-36 (Cont'd.)

SOLUTION EXHIBIT 17-36A

Steps 1 and 2: Summarize Output in Physical Units and Compute Equivalent Units
Finishing Department of Star Toys for April 19_7

| | (Step 1) | (Step 2) Equivalent Units | | |
Flow of Production	Physical Units	Transferred-in Costs	Direct Materials	Conversion Costs
Completed and transferred out during current period	2,100	2,100	2,100	2,100
Add work in process, ending*	400			
(400 × 100%; 400 × 0%; 400 × 30%)		400	0	120
Total accounted for	2,500	2,500	2,100	2,220
Deduct work in process, beginning ‖	500			
(500 × 100%; 500 × 0%; 500 × 60%)		500	0	300
Transferred in during current period	2,000			
Work done in current period only		2,000	2,100	1,920

* Degree of completion in this department: transferred-in costs, 100%; direct materials, 0%; conversion costs, 30%.

‖Degree of completion in this department: transferred-in costs, 100%; direct materials, 0%; conversion costs, 60%.

SOLUTION EXHIBIT 17-36B

Step 3: Compute Equivalent Unit Costs Under the Weighted-Average Method
Finishing Department of Star Toys for April 19-7

	Transferred-in Costs	Direct Materials	Conversion Costs
Equivalent unit costs of beginning work in process			
Work in process, beginning (given)	$ 17,750	—	$ 7,250
Divide by equivalent units of beginning work in process (from Solution Exhibit 17-36A)	÷ 500	—	÷ 300
Cost per equivalent unit of beginning work in process	$ 35.50	—	$24.167
Equivalent unit costs of work done in current period only			
Costs added in current period (given)	$104,000	$23,100	$38,400
Divide by equivalent units of work done in current period (from Solution Exhibit 17-36A)	÷ 2,000	÷ 2,100	÷ 1,920
Cost per equivalent unit of work done in current period only	$ 52	$ 11	$ 20

17-23

SOLUTION EXHIBIT 17-36C

Step 4: Summarize Total Costs to Account For and Assign These Costs to Units Completed, and Units in Ending Work in Process Using the Weighted-Average Method Finishing Department of Star Toys for April 19_7

	Transferred-in Costs			Direct Materials			Conversion Costs			Total Production Costs
	Equivalent Unit (1)	Cost per Equivalent Unit (2)	Total Costs (3)=(1)×(2)	Equivalent Unit (4)	Cost per Equivalent Unit (5)	Total Costs (6)=(4)×(5)	Equivalent Unit (7)	Cost per Equivalent Unit (8)	Total Costs (9)=(7)×(8)	(10)=(3)+(6)+(9)
Panel A: Total Costs to Account for:										
Work in process, beginning (from Solution Exhibit 17-36B)	500	$35.50	$ 17,750	0	—	$ 0	300	$24.167	$ 7,250	$ 25,000
Work done in current period only (from Solution Exhibit, 17-36B)	2,000	$52.00	104,000	2,100	$11	23,100	1,920	$20	38,400	165,500
To account for	2,500	$48.70*	$121,750	2,100	$11†	$23,100	2,220	$20.563‡	$45,650	$190,500
Panel B: Assignment of Costs										
Completed and transferred out: (2,100 physical units)	2,100§	$48.70	$102,270	2,100§	$11	$23,100	2,100§	$20.563	$43,182	$168,552
Work in process, ending (400 physical units)	400§	$48.70	19,480	0§	—	0	120§	$20.563	2,468	21,948
Accounted for	2,500		$121,750	2,100		$23,100	2,220		$45,650	$190,500

* Weighted-average cost per equivalent unit of transferred-in costs = Total transferred-in costs divided by total equivalent units of transferred-in costs = $121,750 ÷ 2,500 = $48.70
† Weighted-average cost per equivalent unit of direct materials = Total direct materials costs divided by total equivalent units of direct materials = $23,100 ÷ 2,100 = $11.
‡ Weighted-average cost per equivalent unit of conversion costs = Total conversion costs divided by total equivalent units of conversion costs = $45,650 ÷ 2,220 = $20.563.
§ From Exhibit 17-36A.

17-38 (45 min.) Transferred-in costs, weighted-average and FIFO.

1.   Solution Exhibit 17-38A computes the equivalent units of work done in week 37 in the Drying and Packaging Department for transferred-in costs, direct materials, and conversion costs.

2.   Solution Exhibit 17-38B calculates the cost per equivalent unit of beginning work in process and of work done in week 37 in the Drying and Packaging Department for transferred-in costs, direct materials, and conversion costs.

Solution Exhibit 17-38C summarizes total drying and packaging Department costs for week 37, and assigns these costs to units completed and transferred out and to units in ending work in process using the weighted-average method.

3.   Solution Exhibit 17-38D calculates the cost per equivalent unit of beginning work in process and of work done in week 37 in the Drying and Packaging Department for transferred-in costs, direct materials, and conversion costs.

Solution Exhibit 17-38E summarizes total Drying and Packaging Department costs for week 37, and assigns these costs to units completed and transferred out and to units in ending work in process using the FIFO method.

17-38 (Cont'd.)

SOLUTION EXHIBIT 17-38A
Steps 1 and 2: Summarize Output in Physical Units and Compute Equivalent Units
Drying and Packaging Department of Frito-Lay Inc. for Week 37

| | (Step 1) | (Step 2) Equivalent Units | | |
| | Physical | Transferred- | Direct | Conversion |
Flow of Production	Units	in Costs	Materials	Costs
Completed and transferred out during current period	5,250	5,250	5,250	5,250
Add work in process, ending*	1,000			
(1,000 × 100%; 1,000 × 0%;1,000 × 40%)		1,000	0	400
Total accounted for	6,250	6,250	5,250	5,650
Deduct work in process, beginning[‖]	1,250			
(1,250 × 100%; 1,250 × 0%; 1,250 × 80%)		1,250	0	1,000
Transferred in during current period	5,000			
Work done in current period only		5,000	5,250	4,650

*Degree of completion in this department: transferred-in costs, 100%; direct materials, 0%; conversion costs, 40%.

[‖]Degree of completion in this department: transferred-in costs, 100%; direct materials, 0%; conversion costs, 80%.

SOLUTION EXHIBIT 17-38B
Step 3: Compute Equivalent Unit Costs Under the Weighted-Average Method
Drying and Packaging Department of Frito-Lay Inc. for Week 37

	Transferred-in Costs	Direct Materials	Conversion Costs
Equivalent unit costs of beginning work in process			
Work in process, beginning (given)	$29,000	—	$ 9,060
Divide by equivalent units of beginning work in process (from Solution Exhibit 17-38A)	÷ 1,250	—	÷ 1,000
Cost per equivalent unit of beginning work in process	$ 23.20	—	$ 9.06
Equivalent unit costs of work done in current period only			
Costs added in current period (given)	$96,000	$25,200	$38,400
Divide by equivalent units of work done in current period (from Solution Exhibit 17-38A)	÷ 5,000	÷ 5,250	÷ 4,650
Cost per equivalent unit of work done in current period only	$ 19.20	$ 4.80	$ 8.258

SOLUTION EXHIBIT 17-38C
Step 4: Summarize Total Costs to Account For and Assign These Costs to Units Completed, and Units in Ending Work in Process Using the Weighted-Average Method Drying and Packaging Department of Frito-Lay for Week 37

	Transferred-in Costs			Direct Materials			Conversion Costs			Total Production Costs
	Equivalent Units (1)	Cost per Equivalent Unit (2)	Total Costs (3)=(1)×(2)	Equivalent Units (4)	Cost per Equivalent Unit (5)	Total Costs (6)=(4)×(5)	Equivalent Units (7)	Cost per Equivalent Unit (8)	Total Costs (9)=(7)¥(8)	(10)= (3)+(6)+(9)
Panel A: Total Costs to Account For										
Work in process, beginning (from Solution Exhibit 17-38B)	1,250	$23.20	$ 29,000	0	—	$ 0	1,000	$9.060	$ 9,060	$ 38,060
Work done in current period only (from Solution Exhibit 17-38B)	5,000	$19.20	96,000	5,250	$4.80	25,200	4,650	$8.258	38,400	159,600
To account for	6,250	$20.00*	$125,000	5,250	$4.80†	$25,200	5,650	$8.400‡	$47,460	$197,660
Panel B: Assignment of Costs										
Completed and transferred out: (5,250 physical units)	5,250**	$20.00	$105,000	5,250**	$4.80	$25,200	5,250**	$8.400	$44,100	$174,300
Work in process, ending (1,000 physical units)	1,000**	$20.00	20,000	0**	—	0	400**	$8.400	3,360	23,360
Accounted for	6,250		$125,000	5,250		$25,200	5,650		$47,460	$197,660

*Weighted-average cost per equivalent unit of transferred-in costs = Total transferred-in costs divided by total equivalent units of transferred-in costs
= $125,000 ÷ 6,250 = $20.

†Weighted average costs per equivalent unit of direct materials = Total direct materials costs divided by total equivalent units of direct materials
= $25,200 ÷ 5,250 = $4.80.

‡Weighted-average cost per equivalent unit of conversion costs = Total conversion costs divided by total equivalent units of conversion costs
= $47,460 ÷ 5,650 = $8.40.

**From Solution Exhibit 17-38A.

17-38 (Cont'd.)

SOLUTION EXHIBIT 17-38D
Step 3: Compute Equivalent Unit Costs Under the FIFO Method
Drying and Packaging Department of Frito-Lay Inc. for Week 37

	Transferred-in Costs	Direct Materials	Conversion Costs
Equivalent unit costs of beginning work in process			
Work in process, beginning (given)	$28,920	—	$ 9,060
Divide by equivalent units of beginning work in process (from Solution Exhibit 17-38A)	÷ 1,250	—	÷ 1,000
Cost per equivalent unit of beginning work in process	$23.136	—	$ 9.06
Equivalent unit costs of work done in current period only			
Costs added in current period (given)	$94,000	$25,200	$38,400
Divide by equivalent units of work done in current period (from Solution Exhibit 17-38A)	÷ 5,000	÷ 5,250	÷ 4,650
Cost per equivalent unit of work done in current period only	$ 18.80	$ 4.80	$ 8.258

SOLUTION EXHIBIT 17-38E
Step 4: Summarize Total Costs to Account For and Assign These Costs to Units Completed, and Units in Ending Work in Process Using the FIFO Method
Drying and Packaging Department of Frito-Lay Inc. for Week 37

	Transferred-in Costs			Direct Materials			Conversion Costs			Total Production Costs
	Equivalent Units (1)	Cost per Equivalent Unit (2)	Total Costs (3)=(1)×(2)	Equivalent Units (4)	Cost per Equivalent Unit (5)	Total Costs (6)=(4)×(5)	Equivalent Units (7)	Cost per Equivalent Unit (8)	Total Costs (9)=(7)×(8)	(10)= (3)+(6)+(9)
Panel A: Total Costs to Account For										
Work in process, beginning (from Solution Exhibit 17-38D)	1,250	$23.136	$ 28,920	0	—	$ 0	1,000	$9.06	$ 9,060	$ 37,980
Work done in current period only (from Solution Exhibit 17-38D)	5,000	$18.80	94,000	5,250	$4.80	25,200	4,650	$8.258	38,400	157,600
To account for	6,250		$122,920	5,250		$25,200	5,650		$47,460	$195,580
Panel B: Assignment of Costs										
Completed and transferred out: (5,250 physical units)										
Work in process, beginning (1,250 physical units)	1,250	$23.136	$ 28,920	0	—	$ 0	1,000	$9.06	$ 9,060	$ 37,980
Work done in current period to complete beginning work in process	0*		0	1,250†	$4.80	6,000	250†	$8.258	2,065	8,065
Total from beginning inventory	1,250		28,920	1,250		6,000	1,250		11,125	46,045
Started and completed (4,000 physical units)	4,000"	$18.80	75,200	4,000"	$4.80	19,200	4,000"	$8.258	33,032	127,432
Total completed and transferred out (5,250 physical units)	5,250§		104,120	5,250§		25,200	5,250§		44,157	173,477
Work in process, ending (1,000 physical units)	1,000§	$18.80	18,800	0§	$4.80	0	400§	$8.258	3,303	22,103
Accounted for	6,250		$122,920	5,250§		$25,200	5,650		$47,460	$195,580

* Beginning work in process is 100% complete as to transferred-in costs so zero equivalent units of transferred-in costs need to be added to complete beginning work in process.

† Beginning work in process is 0% complete as to direct materials, which equals 0 equivalent units of direct materials. To complete the 1,250 physical units of beginning work in process, 1,250 equivalent units of direct materials need to be added.

‡ Beginning work in process is 80% complete as to conversion costs, which equals 1,000 equivalent units of conversion costs. To complete the 1,250 physical units of beginning work in process, 250 (1,250 − 1,000) equivalent units of conversion costs need to be added.

" 5,250 total equivalent units completed and transferred out (Solution Exhibit 17-38A) minus 1,250 equivalent units completed and transferred from beginning inventory equals 4,000 equivalent units.

§ From Solution Exhibit 17-38A.

17-40 (20–25 min.) **Equivalent unit computations, benchmarking, ethics.**

1.   The reported monthly cost per equivalent unit of either direct materials or conversion costs is lower when the plant manager overestimates the percentage of completion of ending work in process; the overestimate increases the denominator and, thus, decreases the cost per equivalent whole unit. By reporting a lower cost per equivalent unit, the plant manager increases the likelihood of being in the top three ranked plants for the benchmarking comparisons.

A plant manager can manipulate the monthly estimate of percentage of completion by understating the number of steps yet to be undertaken before a suit becomes a finished good.

2.   There are several options available:
   a.   Major shows the letters to the line executive to whom the plant managers report in a hard-line way (say, the corporate manager of manufacturing). This approach is appropriate if the letters allege it is the plant managers who are manipulating the percentage of completion estimates.
   b.   Major, herself, shows the letters to the plant managers. This approach runs the danger of the plant managers ignoring or reacting negatively to someone to whom they do not report in a line-mode questioning their behavior. Much will depend here on how Major raises the issue. Unsigned letters need not have much credibility unless they contain specific details.
   c.   Major discusses the letters with the appropriate plant controllers without including the plant manager in the discussion. While the plant controller has responsibility for preparing the accounting reports from the plant, the plant controller, in most cases, reports hard-line to the plant manager. If this reporting relationship exists, Major may create a conflict of interest situation for the plant controller. Only if the plant controller reports hard-line to the corporate controller and dotted-line to the plant manager should Major show the letters to the plant controller without simultaneously showing them to the plant manager.

3.   The plant controller's ethical responsibilities to Major and to Leisure Suits should be the same. These include:
   •   Competence: The plant controller is expected to have the competence to make equivalent unit computations. This competence does not always extend to making estimates of the percentage of completion of a product. In Leisure Suits' case, however, the products are probably easy to understand and observe. Hence, a plant controller could obtain reasonably reliable evidence on percentage of completion at a specific plant.
   •   Objectivity: The plant controller should not allow the possibility of the division being written up favorably in the company newsletter to influence the way equivalent unit costs are computed.

4. Major could seek evidence on possible manipulations as follows:

   a. Have plant controllers report detailed breakdowns on the stages of production and then conduct end-of-month audits to verify the actual stages completed for ending work in process.

   b. Examine trends over time in ending work in process. Divisions that report low amounts of ending work in process relative to total production are not likely to be able to greatly affect equivalent cost amounts by manipulating percentage of completion estimates. Divisions that show sizable quantities of total production in ending work in process are more likely to be able to manipulate equivalent cost computations by manipulating percentage of completion estimates.

CHAPTER 18 SOLUTION
SPOILAGE, REWORKED UNITS, AND SCRAP

18-2 Spoilage – unacceptable units of production that are discarded or sold for net disposal proceeds.

Reworked units – unacceptable units of production that are subsequently reworked and sold as acceptable finished goods.

Scrap – product that has minimal (frequently zero) sales value compared with the sales value of the main or joint product(s).

18-4 Abnormal spoilage is spoilage that is not expected to arise under efficient operating conditions. Costs of abnormal spoilage are "lost costs," measures of inefficiency that should be written off directly as losses for the accounting period.

18-6 Normal spoilage typically is expressed as a percentage of good units passing the inspection point. Given actual spoiled units, we infer abnormal spoilage as follows:

Abnormal spoilage = Actual spoilage – Normal spoilage

18-8 Yes. Normal spoilage rates should be computed from the good output or from the normal input, not the total input. Normal spoilage is a given percentage of a certain output base. This base should never include abnormal spoilage, which is included in total input. Abnormal spoilage does not vary in direct proportion to units produced, and to include it would cause the normal spoilage count to fluctuate irregularly but not vary in direct proportion to the output base.

18-10 No. If abnormal spoilage is detected at a different point in the production cycle than normal spoilage, then unit costs would differ. If, however normal and abnormal spoilage are detected at the same point in the production cycle, their unit costs would be the same.

18-12 No. Unless there are special reasons for charging rework to jobs that contained the bad units, the costs of extra materials, labor, and so on are usually charged to manufacturing overhead and allocated to all jobs.

18-14 A company is justified in inventorying scrap when its estimated net realizable value is significant and the time between storing it and selling or reusing it may be quite long.

18-16 (5-10 min.) Normal and abnormal spoilage in units.

1. Total spoiled units 12,000
    Normal spoilage in units 5% × 132,000 6,600
    Abnormal spoilage in units 5,400

2. Abnormal spoilage, 5,400 × $10 $ 54,000
    Normal spoilage, 6,600 × $10 66,000
    Potential savings, 12,000 × $10 $120,000

Regardless of the targeted normal spoilage, abnormal spoilage is non-recurring and avoidable. The targeted normal spoilage rate is subject to change. Many companies have reduced their spoilage to almost zero, which would realize all potential savings. Of course, zero spoilage usually means higher-quality products, more customer satisfaction, more employee satisfaction, and various effects on nonmanufacturing (for example, purchasing) costs of direct materials.

18-18 (30 min.) **Weighted-average method, spoilage.**

1.   Solution Exhibit 18-18A calculates the cost per equivalent unit of beginning work in process and of work done in the current period for direct materials and conversion costs.

2.   Solution Exhibit 18-18B summarizes the total costs to account for and assigns these costs to units completed, normal spoilage, abnormal spoilage, and ending work in process using the weighted-average method.

3.   From Solution Exhibit 18-18B, under the weighted-average method,

$$\text{Cost of a good unit completed (and transferred out)} = \frac{\text{Total production costs of good units transferred out}}{\text{Number of good units completed}}$$

$$= \frac{\$431,250}{20,000} = \$21.5625$$

Note that this cost is higher than the cost per equivalent unit of $18.75 (direct materials, $8.25 and conversion costs, $10.50). Why? Because the cost of good units completed and transferred out also includes the cost of normal spoilage of 15%. The cost of a good unit completed and transferred out equals $18.75 + 15% of $18.75 = $21.5625.

SOLUTION EXHIBIT 18-18A
Step 3: Compute Equivalent Unit Costs
Molding Department of Anderson Plastics for April 19_8

	Direct Materials	Conversion Costs
Equivalent unit costs of beginning work in process		
Work in process, beginning (given)	$120,000	$140,000
Divide by equivalent units in beginning work in process	÷ 15,000	÷ 14,000
Cost per equivalent unit of beginning work in process	$ 8	$ 10
Equivalent unit costs of work done in current period only		
Costs added in current period (given)	$210,000	$301,000
Divide by equivalent units of work done in current period	÷ 25,000	÷ 28,000
Cost per equivalent unit of work done in current period only	$ 8.40	$ 10.75

18-18 (Cont'd.)

SOLUTION EXHIBIT 18-18B
Step 4: Summarize Total Costs to Account For and Assign These Costs to Units Completed, Units Spoiled, and Units in Ending Work in Process Using the Weighted-Average Method
Molding Department of Anderson Plastics for April 19_8

		Direct Materials			Conversion Costs			Total Production Costs
		Equivalent Units (1)	Cost per Equivalent Unit (2)	Total Costs (3) = (1) × (2)	Equivalent Units (4)	Cost per Equivalent Unit (5)	Total Costs (6) = (4) × (5)	(7) = (3) + (6)
Panel A:	Total Costs to Account For							
	Work in process, beginning (from Solution Exhibit 18-18A)	15,000	$8.00	$120,000	14,000	$10.00	$140,000	$260,000
	Work done in current period only (from Solution Exhibit 18-18A)	25,000	$8.40	210,000	28,000	$10.75	301,000	511,000
	To account for	40,000	$8.25*	$330,000	42,000	$10.50†	$441,000	$771,000
Panel B:	Assignment of Costs							
	Good units completed and transferred out (20,000 units):							
	Costs before adding normal spoilage	20,000	$8.25	$165,000	20,000	$10.50	$210,000	$375,000
	Normal spoilage (15% of good units)	3,000	$8.25	24,750	3,000	$10.50	31,500	56,250
(A)	Total costs of good units transferred out			189,750			241,500	431,250
(B)	Abnormal spoilage (4,000 – normal spoilage)	1,000	$8.25	8,250	1,000	$10.50	10,500	18,750
(C)	Work in process, ending	16,000	$8.25	132,000	18,000	$10.50	189,000	321,000
(A)+(B)+(C)	Accounted for	40,000		$330,000	42,000		$441,000	$771,000

*Weighted-average cost per equivalent unit of direct materials = Total costs of direct materials divided by total equivalent units of direct materials
= $330,000 ÷ 40,000 = $8.25
†Weighted-average cost per equivalent unit of conversion costs = Total conversion costs divided by total equivalent units of conversion costs
= $441,000 ÷ 42,000 = $10.50

18-20 (30 min.) Standard costing method.

1. The cost per equivalent unit for direct materials and conversion costs equal the standard cost per unit given in the problem: direct materials, $8.20 per equivalent unit for direct materials in both beginning inventory and work done in the current period and $10.20 per equivalent unit for conversion costs in both beginning inventory and work done in the current period.

2. Solution Exhibit 18-20 summarizes the total costs to account for and assigns these costs to units completed, normal spoilage, abnormal spoilage and ending work in process using the standard costing method.

Total direct materials variance
= Actual costs – Standard costs
= $330,000 – $328,000 = $ 2,000 U

Total conversion costs variance
= Actual costs – Standard costs
= $441,000 – $428,400 = $12,600 U

3. From Solution Exhibit 18-20, under the standard costing method,

$$\text{Cost of a good unit completed (and transferred out)} = \frac{\text{Total production costs of good units transferred out}}{\text{Number of good units completed}}$$

$$= \frac{\$423,200}{20,000} = \$21.16$$

Note that this cost is higher than the cost per equivalent of $18.40 (direct materials, $8.20 and conversion costs, $10.20). Why? Because the cost of good units completed and transferred out also includes the cost of normal spoilage of 15%. The cost of a good unit completed and transferred out equals $18.40 + 15% of 18.40 = $21.16.

18-20 (Cont'd.)

SOLUTION EXHIBIT 18-20

Step 4: Summarize Total Costs to Account For and Assign These Costs to Units Completed, Units Spoiled, and Units in Ending Work in Process Using Standard Costs
Molding Department of Anderson Plastics for April 19_8

	Direct Materials			Conversion Costs			Total Production Costs
	Equivalent Units (Solution Exhibit 18-18A) (1)	Cost per Equivalent Unit (2)	Total Costs (3) = (1) × (2)	Equivalent Units (Solution Exhibit 18-18A) (4)	Cost per Equivalent Unit (5)	Total Costs (6) = (4) × (5)	(7) = (3) + (6)
Panel A: Total Costs to Account For							
Work in process, beginning	15,000	$8.20	$123,000	14,000	$10.20	$142,800	$265,800
Work done in current period only	25,000	$8.20	205,000	28,000	$10.20	285,600	490,600
To account for	40,000	$8.20	$328,000	42,000	$10.20	$428,400	$756,400
Panel B: Assignment of Costs							
Good units completed and transferred out (20,000 units):							
Costs before adding normal spoilage	20,000	$8.20	$164,000	20,000	$10.20	$204,000	$368,000
Normal spoilage (15% of good units)	3,000	$8.20	24,600	3,000	$10.20	30,600	55,200
(A) Total costs of good units transferred out			188,600			234,600	423,200
(B) Abnormal spoilage (4,000 – normal spoilage)	1,000	$8.20	8,200	1,000	$10.20	10,200	18,400
(C) Work in process, ending	16,000	$8.20	131,200	18,000	$10.20	183,600	314,800
(A)+(B)+(C) Accounted for	40,000		$328,000	42,000		$428,400	$756,400

18-22 (25 min.) **FIFO method, spoilage**

1.   The equivalent units of work done in the Microchip Department in September 19_7 for direct materials and conversion costs are the same as in problem 18-21 and are shown in Solution Exhibit 18-21A.

2.   The cost per equivalent unit of beginning inventory and of work done in the Microchip Department in September 19_7 for direct materials and conversion costs are calculated in problem 18-21 in Solution Exhibit 18-21B.

3.   Solution Exhibit 18-22 summarizes the total Microchip Department costs for September 19_7 and assigns these costs to units completed (and transferred out), normal spoilage, abnormal spoilage, and units in ending work in process under the FIFO method.

18-22 (Cont'd.)

SOLUTION EXHIBIT 18-21A
Steps 1 and 2: Summarize Output in Physical Units and Compute Equivalent Units
Microchip Department of Superchip Company for September 19_7

| | (Step 1) | (Step 2) Equivalent Units | |
Flow of Production	Physical Units	Direct Materials	Conversion Costs
Good units completed and transferred out during current period	1,400	1,400	1,400
Normal spoilage†	210		
210 × 100%; 210 × 100%		210	210
Abnormal spoilage‡	190		
190 × 100%; 190 × 100%		190	190
Work in process, ending§	300		
300 ×100%; 300 × 40%	___	300	120
Total accounted for	2,100	2,100	1,920
Deduct work in process, beginning≠	400		
400 × 100%; 400 × 30%	___	400	120
Started during current period	1,700	___	___
Work done in current period only		1,700	1,800

† Normal spoilage is 15% of good units transferred out: 15% × 1,400 = 210 units; Degree of completion of normal spoilage in this department: direct materials, 100%; conversion costs, 100%.

‡ Actual spoilage = Beginning WIP + Units started – Units completed – Ending WIP
= 400 + 1,700 – 1,400 – 300 = 400.
Abnormal spoilage = Actual spoilage – Normal spoilage = 400 – 210 = 190 units; Degree of completion of abnormal spoilage in this department: direct materials, 100%; conversion costs, 100%.

§ Degree of completion in this department: direct materials, 100%; conversion costs, 40%.

≠ Degree of completion in this department: direct materials, 100%; conversion costs, 30%.

SOLUTION EXHIBIT 18-21B
Step 3: Compute Equivalent Unit Costs
Microchip Department of Superchip Company for September 19_7

	Direct Materials	Conversion Costs
Equivalent unit costs of beginning work in process		
Work in process, beginning (given)	$ 64,000	$ 10,200
Divide by equivalent units in beginning work in process (from Solution Exhibit 18-21A)	÷ 400	÷ 120
Cost per equivalent unit of beginning work in process	$ 160	$ 85
Equivalent unit costs of work done in current period only		
Costs added in current period (given)	$378,000	$153,600
Divide by equivalent units of work done in current period (from Solution Exhibit 18-21A)	÷ 1,700	÷ 1,800
Costs per equivalent unit of work done in current period only	$222.353	$ 85.333

18-22 (Cont'd.)

SOLUTION EXHIBIT 18-22

Step 4: Summarize Total Costs to Account For and Assign These Costs to Units Completed, Units Spoiled, and Units in Ending Work in Process Using the FIFO Method

Microchip Department of Superchip for September 19_7

	Direct Materials			Conversion Costs			Total Production Costs
	Equivalent Units (1)	Cost per Equivalent Unit (2)	Total Costs (3)= (1) x (2)	Equivalent Units (4)	Cost per Equivalent Unit (5)	Total Costs (6)=(4)x(5)	(7)= (3)+(6)
Panel A: Total Costs to Account For							
Work in process, beginning (from Solution Exhibit 18-21B)	400	$160	$ 64,000	120	$85	$ 10,200	$ 74,200
Work done in current period only (from Solution Exhibit 18-21B)	1,700	$222.353	378,000	1,800	$85.333	153,600	531,600
To account for	2,100		$442,000	1,920		$163,800	$605,800
Panel B: Assignment of Costs							
Good units completed and transferred out (1,400 physical units):							
Work in process, beginning (400 physical units)	400	$160	$ 64,000	120	$85	$ 10,200	$ 74,200
Work done in current period to complete beginning work in process	0*	$222.353	0	280†	$85.333	23,893	23,893
Total from beginning inventory before normal spoilage	400		64,000	400		34,093	98,093
Started and completed before normal spoilage (1,000 units)	1,000‡	$222.353	222,353	1,000‡	$85.333	85,333	307,686
Normal spoilage (210 units)	210§	$222.353	46,694	210§	$85.333	17,920	64,614
(A) Total costs of good units transferred out			333,047			137,346	470,393
(B) Abnormal spoilage (190 units)	190§	$222.353	42,247	190§	$85.333	16,214	58,461
(C) Work in process, ending (300 units)	300§	$222.353	66,706	120§	$85.333	10,240	76,946
(A)+(B)+(C) Accounted for	2,100		$442,000	1,920		$163,800	$605,800

* Beginning work in process is 100% complete as to direct materials so zero equivalent units of direct materials need to be added to complete beginning work in process.

† Beginning work in process is 30% complete as to conversion costs, which equals 120 equivalent units of conversion costs. To complete the 400 physical units of beginning work in process, 280 (400 − 120) equivalent units of conversion costs need to be added.

‡ 1,400 total equivalent units completed and transferred out (Solution Exhibit 18-21A) minus 400 equivalent units completed and transferred out from beginning inventory equal to 1,000 equivalent units.

§ From Solution Exhibit 18-21A.

18-24 (20-30 min.) **Spoilage and job costing.**

1. Cash   200
    Loss from Abnormal Spoilage   1,000
        Work in Process Control   1,200
    ($6.00)(200) – $200 = $1,000

Remaining cases cost = $6.00 per case. The cost of these cases are unaffected by the loss from abnormal spoilage.

2. a. Cash   400
            Work in Process Control   400

The cost of the remaining good cases = [($6.00 × 2,500) – $400] = $14,600
The unit cost of a good case now becomes $14,600 ÷ 2,300 = $6.3478

    b. Cash   400
        Manufacturing Department Overhead Control   800
            Work in Process Control   1,200

The unit cost of a good case remains at $6.00.

The unit cost in the cases 2(a) and 2(b) are different because in case (a), the normal spoilage cost, due to the exacting specifications of this particular job, is charged as a cost of this job. In case (b), the normal spoilage is due to the production process (not the particular attributes of this specific job). These costs are, therefore, charged as part of manufacturing overhead. The manufacturing overhead cost of $1 per case already includes a provision for normal spoilage.

3. a. Work in Process Control   200
            Materials Control, Wages Payable Control,
            Manufacturing Overhead Allocated   200

The cost of the good cases = [($6.00 × 2,500) + $200] = $15,200
The unit cost of a good case is $15,200 ÷ 2,500 = $6.08

    b. Manufacturing Department Overhead Control   200
            Materials Control, Wages Payable Control,
            Manufacturing Overhead Allocated   200
The unit cost of a good case = $6.00 per case
The unit cost in the cases 3(a) and 3(b) are different because in case (a), the normal rework cost, due to the exacting specifications of this particular job, is charged as a cost of this job. In case (b), the normal rework is due to the production process (not the particular attributes of this specific job). These costs are, therefore, charged as part of manufacturing overhead. The manufacturing overhead cost of $1 per case already includes a provision for this normal rework.

18-26 (25 min.) **Scrap, job-order costing.**

1.   Journal entry to record scrap generated by a specific job and accounted for at the time scrap is sold is:

Cash or Accounts Receivable	490	
Work in Process Control		490

To recognize asset from sale of scrap.
A posting is made to the specific job record.

2.   Scrap common to various jobs and accounted for at the time of its sale can be accounted for in two ways:

a.   Regard scrap sales as a separate line item of revenues:

Cash or Accounts Receivable	4,000	
Sale of Scrap		4,000

To recognize revenue from sale of scrap.

b.   Regard scrap sales as offsets against manufacturing overhead:

Cash or Accounts Receivable	4,000	
Manufacturing Department Overhead Control		4,000

To recognize revenue from sale of scrap.

3.   Journal entry to record scrap common to various jobs at the time scrap is returned to storeroom is:

Materials Control	4,000	
Manufacturing Department Overhead Control		4,000

To record value of scrap returned to storeroom.

When the scrap is reused as direct material on a subsequent job, the journal entry is:

Work in Process Control	4,000	
Materials Control		4,000

To record reuse of scrap on a job.

Explanations of journal entries are provided here but are not required.

18-28 (30 min.) Weighted-average method, spoilage.

1.   Solution Exhibit 18-28A calculates the equivalent units of work done for each cost element; Solution Exhibit 18-28B presents computations of the cost per equivalent unit of beginning inventory and of work done in the current period for each cost element under the weighted-average method; Solution Exhibit 18-28C presents a summary of total costs to account for and assigns these costs to units completed, normal spoilage, abnormal spoilage, and to units in ending work in process using the weighted-average method.

2.   From Solution Exhibit 18-28C, under the weighted-average method,

$$\text{Cost of a good unit completed (and transferred out)} = \frac{\text{Total production costs of good units transferred out}}{\text{Number of good units completed}}$$

$$= \frac{\$2,166,720}{61,000} = \$35.52$$

Note that this cost is higher than the cost per equivalent unit of $32 (direct materials, $20 and conversion costs, $12). Why? Because the cost of good units completed and transferred out also includes the cost of normal spoilage of 11%. The cost of a good unit completed and transferred out equals $32 + 11% of $32 = $35.52.

18-28 (Cont'd.)

SOLUTION EXHIBIT 18-28A
Steps 1 and 2: Summarize Output in Physical Units and Compute Equivalent Units
Cooking Department of Spicer Company for January

	(Step 1)	(Step 2) Equivalent Units	
Flow of Production	Physical Units	Direct Materials	Conversion Costs
Good units completed and transferred out during current period	61,000	61,000	61,000
Normal spoilage†	6,710		
6,710 × 100%; 6,710 × 100%		6,710	6,710
Abnormal spoilage‡	1,290		
1,290 × 100%; 1,290 × 100%		1,290	1,290
Work in process, ending§	16,000		
16,000 ×100%; 16,000 × 75%		16,000	12,000
Total accounted for	85,000	85,000	81,000
Deduct work in process, beginning≠	11,000		
11,000 × 100%; 11,000 × 25%		11,000	2,750
Started during current period	74,000		
Work done in current period only		74,000	78,250

† Normal spoilage is 11% of good units transferred out: 11% × 61,000 = 6,710 units; Degree of completion of normal spoilage in this department: direct materials, 100%; conversion costs, 100%.

‡ Abnormal spoilage = Actual spoilage – Normal spoilage = 8,000 – 6,710 = 1,290 units; Degree of completion of abnormal spoilage in this department: direct materials, 100%; conversion costs, 100%.

§ Degree of completion in this department: direct materials, 100%; conversion costs, 75%.

≠ Degree of completion in this department: direct materials, 100%; conversion costs, 25%.

SOLUTION EXHIBIT 18-28B
Step 3: Compute Equivalent Unit Costs
Cooking Department of Spicer Company for January

	Direct Materials	Conversion Costs
Equivalent unit costs of beginning work in process		
Work in process, beginning (given)	$ 220,000	$ 30,000
Divide by equivalent units in beginning work in process (from Solution Exhibit 18-28A)	÷ 11,000	÷ 2,750
Cost per equivalent unit of beginning work in process	$ 20	$ 10.909
Equivalent unit costs of work done in current period only		
Costs added in current period (given)	$1,480,000	$ 942,000
Divide by equivalent units of work done in current period (from Solution Exhibit 18-28A)	÷ 74,000	÷ 78,250
Costs per equivalent unit of work done in current period only	$ 20	$12.03834

18-13

18-28 (Cont'd.)

SOLUTION EXHIBIT 18-28C
Step 4: Summarize Total Costs to Account For and Assign These Costs to Units Completed, Units Spoiled, and Units in Ending Work in Process Using the Weighted-Average Method
Cooking Department of Spicer Company for January 19_7

	Direct Materials			Conversion Costs			Total Production Costs
	Equivalent Units (1)	Cost per Equivalent Unit (2)	Total Costs (3)=(1)x(2)	Equivalent Units (4)	Cost per Equivalent Unit (5)	Total Costs (6)=(4)x(5)	(7)=(3)+(6)
Panel A: Total Costs to Account For							
Work in process, beginning (from Solution Exhibit 18-28B)	11,000	$20	$ 220,000	2,750	$10.909	$ 30,000	$ 250,000
Work done in current period only (from Solution Exhibit 18-28B)	74,000	$20	1,480,000	78,250	$12.038	942,000	2,422,000
To account for	85,000	$20*	$1,700,000	81,000	$12†	$972,000	$2,672,000
Panel B: Assignment of Costs							
Good units completed and transferred out (61,000 units):							
Costs before adding normal spoilage	61,000‡	$20	$1,220,000	61,000‡	$12	$732,000	$1,952,000
Normal spoilage	6,710‡	$20	134,200	6,710‡	$12	80,520	214,720
(A) Total costs of good units transferred out			1,354,200			812,520	2,166,720
(B) Abnormal spoilage	1,290‡	$20	25,800	1,290‡	$12	15,480	41,280
(C) Work in process, ending	16,000‡	$20	320,000	12,000‡	$12	144,000	464,000
(A)+(B)+(C) Accounted for	85,000		$1,700,000	81,000		$972,000	$2,672,000

* Weighted-average cost per equivalent unit of direct materials = Total costs of direct materials divided by total equivalent units of direct materials = $1,700,000 ÷ 85,000 = $20.

† Weighted-average cost per equivalent unit of conversion costs = Total conversion costs divided by total equivalent units of conversion costs = $ 972,000 ÷ 81,000 = $12.

‡ From Solution Exhibit 18-28A.

18-30 (30 min.) **Standard costing method, spoilage.**

1.   Solution Exhibit 18-28A shows the computation of the equivalent units of work done in January for direct materials (74,000 units) and conversion costs (78,250 units).

The cost per equivalent unit of beginning work in process and of work done in the current period are the standard costs given in the problem, direct materials, $20 per unit, and conversion costs, $11 per unit.

Solution Exhibit 18-30 summarizes the total costs to account for and assigns these costs to units completed, normal spoilage, abnormal spoilage and ending work in process using the standard costing method.

2.   From Solution Exhibit 18-30, under the standard costing method,

$$\text{Standard cost of a good unit completed (and transferred out)} = \frac{\text{Total production costs of good units transferred out}}{\text{Number of good units completed}}$$

$$= \frac{\$2,099,010}{61,000} = \$34.41$$

Note that this cost is higher than the standard cost per equivalent unit of $31 (direct materials, $20 plus conversion costs, $11). Why? Because the cost of good units completed and transferred out also includes the cost of normal spoilage of 11%. The cost of good units completed and transferred out equals $31 + 11% of $31 = $34.41.

18-30 (Cont'd.)

SOLUTION EXHIBIT 18-30
Step 4: Summarize Total Costs to Account For and Assign These Costs to Units Completed, Units Spoiled, and Units in Ending Work in Process Using Standard Costs
Cooking Department of Spicer Company for January 19_7

		Direct Materials			Conversion Costs			Total Production Costs
		Equivalent Units (Solution Exhibit 18-28A) (1)	Cost per Equivalent Unit (2)	Total Costs (3) = (1) x (2)	Equivalent Units (Solution Exhibit 18-28A) (4)	Cost per Equivalent Unit (5)	Total Costs (6) = (4)x(5)	(7) = (3)+(6)
Panel A:	Total Costs to Account For							
	Work in process, beginning	11,000	$20	$ 220,000	2,750	$11	$ 30,250	$ 250,250
	Work done in current period only	74,000	$20	1,480,000	78,250	$11	860,750	2,340,750
	To account for	85,000	$20	$1,700,000	81,000	$11	$891,000	$2,591,000
Panel B:	Assignment of Costs							
	Good units completed and transferred out (61,000 units):							
	Costs before adding normal spoilage	61,000	$20	$1,220,000	61,000	$11	$671,000	$1,891,000
	Normal spoilage	6,710	$20	134,200	6,710	$11	73,810	208,010
(A)	Total costs of good units transferred out			1,354,200			744,810	2,099,010
(B)	Abnormal spoilage	1,290	$20	25,800	1,290	$11	14,190	39,990
(C)	Work in process, ending	16,000	$20	320,000	12,000	$11	132,000	452,000
(A)+(B)+(C)	Accounted for	85,000		$1,700,000	81,000		$891,000	$2,591,000

18-32 (25 min.) **FIFO method, spoilage.**

The equivalent units of work done in the Cleaning Department of the Alston Company in May for direct materials and conversion costs are the same as in problem 18-31 and are shown in Solution Exhibit 18-31A. The cost per equivalent unit of beginning inventory and of work done in the Cleaning Department in May for direct materials and conversion costs are calculated in problem 18-31 in Solution Exhibit 18-31B. Solution Exhibit 18-32 summarizes the total Cleaning Department costs for May and assigns these costs to units completed (and transferred out), normal spoilage, abnormal spoilage, and units in ending work-in-process under the FIFO method.

SOLUTION EXHIBIT 18-31A
Steps 1 and 2: Summarize Output in Physical Units and Compute Equivalent Units
Cleaning Department of Alston Company for May

	(Step 1) Physical Units	(Step 2) Equivalent Units	
Flow of Production		**Direct Materials**	**Conversion Costs**
Good units completed and transferred out during current period	7,400	7,400	7,400
Normal spoilage†	740		
740 × 100%; 740 × 100%		740	740
Abnormal spoilage‡	260		
260 × 100%; 260 × 100%		260	260
Work in process, ending§	1,600		
1,600 ×100%; 1,600 × 25%		1,600	400
Total accounted for	10,000	10,000	8,800
Deduct work in process, beginning≠	1,000		
1,000 × 100%; 1,000 × 80%		1,000	800
Started during current period	9,000		
Work done in current period only		9,000	8,000

† Normal spoilage is 10% of good units transferred out: 10% × 7,400 = 740 units; Degree of completion of normal spoilage in this department: direct materials, 100%; conversion costs, 100%.

‡ Degree of completion of abnormal spoilage in this department: direct materials, 100%; conversion costs, 100%.

§ Degree of completion in this department: direct materials, 100%; conversion costs, 25%.

≠ Degree of completion in this department: direct materials, 100%; conversion costs, 80%.

SOLUTION EXHIBIT 18-31B
Step 3: Compute Equivalent Unit Costs
Cleaning Department of Alston Company for May

	Direct Materials	Conversion Costs
Equivalent unit costs of beginning work in process		
Work in process, beginning (given)	$1,000	$ 800
Divide by equivalent units in beginning work in process (from Solution Exhibit 18-31A)	÷1,000	÷ 800
Cost per equivalent unit of beginning work in process	$ 1	$ 1
Equivalent unit costs of work done in current period only		
Costs added in current period (given)	$9,000	$8,000
Divide by equivalent units of work done in current period (from Solution Exhibit 18-31A)	÷9,000	÷8,000
Costs per equivalent unit of work done in current period only	$ 1	$ 1

18-32 (Cont'd.)

SOLUTION EXHIBIT 18-32

Step 4: Summarize Total Costs to Account For and Assign These Costs to Units Completed, Units Spoiled, and Units in Ending Work in Process Using the FIFO Method
Cleaning Department of Alston for May

	Direct Materials			Conversion Costs			Total Production Costs
	Equivalent Units (1)	Cost per Equivalent Unit (2)	Total Costs (3)=(1) x (2)	Equivalent Units (4)	Cost per Equivalent Unit (5)	Total Costs (6)=(4)x(5)	(7)=(3)+(6)
Panel A: Total Costs to Account For							
Work in process, beginning (from Solution Exhibit 18-30B)	1,000	$1	$ 1,000	800	$1	$ 800	$ 1,800
Work done in current period only (from Solution Exhibit 18-30B)	9,000	$1	9,000	8,000	$1	8,000	17,000
To account for	10,000		$10,000	8,800		$8,800	$18,800
Panel B: Assignment of Costs							
Good units completed and transferred out (7,400 physical units):							
Work in process, beginning (1,000 physical units)	1,000	$1	$ 1,000	800	$1	$ 800	$ 1,800
Work done in current period to complete beginning work in process	0*	$1	0	200†	$1	200	200
Total from beginning inventory before normal spoilage			1,000			1,000	2,000
Started and completed before normal spoilage (6,400 units)	6,400‡	$1	6,400	6,400‡	$1	6,400	12,800
Normal spoilage (740 units)	740§	$1	740	740§	$1	740	1,480
(A) Total costs of good units transferred out			8,140			8,140	16,280
(B) Abnormal spoilage (260 units)	260§	$1	260	260§	$1	260	520
(C) Work in process, ending (1,600 units)	1,600§	$1	1,600	400§	$1	400	2,000
(A)+(B)+(C) Accounted for	10,000		$10,000	8,800		$8,800	$18,800

* Beginning work in process is 100% complete as to direct materials so zero equivalent units of direct materials need to be added to complete beginning work in process.
† Beginning work in process is 80% complete as to conversion costs, which equals 800 equivalent units of conversion costs. To complete the 1,000 physical units of beginning work in process, 200 (1,000 – 800) equivalent units of conversion costs need to be added.
‡ 7,400 total equivalent units completed and transferred out (Solution Exhibit 18-31A) minus 1,000 equivalent units completed and transferred out from beginning inventory equal to 6,400 equivalent units.
§ From Solution Exhibit 18-31A.

18-34 (25 min.) **FIFO method, Milling Department.**

The equivalent units of work done in the Milling Department in May for transferred-in costs, direct materials and conversion costs are the same as in problem 18-33 and are shown in Solution Exhibit 18-33A. The cost per equivalent unit of beginning inventory and of work done in the Cooking Department in January for transferred-in costs, direct materials and conversion costs are calculated in problem 18-33 in Solution Exhibit 18-33B. Solution Exhibit 18-34 summarizes the total Milling Department costs for May and assigns these costs to units completed (and transferred out), normal spoilage, abnormal spoilage, and units in ending work-in-process under the FIFO method.

SOLUTION EXHIBIT 18-33A
Steps 1 and 2: Summarize Output in Physical Units and Compute Equivalent Units
Milling Department of Alston Company for May

| | (Step 1) | (Step 2) Equivalent Units | | |
| | Physical | Transferred | Direct | Conversion |
Flow of Production	Units	-in Costs	Materials	Costs
Good units completed and transferred out during current period	6,000	6,000	6,000	6,000
Normal spoilage†	300			
300 × 100%; 300 × 100%; 300 × 100%		300	300	300
Abnormal spoilage‡	100			
100 × 100%; 100 × 100%; 100 × 100%		100	100	100
Work in process, ending§	4,000			
4,000 ×100%; 4,000 × 0%; 4,000 × 25%		4,000	0	1,000
Total accounted for	10,400	10,400	6,400	7,400
Deduct work in process, beginning≠	3,000			
3,000 × 100%; 3,000 × 0%; 3,000 × 80%		3,000	0	2,400
Started during current period	7,400			
Work done in current period only		7,400	6,400	5,000

†Normal spoilage is 5% of good units transferred out: 5% × 6,000 = 300 units; Degree of completion of normal spoilage in this department: transferred-in costs, 100%; direct materials, 100%; conversion costs, 100%.

‡Degree of completion of abnormal spoilage in this department: transferred-in costs, 100%; direct materials, 100%; conversion costs, 100%.

§Degree of completion in this department: transferred-in costs, 100% direct materials, 0%; conversion costs, 25%.

≠Degree of completion in this department: transferred-in costs, 100% direct materials, 0%; conversion costs, 80%.

18-34 (Cont'd.)

SOLUTION EXHIBIT 18-33B
Step 3: Compute Equivalent Unit Costs
Milling Department of Alston Company for May

	Transferred -in Costs	Direct Materials	Conversion Costs
Equivalent unit costs of beginning work in process			
Work in process, beginning (Solution Exhibit 18-31C)	$ 6,450	—	$2,450
Divide by equivalent units in beginning work in process (from Solution Exhibit 18-33A)	÷ 3,000	—	÷2,400
Cost per equivalent unit of beginning work in process	$ 2.15	—	$1.021
Equivalent unit costs of work done in current period only			
Costs added in current period (Solution Exhibit 18-31C)	$16,280	$ 640	$4,950
Divide by equivalent units of work done in current period (from Solution Exhibit 18-33A)	÷ 7,400	÷6,400	÷5,000
Costs per equivalent unit of work done in current period only	$ 2.20	$ 0.10	$ 0.99

18-34 (Cont.d)

SOLUTION EXHIBIT 18-34

Step 4: Summarize Total Costs to Account For and Assign These Costs to Units Completed, Units Spoiled, and Units in Ending Work in Process Using the FIFO Method
Milling Department of Alston for May

	Transferred-in Costs			Direct Materials			Conversion Costs			Total Production Cost
	Equivalent Unit (1)	Cost per Equivalent Unit (2)	Total Costs (3)=(1)×(2)	Equivalent Unit (4)	Cost per Equivalent Unit (5)	Total Costs (6)=(4)×(5)	Equivalent Unit (7)	Cost per Equivalent Unit (8)	Total Costs (9)=(7)×(8)	(10)=(3)+(6)+(9)
Panel A: Total Costs to Account For:										
Work in process, beginning (from Solution Exhibit 18-33B)	3,000	$2.15	$ 6,450	—	—	—	2,400	$1.021	$2,450	$ 8,900
Work done in current period only (from Solution Exhibit, 18-33B)	7,400	$2.20	16,280	6,400	$0.10	$640	5,000	$0.99	4,950	21,870
To account for	10,400		$22,730	6,400		$640	7,400		$7,400	$30,770
Panel B: Assignment of Costs										
Good units completed and transferred out (6,000 physical units):										
Work in process, beginning (3,000 physical units)	3,000	$2.15	$ 6,450	—	—	—	2,400	$1.021	$2,450	$ 8,900
Work done in current period to complete beginning WIP	0#	$2.20	0	3,000*	$0.10	$300	600†	$0.99	594	894
Total from beginning inventory before normal spoilage	3,000		6,450	3,000		300	3,000		3,044	9,794
Started and completed before normal spoilage (3,000 units)	3,000‡	$2.20	6,600	3,000‡	$0.10	300	3,000‡	$0.99	2,970	9,870
Normal spoilage (300 units)	300§	$2.20	660	300§	$0.10	30	300§	$0.99	297	987
(A) Total costs of good units tfd. out			13,710			630			6,311	20,651
(B) Abnormal spoilage (100 units)	100§	$2.20	220	100§	$0.10	10	100§	$0.99	99	329
(C) Work in process, ending	4,000§	$2.20	8,800	0§	$0.10	0	1,000§	$0.99	990	9,790
(A)+(B)+(C) Accounted for	10,400		$22,730	6,400		$640	7,400		$7,400	$30,770

Beginning work in process is 100% complete as to transferred-in costs so zero equivalent units of transferred-in costs need to be added to complete beginning work in process.

* Beginning work in process is 0% complete as to direct materials so 3,000 equivalent units of direct materials need to be added to complete the 3,000 physical units of beginning work in process.

† Beginning work in process is 80% complete as to conversion costs, which equals 2,400 equivalent units of conversion costs. To complete the 3,000 physical units of beginning work in process, 600 (3,000 – 2,400) equivalent units of conversion costs need to be added.

‡ 6,000 total equivalent units completed and transferred out (Solution Exhibit 18-33A) minus 3,000 equivalent units completed and transferred out from beginning inventory equal to 3,000 equivalent units.

§ From Solution Exhibit 18-33A.

18-36 (30 min.) **Job costing, rework.**

1.

Work in Process Control (SM-5 motors) ($550 × 80)	44,000	
Materials Control ($300 × 80)		24,000
Wages Payable ($60 × 80)		4,800
Manufacturing Overhead Allocated ($190 × 80)		15,200

Total costs assigned to 80 spoiled units of SM-5 Motors before
  considering rework costs.

Manufacturing Department Overhead Control (rework)	9,000	
Materials Control ($60 × 50)		3,000
Wages Payable ($45 × 50)		2,250
Manufacturing Overhead Allocated ($75 × 50)		3,750

Normal rework on 50 units, but not attributable specifically to the
  SM-5 motor batches or jobs.

Loss from Abnormal Rework ($180 × 30)	5,400	
Materials Control ($60 × 30)		1,800
Wages Payable ($45 × 30)		1,350
Manufacturing Overhead Allocated ($75 × 30)		2,250

Total costs of abnormal rework on 30 units
(Abnormal rework = Actual rework – Normal rework
= 80 – 50 = 30 units) of SM-5 Motors.

Work in Process Control (SM-5 motors)	6,000	
Work in Process Control (RW-8 motors)	3,000	
Manufacturing Department Overhead Allocated (rework)		9,000

(Allocating manufacturing department rework costs to SM-5 and
  RW-8 in the proportion 1,000:500 since each motor requires the
  same number of machine hours.)

2. Total rework costs for SM-5 motors in February 19_8 are as follows:

Normal rework costs allocated to SM-5	$6,000
Abnormal rework costs for SM-5	5,400
Total rework costs	$11,400

We emphasize two points:

a. Only $6,000 of the normal rework costs are allocated to SM-5 even though the normal rework costs of the 50 SM-5 motors reworked equal $9,000. The reason is that the normal rework costs are not specifically attributable to SM-5. For example, the machines happened to malfunction when SM-5 was being made but the rework was not caused by the specific requirements of SM-5. If it were, then all $9,000 would be charged to SM-5.

b. Abnormal rework costs of $5,400 are pegged to SM-5 in the management control system, even though for financial reporting purposes, the abnormal rework costs are written off to the income statement.

18-38 (25-35 min.) **Weighted-average, inspection at 80% completion.**

The computation and allocation of spoilage is the most difficult part of this problem. The units in the ending inventory have passed inspection. Therefore, of the 80,000 units to account for (10,000 beginning + 70,000 started), 10,000 must have been spoiled in June [80,000 − (50,000 completed + 20,000 ending inventory)]. Normal spoilage is 7,000 [0.10 × (50,000 + 20,000)]. The 3,000 remainder is abnormal spoilage (10,000 − 7,000).

Solution Exhibit 18-38A calculates the equivalent units of work done for each cost element. We comment on several points in this calculation:

- Ending work in process includes an element of normal spoilage since all the ending WIP have passed the point of inspection—inspection occurs when production is 80% complete, while the units in ending WIP are 95% complete.
- Spoilage includes no direct materials units because spoiled units are detected and removed from the finishing activity when inspection occurs at the time production is 80% complete. Direct materials are added only later when production is 90% complete.
- Direct materials units are included for ending work in process, which is 95% complete, but not for beginning work in process, which is 25% complete. The reason is that direct materials are added when production is 90% complete. The ending work in process, therefore contains direct materials units, the beginning work in process does not.

Solution Exhibit 18-38B presents computations of the cost per equivalent unit of beginning inventory and of work done in the current period for each cost element under the weighted-average method.

Solution Exhibit 18-38C presents a summary of total costs to account for and assigns these costs to units completed, normal spoilage, abnormal spoilage, and to units in ending work in process using the weighted-average method. The cost of ending work in process includes the assignment of normal spoilage costs since these units have passed the point of inspection. The costs assigned to each cost element are as follows:

Cost of good units completed and transferred out (including normal spoilage costs on good units)	$1,877,350
Abnormal spoilage	67,710
Cost of ending work in process (including normal spoilage costs on ending work in process)	734,140
Total costs assigned and accounted for	$2,679,200

18-38 (Cont'd.)

SOLUTION EXHIBIT 18-38A

Steps 1 and 2: Summarize Output in Physical Units and Compute Equivalent Units
Finishing Department of Ottawa Manufacturing for June

Flow of Production	(Step 1) Physical Units	(Step 2) Equivalent Units		
		Transferred -in Costs	Direct Materials	Conversion Costs
Good units completed and transferred out during current period	50,000	50,000	50,000	50,000
Normal spoilage on good units[†]	5,000			
$5,000 \times 100\%; 5,000 \times 0\%; 5,000 \times 80\%$		5,000	0	4,000
Work in process, ending[§]	20,000			
$20,000 \times 100\%; 20,000 \times 100\%; 20,000 \times 95\%$		20,000	20,000	19,000
Normal spoilage on ending WIP[†]	2,000			
$2,000 \times 100\%; 2,000 \times 0\%; 2,000 \times 80\%$		2,000	0	1,600
Abnormal spoilage[‡]	3,000			
$3,000 \times 100\%; 3,000 \times 0\%; 3,000 \times 80\%$		3,000	0	2,400
Total accounted for	80,000	80,000	70,000	77,000
Deduct work in process, beginning[≠]	10,000			
$10,000 \times 100\%; 10,000 \times 0\%; 10,000 \times 25\%$		10,000	0	2,500
Started during current period	70,000			
Work done in current period only		70,000	70,000	74,500

[†] Normal spoilage is 10% of good units that pass inspection, which occurs when production is 80% complete: $10\% \times 70,000 = 7,000$ units; Degree of completion of normal spoilage in this department: transferred-in costs, 100%; direct materials, 0%; conversion costs, 80%.

[§] Degree of completion in this department: transferred-in costs, 100%; direct materials, 100%; conversion costs, 95%.

[‡] Abnormal spoilage = Actual spoilage – Normal spoilage = $10,000 – 5,000 – 2,000 = 3,000$. Degree of completion of abnormal spoilage in this department: transferred-in costs, 100%; direct materials, 0%; conversion costs, 80%.

[≠] Degree of completion in this department: transferred-in costs, 100%; direct materials, 0%; conversion costs, 25%.

18-38 (Cont'd.)

SOLUTION EXHIBIT 18-38B
Step 3: Compute Equivalent Unit Costs
Finishing Department of Ottawa Manufacturing for June

	Transferred -in Costs	Direct Materials	Conversion Costs
Equivalent unit costs of beginning work in process			
Work in process, beginning (given)	$ 82,900	—	$ 42,000
Divide by equivalent units in beginning work in process (from Solution Exhibit 18-38A)	÷ 10,000	—	÷ 2,500
Cost per equivalent unit of beginning work in process	$ 8.29	—	$ 16.80
Equivalent unit costs of work done in current period only			
Costs added in current period (given)	$647,500	$655,200	$1,251,600
Divide by equivalent units of work done in current period (from Solution Exhibit 18-38A)	÷ 70,000	÷ 70,000	÷ 74,500
Costs per equivalent unit of work done in current period only	$ 9.25	$ 9.36	$ 16.80

SOLUTION EXHIBIT 18-38C

Step 4: Summarize Total Costs to Account For and Assign These Costs to Units Completed, Units Spoiled, and Units in Ending Work in Process Using the Weighted-Average Method, Finishing Department of Ottawa Manufacturing for June

	Transferred-in Costs			Direct Materials			Conversion Costs			Total Production Cost
	Equivalent Units (1)	Cost per Equivalent Unit (2)	Total Costs (3)=(1)×(2)	Equivalent Units (4)	Cost per Equivalent Unit (5)	Total Costs (6)=(4)×(5)	Equivalent Units (7)	Cost per Equivalent Unit (8)	Total Costs (9)=(7)×(8)	(10)=(3)+(6)+(9)
Panel A: Total Costs to Account For:										
Work in process, beginning (from Solution Exhibit 18-38B)	10,000	$8.29	$ 82,900	—	—	—	2,500	$16.80	$ 42,000	$ 124,900
Work done in current period only (from Solution Exhibit 18-38B)	70,000	$9.25	647,500	70,000	$9.36	$655,200	74,500	$16.80	1,251,600	2,554,300
To account for	80,000	$9.13#	$730,400	70,000	$9.36*	$655,200	77,000	$16.80†	$1,293,600	$2,679,200
Panel B: Assignment of Costs										
Good units completed and transferred out (50,000 units):										
Costs before adding norml. splge.	50,000‡	$9.13	$456,500	50,000‡	$9.36	$468,000	50,000‡	$16.80	$ 840,000	$1,764,500
Normal spoilage	5,000‡	$9.13	45,650	0‡	$9.36	0	4,000‡	$16.80	67,200	112,850
(A) Total costs of good units tranfd.			502,150			468,000			907,200	1,877,350
(B) Abnormal spoilage	3,000‡	$9.13	27,390	0‡	$9.36	0	2,400‡	$16.80	40,320	67,710
Work in process, ending										
WIP ending, before nrml. splge.	20,000‡	$9.13	182,600	20,000‡	$9.36	187,200	19,000‡	$16.80	319,200	689,000
Nrml. spoilage on ending WIP	2,000‡	$9.13	18,260	0‡	$9.36	0	1,600‡	$16.80	26,880	45,140
(C) Total costs of ending WIP			200,860			187,200			346,080	734,140
(A)+(B)+(C) Accounted for	80,000		$730,400	70,000		$655,200	77,000		$1,293,600	$2,679,200

#Weighted-average cost per equiv. unit of transferred-in costs = Total transferred-in costs divided by total equiv. units of transferred-in costs = $730,400 ÷ 80,000 = $9.13.

*Weighted-average cost per equivalent unit of direct materials = Total direct materials costs divided by total equivalent units of direct materials = $655,200 ÷ 70,000 = $9.36.

†Weighted-average cost per equivalent unit of conversion costs = Total conversion costs divided by total equivalent units of conversion costs = $1,293,600 ÷ 77,000 = $16.80.

‡From Solution Exhibit 18-38A.

18-40 (40 min.) Job costing, spoilage.

1. Analysis of the 5,000 units rejected by Richport Company for Job No. N1192-122 yields the following breakdown between normal and abnormal spoilage.

	Units
Normal spoilage*	3,000
Abnormal spoilage:	
Design defect	900
Other [5,000 – (3,000 + 900)]	1,100
Total units rejected	5,000

* Normal spoilage = 0.025 of normal input
   When output equals 117,000 units,
     Normal input = $117,000 \div (1 - 0.025)$
              = 120,000 units

   Normal spoilage = $120,000 \times 0.025$
                = 3,000 units

2. The journal entries required to properly account for Job No. N1192-122 are presented below and use an average cost per unit of $57 ($6,954,000 ÷ 122,000).

Materials control (or A/R or cash)[1]	28,700	
Abnormal loss[2]	107,500	
WIP control[3]		135,000
Cash[4]		1,200

To account for 5,000 units rejected.

Finished good inventory	6,819,000	
WIP control		6,819,000

To transfer 117,000 units to finished goods inventory.

[1] Units for sale 4,100 units sold at $7 each.
[2] Loss from abnormal spoilage:

2,000 units at $57	$114,000
Disposal cost	1,200
Cost recovery (1,100 × $7)	(7,700)
	$107,500

[3] WIP control:

900 defective units at $57	$51,300
1,100 other rejected units at $57	62,700
3,000 normal units at $7	21,000
	$135,000

[4] Additional cost to dispose of 900 units rejected because of design defect.

3.   One interpretation of the data could be that the abnormal loss ($107,500) is not large relative to the total manufacturing costs ($6,954,000), or around 1.5%. But this could be important if Richmond's profit margins are small. Also, the abnormal spoilage comes on top of a 2.5% allowance for normal spoilage. The total costs of spoilage may, therefore, be significant.

The accounting for spoilage reveals a loss due to abnormal spoilage. Richmond Company's management would need to understand and analyze the reasons for this loss. In order to be responsive to its customers, Richmond must often make specification changes or modifications to its products. But it cannot afford to have design defects of the kind that resulted in the first 900 units of the current job being rejected. Management would need to understand why the defects were not detected earlier, say, after the first 50 or 100 units were produced.

Richmond's management should also be concerned that Rose Duncan, one of the company's inspection managers, was not able to identify a rejection pattern, and in particular the reasons for the rejection of the remaining 4,100 units. To improve quality, companies pay special attention to identifying the reasons for and the root causes of quality problems. They often find that a few key causes are responsible for the great majority of defects. They then go about solving the problems that caused these defects, for example, by changing product designs, methods of manufacture, investing in new equipment, or training the work force better.

If it can reduce the amounts of abnormal spoilage, Richmond's management can seek to reduce the levels of acceptable or normal spoilage, perhaps from 2.5% of normal inputs to 1%. Many companies have a goal of reducing defects to zero.

4.   As indicated in the response to requirement 3, Richmond needs to do a better job of managing spoilage and quality. The amount of abnormal spoilage is a concern, as are the facts that a large quantity of first units were rejected and that no clear understanding exists for the reasons that caused other units to be rejected. Management needs to aggressively pursue a policy of reducing both normal and abnormal spoilage.

CHAPTER 19
COST MANAGEMENT: QUALITY, TIME, AND THE THEORY OF CONSTRAINTS

19-2 Quality of design measures how closely the characteristics of products or services match the needs and wants of customers. Conformance quality measures whether the product has been made according to design, engineering and manufacturing specifications.

19-4 An internal failure cost differs from an external failure cost on the basis of when the nonconforming product is detected. An internal failure is detected *before* a product is shipped to a customer, whereas an external failure is detected *after* a product is shipped to a customer.

19-6 No, companies should emphasize financial as well as nonfinancial measures of quality, such as yield and defect rates. Nonfinancial measures are not directly linked to bottom-line performance but they indicate and direct attention to the specific areas that need improvement. Tracking nonfinancial measures over time directly reveals whether these areas have, in fact, improved over time. Nonfinancial measures are easy to quantify and easy to understand.

19-8 Examples of nonfinancial measures of internal performance are:
1. The number of defects for each product line.
2. Process yield (rates of good output to total output at a particular process).
3. Manufacturing lead time (the time taken to convert direct materials into finished output).
4. Employee turnover (ratio of the number of employees who left the company in a year, say, to the total number of employees who worked for the company in that year).

19-10 No. There is a trade-off between customer-response time and on-time performance. Simply scheduling longer customer-response time makes achieving on-time performance easier. Companies should, however, attempt to reduce uncertainty of arrival of orders, manage bottlenecks, reduce setup and processing time, and run smaller batches. This would have the effect of reducing both customer-response time and improving on-time performance.

19-12 No. Adding a product when capacity is constrained and the timing of customer orders is uncertain causes delays in delivering all existing products. If the revenue losses from delays in delivering existing products and the increase in carrying costs of the existing products exceed the positive contribution earned by the product that was added, then it is not worthwhile to make and sell the new product, despite its positive contribution margin. The chapter describes the negative effects (negative externalities) that one product can have on others when products share common manufacturing facilities.

19-14   The four key steps in managing bottleneck resources are:

Step 1: Recognize that the bottleneck operation determines throughput contribution.

Step 2: Search for and find the bottleneck.

Step 3: Keep the bottleneck busy and subordinate all nonbottleneck operations to the bottleneck operation.

Step 4: Increase bottleneck efficiency and capacity.

19-16   (15 min.)   **Cost of quality program, nonfinancial quality measures.**

1.   (i)   Prevention cost:
   d: Labor cost of product designer of Baden Engineering
   f: Seminar costs for "Vendor Day" a program aimed at communicating to vendors the new quality requirements for purchased components

   (ii)   Appraisal cost:
   a: Cost of inspecting products on the production line by Baden quality inspectors

   (iii)   Internal failure cost:
   c: Costs of reworking defective parts detected by Baden Engineering quality assurance group
   g: Costs of spoiled parts

   (iv)   External failure cost:
   b: Payment of travel costs for a Baden Engineering customer representative to meet with a customer who detected a defective product
   e: Cost of automotive parts returned by customer

2.   Example of nonfinancial performance measures Baden could monitor include:
   • first-pass calibration yield
   • outgoing quality yield for each product
   • returned merchandise %
   • customer report card
   • competitive rank
   • on-time delivery

19-18 (30–40 min.) **Costs of quality analysis, nonfinancial quality measures.**

1. & 2.

Sales, Costs of Quality and Costs of Quality as a Percentage of Sales for Olivia

Sales = $2,000 × 10,000 units = $20,000,000

Costs of Quality	Cost (1)	Percentage of Sales (2) = (1) ÷ $20,000,000
Prevention costs		
Design engineering ($75 × 6,000 hours)	$ 450,000	2.25%
Appraisal costs		
Testing and inspection ($40 × 1 hour × 10,000 units)	400,000	2.00%
Internal failure costs		
Rework ($500 × 5% × 10,000 units)	250,000	1.25%
External failure costs		
Repair ($600 × 4% × 10,000 units)	240,000	1.20%
Total costs of quality	$1,340,000	6.70%

Sales, Costs of Quality and Costs of Quality as a Percentage of Sales for Solta

Sales: $1,500 × 5,000 units = $7,500,000

Costs of Quality	Costs (1)	Percentage of Sales (2)=(1)÷$7,500,000
Prevention costs		
Design engineering ($75 × 1,000 hours)	$ 75,000	1.00%
Appraisal costs		
Testing and inspection ($40 × 0.5 × 5,000 units)	100,000	1.33%
Internal failure costs		
Rework ($400 × 10% × 5,000 units)	200,000	2.67%
External failure costs		
Repair ($450 × 8% × 5,000 units)	180,000	2.40%
Estimated forgone contribution margin on lost sales [($1,500 – $800) × 300]	210,000	2.80%
Total external failure costs	390,000	5.20%
Total costs of quality	$765,000	10.20%

Costs of quality as a percentage of sales are significantly different for Solta (10.20%) compared with Olivia (6.70%). Ontario spends very little on prevention and appraisal activities for Solta, and incurs high costs of internal and external failures. Ontario follows a different strategy with respect to Olivia, spending a greater percentage of sales on prevention and appraisal activities. The result: fewer internal and external failure costs and lower overall costs of quality as a percentage of sales compared with Solta.

3.   Examples of nonfinancial quality measures that Ontario Industries could monitor as part of a total-quality-control effort are
   a.   Outgoing quality yield for each product.
   b.   Returned refrigerator percentage for each product.
   c.   On-time delivery.
   d.   Employee turnover.

19-20   (25 min.)   **Quality improvement, relevant costs, and relevant revenues.**

1.   Incremental costs over the next year of choosing the new lens $= \$50 \times 20{,}000$ copiers $= \$1{,}000{,}000$

2.

	Incremental Benefits Over the Next Year of Choosing the New Lens
Costs of quality items	
Savings on rework costs	
$\$1{,}600 \times 300$ fewer copiers reworked	$ 480,000
Savings in customer-support costs	
$\$80 \times 200$ fewer copiers repaired	16,000
Savings in transportation costs for parts	
$\$180 \times 200$ fewer copiers repaired	36,000
Savings in warranty repair costs	
$\$1{,}800 \times 200$ fewer copiers repaired	360,000
Opportunity costs	
Contribution margin from increased sales	
$100 \times \$6{,}000$	600,000
Cost savings and additional contribution margin	$1,492,000

3.   Since the expected benefits of $1,492,000 (requirement 2) exceed the costs of the new lens of $1,000,000 (requirement 1), Photon should introduce the new lens. Note that the opportunity cost benefits in the form of higher contribution margin from increased sales is an important component for justifying the investment in the new lens. The incremental cost of the new lens of $1,000,000 is greater than the incremental savings in rework and repair costs of $892,000. Investing in the new lens is beneficial provided it generates additional contribution margin of at least $108,000 ($1,000,000 – $892,000), that is, additional sales of at least $108,000 ÷ $6,000 = 18 copiers.

19-22   (20–25 min.)   **Waiting time, relevant costs, and relevant revenues.**

1.   If the branch expects to receive 60 customers each day and it takes 4 minutes to serve a customer, the average time that a customer will wait in line before being served is:

$$= \frac{[60 \times (4)^2]}{2 \times [300 - (60 \times 4)]} = \frac{(60 \times 16)}{2 \times (300 - 240)} = \frac{60 \times 16}{2 \times 60} = \frac{960}{120} = 8 \text{ minutes}$$

2.   Suppose the bank counter is kept open for X minutes. Then we want

$$\frac{[60 \times (4)^2]}{2 \times [X - (60 \times 4)]} = 5 \text{ minutes}$$

that is,

$$60 \times 16 = 10(X - 240)$$

$$X - 240 = (60 \times 16) \div 10 = 96$$

$$X = 336 \text{ minutes}$$

The counter must be kept open for 336 minutes to reduce average waiting time to 5 minutes.

3.
Incremental operating income from providing new services	$30
Incremental teller cost	
(1 additional hour × $10 per hour)	10
Net increase in operating income	
from providing new services	$20

Yes, the bank should offer the new services since the relevant benefits exceed the relevant costs.

19-24 (15 min.) **Theory of constraints, throughput contribution, relevant costs.**

1.   Finishing is a bottleneck operation. Hence, getting an outside contractor to produce 12,000 units will increase throughput contribution.

Increase in throughput contribution ($72 – $32) × 12,000	$480,000
Incremental contracting costs $10 × 12,000	120,000
Net benefit of contracting 12,000 units of finishing	$360,000

Mayfield should contract with an outside contractor to do 12,000 units of finishing at $10 per unit because the benefit of higher throughput contribution of $480,000 exceeds the cost of $120,000. The fact that the costs of $10 are double Mayfield's finishing costs of $5 per unit are irrelevant.

2.   Operating costs in the Machining Department of $640,000, or $8 per unit, are fixed costs. Mayfield will not save any of these costs by subcontracting machining of 4,000 units to Hunt Corporation. Total costs will be greater by $16,000 ($4 per unit × 4,000 units) under the subcontracting alternative. Machining more filing cabinets will not increase throughput contribution, which is constrained by the finishing capacity. Mayfield should not accept Hunt's offer. The fact that Hunt's costs of machining per unit are half of what it costs Mayfield in-house is irrelevant.

19-26 (30 min.) **Quality improvement, relevant costs, and relevant revenues.**

One way to present the alternatives is via a decision tree, as shown below.

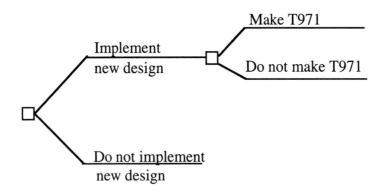

The idea is to first evaluate the best action that Thomas should take if it implements the new design (that is, make or not make T971). Thomas can then compare the best mix of products to produce if it implements the new design against the status quo of not implementing the new design.

1.   Thomas has capacity constraints. Demand for V262 valves (370,000 valves) exceeds production capacity of 330,000 valves (3 valves per hour × 110,000 machine-hours). Since capacity is constrained, Thomas will choose to sell the product that maximizes contribution margin per machine-hour (the constrained resource).

19-26 (Cont'd.)

Contribution margin per
machine-hour for V262 $= \$8$ per valve $\times$ 3 valves per hour $= \$24$

Contribution margin per
machine-hour for T971 $= \$10$ per valve $\times$ 2 valves per hour $= \$20$.

Thomas should reject Jackson Corporation's offer and continue to only manufacture V262 valves.

2. Now compare the alternatives of (a) not implementing the new design versus (b) implementing the new design. By implementing the new design, Thomas will save 10,000 machine-hours of rework time. This time can then be used to make and sell 30,000 (3 valves per hour $\times$ 10,000 hours) additional V262 valves. The relevant costs and benefits of implementing the new design follow:

The <u>relevant costs</u> of implementing the new design	$(315,000)
Relevant benefits:	
(a) Savings in rework costs ($3[a] per V262 valve $\times$ 30,000 valves)	90,000
(b) Additional contribution margin from selling another 30,000 V262 valves (3 valves per hour $\times$ 10,000 hours) because capacity previously used for rework is freed up ($8 per valve $\times$ 30,000 units)	240,000
Net relevant benefit (cost)	$ 15,000

Thomas should implement the new design since the relevant benefits exceed the relevant costs by $15,000.

[a] Note that the fixed rework costs of equipment rent and allocated overhead are irrelevant, because these costs will be incurred whether Thomas implements or does not implement the new design.

3. Thomas Corporation should also consider other benefits of improving quality. For example, the process of quality improvement will help Thomas's managers and workers gain expertise about the product and the manufacturing process that may lead to further cost reductions in the future. Improving quality within the plant is also likely to translate into delivering better quality products to customers. The increased reputation and customer goodwill may well lead to higher future revenues through greater unit sales and higher sales prices.

19-28   (30–40 min.)   **Statistical quality control, airline operations.**

1.   The $\pm 2\sigma$ rule will trigger a decision to investigate when the round-trip fuel usage is outside the control limit:

$$\text{Mean} \pm 2\sigma = 100 \pm 2\sigma = 100 \pm (2 \times 10) \text{ or } 80 \text{ to } 120 \text{ gallon-units}$$

Any fuel usage less than 80 gallon-units or greater than 120 gallon-units will trigger a decision to investigate.

The only plane to be outside the specified $\mu \pm 2\sigma$ fuel usage control limit is the Spirit of Manchester on flights #5 (122 gallon-units), #7 (126 gallon-units), and #10 (123 gallon-units).

2.   Solution Exhibit 19-21 presents the SQC charts for each of the three 747s.

The Spirit of Birmingham has no observation outside the $\mu \pm 2\sigma$ control limits. However, there was an increase in fuel use in each of the last eight round-trip flights. The probability of eight consecutive increases from an in-control process is very low.

The Spirit of Glasgow appears in control regarding fuel usage.

The Spirit of Manchester has three observations outside the $\mu + 2\sigma$ control limits. Moreover, the mean on the last six flights is 120 compared to a mean of 104 for the first four flights.

3.   The advantage of using dollar fuel costs as the unit of analysis in an SQC chart is that it focuses on a variable of overriding concern to top managers (operating costs).

However, the disadvantages of using dollar fuel costs are:
   a.   Split responsibilities. Operations managers may not control the purchase of fuel, and may want to exclude from their performance measures any variation stemming from factors outside their control.
   b.   Offsetting factors may mask important underlying trends when the quantity used and the price paid are combined in a single observation. For example, decreasing gallon usage may be offset by increasing fuel costs. Both of these individual patterns are important in budgeting for an airline.
   c.   The distribution of fuel usage in gallons may be different from the distribution of fuel prices per gallon. More reliable estimates of the μ and σ parameters might be obtained by focusing separately on the individual usage and price distributions.

Note: The above disadvantages are most marked if actual fuel prices are used. The use of standard fuel prices can reduce many of these disadvantages.

19-28 (Cont'd.)

SOLUTION EXHIBIT 19-28
Plots of round-trip fuel usage for People's Skyway

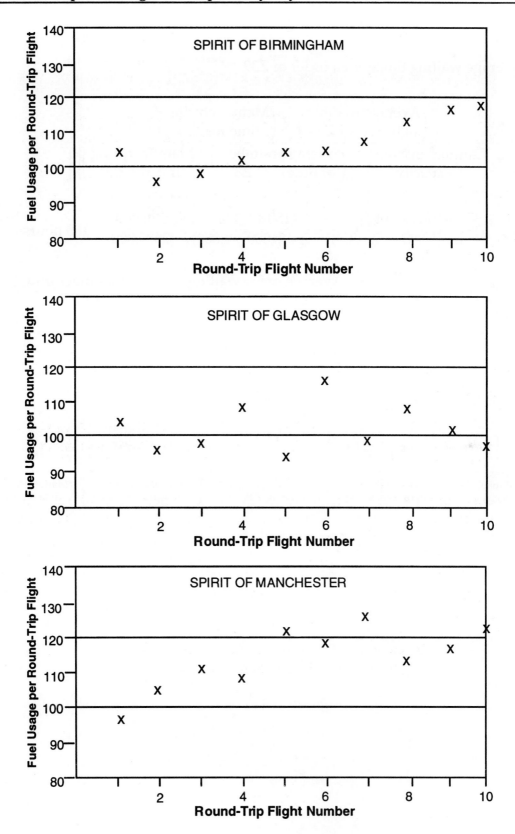

19-30 (40 min.) **Waiting times, manufacturing lead times.**

1. SRG expects to use 4,000 (80 hours per order × 50 orders) hours of total capacity of 5,000 hours equal to $\frac{4,000}{5,000} = 80\%$.

2. Average waiting time for an order of Z39

$$= \frac{\left(\begin{array}{c}\text{Average number}\\\text{of orders of Z39}\end{array}\right) \times \left(\begin{array}{c}\text{Manufacturing}\\\text{time for Z39}\end{array}\right)^2}{2 \times \left[\begin{array}{c}\text{Annual machine}\\\text{capacity}\end{array} - \left[\left(\begin{array}{c}\text{Average number}\\\text{of orders of Z39}\end{array}\right) \times \left(\begin{array}{c}\text{Manufacturing}\\\text{time for Z39}\end{array}\right)\right]\right]}$$

$$= \frac{[50 \times (80)^2]}{2 \times [5,000 - (50 \times 80)]} = \frac{(50 \times 6,400)}{2 \times (5,000 - 4,000)} = \frac{320,000}{(2 \times 1,000)} = 160 \text{ hours}$$

$$\begin{array}{c}\text{Average manufacturing}\\\text{lead time for Z39}\end{array} = \begin{array}{c}\text{Average order waiting}\\\text{time for Z39}\end{array} + \begin{array}{c}\text{Order manufacturing time}\\\text{for Z39}\end{array}$$

$$= 160 \text{ hours} + 80 \text{ hours} = 240 \text{ hours}$$

3. Average waiting time for Z39 and Y28

$$\frac{\left[\left(\begin{array}{c}\text{Average number}\\\text{of orders of Z39}\end{array}\right) \times \left(\begin{array}{c}\text{Manufacturing}\\\text{time for Z39}\end{array}\right)^2\right] + \left[\left(\begin{array}{c}\text{Average number}\\\text{of orders of Y28}\end{array}\right) \times \left(\begin{array}{c}\text{Manufacturing}\\\text{time for Y28}\end{array}\right)^2\right]}{2 \times \left[\begin{array}{c}\text{Annual machine}\\\text{capacity}\end{array} - \left[\left(\begin{array}{c}\text{Average number}\\\text{of orders of Z39}\end{array}\right) \times \left(\begin{array}{c}\text{Manufacturing}\\\text{time for Z39}\end{array}\right)\right] - \left[\left(\begin{array}{c}\text{Average number}\\\text{of orders of Y28}\end{array}\right) \times \left(\begin{array}{c}\text{Manufacturing}\\\text{time for Y28}\end{array}\right)\right]\right]}$$

$$= \frac{[50 \times (80)^2] + [25 \times (20)^2]}{2 \times [5,000 - (50 \times 80) - (25 \times 20)]} = \frac{[(50 \times 6,400) + (25 \times 400)]}{2 \times [5,000 - 4,000 - 500]} = \frac{(320,000 + 10,000)}{2 \times 500}$$

$$= \frac{330,000}{1,000} = 330 \text{ hours}$$

●

Average manufacturing lead time for Z39 $=$ Average order waiting time $+$ Order manufacturing time for Z39

$=$ 330 hours + 80 hours = 410 hours

Average manufacturing lead time for Y28 $=$ Average order waiting time $+$ Order manufacturing time for Y28

$=$ 330 hours + 20 hours = 350 hours

4. $\dfrac{\text{Average waiting time}}{\text{Average throughput time for Y28}} = \dfrac{330}{350} = 94\%$

Part Y28 spends 94% of the time in the plant, on average, just waiting to be processed!

5.   Delays occur in the processing of Z39 and Y28 because (a) uncertainty about how many orders SRG will actually receive (SRG expects to receive 50 orders of Z39 and 25 orders of Y28), and (b) uncertainty about the actual dates when SRG will receive the orders. The uncertainty (randomness) about the quantity and timing of customer orders means that SRG may receive customer orders while another order is still being processed. Orders received while the machine is actually processing another order must wait in queue for the machine to be free. As average capacity utilization of the machine increases, there is less slack and a greater chance that a machine will be busy when another order arrives.

●

●

19-32 (20 min.) **Waiting times, manufacturing lead times.**

1. Average waiting time for G72 and R76

$$\frac{\left[\left(\substack{\text{Average number} \\ \text{of orders of G72}}\right) \times \left(\substack{\text{Manufacturing} \\ \text{time for G72}}\right)^2\right] + \left[\left(\substack{\text{Average number} \\ \text{of orders of R76}}\right) \times \left(\substack{\text{Manufacturing} \\ \text{time for R76}}\right)^2\right]}{2 \times \left[\substack{\text{Annual machine} \\ \text{capacity}} - \left[\left(\substack{\text{Average number} \\ \text{of orders of G72}}\right) \times \left(\substack{\text{Manufacturing} \\ \text{time for G72}}\right)\right] - \left[\left(\substack{\text{Average number} \\ \text{of orders of R76}}\right) \times \left(\substack{\text{Manufacturing} \\ \text{time for R76}}\right)\right]\right]}$$

$$= \frac{[125 \times (40)^2] + [10 \times (50)^2]}{2 \times [6,000 - (125 \times 40) - (10 \times 50)]}$$

$$= \frac{[(125 \times 1,600) + (10 \times 2,500)]}{2 \times [6,000 - 5,000 - 500]} = \frac{(200,000 + 25,000)}{2 \times 500}$$

$$= \frac{225,000}{1,000} = 225 \text{ hours}$$

$$\substack{\text{Average manufacturing} \\ \text{lead time for G72}} = \substack{\text{Average order waiting} \\ \text{time}} + \substack{\text{Order manufacturing} \\ \text{time for G72}}$$

$$= 225 \text{ hours} + 40 \text{ hours} = 265 \text{ hours}$$

$$\substack{\text{Average manufacturing} \\ \text{lead time for R76}} = \substack{\text{Average order waiting} \\ \text{time}} + \substack{\text{Order manufacturing} \\ \text{time for R76}}$$

$$= 225 \text{ hours} + 50 \text{ hours} = 275 \text{ hours}$$

2. Average waiting time for an order of G72

$$= \frac{\left(\substack{\text{Average number} \\ \text{of orders of G72}}\right) \times \left(\substack{\text{Manufacturing} \\ \text{time for G72}}\right)^2}{2 \times \left[\substack{\text{Annual machine} \\ \text{capacity}} - \left[\left(\substack{\text{Average number} \\ \text{of orders of G72}}\right) \times \left(\substack{\text{Manufacturing} \\ \text{time for G72}}\right)\right]\right]}$$

$$= \frac{[125 \times (40)^2]}{2 \times [6,000 - (125 \times 40)]} = \frac{(125 \times 1,600)}{2 \times (6,000 - 5,000)} = \frac{200,000}{(2 \times 1,000)} = 100 \text{ hours}$$

$$\substack{\text{Average manufacturing} \\ \text{lead time for G72}} = \substack{\text{Average order waiting} \\ \text{time for G72}} + \substack{\text{Order manufacturing time} \\ \text{for G72}}$$

$$= 100 \text{ hours} + 40 \text{ hours} = 140 \text{ hours}$$

19-34 (20 min.) **Theory of constraints, throughput contribution, relevant costs.**

1.   It will cost Colorado $50 per unit to reduce manufacturing time. But manufacturing is not a bottleneck operation, installation is. Therefore, manufacturing more equipment will not increase sales and throughput contribution. Colorado Industries should not implement the new manufacturing method.

2.   Additional relevant costs of new direct materials, $2,000 × 320 units, $640,000
       Increase in throughput contribution, $25,000 × 20 units, $500,000
The additional incremental costs exceed the benefits from higher throughput contribution by $140,000, so Colorado Industries should not implement the new design.

       Alternatively, compare throughput contribution under each alternative.
       Current throughput contribution is $25,000 × 300 $7,500,000
       With the modification, throughput contribution is $23,000 × 320 $7,360,000
The current throughput contribution is greater than the throughput contribution resulting from the proposed change in direct materials. Hence, Colorado Industries should not implement the new design.

3.   Increase in throughput contribution, $25,000 × 10 units $250,000
       Increase in relevant costs $ 50,000
The additional throughput contribution exceeds incremental costs by $200,000 so Colorado Industries should implement the new installation technique.

4.   Motivating installation workers to increase productivity is worthwhile because installation is a bottleneck operation and any increase in productivity at the bottleneck will increase throughput contribution. On the other hand, motivating workers in the manufacturing department to increase productivity is not worthwhile. Manufacturing is not a bottleneck operation, so any increase in output will only result in extra inventory of equipment. Colorado Industries should only encourage manufacturing to produce as much equipment as the installation department needs, not to produce as much as it can. Under these circumstances, it would not be a good idea to evaluate and compensate manufacturing workers on the basis of their productivity.

19-36 (25 min.)   **Quality improvement, Pareto charts, fishbone diagrams.**

1.   Examples of failures in accounts receivable management are:
   a.   Uncollectible amounts or bad debts
   b.   Delays in receiving payments

2.   Prevention activities that could reduce failures in accounts receivable management include:
   a.   Credit checks on customers
   b.   Shipping the correct copier to the customer
   c.   Supporting installation of the copier and answering customer questions
   d.   Sending the correct invoice, in the correct amount, and to the correct address, promptly
   e.   Following up to see if the machine is functioning smoothly

3.   A Pareto diagram for the problem of delays in receiving customer payments might look like the following:

SOLUTION EXHIBIT 19-36A
Pareto Diagram for Failures in Accounts Receivables at Murray Corporation

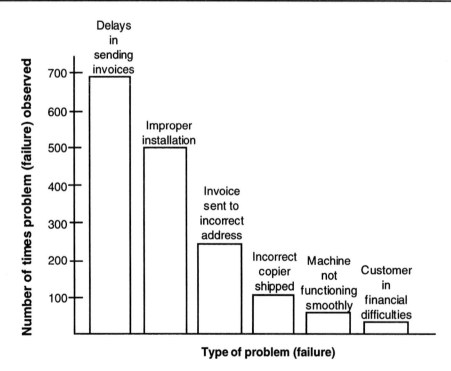

19-36 (Cont'd.)

A cause-and-effect or fishbone diagram for the problem of delays in sending invoices may appear as follows:

SOLUTION EXHIBIT 19-36B
Cause-and-Effect Diagram
For Problem of Delays in Sending Invoices at Murray Corporation

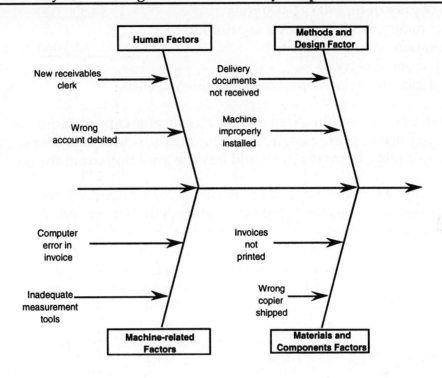

19-38 (45–50 min.) **Quality improvement, relevant costs, and relevant revenues.**

1. Consider the incremental revenues and incremental costs to Wellesley Corporation of purchasing grey cloth from outside suppliers.

Incremental revenues, $1,250 × (5,000 rolls × 0.90)		$5,625,000
Incremental costs:		
Cost of gray cloth, $900 × 5,000 rolls	$4,500,000	
Direct materials variable costs at printing		
operation, $100 × 5,000 rolls	500,000	
Incremental costs		5,000,000
Excess of incremental revenues over incremental costs		$ 625,000

Note that, since the printing department has surplus capacity equal to 5,500 (15,000 – 9,500) rolls per month, purchasing grey cloth from outside entails zero opportunity costs. Yes, the Printing Department should buy the grey cloth from the outside supplier.

2. By producing a defective roll in the Printing Department, Wellesley Corporation is worse off by the entire amount of revenue forgone of $1,250 per roll. Note that, since the weaving operation is a constraint, any rolls received by the Printing Department that are scrapped result in lost revenue to the firm. All costs already incurred in manufacturing the roll (Weaving Department direct materials variable costs, $500, Weaving Department other operating costs, $285, Printing Department direct materials variable costs, $100, and Printing Department other operating costs, $45) are past costs and, hence, irrelevant.

An alternative approach to analyzing the problem is to focus on scrap costs and the benefits of reducing scrap.

The relevant costs of Printing Department scrap are:		
(a) Direct materials variable costs in the Weaving Department		$ 500
(b) Direct materials variable costs in the Printing Department		100
(c) Contribution margin forgone from not selling one roll		
$1,250 – $500 – $100		650
Amount by which Wellesley Corporation is worse off as a		
result of Printing Department scrap		$1,250

Note that only the variable scrap costs of $600 per roll (direct materials in the Weaving Department, $500 per roll and direct materials in the Printing Department, $100 per roll) are relevant because improving quality will save these costs. Fixed scrap costs attributable to other operating costs are irrelevant because these costs will be incurred whether Wellesley Corporation reduces scrap in the Printing Department or not.

19-38 (Cont'd.)

3. To determine how much Wellesley Corporation is worse off by producing a defective roll in the Weaving Department, consider the payoff to Wellesley from not having a defective roll produced in the Weaving Department. The good roll produced in the Weaving Department will be sent for further processing in the Printing Department. The relevant costs and benefits of printing and selling this roll follow:

Additional direct materials variable costs incurred in the Printing Department	$ (100)
Expected revenue from selling the finished product, 0.9 × $1,250 (since 10% of the Printing Department output will need to be scrapped and earn zero revenue)	1,125
Net expected benefit of producing a good roll in the Weaving Department	$1,025

By producing a defective roll in the Printing Department, Wellesley Corporation is worse off by $1,025 per roll. Note that, since the weaving operation is a constraint, any rolls that are scrapped result in lost revenue to the firm. All costs already incurred in manufacturing the roll (Weaving Department direct materials variable costs, $500, Weaving Department other operating costs, $285) and future costs that will not change whether a roll is scrapped or not at the Weaving Department (for example, other operating costs in the Printing Department, $45) are irrelevant.

An alternative approach to analyzing the problem is to focus on scrap costs and the benefits of reducing scrap.

The relevant costs of Weaving Department scrap are:	
(a) Direct materials variable costs in the Weaving Department	$ 500
(b) Expected unit contribution margin forgone from not selling one roll, ($1,250 × 0.9) – $500 – $100	525
Amount by which Wesley Corporation is worse off as a result of Weaving Department scrap	$1,025

Note that only the variable scrap costs of $500 per roll (direct materials in the Weaving Department) are relevant because improving quality will save these costs. Fixed scrap costs attributable to other operating costs are irrelevant because these costs will be incurred whether Wellesley Corporation reduces scrap in the Weaving Department or not.

4. Wellesley Corporation should make the proposed modifications in the Weaving Department because the incremental benefits exceed the incremental costs by $125,000 per month:

Incremental benefits of reducing scrap in the Printing Department by 4% (from 10% to 6%)	
4% × 9,500 rolls × $1,250 per roll (computed in requirement 2)	$475,000
Incremental costs of the modification	350,000
Excess of incremental benefits over incremental costs	$125,000

19-38 (Cont'd.)

5. Wellesley Corporation should make the proposed improvements in the Printing Department because the incremental benefits exceed the incremental costs by $30,000 per month:

    Incremental benefits of reducing scrap in the Weaving Department
       by 2% (from 5% to 3%)

2% × 10,000 rolls × $1,025 per roll (computed in requirement 3)	$205,000
Incremental costs of the improvements	175,000
Excess of incremental benefits over incremental costs	$ 30,000

6. Poor quality is often more costly at a bottleneck operation than it is at a nonbottleneck operation. The cost of poor quality at a nonbottleneck operation is largely the cost of materials wasted. No throughput contribution is forgone as a result of poor quality at a nonbottleneck operation. At a bottleneck operation, the cost of poor quality is the cost of materials wasted plus the opportunity cost of lost throughput contribution. At both the Weaving and the Printing Department, capacity not wasted in producing defective units could be used to generate additional sales and throughput contribution. Companies implementing quality programs should especially look at improving the quality of parts or products manufactured at the bottleneck operation.

CHAPTER 20
OPERATION COSTING, JUST-IN-TIME SYSTEMS, AND BACKFLUSH COSTING

20-2 Not quite. Operations are usually conducted within departments. For example, a company may have its machining and assembly operations within one department. The term operation, however, is often used loosely as a synonym for a department or process. A company may call its assembly department an assembly operation.

20-4 Industries likely to use operation costing include automotive, processed vegetables, and clothing manufacturing.

20-6 JIT production systems simplify job costing because direct materials are rapidly converted to finished goods that are immediately sold. The absence of inventories means that cost-flow assumptions (e.g., weighted-average or first-in, first out) or inventory costing methods (absorption or variable costing) are unimportant. When inventories are low, managers may not find it worthwhile to spend resources tracking costs through Work in Process, Finished Goods and Cost of Goods Sold. Job-costing systems can be simplified using backflush costing.

20-8 The five major features of JIT production systems are:

1. Production is organized in manufacturing cells, a grouping of all the different types of equipment used to manufacture a given product.
2. Workers are trained to be multiskilled so that they are capable of performing a variety of operations and tasks.
3. Total quality management is aggressively pursued to eliminate defects.
4. Emphasis is placed on reducing setup time and manufacturing lead time.
5. Suppliers are carefully selected to obtain delivery of quality-tested parts in a timely manner.

20-10 Just-in-time systems facilitate the direct tracing of some costs that were formerly classified as overhead. For example, the use of manufacturing cells makes it easy to trace materials handling and machine operating costs as direct costs of specific products or product families made in specific cells. Multiskilled workers in cells also perform their own setups, maintenance and quality inspection so that these costs become easily traced, direct costs of products made in specific cells.

20-12 Backflush-costing delays the recording of journal entries until after the physical sequences have occurred. Typically, no record of work in process appears in the accounting system.

20-14 Backflush costing systems can differ in both the number and the placement of trigger points for making journal entries in the accounting system:

Example	Number of Journal Entry Trigger Points	Location of Journal Entry Trigger Points
1.	2	1. Purchase of direct (raw) materials 2. Completion of good finished units of product
2.	2	1. Purchase of direct (raw) materials 2. Sale of good finished units of product
3.	1	1. Completion of good finished units of product

20-16 (20 mins.) Operation costing.

1.   Conversion costs of each operation, the total units produced and the conversion cost per unit for the month of June are as follows:

	Framing	Assembly	Staining	Painting
Conversion costs	$75,000	$105,000	$36,000	$54,000
Total units produced	3,000	3,000	1,500	1,500
Conversion cost per unit	$25	$35	$24	$36

2.   Costs of Work Order 626 and Work Order 750 are as follows:

	Work Order 626	Work Order 750
Number of windows	50	100
Direct materials costs	$ 5,500	$ 9,800
Conversion costs:		
Framing (50; 100 × $25)	1,250	2,500
Assembly (50; 100 × $35)	1,750	3,500
Staining (100 × $24)	–	2,400
Painting (50 × $36)	1,800	–
Total costs	$10,300	$18,200
Total cost per window	$\frac{\$10,300}{50} = \$206$	$\frac{\$18,200}{100} = \$182$

20-18 (25–40 min.) **Operation costing.**

1.

	Cutting	Assembly	Finishing
Conversion Costs:			
Direct manufacturing labor costs	$ 2,600	$16,500	$4,800
Manufacturing overhead costs	3,000	22,900	3,300
Conversion costs	$ 5,600	$39,400	$8,100
Total units produced:			
1,200 + 600 + 200	2,000	2,000	
1,200 + 600			1,800
Conversion cost per unit	$ 2.80	$ 19.70	$ 4.50

2.

	Standard	Home	Industrial
Tool Box Costs:			
Direct materials costs	$18,000	$ 6,660	$5,400
Conversion costs:			
Cutting, (1,200; 600; 200 × $2.80)	3,360	1,680	560
Assembly, (1,200; 600; 200 × $19.70)	23,640	11,820	3,940
Finishing, (1,200; 600 × $4.50)	5,400	2,700	--
Total costs	$50,400	$22,860	$9,900
Divided by quantity produced	1,200	600	200
Cost per unit	$ 42.00	$ 38.10	$49.50

20-20 (15–30 min.) Operation costing.

1. Conversion costs of each operation, the total units produced and the conversion cost per unit for the month of October are as follows:

	Extrude	Form	Trim	Finish
Direct manufacturing labor	$ 55,000	$ 30,000	$ 20,000	$ 40,000
Manufacturing overhead	270,000	90,000	40,000	60,000
Conversion costs	$325,000	$120,000	$ 60,000	$100,000
Total units produced	13,000			
13,000 – 10,000		3,000	3,000	
13,000 – 10,000 – 1,000				2,000
Conversion cost per unit	$25	$40	$20	$50

2. Manufacturing product costs for October are as follows:

	10,000 Plastic Sheets Sold Outside	1,000 Firewalls	2,000 Dashboards	Total Costs Accounted for
Direct materials:				
For sheets @ $50	$500,000	$ 50,000	$100,000	$ 650,000
Additional materials	–	–	80,000	80,000
Conversion costs:				
Extrude (10,000; 1,000; 2,000 × $25)	250,000	25,000	50,000	325,000
Form (1,000; 2,000 × $40)	–	40,000	80,000	120,000
Trim (1,000; 2,000 × $20)	–	20,000	40,000	60,000
Finish (2,000 × $50)	–	–	100,000	100,000
Total costs	$750,000	$135,000	$450,000	$1,335,000
Units produced	10,000	1,000	2,000	
Total cost per unit	$75	$135	$225	

20-22 (20 min.) **Backflush costing and JIT production.**

1.   Journal entries for August are as follows:

Entry (a) Inventory: Raw and In-Process Control   550,000
               Accounts Payable Control   550,000
         (raw materials and components purchased)

Entry (b) Conversion Costs Control   440,000
               Various Accounts (such as Accounts
               Payable Control and Wages Payable)   440,000
         (conversion costs incurred)

Entry (c) Finished Goods Control   945,000
               Inventory: Raw and In-Process Control   525,000
               Conversion Costs Allocated   420,000
         (standard costs of 21,000 units of finished goods produced
         at $45 per unit; direct materials, $25 per unit;
         conversion costs, $20 per unit)

Entry (d) Cost of Goods Sold   900,000
               Finished Goods Control   900,000
         (standard costs of 20,000 units of finished goods sold
         at $45 per unit

2.

	Inventory: Raw and In-Process Control		Finished Goods Control		Cost of Goods Sold
Direct Materials →	(a) 550,000	(c) 525,000 →	(c) 945,000	(d) 900,000 →	(d) 900,000
	Bal. 25,000		Bal. 45,000		

Conversion Costs Allocated

	(c) 420,000

Conversion
Costs →

Conversion Costs Control

(b) 440,000

20-24 (20 min.) Backflush, one trigger point.

1.   Journal entries for August are as follows:

Entry (a) to record purchase of direct materials is not made.

Entry (b) Conversion Costs Control   440,000
             Various Accounts (such as Accounts
               Payable Control and Wages Payable)   440,000
           (conversion costs incurred)

Entry (c) Finished Goods Control   945,000
             Accounts Payable Control   525,000
             Conversion Costs Allocated   420,000
           (standard costs of 21,000 units of finished goods produced
           at $45 per unit; direct materials, $25 per unit;
           conversion costs, $20 per unit)

Entry (d) Cost of Goods Sold   900,000
             Finished Goods Control   900,000
           (standard costs of 20,000 units of finished goods sold
           at $45 per unit)

Entry (e) Conversion Costs Allocated   420,000
           Cost of Goods Sold   20,000
             Conversion Costs Control   440,000
           (underallocated conversion costs written off)

2.

Finished Goods Control	Cost of Goods Sold

Direct Materials

Conversion Costs Allocated
(e) 420,000 | (c) 420,000

Conversion Costs

Conversion Costs Control
(b) 440,000 | (e) 440,000

(c) 945,000 | (d) 900,000 ➔ (d) 900,000

(e) 900,000

20-26 (25–35 min.) **Operation costing with ending work in process and journal entries.**

The objective of this problem is to give the student a sense of how cost accounting copes with the costs of multiple products and multiple operations that are commonplace in today's world.

1. $$\text{Budgeted conversion costs rate for } 19\_7 = \frac{\$100,000 + \$440,000}{180,000} = \$3 \text{ per unit}$$

    Conversion costs of 1,000 Deluxe units in Operation 2   = $1,000 \times \$3 = \$3,000$
    Conversion costs of 500 Superdeluxe units in Operation 2   = $500 \times \$3 = \$1,500$

2.

	Deluxe Units	Superdeluxe Units
Direct materials	$50,000	$54,000
Conversion costs:		
Operation 1	20,000	10,000
Operation 2	3,000	1,500
Operation 3	–	5,000
Total manufacturing costs	$73,000	$70,500
Divided by total units	÷ 1,000	÷ 500
Total manufacturing cost per unit	$ 73	$ 141

3.

Work in Process, Operation 1	50,000	
Materials Inventory		50,000
Work in Process, Operation 1	20,000	
Conversion Costs Allocated		20,000
Work in Process, Operation 2	70,000	
Work in Process, Operation 1		70,000
Work in Process, Operation 2	3,000	
Conversion Costs Allocated		3,000
Finished Goods	73,000	
Work in Process, Operation 2		73,000

($70,000 + $3,000 = $73,000

4.

	Deluxe Units	Superdeluxe Units
Direct materials:		
$50,000 × 500/1,000	$25,000	
($54,000 – $4,000) × 300/500		$30,000
Conversion costs:		
Operation 1:		
(500/1,000 × $20,000)	10,000	
(300/500 × $10,000)		6,000
Operation 2:		
(300/500 × $1,500)	–	900
Total costs of work in process, $71,900	$35,000	$36,900

20-28 (20–25 min.) **Backflush costing and JIT production.**

1.

Entry (a) Inventory: Raw and In-Process Control   5,300,000
        Accounts Payable Control   5,300,000
        (raw materials purchased)

Entry (b) Conversion Costs Control   3,080,000
        Various Accounts   3,080,000
        (conversion costs incurred)

Entry (c) Finished Goods Control   8,200,000
        Inventory: Raw and In-Process Control   5,200,000
        Conversion Costs allocated   3,000,000
        (standard costs of 200,000 finished goods
        produced at $41 per unit; direct
        materials, $26 per unit, conversion costs,
        $15 per unit)

Entry (d) Cost of Goods Sold   7,872,000
        Finished Goods Control   7,872,000
        (standard costs of 192,000 units sold at
        $41 per unit)

2.

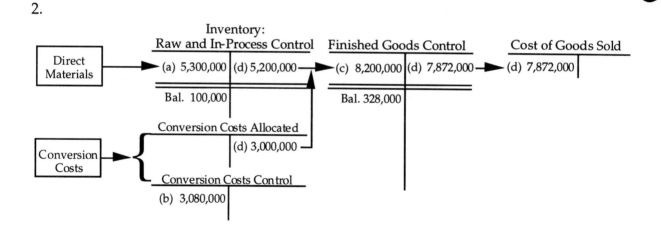

20-8

20-30 (20–25 min.) **Backflush, one trigger point.**

1. Journal entries for June are as follows:

Entry (a) to record purchase of direct materials is not made.

Entry (b)	Conversion Costs Control	3,080,000	
	Various Accounts		3,080,000
	(conversion costs incurred)		

Entry (c)	Finished Goods Control	8,200,000	
	Accounts Payable Control		5,200,000
	Conversion Costs Allocated		3,000,000
	(standard costs of 200,000 units of		
	finished goods produced at $41 per		
	unit, direct materials, $26, conversion		
	costs, $15)		
Entry (d)	Cost of Goods Sold	7,872,000	
	Finished Goods Control		7,872,000
	(standard costs of 192,000 units of		
	finished goods sold at $41 per unit)		
Entry (e)	Conversion Costs Allocated	3,000,000	
	Cost of Goods Sold	80,000	
	Conversion Costs Control		3,080,000
	(underallocated conversion costs		
	written off)		

2.

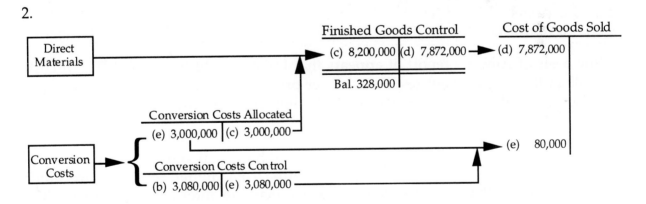

The $328,000 ending balance of Finished Goods Control consists of the 8,000 units of finished goods units in inventory at the standard cost of $41 per unit. Since there is only one trigger point, the $100,000 of direct materials on hand (as shown in solution to Problem 20-28) are not recorded as inventory. In this version, if backflush costing, direct materials purchases are only recorded when finished goods are produced.

20-30 (Cont'd.)

3.   The key difference between the accounting in Problem 20-28 and the accounting here is the absence of the Inventory: Raw and In-Process Control Account. As a result, at the end of June, $100,000 of direct materials purchased but not yet manufactured into finished units have not been entered into the Inventory Control account. (Direct materials purchased is $5,300,000.) This variation of backflush costing is suitable for a production system that has virtually no direct materials inventory and minimum work-in-process inventories. It is less feasible otherwise.

20-32   (30 min.)   **Just-in-time systems, ethics.**

1.   Plant profitability in the first year after implementation and in subsequent years based on Anwar's report will be as follows:

	First-Year After Implementation	Subsequent Years
Annual expected benefits:		
Lower investment in inventories	$ 290,000	$ 350,000
Reductions in setup costs	110,000	150,000
Reduction in costs of waste, spoilage and rework	200,000	250,000
Higher revenues from responding faster to customers	180,000	300,000
Total annual expected benefits	780,000	1,050,000
Annual expected costs of JIT implementation	950,000	750,000
Operating profit (loss) from JIT implementation	$(170,000)	$ 300,000

On the basis of Anwar's report, it appears that Daisy should implement JIT. It costs $170,000 in the first year but results in higher profits of $300,000 in subsequent years. In the long run, the benefits appear to clearly outweigh the costs.

2.   Daly is correct in characterizing some of the financial benefits as 'soft'. She is probably referring to operating income from higher revenues as a result of responding faster to customers. Higher profits from higher revenues are much harder to predict than cost savings. Cost savings are internal to the firm. The benefits from higher revenues depend on the reactions of customers and the responses of competitors.

     If the revenue benefits are not realized, losses in the first year after JIT implementation will increase to $350,000 (presently estimated loss of $170,000 plus $180,000). Furthermore, no net benefit will accrue in subsequent years (currently estimated operating profit of $300,000 minus the $300,000 loss in operating profits if the 'soft' revenue benefits are not realized). Without the revenue gains, JIT does not appear to be worthwhile.

20-32 (Cont'd.)

Students might also raise questions as to whether Anwar has correctly estimated the likely cost savings. For example, suppose setup costs include a labor component. Then, even if setups are performed more efficiently, setup cost savings may not occur if labor agreements make laying off workers difficult.

3.   It is unfortunate that the first year of JIT implementation (when costs of JIT implementation are likely to exceed benefits) happens to coincide with Gail Daly's last year with Daisy. In this sense, it does appear that Daly is being unfairly penalized if she implements JIT—she would bear the costs while the incoming manager would get the benefits.

Daly should indicate these circumstances to the senior management at Daisy and see if she can renegotiate the terms. For example, she might ask senior management to evaluate her performance after adjusting for the decline in plant profitability resulting from implementing JIT. Asking Anwar to change the numbers to make the JIT program look worse and to, hence, postpone implementation is unethical.

Any attempt by Anwar to use alternative numbers to manipulate the benefits from JIT implementation is unethical because it violates the Standards of Ethical Conduct for Management Accountants. The competence standard is violated because of failure to comply with technical standards and lack of appropriate analysis. The integrity standard is violated because it subverts the attainment of an organization's objectives and discredits the profession. The objectivity standard is violated because of the failure to communicate information fully and fairly.

The Standards of Ethical Conduct for Management Accountants describes the steps that Anwar should take to resolve the ethical conflict.

- If Anwar is certain that her numbers are correct, she should inform Daly about it.
- If Daly continues to pressure her, Anwar should present the situation to the next higher level, the vice-president of manufacturing, for resolution.
- If Anwar does not receive a satisfactory response, she should continue to successive higher levels including the Audit Committee and the Board of Directors.
- Anwar should clarify the concepts of the issue at hand in a confidential discussion with an objective advisor, that is, a peer.
- If the situation is still unresolved after exhausting all levels of internal review, Anwar will have no recourse but to resign and submit an informative memorandum to an appropriate representative of the organization.
- Unless legally bound (which does not appear to be the case in this situation), it is inappropriate to have communication about this situation with authorities and individuals not employed or engaged by the organization.

CHAPTER 21
INVENTORY MANAGEMENT AND JUST-IN-TIME

21-2 Cost of goods sold (in retail organizations) or direct materials costs (in organizations with a manufacturing function) as a percentage of sales frequently exceeds net income as a percentage of sales by many orders of magnitude. In the Kroger grocery store example cited in the text, cost of goods sold to sales is 75.8%, and net income to sales is 1.2%. Thus, a 10% reduction in the ratio of cost of goods sold to sales (75.8 to 68.2%) without any other changes can result in a 633% increase in net income to sales (1.2% to 8.8%).

21-4 The decisions central to the management of goods for sale in a retail organization are:
1. How much to order (the economic-order-quantity (EOQ) decision)?
2. When to order (the reorder decision)?

21-6 Costs included in the carrying costs of inventory are *incremental costs* for such items as insurance, rent, obsolescence, spoilage, and breakage plus the *opportunity cost* of capital (or required return on investment).

21-8 Examples of opportunity costs relevant to the EOQ decision model but typically not recorded in accounting systems are:
1. the return forgone by investing capital in inventory,
2. lost contribution margin on existing sales when a stockout occurs, and
3. lost contribution margin on potential future sales that will not be made to disgruntled customers.

21-10 Many solutions near the optimal EOQ have very similar total relevant costs.

21-12 Two cost factors that can lead organizations to make smaller and more frequent purchase orders are:
1. A decrease in the estimated cost of placing each purchase order, and
2. An increase in the estimated cost of holding goods in inventory.
   Recognition of how costs of quality increase with higher inventory levels is also motivating organizations to make smaller and more frequent purchase orders.

21-14 In choosing suppliers, organizations should look at more than the lowest price. Quality and delivery reliability are very important considerations, particularly as purchasing companies adopt JIT. For example, better quality reduces costs of incoming inspection and customer returns, while reliable delivery reduces stockout costs.

21-16 (15 min.) **EOQ for a retailer.**

1. D = 20,000, P = $160, C = 20% × $8 = $1.60

$$EOQ = \sqrt{\frac{2DP}{C}} = \sqrt{\frac{2(20,000)\$160}{\$1.60}} = 2,000 \text{ yards}$$

2. Number of orders per year: $\dfrac{D}{EOQ} = \dfrac{20,000}{2,000} = 10$ orders

3. Demand each working day $= \dfrac{D}{\text{Number of working days}}$

$$= \frac{20,000}{250}$$

= 80 yards per day
= 400 yards per week

Purchasing lead time = 2 weeks
Reorder point = 400 × 2 = 800 yards

21-18 (20 min.) **EOQ, ordering and carrying costs.**

1. $\quad EOQ = \sqrt{\dfrac{2DP}{C}}$

D = 8,000; P = $100; C = $10

$$EOQ = \sqrt{\frac{2(8,000)(\$100)}{\$10}} = \sqrt{160,000} = 400 \text{ units}$$

Richmond's ordering policy is not optimal because Richmond orders 200 units at a time instead of the economic order quantity of 400 units.

For the economic order quantity, Q = 400 units

$$TRC = \frac{DP}{Q} + \frac{QC}{2}$$

$$= \frac{8,000 \times \$100}{400} + \frac{400 \times \$10}{2} = \$4,000$$

2. Under Richmond's policy of placing 200 orders at a time, Q = 200

$$TR = \frac{DP}{Q} + \frac{QC}{2} = \frac{8,000 \times \$100}{200} + \frac{200 \times \$10}{2}$$

$$= \$4,000 + \$1,000 = \$5,000$$

3. Richmond's ordering policy results in an annual loss of $1,000 [$5,000 (requirement 2) minus $4,000 (requirement 1)].

21-20 (20 min.) **Production batch size, EOQ.**

1. Adam Furniture Company would be attempting to balance total setup costs and total carrying costs. These costs are equal at the production run quantity that minimizes the sum of these two costs.

2. Incremental manufacturing costs

Direct materials	$ 30
Direct manufacturing labor	14
Variable overhead	6
Total incremental manufacturing costs	$ 50

$D = 18,000$; $P = \$600$; $C = 10.8\% \times \$50 = \$5.40$

$$\text{Economic production run quantity} = \sqrt{\frac{2\,DP}{C}}$$

$$= \sqrt{\frac{2\,(18,000)\,(\$600)}{\$5.40}}$$

$$= \sqrt{4,000,000}$$

$$= 2,000 \text{ desks}$$

3.

$$\text{Number of production runs per year} = \frac{\text{Annual demand}}{\text{Economic production run quantity}}$$

$$= \frac{18,000}{2,000}$$

$$= 9 \text{ production runs}$$

21-22 (30 min.) **JIT purchasing, relevant benefits, relevant costs.**

1. Solution Exhibit 21-22 presents the $43,000 cash savings of AgriCorp's Service Division for 19_7 from adopting the just-in-time inventory program.

2. Other nonfinancial and qualitative factors that should be considered before a company implements a just-in-time inventory program include :

    a.   Customer dissatisfaction that may result from stockouts of finished goods and/or spare parts resulting in customers' downtime that may not be acceptable and may also be costly.

    a.   Stockouts of spare parts and/or finished goods can impair the manufacturer's image with its distributors who represent the direct contacts with the ultimate (customer) users.

    c.   Placement of smaller and more frequent orders can result in higher material and delivery costs from suppliers. Additionally, given required changes in the suppliers' production and procurement processes, suppliers may choose to discontinue being suppliers to a just-in-time customer.

    d.   The marketplace will determine the impact of service degradation due to stockouts. Brand loyalty can deteriorate when service standards are lowered.

SOLUTION EXHIBIT 21-22
Annual Relevant Costs of Current Purchasing Policy and JIT Purchasing Policy for AgriCorp's Service Division

	Incremental Costs Under Current Purchasing Policy	Incremental Costs Under JIT Purchasing Policy
Required return on investment		
15% per year × $550,000 of average inventory per year	$ 82,500	
15% per year × $150,000 of average inventory per year		$ 22,500
Annual insurance costs	80,000	32,000[a]
Warehouse rent	11,200	(3,800)[b]
Overtime costs		
No overtime	0	
Overtime premium ($5.60 × 7,500 units)		42,000
Stockout costs		
No stockouts	0	
$10 contribution margin per unit × 3,800 units		38,000
Total incremental costs	$173,700	$130,700
Difference in favor of JIT purchasing	↑ $43,000 ↑	

[a]$80,000 × (1 − 0.60) = $32,000.

[b]$(3,800) = Warehouse rent, $11,200 − sublet revenues, $15,000.

Note that the incremental cost of $5.60 per unit for overtime is less than the additional $10.00 per unit contribution margin for the 7,500 units that would have been lost sales. Agricorp would rather incur overtime than lose sales. Also note that the cost of the two warehouse employees is irrelevant. The same salary costs of $35,000 will be incurred under both alternatives.

21-24 (20 min.) JIT production, relevant benefits, relevant costs.

1. Solution Exhibit 21-24 presents the annual net benefit of $154,000 to Evans Corporation of implementing a JIT production system.

2. Other nonfinancial and qualitative factors that Evans should consider in deciding whether it should implement a JIT system include:

    a. The possibility of developing and implementing a detailed system for integrating the sequential operations of the manufacturing process. Direct materials must arrive when needed for each subassembly so that the production process functions smoothly.

    b. The ability to design products that use standardized parts and reduce manufacturing time.

    c. The ease of obtaining reliable vendors who can deliver quality direct materials on time with minimum lead time.

    d. Willingness of suppliers to deliver smaller and more frequent orders.

    e. The confidence of being able to deliver quality products on time. Failure to do so would result in customer dissatisfaction.

    f. The skill levels of workers to perform multiple tasks such as minor repairs and maintenance, and quality testing and inspection.

SOLUTION EXHIBIT 21-24
Annual Relevant Costs of Current Production System and JIT Production System for Evans Corporation

Relevant Items	Incremental Costs Under Current Production System	Incremental Costs Under JIT Production System
Annual tooling costs	–	$150,000
Required return on investment		
12% per year × $900,000 of average inventory per year	$108,000	
12% per year × $200,000 of average inventory per year		24,000
Insurance, space, materials handling and setup costs	200,000	140,000[a]
Rework costs	350,000	280,000[b]
Incremental revenues from higher selling prices	–	(90,000)[c]
Total net incremental costs	$658,000	$504,000
Annual difference in favor of JIT production	⌐ $154,000 ⌐	

[a] $200,000 (1 – 0.30) = $140,000
[b] $350,000 (1 – 0.20) = $280,000
[c] $3 × 30,000 units = $90,000

21-5

21-26 (25–30 min.) **EOQ, quantity discounts.**

1. $D = 10,000$, $P = \$120$, $C = 30\% \times \$8 = \$2.40$

$$EOQ = \sqrt{\frac{2DP}{C}} = \sqrt{\frac{2(10,000)\,\$120}{\$2.40}} = \sqrt{1,000,000} = 1,000 \text{ leashes}$$

2.   For the EOQ model, we have

Total purchasing costs per year, $\$8 \times 10,000$	\$80,000
Total ordering costs per year $(D/Q) \times P$, $\dfrac{10,000 \times \$120}{1,000}$	1,200
Total carrying costs per year $(Q/2) \times C$, $\dfrac{1,000 \times \$2.40}{2}$	1,200
Total costs	\$82,400

3a.   If the order size Q is 2,000 units, we have

Total purchasing costs per year, $\$7.90 \times 10,000$	\$79,000
Total ordering costs per year $(D/Q) \times P$, $\dfrac{10,000 \times \$120}{2,000}$	600
Total carrying costs per year $(Q/2) \times C$, $\dfrac{2,000 \times \$2.40}{2}$	2,400
Total costs	\$82,000

b.   If the order size Q is 2,500 units, we have

Total purchasing costs per year, $\$7.90 \times 10,000$	\$79,000
Total ordering costs per year $(D/Q) \times P$, $\dfrac{10,000 \times \$120}{2,500}$	480
Total carrying costs per year $(Q/2) \times C$, $\dfrac{2,500 \times \$2.40}{2}$	3,000
Total costs	\$82,480

4.   Crofton should choose an order size of 2,000 leashes. This is the minimum order size that entitles Crofton to the $0.10 per leash discount, saving $1,000 in purchasing costs. The order size of 2,000 leashes per order is larger than the economic order quantity (EOQ) of 1,000 leashes per order, resulting in $600 ($3,000 – $2,400) more in ordering and carrying costs. The savings in purchasing costs of $1,000 exceeds the higher ordering and carrying costs of $600, yielding a $400 savings if Crofton purchases leashes in order sizes of 2,000 rather than in the EOQ of 1,000. Choosing an order size greater than 2,000 leashes (2,001 leashes and greater) causes the order size to deviate even more from the EOQ and leads to even higher carrying and ordering costs (see Exhibit 21-1 in text) without any further savings in purchasing costs. For example, at an order size of 2,500 leashes, ordering and carrying costs equal $3,480 (which is greater than the ordering and carrying costs of $3,000 at an order size of 2,000). An order size of 2,000 achieves the purchase discount yet minimizes the deviation from the EOQ.

21-28 (20–30 min.) **EOQ, cost of prediction error.**

1. EOQ $= \sqrt{\dfrac{2DP}{C}}$

    $D = 2{,}000;\ P = \$40;\ C = \$4 + (10\% \times \$50) = \$9$

    EOQ $= \sqrt{\dfrac{2(2000)\$40}{\$9}} = 133.333$ tires $\simeq 133$ tires

    TRC $= \dfrac{DP}{Q} + \dfrac{QC}{2}$ where Q can be any quantity, including the EOQ

    $ = \dfrac{2{,}000 \times \$40}{133.3} + \dfrac{133.3 \times \$9}{2} = \$600 + \$600 = \$1{,}200$

    If students used an EOQ of 133 tires (order quantities rounded to the nearest whole number),

    TRC $= \dfrac{2{,}000 \times \$40}{133} + \dfrac{133 \times \$9}{2} = \$601.5 + \$598.5 = \$1{,}200.$

    Sum of annual relevant ordering and carrying costs equal $1,200.

2. The prediction error affects C, which is now:

    $C = \$4 + (10\% \times \$30) = \$7$

    $D = 2{,}000,\ P = \$40,\ C = \$7$

    EOQ $= \sqrt{\dfrac{2(2{,}000)\$40}{\$7}} = 151.186$ tires $\simeq 151$ tires

The cost of the prediction error can be calculated using a three-step procedure:

Step 1: Compute the monetary outcome from the best action that could have been taken, given the actual amount of the cost input.

    TRC $= \dfrac{DP}{Q} + \dfrac{QC}{2}$

    $ = \dfrac{2{,}000 \times \$40}{151.186} + \dfrac{151.186 \times \$7}{2}$

    $ = \$529.15 + \$529.15 = \$1{,}058.30$

21-28 (Cont'd.)

Step 2: Compute the monetary outcome from the best action based on the incorrect amount of the predicted cost input.

$$\text{TRC} = \frac{DP}{Q} + \frac{QC}{2}$$

$$= \frac{2,000 \times \$40}{133.333} + \frac{133.333 \times \$7}{2}$$

$$= \$600 + \$466.67 = \$1,066.67$$

Step 3: Compute the difference between the monetary outcomes from Step 1 and Step 2:

	Monetary Outcome
Step 1	$1,058.30
Step 2	1,066.67
Difference	$ (8.37)

The cost of the prediction error is $8.37.

Note: The $20 prediction error for the purchase price of the heavy-duty tires is irrelevant in computing purchase costs under the two alternatives because the same purchase costs will be incurred whatever the order size.

Some students may prefer to round off the EOQs to 133 tires and 151 tires, respectively. The calculations under each step in this case follows:

Step 1: $\text{TRC} = \dfrac{2,000 \times \$40}{151} + \dfrac{151 \times \$7}{2} = \$529.80 + \$528.50 = \$1058.30$

Step 2: $\text{TRC} = \dfrac{2,000 \times \$40}{133} + \dfrac{133 \times \$7}{2} = \$601.50 + \$465.50 = \$1067.00$

Step 3: Difference = $1,058.30 – $1,067.00 = $8.70

21-30 (30 min.) **Choosing suppliers for JIT purchasing.**

1. Solution Exhibit 21-30 presents the costs to Chang if he purchases the paper from Savoy and if he purchases the paper from Bond. On the basis of the financial numbers, it costs Chang $44,850 less to purchase the paper from Savoy.

2. Other factors that Chang should consider before choosing a supplier are:

   a. The supplier's flexibility to supply different types of paper that Chang may need from time to time.
   b. The supplier's ability to deliver printing paper at short notice, if Chang needs supplies urgently.
   c. The emphasis that the supplier places on continuous improvement in costs, quality and delivery.
   d. Chang's confidence in building a long-term relationship with the supplier based on trust and the willingness to share confidential information with each other.
   e. Chang's confidence in his own estimates and the need to perform sensitivity analysis.

SOLUTION EXHIBIT 21-30
Annual Relevant Costs of Purchasing From Savoy and Bond

	Incremental Costs of Purchasing from Savoy	Incremental Costs of Purchasing from Bond
Purchase costs		
$100 per box × 100,000 boxes	$10,000,000	
$95 per box × 100,000 boxes		$ 9,500,000
Required return on investment		
15% per year × $100 × 200[a] boxes of average inventory per year	3,000	
15% per year × $95 × 200[a] boxes of average inventory per year		2,850
Overtime and subcontracting costs		
No overtime necessary	0	
Overtime due to late deliveries ($30,000 × 10 jobs)		300,000
Costs of poor quality and smudging	0	245,000[b]
Total relevant costs	$10,003,000	$10,047,850
Difference in favor of Savoy	↑ $44,850 ↑	

[a] Order quantity ÷ 2 = 400 ÷ 2 = 200.

[b]The relevant costs of poor quality and smudging per job are:

Additional costs of printing paper ($110 per box × 400 boxes)	$ 44,000
Additional other direct materials (ink and so on)	2,000
Additional variable printing overhead	3,000
Total relevant costs of poor quality per job	$ 49,000
Relevant costs of poor quality for 5 jobs during the year ($49,000 × 5)	$245,000

21-32 (20 min.)   **Inventory management, ethics.**

1.   Showing supplies purchased in 19_8 as equipment purchases increases Belco's 19_8 operating income by $2,700,000 as follows:

Reduced supplies expense in 19_8	$3,000,000
Increased depreciation expense in 19_8	
$3,000,000 ÷ 10	(300,000)
Net reduction in operating expense or increase in operating income	$2,700,000

Yes, as Gary Wood states, costs related to revenue should be expensed in the period in which the revenue is recognized. Generally, supplies are purchased for use in the current period, will not provide benefits in future periods, and should be matched against the revenue recognized in the current period. The accounting treatment for the supplies was not in accordance with generally accepted accounting principles.

2.   The use of alternative accounting methods to manipulate reported earnings is unethical because it violates the Standards of Ethical Conduct for Management Accountants. The competence standard is violated because of failure to comply with technical standards and lack of appropriate analysis. The integrity standard is violated because this action puts extreme management pressure on persons to carry out unethical duties, subverts the attainment of an organization's objectives, and discredits the profession. The objectivity standard is violated because of the failure to communicate information fully and fairly.

3.   Gary Woods' actions were appropriate. The Standards of Ethical Conduct for Management Accountants describe steps to be taken in the resolution of ethical conflict, and Wood has followed these steps. Upon discovering the change in the method of accounting for supplies, Wood brought the matter to the attention of his immediate superior, Kern. Upon learning of the arrangement with Pristeel, Wood told Kern that action was improper and requested that the accounts be corrected and the arrangement discontinued. Wood clarified the situation with a qualified and objective peer (advisor) before disclosing Kern's arrangement with Pristeel to Belco's president, Kern's immediate superior. The Standards state that contact with levels above the immediate superior should be initiated only with the superior's knowledge, assuming the superior is not involved. In this case, the superior is involved. Therefore, Wood has acted appropriately by approaching North without Kern's knowledge.

CHAPTER 22
CAPITAL BUDGETING AND COST ANALYSIS

22-2 The six stages in capital budgeting are:

1. An *identification stage* to distinguish which capital expenditure projects will accomplish organization objectives.
2. A *search stage* that explores several potential capital expenditure investments that will achieve organization objectives.
3. An *information-acquisition stage* to consider the consequences of alternative capital investments.
4. A *selection stage* to choose projects for implementation.
5. A *financing stage* to obtain project financing.
6. An *implementation and control* stage to put the project in motion and monitor its performance.

22-4 No. Only quantitative outcomes are formally analyzed in capital budgeting decisions. Many effects of capital budgeting decisions, however, are difficult to quantify in financial terms. These nonfinancial or qualitative factors, for example, the number of accidents in a manufacturing plant, or employee morale, are important to consider in making capital budgeting decisions.

22-6 The payback method measures the time it will take to recoup, in the form of net cash inflows, the total dollars invested in a project. The payback method is simple and easy to understand. It is a handy method when precision in estimates of profitability is not crucial and when predicted cash flows in later years are highly uncertain. The main weakness of the payback method is its neglect of profitability and the time value of money.

22-8 The breakeven time (BET) method differs from the payback method in two ways.

1. BET counts time from when management first approves the project while payback counts time from when the initial investment was made.

2. BET method discounts future cash inflows to calculate BET; the payback method does not discount future cash inflows.

22-10 No. The discounted cash-flow techniques implicitly consider depreciation in rate of return computations; the compound interest tables automatically allow for recovery of investment. The net initial investment of an asset is usually regarded as a lump-sum outflow at time zero.

22-12 No. If managers are evaluated on the accrual accounting rate of return, they may not use the NPV method for capital-budgeting decisions. Instead, managers will choose investments that maximize the accrual accounting rate of return.

22-14 A postinvestment audit compares the predictions of investment costs and outcomes made at the time a project was selected to the actual results. It is important because it provides management feedback about performance. For example, if actual outcomes are much lower than predicted outcomes, management will investigate whether this occurred because the original estimates were overly optimistic or because of problems in implementing the project.

22-16 Exercises in compound interest.

The answers to these exercises are printed after the last problem, at the end of the chapter.

22-18 (30 min.) **Comparison of approaches to capital budgeting.**

The table for the present value of annuities (Appendix C, Table 4) shows: 10 periods at 14% = 5.216

1. Payback period $= \dfrac{\$110,000}{\$28,000} = 3.93$ years

2. Net present value $= \$28,000(5.216) - \$110,000$
$= \$146,048 - \$110,000 = \$36,048$

3. Internal rate of return:
$\$110,000 \ = \ $ Present value of annuity of $28,000 at x% for 10 years, or what factor (F) in the table of present values of an annuity (Appendix C, Table 4) will satisfy the following equation.

$\$110,000 \ = \$28,000F$

$F \ = \dfrac{\$110,000}{\$28,000} = 3.929$

On the 10-year line in the table for the present value of annuities (Appendix C, Table 4), find the column closest to 3.929; 3.929 is between a rate of return of 20% and 22%.

Interpolation can be used to determine the exact rate:

	Present Value Factors	
20%	4.192	4.192
IRR rate	—	3.929
22%	3.923	—
Difference	0.269	0.263

Internal rate of return $= 20\% + \left[\dfrac{0.263}{0.269} \right] (2\%)$

$= 20\% + (0.978)\,(2\%) \ = 21.96\%$

22-18 (Cont'd.)

4. Accrual accounting rate of return based on net initial investment:

    Net initial investment $= \$110,000$
    Estimated useful life $= 10$ years
    Annual straight-line depreciation $= \$110,000 \div 10 = \$11,000$

    Accrual accounting rate of return $= \dfrac{\$28,000 - \$11,000}{\$110,000}$

    $\qquad\qquad\qquad\qquad\qquad\qquad = \dfrac{\$17,000}{\$110,000} = 15.46\%$

22-20 (20–30 min.) **Net present value, internal rate of return, sensitivity analysis.**

1a. The table for the present value of annuities (Appendix C, Table 4) shows:
     16 periods at 14% = 3.889

     Net present value $= \$40,000 \, (3.889) - \$120,000$

     $\qquad\qquad\qquad\quad = \$155,560 - \$120,000 = \$35,560$

b. Internal rate of return:
    $\$120,000$ = Present value of annuity of \$40,000 at $X\%$ for 6 years, or what factor (F) in the table of present values of an annuity (Appendix C, Table 4) will satisfy the following equation.

    $\$120,000 = \$40,000F$

    $F \qquad = \dfrac{\$120,000}{\$40,000} = 3.0$

On the six-year line in the table for the present value of annuities (Appendix C, Table 4), find the column closest to 3.0; 3.0 is between a rate of return of 24% and 26%.

Interpolation is necessary:

	Present Value Factors	
24%	3.020	3.020
IRR rate	—	3.000
26%	2.885	—
Difference	0.135	0.020

Internal rate of return $= 24\% + \left[\dfrac{0.020}{0.135}\right](2\%)$

$\qquad\qquad\qquad\qquad\qquad = 24\% + (0.148) \, (2\%) = 24.30\%$

22-20 (Cont'd.)

2.   Let the minimum annual cash savings be $X.
        Then we want $X (3.889)   = $120,000

$$X = \frac{\$120,000}{3.889} = \$30,856$$

      Johnson Corporation would want annual cash savings of at least $30,856 for the net present value of the investment to equal zero. This amount of cash savings would justify the investment in financial terms.

3.   When the manager is uncertain about future cash flows, the manager would want to do sensitivity analysis, a form of which is described in requirement 2. Calculating the minimum cash flows necessary to make the project desirable gives the manager a feel for whether the investment is worthwhile or not. If the manager were quite certain about the future cash-operating cost savings, the approaches in requirement 1 would be preferred.

22-22   (22–30 min.) DCF, accrual accounting rate of return, working capital, evaluation of performance.

1a.   A summary of cash inflows and outflows (in thousands) are:

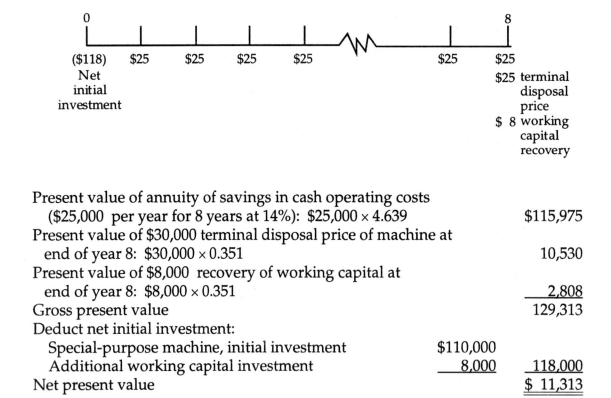

Present value of annuity of savings in cash operating costs ($25,000 per year for 8 years at 14%): $25,000 × 4.639	$115,975
Present value of $30,000 terminal disposal price of machine at end of year 8: $30,000 × 0.351	10,530
Present value of $8,000 recovery of working capital at end of year 8: $8,000 × 0.351	2,808
Gross present value	129,313

Deduct net initial investment:		
Special-purpose machine, initial investment	$110,000	
Additional working capital investment	8,000	118,000
Net present value		$ 11,313

22-22 (Cont'd.)

b. Use a trial-and-error approach. First, try a 16% discount rate:

$25,000 × 4.344	$108,600
($30,000 + $8,000) × .305	11,590
Gross present value	120,190
Deduct net initial investment	(118,000)
Net present value	$ 2,190

Second, try an 18% discount rate:

$25,000 × 4.078	$101,950
($30,000 + $8,000) × .266	10,108
Gross present value	112,058
Deduct net initial investment	(118,000)
Net present value	$ (5,942)

By interpolation:

$$\text{Internal rate of return} = 16\% + \left(\frac{2,190}{2,190 + 5,942} \right)(2\%)$$

$$= 16\% + (.269)\,(2\%) = 16.54\%$$

2.   Accrual accounting rate of return based on net initial investment:

Net initial investment = $110,000 + $8,000
= $118,000

Annual depreciation
($110,000 – $30,000) ÷ 8 years   = $10,000

$$\text{Accrual accounting rate of return} = \frac{\$25,000 - \$10,000}{\$118,000} = 12.71\%$$

3.   If your decision is based on the DCF model, the purchase would be made because the net present value is positive, and the 16.54% internal rate of return exceeds the 14% required rate of return. However, you may believe that your performance may actually be measured using accrual accounting. This approach would show a 12.71% return on the initial investment, which is below the required rate. Your reluctance to make a "buy" decision would be quite natural unless you are assured of reasonable consistency between the decision model and the performance evaluation method.

22-24 (30 min.) **Sporting contract, net present value, payback, breakeven time.**

1. a. Summary of cash inflows and outflows (in millions) follows:

	Cash Outflows	Cash Inflows	Net Cash Inflows
1998 (start)	$3.000	$ 0	$(3.000)
1998 (end)	5.500	5.600	0.100
1999 (end)	6.200	8.300	2.100
2000 (end)	7.300	9.100	1.800
2001 (end)	7.900	9.700	1.800

Year	P.V. Discount Factor	Cash Outflows	P.V. of Cash Outflows	Cash Inflows	P.V. of Cash Inflows
0:1998 (start)	1.000	$3.000	$ 3.0000	$ 0	$ 0
1:1998 (end)	0.893	5.500	4.9115	5.600	5.0008
2:1999 (end)	0.797	6.200	4.9414	8.300	6.6151
3:2000 (end)	0.712	7.300	5.1976	9.100	6.4792
4:2001 (end)	0.636	7.900	5.0244	9.700	6.1692
			$23.0749		$24.2643

The net present value of the Bebeto contract is $1.1894 ($24.2643 − $23.0749) million.

An alternative approach to determine the NPV of the Bebeto contract follows:

End of Year	Total Present Value (in millions)	Present Value of $1 Discounted at 12%	Sketch of Relevant Cash Flows				
			1998 (start)	1998 (end)	1999 (end)	2000 (end)	2001 (end)
1. Initial signing bonus	$(3.0000)←— 1.000←—— $(3.0)						
2. Recurring operating cash flows	0.0893←— 0.893←——————————$0.1						
	1.6737←— 0.797←———————————————$2.1						
	1.2816←— 0.712←———————————————————————$1.8						
	1.1448←— 0.636←———————————————————————————————$1.8						
Net present value	$1.1894						

b. Payback period:

Year	Net Cash Inflows	Cumulative Net Cash Inflows	Cash Investment Yet To Be Recovered at End of Year
0: 1998 (start)	–	–	$3.000
1: 1998 (end)	$0.100	$0.100	2.900
2: 1999 (end)	2.100	2.200	0.800
3: 2000 (end)	1.800	4.000	–
4: 2001 (end)	1.800	5.800	–

$$\text{Payback period} = 2 \text{ years} + \left[\frac{\$0.800}{\$1.800}\right] = 2.44 \text{ years}$$

c. Breakeven time:

Year	PV Discount Factor at 12% (1)	Investment Cash Outflows (2)	PV of Investment Cash Outflows* (3)=(1) x(2)	Cumulative PV of Investment Cash Outflows* (4)	Cash Inflows from Signing (5)	PV of Product Cash Inflows* (6)=(1) × (5)	Cumulative PV of Product Cash & Inflows* (7)
1998 (start)	1.000	$(3.000)	$(3.000)	$(3.000)			
1998 (end)	0.893				$0.100	$0.0893	$0.0893
1999 (end)	0.797				2.100	1.6737	1.7630
2000 (end)	0.712				1.800	1.2816	3.0446
2001 (end)	0.636				1.800	1.1448	4.1894

* at January 1, 1998

In present value terms, Milano Capri will recover $1,763 million of its investment through cash inflows by Dec. 31,1999 and $3.0446 million by Dec. 31, 2000. Milano Capri's present value of estimated cash inflows during the year 2000 is $1.2816 million and it needs $1.237 million ($3.0 million – $1.763 million) to recover its investment. Milano Capri will, thus, take 2.97 years to recover the cumulative present value of initial investment:

$$2 \text{ years (up to December 31, 1999)} + \frac{\$1.237 \text{ million}}{\$1.2816 \text{ million}} = 2.97 \text{ years}.$$

2. Other factors Agnelli might consider include:

a. Uncertainty over the predicted cash inflows for 1998 to 2001. A key factor here is the possible risk of injury to Bebeto or a diminishing of his soccer ability.
b. Increase in number of championships Milano Capri wins.
c. Increase in community pride that accompanies a championship team.
d. Agnelli's own personal prestige of being president of a championship club.
e. The effect the signing would have on Milano Capri's ability to sign other players.

22-26 (15–20 min.) **Basic job project cost control**.

1. Job project-performance cost variance is ACWP – BCWP:
   ($70 × 14,300 hours) – ($70 × 13,750 hours)   = $1,001,000 – $962,500
                                                   = $38,500 U

   Job project-schedule cost variance is BCWP – BCWS:
   ($70 × 13,750 hours) – ($70 × 15,000 hours)   = $962,500 – $1,050,000
                                                   = $87,500 U

2.

Original budget, 25,000 hours × $70	$1,750,000
Add: Unfavorable job project-performance cost variance to date	38,500
Sub-total	1,788,500
Add: Additional unfavorable job project-performance cost variance expected	31,500*
Revised budget, final cost	$1,820,000

*14,300 –13,750 = 550 hours, which is 4% of 13,750;
0.04 × 25,000 × $70 = $70,000
$70,000 – $38,500 = $31,500
or (25,000 – 13,750) × $70 × 0.04 = $31,500
Alternatively budgeted additional hours to complete project, 25,000 – 13,750 = 11,250 hours
Overruns on 13,750 budgeted hours is $38,500
So overruns on 11,250 budgeted hours is (11,250 ÷ 13,750) × $38,500 = $31,500.

The revised budget, by itself, does not show a revised schedule. The project is already 550 (14,300 – 13,750) hours behind schedule. A late completion date may be in the offing. Extra costs might have to be incurred in order to attain the original completion date.

22-28 (22–30 min.) Payback, net present value, relevant costs, sensitivity analysis.

All amounts are in thousands.

1. Old cash flow: Cash revenues, $120 – Cash costs, $124 $ (4)
    New cash flow: 10% of $80   8
    Expected increase in recurring operating
       cash flows for 10 years $12

2. Initial machine investment $64
    Deduct current disposal price of old equipment   (4)
    Net initial investment $60

    Payback period: $60 ÷ $12 = 5 years

3. NPV of cash inflows and outflows (in thousands):

End of Year	Total Present Value	Present Value Discount Factor at 14%	Sketch of Relevant Cash Flows				
			0	1		9	10
1. Initial machine investment			$(64)				
2. Current disposal price of old equipment			$ 4				
Net initial investment	$(60.00) ←— 1.00 ←—		$(60)				
3. Recurring operating cash flows	62.40 ←— 5.20←			$12·········	····················$12	$12	
4. Terminal disposal price of machine	1.35 ←— 0.27 ←						$ 5
Net present value	$ 3.75						

4. Let X = Annual gross vending machine receipts.

    $$
    \begin{aligned}
    (0.10X + \$4)(5.20) \quad + \quad \$1.35 &= \$60 \\
    0.52X \quad + \quad \$20.80 &= \$60 - \$1.35 \\
    0.52X &= \$58.65 - \$20.80 = \$37.85 \\
    X &= \$37.85 \div 0.52 \\
    &= \$72.788 \text{ (or } \$72,788)
    \end{aligned}
    $$

    Proof:
$72,788 × 10%	$ 7,278.80
Add	4,000.00
Total	11,278.80
Multiply by	5.20
Total	58,650.00
Disposal price, $5,000 × 0.27	1,350.00
Total	60,000.00
Deduct investment	(60,000.00)
Difference	$ 0

Note: Both the book value and the depreciation on the old equipment are irrelevant.

22-30 (30 min.) **Special order, relevant costs, capital budgeting.**

1. Relevant cash inflow from accepting the special order

	Relevant cash flows	
	Per Car	Total
	(1)	(2)=(1) × 100,000
Incremental revenues (cash inflows)	$50	$5,000,000
Incremental costs (cash outflows)		
Neon paint	6	600,000
Boxes	3	300,000
Direct manufacturing labor	8	800,000
Total incremental costs	17	1,700,000
Net incremental benefit	$33	$3,300,000

Notes:

a. The costs of plastic cars are irrelevant because these cars have already been purchased and, so, entail no incremental cash flow.

b. Vat depreciation is irrelevant because it is a past cost.

c. Allocated plant manager's salary is irrelevant because it will not change whether or not the special order is accepted.

d. Variable marketing costs are not deducted because they will not be incurred on the special order.

(e) Fixed marketing costs are irrelevant because they will not change whether or not the special order is accepted.

If it must offer the same $50 price to its other customers, Toys Inc. will lose cash flow of $9 × 130,000 = $1,170,000 per year for 4 years from its existing customers.

Note that whatever incremental costs Toys incurs on sales to its existing customers is irrelevant. These costs would continue to be incurred whether Toys prices the cars at $50 or $59. You can verify that Toys generates positive contribution margin at a price of $50 and, so, should continue to sell to its existing customers.

From Appendix C, Table 4, the present value of a stream of $1,170,000 payments for 4 years discounted at 16% is $1,170,000 × 2.798 = $3,273,660.

The net relevant benefit of accepting the special order is $3,300,000 – $3,273,660 = $26,340. Therefore, Toys, Inc. should accept the special order.

22-30 (Cont'd.)

2.   Let the dollar discount from the current $59 price offered to existing customers be $X

Then $X (130,000) (2.798)   =   3,300,000

$$X = \frac{3,300,000}{(130,000)(2.798)} = \$9.0724$$

At a price of $49.9276 ($59 – $9.0724) per car to its existing customers, Toys would just be indifferent between accepting and rejecting Tiny Tot's special order.

22-32   (25 min.)   Capital budgeting, computer-integrated manufacturing, sensitivity.

1.   The net present value analysis of the CIM proposal follows. We consider the differences in cash flows if the machine is replaced. (All values in millions.)

	Relevant Cash Flows	Present Value Discount Factors at 14%	Total Present Value
1. Initial investment in CIM today	$(45)	1.000	$(45.000)
2a. Current disposal price of old production line	5	1.000	5.000
2b. Current recovery of working capital ($6 – $2)	4	1.000	4.000
3 Recurring operating cash savings			
$4[1] each year for 10 years	4	5.216	20.864
4a. Higher terminal disposal price of machines			
($14 – $0) in year 10	14	0.270	3.780
b. Reduced recovery of working capital			
($2 – $6) in year 10	(4)	0.270	(1.080)
Net present value of CIM investment			$(12.436)

[1] Recurring operating cash flows are as follows:

Cost of maintaining software programs and CIM equipment	$(1.5)
Reduction in lease payments due to reduced floor-space requirements	1.0
Fewer product defects and reduced rework	4.5
Annual recurring operating cash flows	$ 4.0

On the basis of this formal financial analysis, Dynamo should not invest in CIM—it has a negative net present value of $(12.436) million.

2.   Requirement 1 only looked at cost savings to justify the investment in CIM. Burns estimates additional cash revenues net of cash operating costs of $3 million a year as a result of higher quality and faster production resulting from CIM.

From Appendix C, Table 4, the net present value of the $3 million annuity stream for 10 years discounted at 14% is $3 × 5.216 = $15.648. Taking these revenue benefits into account, the net present value of the CIM investment is $3.212 ($15.648 – $12.436) million. On the basis of this financial analysis, Dynamo should invest in CIM.

3.   Let the annual cash flow from additional revenues be X. Then, we want the present value of this cash flow stream to overcome the negative NPV of $(12.436) calculated in requirement 1. Hence,

$$X\ (5.216) \quad = \quad 12.436$$

$$X \quad = \quad \$2.384 \text{ million}$$

An annuity stream of $2.384 million for 10 years discounted at 14% gives an NPV of $2.384 × 5.216 = 12.436 (rounded)

4.

		Relevant Cash Flows	Present Value Discount Factors at 14%	Total Present Value
1.	Initial investment in CIM Today	$(45)	1.000	$(45.000)
2a.	Current disposal price of old production line	5	1.000	5.000
b.	Current recovery of working capital ($6 – $2)	4	1.000	4.000
3a	Recurring operating cash savings 4 each year for 5 years	4	3.433	13.732
b.	Recurring cash flows from additional revenues of $3 each year for 5 years	3	3.433	10.299
4a.	Higher terminal disposal price of machines ($20 – $4) in year 5	16	0.519	8.304
b.	Reduced recovery of working capital ($2 – $6) in year 5	(4)	0.519	(2.076)
	Net present value of CIM investment			$ (5.741)

The use of too short a time horizon such as 5 years biases against the adoption of CIM projects. Before finally deciding against CIM in this case, Burns should consider other factors, including

a.   Sensitivity to different estimates of recurring cash savings or revenue gains.
b.   Accuracy of the costs of implementing and maintaining CIM.
c.   Benefits of greater flexibility that results from CIM and the opportunity to train workers for the manufacturing environment of the future.
d.   Potential obsolescence of the CIM equipment. Dynamo should consider how difficult the CIM equipment would be to modify if there is a major change in CIM technology.
e.   Alternative approaches to achieving the major benefits of CIM such as changes in process or implementation of just-in-time systems.
f.   Strategic factors. CIM may be the best approach to remain competitive against other low-cost producers in the future.

22-34 (15–25 min.) **Project-cost control.**

Basic data follow. Budgeted costs are $120 per hour:

	Hours	Costs	
Original budget to complete	30,000	$3,600,000[a]	
Budgeted for work scheduled to date	21,000	2,520,000[a]	BCWS
Budgeted for work performed to date	22,000	2,640,000[a]	BCWP
Actual hours and costs of work performed to date	21,500	2,795,000	ACWP

[a]Hours times the budgeted costs of $120 per hour.

1. Job project-performance cost variance is ACWP – BCWP:

($130 × 21,500 hours) – ($120 × 22,000 hours) $\quad$ = $\quad$ $2,795,000 –$2,640,000

$\qquad\qquad\qquad\qquad\qquad\qquad\qquad\qquad\qquad$ = $\quad$ $155,000 U

A breakdown of the job project-performance cost variance into efficiency and price variances is:

Efficiency variance:

(22,000 – 21,500) × $120 $\qquad\qquad$ = $\qquad\qquad$ $60,000 F

Price variance, unfavorable:

$\qquad$ (unfavorable job project-performance cost variance – unfavorable efficiency variance) or (unfavorable job project-performance cost variance + favorable efficiency variance)

$\qquad$ $155,000 + $60,000 $\qquad\qquad$ = $\qquad\qquad$ $215,000 U

Job project-schedule cost variance is BCWP – BCWS:

($120 × 22,000) – ($120 × 21,000) $\quad$ = $\quad$ $2,640,000 – $2,520,000

$\qquad\qquad\qquad\qquad\qquad\qquad\qquad\quad$ = $\quad$ $120,000 F

2. The project is ahead of schedule and the underlying work is being performed efficiently. The unfavorable job project-performance cost variance is attributable to the average "price" per hour being $10 higher than anticipated.

$\qquad$ $215,000 ÷ 21,500 actual hours = $10

The manager may find this an acceptable price to pay if the project will be completed ahead of schedule. However, the expected final costs will exceed the original budget of $3,600,000.

Original budget	$3,600,000
Project cost (actual) as a percent of budget:	
$2,795,000 ÷ $2,640,000 = 105.87121%	
105.87121% of $3,600,000 =	
Revised budget, final cost	$3,811,364

22-36 (50 min.) Relevant costs, capital budgeting

1.   Solution Exhibit 22-36 presents an analysis of cash inflows and outflows (in thousands) under the alternatives of (1) cease SPD operations and (2) buy a new machine.

The Special Products Division should buy the new machine rather than cease operations because purchasing the new machine has a higher net present value ($162,160 versus $136,780).

SOLUTION EXHIBIT 22-36
Net Present Value Analysis for Special Products Division
(in thousands)

End of Year	Total Present Value	Present Value of $1 Discounted at 16%	Sketch of Relevant Cash Flows					
			1997	1998	1999	2000	2001	2002
CEASE OPERATIONS								
1. Sell patent	$235.00	←—1.000	←–$235					
2. Recurring operating cash flows								
a. Manager's salary in larger department	(196.44)	←—3.274	←———————— $(60)	$ (60)	$ (60)	$ (60)	$ (60)	
b. Rental income from building space	98.22	←—3.274	←———————— $ 30	$ 30	$ 30	$ 30	$ 30	
Net present value	$136.78							
BUY A NEW MACHINE								
1. Initial machine investment	$(320.00)	←—1.000	←–$(320)					
2. Recurring operating cash flows								
a. Contribution margin from operations[a]	982.20	←—3.274	←————————$ 300	$300	$300	$300	$300	
b. Machine maintenance	(81.85)	←—3.274	←————————$ (25)	$ (25)	$ (25)	$ (25)	$ (25)	
c. Other fixed costs	(49.11)	←—3.274	←————————$ (15)	$ (15)	$ (15)	$ (15)	$ (15)	
d. Manager's salary in Special Products Div.	(180.07)	←—3.274	←————————$ (55)	$ (55)	$ (55)	$ (55)	$ (55)	
e. Manager's salary in larger department	(212.81)	←—3.274	←————————$ (65)	$ (65)	$ (65)	$ (65)	$ (65)	
3. Terminal disposal price of new machine	23.80	←—0.476	←—————————————————————————$50					
Net present value	$162.16							

[a] Contribution margin from operations (in thousands):

Revenues		$1,200
Variable costs:		
Production	$770	
Marketing	130	
Total variable costs		900
Contribution margin		$ 300

22-14

22-36 (Cont'd.)

Note the following:

    a.   The terminal disposal price of $4,000 for the old machine is irrelevant because the old machine will be disposed of under both alternatives—either if SPD ceases operations or if SPD buys a new machine.

    b.   Machine depreciation and patent amortization are noncash costs and, hence, irrelevant for the NPV analysis.

    c.   The allocated building costs of $20,000 are irrelevant for the analysis because the same building costs will be incurred in total under either alternative. The $30,000 additional cash flow that SPD will receive if it ceases operations and rents out the space is relevant in computing the NPV of the "cease operations" alternative, because this cash flow is only received if SPD shuts down operations.

    d.   Machine maintenance costs of $20,000 for the old broken down machine are irrelevant. Machine maintenance costs of $25,000 for the new machine are relevant.

2.   In order to maximize compensation, the decision maker will favor the alternative that maximizes aggregate accounting income in 1998.

	Increase/(Decrease) in Plastics Unlimited's Total Operating Income in 1998 (in thousands)
Effect of ceasing operations on Plastic Unlimited's operating income	
Gain on sale of patent[b]	$110
Manager's salary in larger department	(60)
Rental income	30
Effect on Plastic Unlimited's operating income	$ 80
Effect of buying a new machine on Plastic Unlimited's operating income	
Contribution margin from operations	$300
Machine depreciation ($320 – $50) ÷ 5 years	(54)
Patent amortization	(25)
SPD manager's salary	(55)
Assistant manager's salary in larger department	(65)
Machine maintenance	(25)
Other fixed costs	(15)
Effect on Plastic Unlimited's operating income	$ 61

[b] Proceeds from sale of patent	$235
Deduct book value of patent	125
Gain on sale of patent	$110

To maximize Plastic Unlimited's operating income in 1998, and, hence, bonus, the individual decision maker would prefer to cease SPD's operations even though buying a new machine has a higher NPV.

Note the following:
  a. The data relating to the disposal of the old machine are irrelevant since the old machine will be disposed of under both alternatives.
  b. Depreciation on the new machine and patent amortization are relevant for the operating income computations. These costs will only be incurred if SPD continues operations and buys the new machine.
  c. The allocated building space costs of $20,000 are irrelevant because the same building costs will be incurred in total whether SPD ceases operations or SPD buys a new machine. The rental income of $30,000 by renting out building space if SPD ceases operations is relevant and is, therefore, included in the calculation of operating income under the "cease operations" alternative.

CHAPTER 23
CAPITAL BUDGETING: A CLOSER LOOK

The exercises and problems in this chapter most often use straight-line or accelerated depreciation methods. These two methods are the ones most frequently used in the Modified Accelerated Cost Recovery System. Depreciation regulations based on a specific tax code are not presented. Specific tax regulations are frequently updated and are often out-of-date even before a book is published. Our purpose is to illustrate how a given write-off is incorporated into DCF analysis.

23-2 No. If a company has taxable income and if no changes in future tax rates are anticipated, accelerated write-offs are generally preferable to straight-line write-offs. Although the total dollar tax bills under alternative depreciation methods may be the same when the years are taken together, their present values may differ because early write-offs defer tax outlays to future periods. The measure of this advantage depends on the rate of return that can be gained from the use of funds that otherwise would have been paid as income taxes.

23-4 The total project approach calculates the present value of *all* cash outflows and inflows associated with each alternative. The differential approach analyzes only those cash outflows and inflows that differ between alternatives.

23-6 No. Income taxes also affect the cash-operating flows from an investment and the cash flows from current and terminal disposal of machines in the capital budgeting decision. When a company has positive cash-operating flows and gains on disposal of machines, income taxes reduce the cash flows available to the company from these sources.

23-8 The *real rate of return* is the rate of return required to cover only investment risk. This rate is made up of two elements: (1) a risk-free element, and (2) a business-risk element. The *nominal rate of return* is the rate of return required to cover investment risk and the anticipated decline, due to inflation, in general purchasing power of the cash that the investment generates. This rate is made up of two elements: (1) the real rate of return, and (2) an inflation element.

The *nominal rate of return* and the *real rate of return* are related as follows:

Nominal rate = [(1 + Real rate) (1 + Inflation rate)] − 1

23-10 U.S. tax laws restrict the amount allowed for depreciation to the asset's original cost in *nominal dollars* irrespective of any inflation that occurs from the time when the asset was purchased to the time that the depreciation is claimed. To express these depreciation tax savings in real dollars, we divide the nominal dollars by the cumulative rate of inflation when using the real approach.

23-12 Projects with different levels of risk should have different required rates of return. The higher the risk, the higher the required rate of return.

23-14 Yes. The excess present-value index measures the cash-flow return per dollar invested. The index is helpful in choosing among projects when investment funds are limited because profitability indexes can identify the projects that will generate the most money from the limited capital available. Managers cannot, however, base decisions involving mutually exclusive investments of different sizes solely on the excess present-value index. The net present-value method is the best general guide.

23-16 (10–15 min.) **Recapitulation of role of depreciation in Chapters 11, 22, and 23.**

Many students are confused at this point. A discussion is usually worthwhile. Relevance is defined in Chapter 11 as being those expected future items that will differ among alternative courses of action.

Chapter 11 was confined to an accrual-accounting model, not a discounted cash-flow model. Under the accrual model, depreciation on old equipment is irrelevant because the total book value is ultimately written off regardless of whether it takes the form of annual depreciation or a lump-sum charge. Thus, depreciation on the old equipment is not an element of difference. Depreciation on new equipment is a relevant cost because this is a future cost that will not be incurred if the equipment is not purchased.

Chapter 22 implied that all depreciation was irrelevant under the discounted cash-flow model because, otherwise, the original investment would be counted twice. The investment is incorporated as a one-time outlay at time zero, so it should not be deducted again in the form of depreciation.

Chapter 23 did not state that depreciation was relevant. However, depreciation does provide a basis for predicting income tax cash flows, which are indeed relevant.

23-18 (15–20 min.) **Multiple choice, including straight-line depreciation.**

1. a.

Recurring before-tax cash-operating inflows	$10,000
Income tax cash outflow:	
0.40 [$10,000 – ($30,000 ÷ 6)] = 0.40 ($10,000 – $5,000)	(2,000)
Recurring cash flows from operations, net of income taxes	8,000*
Depreciation	(5,000)
Net income	$ 3,000

Accrual accounting rate of return, $3,000 ÷ $30,000 = 10%

*or

Recurring before-tax cash-operating flows	$10,000
Deduct depreciation: $30,000 ÷ 6	(5,000)
Operating income	5,000
Deduct income tax cash outflow: 0.40 ($5,000)	(2,000)
Net income	3,000
Add back depreciation	5,000
Recurring cash flows from operations, net of income taxes	$ 8,000

2. b.   Payback period = $30,000 ÷ $8,000 = 3.75 years

3. b.   NPV = $8,000 (3.785) – $30,000 = $280

4. b.   Only one payment will be made, which 5 years later, must yield $30,000. Therefore, deduct the value of an annuity of four payments from the value of an annuity of five payments:

$$3.353 - 2.856 = 0.497$$

Note that 3.353 – 2.856 = 0.497 is the present value of a cash outflow of $1 occurring at the end of period 5. Alternatively stated, $1 is the future value of $0.497 invested five years ago. Therefore, to have $30,000 now, we need to invest its present value 5 years ago discounted at 15% equal to:

$$\$30,000 \times 0.497 = \$14,910$$

23-20 (40 min.) **Total project versus differential approach, income taxes, straight-line depreciation.**

a. Total Project Approach
Replace machine

	Relevant Cash Flows	Present Value Discount Factors at 14%	Total Present Value
1. Initial machine-investment	$(63,000)	1.000	$(63,000.00)
2. After-tax cash flow from current disposal of old machine:			
Book value of old machine ($88,000 – $22,000) $66,000			
Current disposal price of old machine 29,000	$ 29,000		
Loss on disposal of machine $37,000			
Tax savings (30% of $37,000 loss)	11,100		
After-tax cash flow from current disposal of old machine	$ 40,100	1.000	40,100.00
3. Recurring cash-operating flows (costs)	$(40,000)		
Deduct income tax savings at 30% of $40,000	12,000		
Recurring after-tax cash-operating flows (costs) for 3 years (excl. deprn. effects)	$(28,000)	2.322	(65,016.00)
4. Income tax savings from depreciation deductions			

Year	Straight-Line Depreciation Rate	Income Tax Depreciation Deduction	Income Tax Cash Savings from Depreciation Deductions at 30%		
1	1/3	$21,000	$6,300	0.877	5,525.10
2	1/3	21,000	6,300	0.769	4,844.70
3	1/3	21,000	6,300	0.675	4,252.50
					14,622.30
Net present value					$(73,293.70)

23-20 (Cont'd.)

Keep machine

	Relevant Cash Flows	Present Value Discount Factors at 14%	Total Present Value
1. Recurring cash-operating flows (costs)	$(60,000)		
Deduct income tax savings at 30% of $60,000	18,000		
Recurring after-tax cash-operating flows (costs) each year for 3 years (excl. deprn. effects)	$(42,000)	2.322	$(97,524.00)
2. Income tax cash savings from depreciation deductions ($88,000 ÷ 4): $22,000			
Income tax cash savings from depreciation deductions each year for 3 years at 30%: $22,000 × 0.30	$ 6,600	2.322	15,325.20
3. After-tax cash flow from terminal disposal of old machine:			
Terminal disposal price of old machine three years hence	$ 6,000		
Deduct book value of old machine at end of year 3	0		
Gain on disposal of machine	6,000		
Deduct taxes on gain (30% of $6,000)	(1,800)		
After-tax cash flow from terminal disposal of old machine	$ 4,200	0.675	2,835.00
Net present value of all cash flows			$(79,363.80)
Net present value difference in favor of replacement ($79,363.80 – $73,293.70)			$ 6,070.10

23-5

b. Differential Approach

	Relevant Cash Flows	Present Value Discount Factors at 14%	Total Present Value
Analysis confined to differences if machine replaced			
1. Initial machine investment	$(63,000)	1.000	$(63,000.00)
2. After-tax cash flow from current disposal of old machine	$ 40,100	1.000	40,100.00
3. Additional recurring before-tax cash-operating savings $60,000 – $40,000	$ 20,000		
Deduct income tax on savings at 30% of $20,000	(6,000)		
Savings in after-tax cash-operating costs each year for 3 years (excl. deprn. effects)	$ 14,000	2.322	32,508.00
4. Income tax savings from depreciation deductions			

Year (1)	Income Tax Depreciation Deduction when Machine Replaced (2)	Income Tax Depreciation Deduction if Old Machine Kept (3)	Additional Income Tax Depreciation Deductions if Machine Replaced (4)	Income Tax Cash Savings from Additional Depreciation Deductions (5) = 30% of (4)		
1	$21,000	$22,000	$(1,000)	$(300)	0.877	(263.10)
2	21,000	22,000	(1,000)	(300)	0.769	(230.70)
3	21,000	22,000	(1,000)	(300)	0.675	(202.50)

5. Increase in after-tax cash flow from terminal disposal if machine replaced, end of year 3:

	Relevant Cash Flows	Discount Factors	Total Present Value
$0 – $4,200	(4,200)	0.675	(2,835.00)
Net present value difference in favor of replacement			$ 6,076.70*

* Differences caused by rounding discount factors.

23-22 (40 min.) Project risk, required rate of return.

1.   Assume an after-tax required rate of return of 12% for both projects.

Drilling equipment project

		Relevant Cash Flows	Present Value Discount Factors at 12%	Total Present Value
1.	Initial drilling equipment investment	$(1,000,000)	1.000	$(1,000,000)
2.	Recurring cash-operating flows	$ 370,000		
	Additional income taxes at 30%	(111,000)		
	Recurring after-tax cash-operating flows each year for 5 years (excl. deprn. effects)	$ 259,000	3.605	933,695
3.	Income tax cash savings from depreciation deductions:			
	Depreciation deductions ($1,000,000 ÷ 5): $200,000 each year			
	Income tax cash savings from depreciation deductions each year for 5 years at 30%:			
	$200,000 × 0.30	$ 60,000	3.605	216,300
	Net present value			$ 149,995

Production equipment project

		Relevant Cash Flows	Present Value Discount Factors at 12%	Total Present Value
1.	Initial production equipment investment	$ (800,000)	1.000	$ (800,000)
2.	Recurring cash-operating flows	$ 300,000		
	Additional income taxes at 30%	(90,000)		
	Recurring after-tax cash-operating flows each year for 4 years (excl. deprn. effects)	$ 210,000	3.037	637,770
3.	Income tax cash savings from depreciation deductions:			
	Depreciation deductions ($800,000 ÷ 4): $200,000 each year			
	Income tax cash savings from depreciation deductions each year for 4 years at 30%:			
	$200,000 × 0.30	$ 60,000	3.037	182,220
	Net present value			$ 19,990

At a 12% discount rate for both projects, the drilling equipment project has the higher NPV and would be preferred.

23-22 (Cont'd.)

2.   We calculate the NPV of the high-risk drilling equipment project assuming a required rate of return of 18%.

		Relevant Cash Flows	Present Value Discount Factors at 18%	Total Present Value
1.	Initial drilling equipment investment	$(1,000,000)	1.000	$(1,000,000)
2.	Recurring cash-operating flows	$ 370,000		
	Additional income taxes at 30%	(111,000)		
	Recurring after-tax cash-operating flows each year for 5 years (excl. deprn. effects)	$ 259,000	3.127	809,893
3.	Income tax cash savings from depreciation deductions:			
	Depreciation deductions ($1,000,000 ÷ 5): $200,000 each year			
	Income tax cash savings from depreciation deductions each year for 5 years at 30%:			
	$200,000 × 0.30	$ 60,000	3.127	187,620
	Net present value			$ (2,487)

The lower-risk production equipment project for the refinery discounted at 12% has an NPV of $19,990 (requirement 1) that is greater than the NPV of $(2,487) for the higher-risk drilling equipment project for oil exploration discounted at 18%.

3.   Esso should favor investing in the production equipment for the refinery because it has a positive NPV. It should not invest in the drilling equipment because this project has a negative NPV when discounted at the risk adjusted 18% required rate of return.

23-24   (25 min.)   Inflation and nonprofit institution, no tax aspects.

1.   The university official calculated the following NPV using the 18.8% discount rate and real cash operating savings.

Year	Relevant Cash-Operating Savings in Real Dollars as of 12-31-94 (1)	Present Value Discount Factors at 18.8% (2)	Present Value of Cash Flows (3) = (1) × (2)
19_5	$1,000	0.842	$ 842
19_6	1,000	0.709	709
19_7	1,000	0.596	596
19_8	1,000	0.502	502
19_9	1,000	0.423	423
Present value of recurring cash-operating savings			3,072
Net initial investment			3,500
Net present value			$ (428)

On the basis of these calculations, the university official would reject the proposal to invest in the photocopying machine. This approach is incorrect because it discounts real cash flows using a nominal discount rate. The official should redo the analysis after restating the real cash savings into nominal cash savings as shown below.

Year	Relevant Cash-Operating Savings in Nominal Dollars (1)	Present Value Discount Factors at 18.8% (2)	Present Value of Nominal Cash Flows (3) = (1) × (2)
19_5	$1,000 × 1.10 = $1,100	0.842	$ 926
19_6	1,000 × (1.10)^2 = 1,210	0.709	858
19_7	1,000 × (1.10)^3 = 1,331	0.596	793
19_8	1,000 × (1.10)^4 = 1,464	0.502	735
19_9	1,000 × (1.10)^5 = 1,611	0.423	681
Present value of recurring cash-operating savings			3,993
Net initial investment			3,500
Net present value			$ 493

The net present value using nominal cash flows and a nominal rate of return is positive, $493. Southern University should invest in the photocopying machine on the basis of financial considerations.

2a. The real rate of return required by Southern University can be computed using the following relationship:

$$(1 + \text{real rate}) = \frac{1 + \text{nominal rate}}{1 + \text{inflation rate}} = \frac{1 + 0.188}{1 + 0.10} = \frac{1.188}{1.10} = 1.08$$

Real rate of return required = 0.08 or 8%

b. The net present value using real operating cash savings and real rates of return are as follows:

Year	Relevant Cash-Operating Savings in Real Dollars as of 12-31-94	Present Value Discount Factors at 8% (2)	Present Value of Real Cash Flows (3) = (1) × (2)
1	$1,000	0.926	$ 926
2	1,000	0.857	857
3	1,000	0.794	794
4	1,000	0.735	735
5	1,000	0.681	681
Present value of recurring cash-operating savings			3,993
Net initial investment			3,500
Net present value			$ 493

3. Requirements 1 and 2, when correctly done, give the same NPV of $493. Consistency is key in capital budgeting. Requirement 1 uses nominal cash flows and nominal rates of return. Requirement 2 uses real cash flows and real rates of return. Both are valid approaches.

23-26 (20–30 min.) **Comparison of projects with unequal lives.**

1. Internal rate of return

Project 1

Let F = Present value factor of $1 at X% received at the end of year 1, Appendix C, Table 2

$$\$10,000 \quad = \quad \text{PV of } \$12,000 \text{ at X\% to be received at the end of year 1}$$
$$F \quad = \quad \frac{\$10,000}{\$12,000} = 0.833$$
$$IRR \quad = \quad 20\%$$

Project 2

Let F = Present value factor of $1 at X% received at the end of year 4, Appendix C, Table 2

$$\$10,000 \quad = \quad \text{PV of } \$17,500 \text{ at X\% to be received at the end of year 4}$$

$$F \quad = \quad \frac{\$10,000}{\$17,500} = 0.571$$

The internal rate of return can be calculated by interpolation:

	Present Value Factors for $1 Received after 4 years	
14%	0.592	0.592
IRR rate	–	0.571
16%	0.552	–
Difference	0.040	0.021

$$\text{IRR rate: } 14\% + \left(\frac{0.021}{0.040}\right)(2\%) = 15.05\%$$

Project 1 is preferable to Project 2 using the IRR criterion.

2. Net present value

Project 1:

Gross present value $=$ PV of $12,000 at 10% to be received at the end of year 1
$= \$12,000 \ (0.909) \quad = \quad \$10,908$
Net present value $= \$10,908 - \$10,000 \quad = \quad \$908$

● Project 2:

Gross present value   = PV of $17,500 at 10% to be received at the end of year 4
                       = $17,500 (0.683)   = $11,952.50
Net present value   = $11,952.50 – $10,000 = $1,952.50

Project 2 is preferable to Project 1 using the net present value criterion.

3.   This problem contrasts the implied reinvestment rates of return under the internal rate of return and net present value methods. Where the economic lives of mutually exclusive projects are unequal, this clash of reinvestment rates may give different conclusions under the two methods. This result occurs because the internal rate of return method assumes that the reinvestment rate is at least equal to the computed rate of return on the project. The net present value method assumes that the funds obtainable from competing projects can be reinvested at the rate of the company's required rate of return. Comparisons follow:

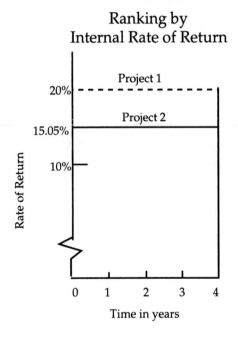

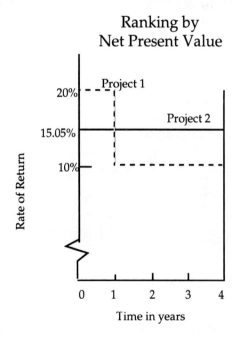

Assumption: Project 1 funds can be reinvested at 20% over the life of the shorter-lived project.

Assumption: Project (1) funds can be reinvested at 10%, the required rate of return.

23-28 (40 min.) **Replacement of a machine, income taxes, straight-line depreciation, sensitivity.**

1.   WRL Company should retain the old equipment because the net present value of the incremental cash flows is negative. The computations are presented below. In this format the present value factors appear at the bottom. All cash flows, year by year, are then converted into present values.

	After-Tax Cash Flows				
	19_5ᵃ	**19_6**	**19_7**	**19_8**	**19_9**
Initial machine investment	$(120,000)				
Current disposal price of old machine	40,000				
Tax savings from loss on disposal of old machineᵇ	4,000				
Recurring after-tax cash-operating savings:					
Variable ($0.06 × 300,000 × 0.6)ᶜ		$10,800	$10,800	$10,800	$10,800
Fixed ($1,000 × 0.6)ᵈ		600	600	600	600
Difference in income tax cash savings from depreciation deductionsᵉ		6,000	6,000	6,000	6,000
Additional after-tax cash flow from terminal disposal of new machine over old machine ($20,000 – $8,200)ᶠ					11,800
Net after-tax cash flows	$(76,000)	$17,400	$17,400	$17,400	$29,200
Present value discount factors	1.000	0.862	0.743	0.641	0.552
Present value	$(76,000)	$14,999	$12,928	$11,153	$16,118
Net present value	$(20,802)				

a. Actually January 2, 19_6

b. Original cost of old machine: $80,000
    Depreciation taken during the first 3 years
    {[(80,000 – 10,000) ÷ 7] × 3}   30,000
    Book value   50,000
    Current disposal price: 40,000
    Loss on disposal $10,000
    Tax rate   × 0.40
    Tax savings from loss on disposal of old machine $ 4,000

c. Difference in recurring after-tax variable cash-operating savings, with 40% tax rate:
    ($0.20 – $0.14) × (300,000)× (1– 0.40) = $10,800

d. Difference in after-tax fixed cost savings, with 40% tax rate:
$$(\$15{,}000 - \$14{,}000) \times (1 - 0.40) = \$600$$

e.

	Old Machine	New Machine
Initial machine investment	$80,000	$120,000
Terminal disposal price at end of useful life	10,000	20,000
Depreciable base	$70,000	$100,000
Annual depreciation using straight-line (7 year life)	$10,000	
Annual depreciation using straight-line (4 year life):		$25,000

Income tax cash savings from differences in depreciation deductions are:

Year (1)	Depreciation on Old Machine (2)	Depreciation on New Machine (3)	Additional Depreciation Deductions on New Machine (4)=(3) – (2)	Income Tax Cash Savings from Differences in Depreciation Deductions at 40% (4) × 40%
19_6	$10,000	$25,000	$15,000	$6,000
19_7	10,000	25,000	15,000	6,000
19_8	10,000	25,000	15,000	6,000
19_9	10,000	25,000	15,000	6,000

f.

	Old Machine	New Machine
Original cost	$80,000	$120,000
Total depreciation	70,000	100,000
Book value of machines on Dec. 31, 19_9	10,000	20,000
Terminal disposal price of machines on Dec. 31,19_9	7,000	20,000
Loss on disposal of machines	3,000	0
Add tax savings on loss (40% of $3,000; 40% of $0)	1,200	0
After-tax cash flow from terminal disposal of machines ($7,000 + $1,200; $20,000 – $0)	$ 8,200	$ 20,000

Additional after-tax cash flow from terminal disposal of machines: $20,000 – $8,200 = $11,800.

23-28 (Cont'd.)

2.   Let the <u>additional</u> recurring after-tax variable cash operating savings required to make NPV = $0 be $X each year.

The present value of an annuity of $1 per year for 4 years discounted at 16% = 2.798 (Appendix C, Table 4)

To make NPV = 0, we need to generate cash savings with NPV of $20,802.

That is $X (2.798)   = $20,802

X   =   20,802 ÷ 2.798 = 7,435

WRL must generate additional annual after-tax variable cash operating savings of $7,435.

3.   The nonquantitative factors that are important to WRL Company's decision include the following:

a.   The lower operating costs (variable and fixed) of the new machine would enable WRL to meet future competitive or inflationary pressures to a greater degree than the business could using the old machine.

b.   If the increased efficiency of the new machine provides a labor or energy cost savings, then additional increases in these costs in the future would make the new machine more attractive.

c.   Maintenance and servicing of both machines should be reviewed in terms of reliability of the manufacturer and the costs.

d.   Potential technological advances in machinery over the next four years should be evaluated.

e.   Space requirements for the new machine should be reviewed and compared with the space requirements of the present equipment to determine if more or less space is required.

23-30 (35 min.) **Capital budgeting, inventory changes.**

1.   A schedule of relevant cash flows follows:

	Sketch of Relevant Cash Flows				
	Year 0	Year 1	Year 2	Year 3	Year 4
Acquire machines	($109,200)				
Sales					
6,000 × $25		$150,000			
6,200 × $25			$155,000		
7,700 × $24				$184,800	
3,100 × $22					$68,200
Manufacturing Costs					
7,000 × $12		(84,000)			
6,500 × $13			(84,500)		
6,500 × $14				(91,000)	
3,000 × $15					(45,000)
Marketing, distribution & customer service costs					
6,000 × $3		(18,000)			
6,200 × $3			(18,600)		
7,700 × $3				(23,100)	
3,100 × $3					(9,300)
Disposal of machine					18,000
Taxes (see schedule)		(14,640)	(12,424)	(9,144)	(1,112)
Net cash flow after tax	($109,200)	$ 33,360	$ 39,476	$ 61,556	$30,788

Income statement for tax purposes:

	Year 1	Year 2	Year 3	Year 4
Sales	$150,000	$155,000	$184,800	$68,200
Cost of goods sold (COGS)	(95,400)[a]	(105,340)[b]	(138,840)[c]	(74,120)[d]
Mkt., Dist., and Cust. serv.	(18,000)	(18,600)	(23,100)	(9,300)
Gain on sale of machines				18,000
Taxable income	$36,600	$ 31,060	$ 22,860	$ 2,780
Tax at 40%	$14,640	$ 12,424	$ 9,144	$ 1,112

a. $$\frac{(7,000 \times \$12) + (\$109,200 \div 4)}{7,000} = \frac{\$84,000 + \$27,300}{7,000} = \$15.90;$$

  COGS = 15.90 × 6,000 = $95,400

b. $$\frac{(6,500 \times \$13) + \$27,300}{6,500} = \frac{84,500 + \$27,300}{6,500} = \$17.20$$

COGS =	1,000 from Year 1 × $15.90 =	$ 15,900
	5,200 from Year 2 × 17.20 =	89,440
		$105,340

23-15

c. $\dfrac{(6{,}500 \times \$14) + \$27{,}300}{6{,}500} = \dfrac{\$91{,}000 + \$27{,}300}{6{,}500} = \$18.20$

$$
\begin{array}{llr}
\text{COGS} = & 1{,}300 \text{ from Year } 2 \times \$17.20 = & \$\ 22{,}360 \\
 & 6{,}400 \text{ from Year } 3 \times\ \ 18.20 = & \underline{116{,}480} \\
 & & \$138{,}840
\end{array}
$$

d. $\dfrac{(3{,}000 \times \$15) + \$27{,}300}{3{,}000} = \dfrac{45{,}000 + \$27{,}300}{3{,}000} = \$24.10$

$$
\begin{array}{llr}
\text{COGS} = & 100 \times \$18.20 \quad = & \$\ 1{,}820 \\
 & 3{,}000 \times\ \ 24.10 \quad = & \underline{72{,}300} \\
 & & \$74{,}120
\end{array}
$$

2. The net present value calculations are as follows:

Year	Relevant Cash Flows (1)	Present Value Discount Factors at 16% (2)	Total Present Value (3) = (1) × (2)
0	$(109,200)	1.000	$(109,200)
1	33,360	0.862	28,756
2	39,476	0.743	29,331
3	61,556	0.641	39,457
4	30,788	0.552	16,995
Net present value			$ 5,339

On the basis of financial considerations, Total Fitness should add the new line of running shoes because the investment has a positive NPV of $5,339.

23-32 (40 min.) **Mining, income taxes, straight-line depreciation, inflation, sensitivity analysis.**

1. <u>Annual cash flow (Years 1-5)</u>

Revenue ($350 × 4,800[a])		<u>$1,680,000</u>
Cash-operating costs		
Variable costs ($100 × 4,800)	480,000	
Technicians ($110,000)	110,000	
Maintenance	<u>50,000</u>	
Total cash-operating costs		<u>640,000</u>
Recurring cash-operating flows		1,040,000
Additional income taxes at 40%		<u>416,000</u>
Recurring after-tax cash-operating flows		
each year for 5 years (excl. deprn. effects)		<u>$ 624,000</u>

Income tax cash savings from depreciation deductions:
Depreciation deductions ($3,000,000 ÷ 5):
   $600,000 each year
Income tax cash savings from depreciation deductions
   each year for 5 years at 40%:

$600,000 × 0.40	<u>$ 240,000</u>
Uniform increase in annual cash flow	<u>$ 864,000</u>

[a] 300 pounds × 16 ounces per pound = 4,800 ounces

The payback period for VanDyk Enterprises' proposed acquisition of the extraction equipment is 3.47 years, calculated as follows.

$$\text{Payback period} = \frac{\text{Net initial investment}}{\text{Uniform increase in annual cash flow}}$$

$$= \frac{\$3,000,000}{\$864,000}$$

$$= 3.47 \text{ years}$$

23-32 (Cont'd.)

2.   The net present value of VanDyk Enterprises' proposed acquisition of the extraction equipment is $114,720, as shown in the following calculation:

	Relevant Cash Flows	Present Value Discount Factors at 12%	Total Present Value
1. Initial equipment investment	$(3,000,000)	1.000	$(3,000,000)
2. Recurring cash-operating flows	$1,040,000		
Additional income taxes at 40%	(416,000)		
Recurring after-tax cash-operating savings each year for 5 years (excl. deprn. effects)	$624,000	3.605	2,249,520
3. Income tax cash savings from depreciation deductions:			
Depreciation deductions ($3,000,000 ÷ 5): $600,000 each year			
Income tax cash savings from depreciation deductions each year for 5 years at 40% $600,000 × 0.40			
Net present value	$240,000	3.605	865,200
			$114,720

3.   In order for VanDyk Enterprises' acquisition of the extraction equipment to break even from a net present value perspective, the revenue per ounce of gold must be at least $338.95, calculated as follows.

$$\frac{\text{Average annual after-tax cash flow}}{\text{required for net present value to equal zero}} = \frac{\text{Initial investment}}{\text{Present value of annuity @ 12\% for 5 years}}$$

$$= \frac{\$3,000,000}{3.605}$$
$$= \$832,178$$

After-tax total cash flow required	$832,178
Less: Income tax cash savings from depreciation deductions each year: $600,000 × 0.40	240,000
Required after-tax cash-operating flows	592,178
Divide by (1 – tax rate) or (1 – 0.4) = 0.6	÷ 0.60
Recurring before-tax cash-operating flows	986,963
Add recurring cash-operating costs	
Variable costs ($100 × 4,800)	480,000
Technicians	110,000
Maintenance	50,000
Cash revenue required for NPV to equal zero	1,626,963
Divide by total number of ounces sold	÷ 4,800
Revenue per ounce required for NPV to be zero	$338.95

23-32 (Cont'd.)

4.   Under the assumptions given here, requirement 2 has already calculated NPV using nominal cash flows and nominal rates of return. It has already taken inflationary effects into consideration. Hence, no new calculations are necessary. The after-tax net present value is $114,720, as calculated in requirement 2.   Some students may question whether the assumptions specified in requirement 4 are appropriate since, despite the 2% inflation per year, the revenues and cash-operating costs are assumed to be the same each year for the 5 years. There is no inconsistency here. Despite the 2% increase in general price levels, the specific revenues per ounce of gold and the specific cash-operating costs in this industry could well be the same either because of contractual reasons or because of the general economic conditions of supply and demand.

23-34   (40 min.)   Ranking projects.

1.   Project B

Let F = Present value factor for an annuity of $1 for 10 years in Appendix C, Table 4

$100,000   = $20,000 F
         F   = 5.000 for ten-year life

The internal rate of return can be calculated by interpolation:

		Present Value Factors for Annuity of $1 for 10 years	
14%		5.216	5.216
IRR		–	5.000
16%		4.833	–
Difference		0.383	0.216

$$\text{IRR} = 14\% + \left(\frac{0.216}{0.383}\right)(2\%) = 15.1\%$$

Project C
      $200,000   = $70,000 F

Let F = Present value factor for an annuity of $1 for 5 years in Appendix C, Table 4

         F   =   2.857 for five-year life

The internal rate of return can be calculated by interpolation:

		Present Value Factors for Annuity of $1 for 5 years	
22%		2.864	2.864
IRR		–	2.857
24%		2.745	–
Difference		0.119	0.007

$$\text{IRR}   =   22\% + \left(\frac{0.007}{0.119}\right)(2\%) = 22.1\%$$

23-19

23-34 (Cont'd.)

<u>Project D</u>: We need to find the discount rate at which:
Initial investment, \$200,000 = PV of a four-year annuity of \$200,000 per year deferred five years since the \$200,000 of cash inflows are received in years 6 through 9.

Trial and error:

	At 18%	**At 20%**	**At 22%**
\$1 per year for 4 years	2.690	2.589	2.494
Multiply by \$200,000, the total value of the annuity	\$538,000	\$517,800	\$498,800
Multiply by the present value of \$1 five years hence	0.437	0.402	0.370
P.V. of annuity in arrears	\$235,106	\$208,156	\$184,556

$$\text{IRR} = 20\% + \left(\frac{\$208,156 - \$200,000}{\$208,156 - \$184,556}\right)(2\%)$$

$$= 20\% + \left(\frac{\$8,156}{\$23,600}\right)(2\%) = 20.7\%$$

<u>Ranking of Projects</u>

Rank	**Project**	**IRR**	**Initial Investment**
1	C	22.1%	\$200,000
2	D	20.7	200,000
3	B	15.1	100,000
4	A	14.0	100,000
5	E	12.6	200,000
6	F	12.0	50,000

2. Budget limit:

\$500,000	**\$550,000**	**\$650,000**
C	C	C
D	D	D
B	B	B
	F	A
		F

3. <u>Ranking by net present value, discounting at 16%:</u>

Rank	**Project**	**Net Present Value**
1	D	\$ 66,370
2	C	29,180
3	B	(3,340)
4	F	(3,384)
5	A	(13,170)
6	E	(35,965)

23-34 (Cont'd.)

Project D is more desirable than Project C because it has a higher NPV. Because 16% is the implicit reinvestment rate, these rankings are different from the rankings made on the basis of internal rates of return in requirement 1.

Computations

Project D

PV of $200,000 per year for four years at 16% = $200,000 (2.798)	$559,600
It is in arrears five years, so PV = $559,600 (0.476)	266,370
Net initial investment	(200,000)
Net present value	$ 66,370

Project C

PV of $70,000 per year for five years at 16% = $70,000 (3.274)	$229,180
Net initial investment	(200,000)
Net present value	$ 29,180

Project B

PV of $20,000 per year for ten years at 16% = $20,000 (4.833)	$ 96,660
Net initial investment	(100,000)
Net present value	$ (3,340)

Project F

PV at 16%:	$23,000 × 0.862	$ 19,826
	20,000 × 0.743	14,860
	10,000 × 0.641	6,410
	10,000 × 0.552	5,520
	Total PV	46,616
Net initial investment		(50,000)
Net present value		$ (3,384)

Project A

PV of annuity of $20,000 for 15 years	= $20,000	× 5.575	$111,500
Deduct deferral of 2 years	= 20,000	× 1.605	(32,100)
PV of annuity in arrears			79,400
PV of $10,000 due in 2 years	= 10,000	× 0.743	7,430
Total PV			86,830
Net initial investment			(100,000)
Net present value			$ (13,170)

23-34 (Cont'd.)

Project E

PV of annuity of $50,000 for 10 years	= $50,000	×	4.833	$241,650
Deduct deferral of 3 years	= 50,000	×	2.246	(112,300)
PV of annuity in arrears				129,350
PV of $30,000 due in 3 years	= 30,000	×	0.641	19,230
PV of $15,000 due in 2 years	= 15,000	×	0.743	11,145
PV of $ 5,000 due in 1 years	= 5,000	×	0.862	4,310
Total PV				164,035
Net initial investment				(200,000)
Net present value				$ (35,965)

4. Other influential factors include:

   a. The risk linked with a given proposal may prompt management to judge it more or less attractive than other proposals that promise a comparable internal rate of return.

   b. Future investment opportunities may affect the current relative attractiveness of alternative proposals. For example, if management expects that, in five years hence, the best available alternatives will bring less than 20%, Project D (which promises an internal rate of return of 20.7% for 9 years) may be preferable to Project C (which promises 22.1% for 5 years). However, if future opportunities are expected to bring equal or higher internal rates of return, a shorter-lived project may be more attractive, even though a longer-lived project may yield a higher rate of return. Thus, if a choice must be made now between E and F, Project F (12.0% for 4 years) may be chosen instead of Project E (12.6%, but it locks in capital for 10 years and necessitates a much larger investment).

23-36 (40–50 min.) Ethics, discounted cash-flow analysis, straight-line depreciation.

1. The new equipment will be depreciated for tax purposes using a 9-year life (n=9) and the straight-line method with zero terminal disposal price assumed. The annual depreciation rate is $900,000 ÷ 9 = $100,000. At the end of Year 6, the book value is $300,000. The net present value computations follow. Dudley should launch the new household product because investing in the product has a positive net present value of $83,010.

		Relevant Cash Flows	Present Value Discount Factors at 12%	Total Present Value
1a.	Initial equipment investment	$ (900,000)		
b.	Initial working capital investment	(200,000)		
	Net initial investment	$ (1,100,000)	1.000	$(1,100,000)
2.	Addl. working capital investment	$ (200,000)	0.797	(159,400)
3a.	Cash flow from canceling lease	$ (30,000)		
	Income tax savings at 36%	10,800		
	After tax cash flow from canceling lease	$ (19,200)	1.000	(19,200)
b.	Recurring rent cash flow forgone	$ (45,000)		
	Income tax savings at 36%	16,200		
	Recurring after-tax rent cash flow forgone each year for 6 years	$ (28,800)	4.111	(118,397)
4.	Market-research and sales-promotion cash flows	$ (300,000)		
	Income tax savings at 36%	108,000		
	After-tax cash flow from market research and sales promotion	$ (192,000)	0.893	(171,456)
5.	Recurring after-tax cash-operating flows (excluding deprn. effects)			

Year (1)	Cash-Operating Flows (2)	After-Tax Cash-Operating Flows (3) = 0.64 × (2)		
1	$400,000	$ 256,000	0.893	228,608
2	400,000	256,000	0.797	204,032
3	600,000	384,000	0.712	273,408
4	600,000	384,000	0.636	244,224
5	600,000	384,000	0.567	217,728
6	100,000	64,000	0.507	32,448

			Relevant Cash Flows	Present Value Discount Factors at 12%	Total Present Value
6.	Income tax cash savings from depreciation deductions				

Year	Straight-Line Depreciation Rate	Income Tax Depreciation Deduction	Income Tax Cash Savings from Depreciation Deductions at 36%		
1	1/9	$100,000	$ 36,000	0.893	$ 32,148
2	1/9	100,000	36,000	0.797	28,692
3	1/9	100,000	36,000	0.712	25,632
4	1/9	100,000	36,000	0.636	22,896
5	1/9	100,000	36,000	0.567	20,412
6	1/9	100,000	36,000	0.507	18,252

7. After-tax cash flow from terminal
   disposal of new equipment:

	Relevant Cash Flows	DF	TPV
Book value of new equipment ($900,000 – $600,000)	$300,000		
Terminal disposal price of new equipment	140,000	$ 140,000	
Loss on disposal of new equipment	$160,000		
Tax savings (36% of $160,000 loss)		57,600	
After-tax cash flow from terminal disposal of old machine		$ 197,600	0.507	100,183

8. After-tax cash flow from terminal
   recovery of working capital ... $ 400,000 ... 0.507 ... 202,800

Net present Value ... $ 83,010

2. If the working capital requirements are $400,000 at the outset and $400,000 at the end of 2 years, the NPV will change as follows:

		Relevant Cash Flows	Present Value Discount Factors at 12%	Total Present Value
1.	Incremental working capital investment at Year 0	$(200,000)	1.00	$(200,000)
2.	Incremental working capital investment at Year 2	(200,000)	0.797	(159,400)
3.	Incremental recovery of working capital in Year 6	400,000	0.507	202,800
Incremental net present value effect				$(156,600)

The overall NPV of the project would then be $83,010 – $156,600 = $(73,590). Griffey is unhappy with Chen's revised analysis because the NPV of the project is now negative, possibly leading to the project being rejected. He would like to resume production in the plant, and reemploy his friends who had been laid off earlier. There is also the possibility that Griffey may be hired as a consultant by the new plant management after he retires next year.

Referring to **Statements of Management Accounting 1C (MC 1C)**, "Standards of Ethical Conduct for Management Accountants," and taking into consideration the specific standards of competence, confidentiality, integrity, and/or objectivity, Andrew Chen should evaluate Eric Griffey's directives as follows.

Competence. Chen has a responsibility to present complete and clear reports and recommendations after appropriate analyses of relevant and reliable information. Griffey does not wish the report to be complete or clear, and has provided some information which is not totally reliable.

Confidentiality. Chen should not disclose confidential information outside of the organization, but it also appears that Griffey wants to refrain from disclosing information to senior management that it should know about.

Integrity. Griffey is engaging in activities that could prejudice him from carrying out his duties ethically.

In evaluating Griffey's directive as it affects Chen, Chen has an obligation to communicate unfavorable as well as favorable information and professional judgments or opinions.

Objectivity. The responsibility to communicate information fairly and objectively, as well as to disclose fully all relevant information that could reasonably be expected to influence an intended user's understanding of the reports and recommendations presented, is being hampered. Management will not have the full scope of information they should have when they are presented with the analysis.

Andrew Chen should take the following steps to resolve this situation.
- Chen should first investigate and see if Dudley Company has an established policy for resolution of ethical conflicts and follow those procedures.
- If this policy does not resolve the ethical conflict, the next step would be for Chen to discuss the situation with his supervisor, Griffey, and see if he can obtain resolution. One possible solution may be to present a "base case" and sensitivity analysis of the investment. Chen should make it clear to Griffey that he has a problem and is seeking guidance.
- If Chen cannot obtain a satisfactory resolution with Griffey, he could take the situation up to the next layer of management, and inform Griffey that he is doing this. If this is not satisfactory, Chen should progress to the next, and subsequent, higher levels of management until the issue is resolved (i.e., the president, Audit Committee, or Board of Directors).
- Chen may want to have a confidential discussion with an objective advisor to clarify relevant concepts and obtain an understanding of possible courses of action. He may want to talk to a close professional friend or the IMA "Ethics Hotline" for this purpose.
- If Chen cannot satisfactorily resolve the situation within the organization, he may resign from the company and submit an informative memo to an appropriate person in Dudley (i.e., the present, Audit Committee, or Board of Directors).

CHAPTER 24
MEASURING INPUT YIELD, MIX, AND PRODUCTIVITY

24-2 Yes. When inputs are substitutable, direct materials efficiency improvement relative to budgeted costs can come from two sources: (1) using less input to achieve a given output, and (2) using a cheaper mix to produce a given output. The direct materials yield and mix variances divide the efficiency variance into two variances: the yield variance focusing on total inputs used and the mix variance focusing on how the substitutable inputs are combined. However, when direct materials inputs are not substitutes, calculating only the direct materials efficiency variance may suffice. Managers control each individual input, and no discretion is permitted regarding the substitution of materials inputs. All deviations from the input-output relationships are due to efficient or inefficient usage of individual direct materials.

24-4 Disagree. Changes in the mix of direct materials from the budgeted mix could improve yield, for example, if the mix of direct materials shifts in favor of using more of the higher quality, more costly materials. This could potentially have the effect of hurting mix but improving yield if the actual total quantity of direct materials used to produce actual output is lower than the budgeted total quantity.

24-6 The direct-labor mix variance helps managers to understand how costs (calculated at budgeted prices) change as the actual mix varies from the budgeted mix. The direct-labor yield variance indicates the total amount of hours taken and costs incurred (at budgeted prices) relative to budgeted hours to complete a given task. If the mix variance is unfavorable, say, but the yield variance is favorable, the manager can evaluate if the mix-versus-yield trade-off reduced cost, that is, improved the direct-labor efficiency variance. If it did not, for example, managers will understand that shifting to a higher skills mix would only be worthwhile if the total time taken can be further reduced. Managers would then have to consider ways to achieve this goal—better training for lower-costs workers, improved work procedures, etc.

24-8 Two possible explanations for the manager's statement are:
1. The plant manager has no leeway in determining the direct material or the direct manufacturing labor content. If a plant is highly automated, it is likely that a computer program would calculate the specific direct materials or manufacturing labor content.
2. The plant manager believes that other (probably nonfinancial) information is sufficient to manage costs on a day-to-day basis.

24-10 Partial productivity of an input is the ratio of the quantity of output produced to the quantity of that *single* input consumed.

$$\text{Partial productivity of input} = \frac{\text{Quantity of output produced}}{\text{Quantity of input used}}$$

24-12 Total factor productivity is the ratio of the quantity of output produced to the quantity of *all* inputs used, where the inputs are combined on the basis of current period prices.

$$\text{Total factor productivity} = \frac{\text{Quantity of output produced}}{\text{Cost of all inputs used}}$$

24-14 One advantage of total factor productivity (TFP) is that it measures the combined productivity of all inputs to produce output and, therefore, explicitly evaluates substitution among inputs. One disadvantage of total factor productivity is that operations personnel find physical rather than the financial numbers of total factor productivity more useful in performing their tasks. Physical measures, unlike TFP, provide direct feedback.

24-16 (20–25 min.) **Direct materials efficiency, yield and mix variances.**

1&2. Actual total quantity of all inputs used and actual input mix percentages for each input are as follows:

Chemical	Actual Quantity	Actual Mix Percentage		
Echol	24,080	24,080 ÷ 86,000	=	0.28
Protex	15,480	15,480 ÷ 86,000	=	0.18
Benz	36,120	36,120 ÷ 86,000	=	0.42
CT-40	10,320	10,320 ÷ 86,000	=	0.12
Total	86,000			1.00

Budgeted total quantity of all inputs allowed and budgeted input mix percentages for each input are as follows:

Chemical	Actual Quantity	Actual Mix Percentage		
Echol	25,200	25,200 ÷ 84,000	=	0.30
Protex	16,800	16,800 ÷ 84,000	=	0.20
Benz	33,600	33,600 ÷ 84,000	=	0.40
CT-40	8,400	8,400 ÷ 84,000	=	0.10
Total	84,000			1.00

24-16 (Cont'd.)

Solution Exhibit 24-16 presents the total direct materials efficiency, yield and mix variances for August 19_7.

Total direct materials efficiency variance can also be computed as:

$$\begin{array}{l}\text{Direct materials} \\ \text{efficiency variance} \\ \text{for each input}\end{array} = \left(\begin{array}{l}\text{Actual} \\ \text{inputs}\end{array} - \begin{array}{l}\text{Budgeted inputs allowed} \\ \text{for actual outputs achieved}\end{array}\right) \times \begin{array}{l}\text{Budgeted} \\ \text{prices}\end{array}$$

Echol	= (24,080 − 25,200) × $0.20	=	$224 F
Protex	= (15,480 − 16,800) × $0.45	=	594 F
Benz	= (36,120 − 33,600) × $0.15	=	378 U
CT40	= (10,320 − 8,400) × $0.30	=	576 U
Total direct materials efficiency variance			$136 U

The total direct materials yield variance can also be computed as the sum of the direct materials yield variances for each input:

$$\begin{array}{l}\text{Direct} \\ \text{materials} \\ \text{yield variance} \\ \text{for each input}\end{array} = \left(\begin{array}{l}\text{Actual total} \\ \text{quantity of all} \\ \text{direct materials} \\ \text{inputs used}\end{array} - \begin{array}{l}\text{Budgeted total quantity} \\ \text{of all direct materials} \\ \text{inputs allowed for} \\ \text{actual output achieved}\end{array}\right) \times \begin{array}{l}\text{Budgeted} \\ \text{direct materials} \\ \text{input mix} \\ \text{percentage}\end{array} \times \begin{array}{l}\text{Budgeted} \\ \text{price of} \\ \text{direct materials} \\ \text{inputs}\end{array}$$

Echol	= (86,000 − 84,000) × 0.30 × $0.20 = 2,000 × 0.30 × $0.20	=	$120 U
Protex	= (86,000 − 84,000) × 0.20 × $0.45 = 2,000 × 0.20 × $0.45	=	180 U
Benz	= (86,000 − 84,000) × 0.40 × $0.15 = 2,000 × 0.40 × $0.15	=	120 U
CT40	= (86,000 − 84,000) × 0.10 × $0.30 = 2,000 × 0.10 × $0.30	=	60 U
Total direct materials yield variance			$480 U

The total direct materials mix variance can also be computed as the sum of the direct materials mix variances for each input:

$$\begin{array}{l}\text{Direct} \\ \text{materials} \\ \text{mix variance} \\ \text{for each input}\end{array} = \left(\begin{array}{l}\text{Actual} \\ \text{direct materials} \\ \text{input mix} \\ \text{percentage}\end{array} - \begin{array}{l}\text{Budgeted} \\ \text{direct materials} \\ \text{input mix} \\ \text{percentage}\end{array}\right) \times \begin{array}{l}\text{Actual total} \\ \text{quantity of all} \\ \text{direct materials} \\ \text{inputs used}\end{array} \times \begin{array}{l}\text{Budgeted} \\ \text{price of} \\ \text{direct materials} \\ \text{inputs}\end{array}$$

Echol	= (0.28 − 0.30) × 86,000 × $0.20 = −0.02 × 86,000 × $0.20	=	$344 F
Protex	= (0.18 − 0.20) × 86,000 × $0.45 = −0.02 × 86,000 × $0.45	=	774 F
Benz	= (0.42 − 0.40) × 86,000 × $0.15 = 0.02 × 86,000 × $0.15	=	258 U
CT40	= (0.12 − 0.10) × 86,000 × $0.30 = 0.02 × 86,000 × $0.30	=	516 U
Total direct materials mix variance			$344 F

24-16 (Cont'd.)

3.   Energy Products used a larger total quantity of direct materials inputs than budgeted, and so showed an unfavorable yield variance. The mix variance was favorable because the actual mix contained more of the cheapest input, Benz, and less of the costliest input, Protex, than the budgeted mix. The favorable mix variance offset some, but not all, of the unfavorable yield variance—the overall efficiency variance was unfavorable. Energy Products will only find it profitable to shift to the cheaper mix, if the yield from this cheaper mix can be improved. Energy Products must also consider the effect on output quality of using the cheaper mix, and the potential consequences for future revenues.

SOLUTION EXHIBIT 24-16
Columnar Presentation of Direct Materials Efficiency, Yield and Mix Variances for The Energy Products Company for August 19_7

	(Actual Total Quantity of All Inputs Used × Actual Input Mix) × Budgeted Prices (1)	(Actual Total Quantity of All Inputs Used × Budgeted Input Mix) × Budgeted Prices (2)	Flexible Budget (Budgeted Total Quantity of All Inputs Allowed for Actual Output Achieved × Budgeted Input Mix) × Budgeted Prices (3)
Echol	$86,000 \times 0.28 \times \$0.20 =$ $ 4,816	$86,000 \times 0.30 \times \$0.20 =$ $ 5,160	$84,000 \times 0.30 \times \$0.20 =$ $ 5,040
Protex	$86,000 \times 0.18 \times \$0.45 =$ 6,966	$86,000 \times 0.20 \times \$0.45 =$ 7,740	$84,000 \times 0.20 \times \$0.45 =$ 7,560
Benz	$86,000 \times 0.42 \times \$0.15 =$ 5,418	$86,000 \times 0.40 \times \$0.15 =$ 5,160	$84,000 \times 0.40 \times \$0.15 =$ 5,040
CT40	$86,000 \times 0.12 \times \$0.30 =$ 3,096	$86,000 \times 0.10 \times \$0.30 =$ 2,580	$84,000 \times 0.10 \times \$0.30 =$ 2,520
	$20,296	$20,640	$20,160

           ↑ $344 F   ↑ $480 U   ↑
               Total mix variance   Total yield variance
           ↑ $136 U   ↑
                       Total efficiency variance

Note that F = favorable effect on operating income; U = unfavorable effect on operating income

24-18 (40 min.) **Direct materials price and efficiency variances, direct materials yield and mix variances, perfume manufacturing.**

1.   The direct materials standard to produce 80 pints of perfume are:

40 pints of Dycone; 30 pints of Cycone; 30 pints of Bycone.

Therefore, budgeted inputs allowed for <u>each pint</u> of perfume are:
Dycone:	40 pints ÷ 80 pints	=	0.500 pints
Cycone:	30 pints ÷ 80 pints	=	0.375 pints
Bycone:	30 pints ÷ 80 pints	=	<u>0.375</u> pints
All fluids:			<u>1.250</u> pints

Budgeted input allowed for 75,000 pints of perfume are:
Dycone:	75,000 × 0.500	=	37,500 pints
Cycone:	75,000 × 0.375	=	28,125 pints
Bycone:	75,000 × 0.375	=	<u>28,125</u> pints
All fluids:			<u>93,750</u> pints

Solution Exhibit 24-18A presents the total direct materials price and efficiency variances for Scent Makers Co. for the week.

The total direct materials price variance can also be computed as:

$$\text{Direct materials price variance for each input} = \left(\begin{array}{c}\text{Actual} \\ \text{price}\end{array} - \begin{array}{c}\text{Budgeted} \\ \text{price}\end{array}\right) \times \begin{array}{c}\text{Actual} \\ \text{inputs}\end{array}$$

Dycone	=	($5.50 – $6.00) × 45,000	=	$22,500 F
Cycone	=	($4.20 – $3.50) × 35,000	=	24,500 U
Bycone	=	($2.75 – $2.50) × 20,000	=	<u>5,000</u> U
Total direct materials price variance				<u>$ 7,000</u> U

The total direct materials efficiency variance can also be computed as:

$$\text{Direct materials efficiency variance for each input} = \left(\begin{array}{c}\text{Actual inputs} \\ \text{used}\end{array} - \begin{array}{c}\text{Budgeted inputs allowed} \\ \text{for actual output achieved}\end{array}\right) \times \begin{array}{c}\text{Budgeted} \\ \text{prices}\end{array}$$

Dycone	=	(45,000 – 37,500) × $6.00	=	$45,000.00 U
Cycone	=	(35,000 – 28,125) × $3.50	=	24,062.50 U
Bycone	=	(20,000 – 28,125) × $2.50	=	<u>20,312.50</u> F
Total direct materials efficiency variance				<u>$48,750.00</u> U

SOLUTION EXHIBIT 24-18A
Columnar Presentation of Direct Materials
Price and Efficiency Variances for Scent Makers Co.

	Actual Costs Incurred: (Actual Inputs × Actual Prices) (1)	Actual Inputs × Budgeted Prices (2)	Flexible Budget: (Budgeted Inputs Allowed for Actual Output Achieved × Budgeted Prices) (3)
Dycone	45,000 × $5.50 = $247,500	45,000 × $6.00 = $270,000	37,500 × $6.00 = $225,000.00
Cycone	35,000 × $4.20 = 147,000	35,000 × $3.50 = 122,500	28,125 × $3.50 = 98,437.50
Bycone	20,000 × $2.75 = 55,000	20,000 × $2.50 = 50,000	28,125 × $2.50 = 70,312.50
All Fluids	$449,500	$442,500	$393,750.00

$7,000 U
Total price variance

$48,750 U
Total efficiency variance

$55,750 U
Total flexible-budget variance

F = favorable effect on operating income; U = unfavorable effect on operating income.

2.   Solution Exhibit 24-18B presents the direct materials yield and mix variances for Dycone, Cycone and Bycone and in total for Scent Makers Co. for the week.

The direct materials yield variances can also be computed as:

$$\begin{pmatrix} \text{Direct} \\ \text{materials} \\ \text{yield variance} \\ \text{for each input} \end{pmatrix} = \begin{pmatrix} \text{Actual total} \\ \text{quantity of} \\ \text{all direct} \\ \text{materials} \\ \text{inputs used} \end{pmatrix} - \begin{pmatrix} \text{Budgeted total} \\ \text{quantity of all} \\ \text{direct materials} \\ \text{inputs allowed} \\ \text{for actual} \\ \text{output achieved} \end{pmatrix} \times \begin{pmatrix} \text{Budgeted} \\ \text{direct materials} \\ \text{input mix} \\ \text{percentage} \end{pmatrix} \times \begin{pmatrix} \text{Budgeted} \\ \text{price of} \\ \text{direct materials} \\ \text{input} \end{pmatrix}$$

Dycone:	= (100,000 − 93,750) × 0.40 × $6.00 = 6,250 × 0.40 × $6.00	=	$15,000.00 U
Cycone:	= (100,000 − 93,750) × 0.30 × $3.50 = 6,250 × 0.30 × $3.50	=	6,562.50 U
Bycone:	= (100,000 − 93,750) × 0.30 × $2.50 = 6,250 × 0.30 × $2.50	=	4,687.50 U
Total direct materials yield variance			$26,250.00 U

24-18 (Cont'd.)

The direct materials mix variances can also be computed as:

| Direct materials mix variance for each input | = | (Actual direct materials input mix percentage | − | Budgeted direct materials input mix percentage) | × | Actual total quantity of all direct materials inputs used | × | Budgeted price of direct materials input |

Dycone   = $(0.45 - 0.40) \times 100{,}000 \times \$6.00$ = $0.05 \times 100{,}000 \times \$6.00$ = $\$30{,}000$ U

Cycone   = $(0.35 - 0.30) \times 100{,}000 \times \$3.50$ = $0.05 \times 100{,}000 \times \$3.50$ = $17{,}500$ U

Bycone   = $(0.20 - 0.30) \times 100{,}000 \times \$2.50$ = $-0.10 \times 100{,}000 \times \$2.50$ = $\underline{25{,}000}$ F

Total direct materials mix variance $\underline{\$22{,}500}$ U

3.   Scent Makers has an unfavorable direct materials price variance of $7,000 and an unfavorable direct materials efficiency variance of $48,750. Both the yield and the mix variances are unfavorable. Scent Makers may have used more quantities of all input fluids because of the lower quality of Dycone and Cycone.

The unfavorable direct materials mix variance occurs with Dycone and Cycone because Scent Makers used a greater percentage of these fluids in its direct materials mix than budgeted. Bycone shows a favorable direct materials mix variance because the actual direct materials mix percentage of Bycone is less than the budgeted direct materials mix percentage. The total direct materials mix variance is unfavorable because the actual mix of direct materials inputs had a greater proportion of the more costly inputs (Dycone and Cycone) than the budgeted mix.

Direct materials yield and direct materials mix variances are especially informative when management can substitute among the individual material inputs. Such substitution is possible in the processing of individual inputs into perfume.

24-18 (Cont'd.)

SOLUTION EXHIBIT 24-18B
Columnar Presentation of Direct Materials
Yield and Mix Variances for Scent Makers Co.

	(Actual Total Quantity of All Inputs Used × Actual Input Mix) × Budgeted Prices (1)		(Actual Total Quantity of All Inputs Used × Budgeted Input Mix) × Budgeted Prices (2)		Flexible Budget (Budgeted Total Quantity of All Inputs Allowed for Actual Output Achieved × Budgeted Input Mix) × Budgeted Prices (3)	
Dycone	$100,000 \times 0.45^a \times \$6.00$	$270,000	$(100,000 \times 0.4^b) \times \$6.00 =$	\$ 240,000	$(93,750 \times 0.4) \times \$6.00 =$	$225,000.00
Cycone	$100,000 \times 0.35^c \times \$3.50$	122,500	$(100,000 \times 0.3^d) \times \$3.50 =$	105,000	$(93,750 \times 0.3) \times \$3.50 =$	98,437.50
Bycone	$100,000 \times 0.20^e \times \$2.50$	50,000	$(100,000 \times 0.3^f) \times \$2.50 =$	75,000	$(93,750 \times 0.3) \times \$2.50 =$	70,312.50
All Fluids		$442,500		\$420,000		$393,750.00

$22,500 U
Total mix variance

$26,250 U
Total yield variance

$48,750 U
Total efficiency variance

F = favorable effect on operating income; U = unfavorable effect on operating income.

Actual Input Mix:
^{a}Dycone = $45,000 \div 100,000 = 45\%$
^{c}Cycone = $35,000 \div 100,000 = 35\%$
^{e}Bycone = $20,000 \div 100,000 = 20\%$

Budgeted Input Mix:
^{b}Dycone = $40 \div 100 = 40\%$
^{d}Cycone = $30 \div 100 = 30\%$
^{f}Bycone = $30 \div 100 = 30\%$

24-20 (40 min.) **Direct distribution labor price, efficiency variances, direct distribution labor yield and mix variances.**

1.　　Solution Exhibit 24-20A presents the total distribution labor price and efficiency variances for the Memphis distribution center of Landeau Manufacturing Company.

The total direct distribution labor price variance can also be computed as:

$$\text{Direct distribution labor price variance for each input} = \left(\begin{array}{c}\text{Actual}\\\text{prices}\end{array} - \begin{array}{c}\text{Budgeted}\\\text{prices}\end{array}\right) \times \begin{array}{c}\text{Actual}\\\text{inputs}\end{array}$$

Class III	=	($12.50 – $12.00) × 550	=	$275 U
Class II	=	($10.50 – $10.00) × 650	=	325 U
Class I	=	($ 8.40 – $ 8.00) × 375	=	150 U
Total direct distribution labor price variance				$750 U

The total direct distribution labor efficiency variance can also be computed as:

$$\text{Direct distribution labor efficiency variance for each input} = \left(\begin{array}{c}\text{Actual}\\\text{inputs}\end{array} - \begin{array}{c}\text{Budgeted inputs allowed}\\\text{for actual outputs achieved}\end{array}\right) \times \begin{array}{c}\text{Budgeted}\\\text{price}\end{array}$$

Class III	=	(550 – 500) × $12.00	=	$ 600 U
Class II	=	(650 – 500) × $10.00	=	1,500 U
Class I	=	(375 – 500) × $ 8.00	=	1,000 F
Total direct distribution labor efficiency variance				$1,100 U

Landeau paid more than the budgeted rate for each class of labor which resulted in an unfavorable price variance. It also used more than the standard quantity of labor resulting in an unfavorable efficiency variance.

24-20 (cont'd.)

SOLUTION EXHIBIT 24-20A
Columnar Presentation of Direct Distribution Labor
Price and Efficiency Variances for Landeau Manufacturing

	Actual Costs Incurred: (Actual Inputs × Actual Prices) (1)		Actual Inputs × Budgeted Prices (2)		Flexible Budget: (Budgeted Inputs Allowed for Actual Outputs Achieved × Budgeted Prices) (3)	
Class III	550 × $12.50 =	$ 6,875	550 × $12.00 =	$ 6,600	500 × $ 12.00 =	$ 6,000
Class II	650 × $10.50 =	6,825	650 × $10.00 =	6,500	500 × $10.00 =	5,000
Class I	375 × $ 8.40 =	3,150	375 × $ 8.00 =	3,000	500 × $ 8.00 =	4,000
		$16,850		$16,100		$15,000

↑ —————— 750 U —————— ↑ —————— 1,100 U —————— ↑

Total price variance   Total efficiency variance

↑ ———————————————— 1,850 U ———————————————— ↑

Total flexible-budget variance

F = favorable effect on operating income; U = unfavorable effect on operating income.

2.   Solution Exhibit 24-20B presents the total direct distribution labor mix and yield variances for the Landeau Manufacturing Company.

The total direct distribution labor mix variance can also be computed as the sum of the direct distribution labor mix variances for each input.

$$
\begin{pmatrix} \text{Direct distribn} \\ \text{labor} \\ \text{mix variance} \\ \text{for each input} \end{pmatrix} = \begin{pmatrix} \text{Actual} \\ \text{distribn labor} \\ \text{input mix} \\ \text{percentage} \end{pmatrix} - \begin{pmatrix} \text{Budgeted} \\ \text{distribn labor} \\ \text{input mix} \\ \text{percentage} \end{pmatrix} \times \begin{pmatrix} \text{Actual total quantity} \\ \text{of all} \\ \text{distribution} \\ \text{labor inputs used} \end{pmatrix} \times \begin{pmatrix} \text{Budgeted} \\ \text{price of} \\ \text{distribution} \\ \text{labor input} \end{pmatrix}
$$

Class III	=	(0.34921 − 0.33333) × 1,575 × $12 =	0.01588 × 1,575 × $12	= $ 300 U
Class II	=	(0.41270 − 0.33333) × 1,575 × $10 =	0.07937 × 1,575 × $10	= 1,250 U
Class I	=	(0.23810 − 0.33333) × 1,575 × $ 8 =	− 0.09523 × 1,575 × $ 8	= 1,200 F
Total direct distribution labor mix variance				$ 350 U

● The total direct distribution labor yield variance can also be computed as the sum of the direct distribution labor yield variances for each input.

$$\begin{pmatrix} \text{Direct distribn} \\ \text{labor} \\ \text{yield variance} \\ \text{for each input} \end{pmatrix} = \begin{pmatrix} \text{Actual total quantity} \\ \text{of all direct distribution} - \\ \text{labor inputs used} \end{pmatrix} \begin{pmatrix} \text{Budgeted total quantity} \\ \text{of all direct distribution} \\ \text{labor inputs allowed} \\ \text{for actual output achieved} \end{pmatrix} \times \begin{pmatrix} \text{Budgeted direct} \\ \text{distribution} \\ \text{labor input} \\ \text{mix percentage} \end{pmatrix} \times \begin{pmatrix} \text{Budgeted} \\ \text{price of} \\ \text{direct distribution} \\ \text{labor input} \end{pmatrix}$$

Class III	=	$(1,575 - 1,500) \times 0.33333 \times \$12$	$= 75 \times 0.33333 \times \$12 =$	\$300 U
Class II	=	$(1,575 - 1,500) \times 0.33333 \times \$10$	$= 75 \times 0.33333 \times \$10 =$	250 U
Class I	=	$(1,575 - 1,500) \times 0.33333 \times \$\ 8$	$= 75 \times 0.33333 \times \$\ 8 =$	200 U
Total direct distribution labor yield variance				\$750 U

The distribution labor mix variance is unfavorable because Landeau used more of the high cost Class III distribution labor than the specified budgeted mix. The total quantity of all distribution labor used was greater than budgeted resulting in an unfavorable yield variance.

SOLUTION EXHIBIT 24-20B
Columnar Presentation of Direct Distribution Labor
Yield and Mix Variances for Landeau Manufacturing

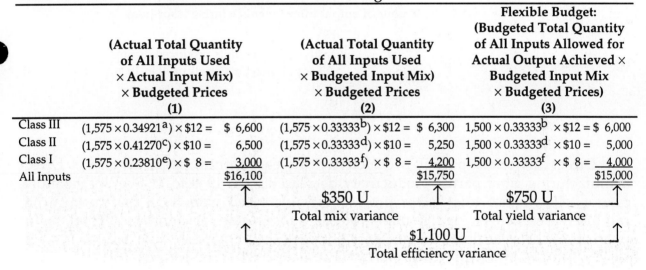

	(Actual Total Quantity of All Inputs Used × Actual Input Mix) × Budgeted Prices (1)	(Actual Total Quantity of All Inputs Used × Budgeted Input Mix) × Budgeted Prices (2)	Flexible Budget: (Budgeted Total Quantity of All Inputs Allowed for Actual Output Achieved × Budgeted Input Mix × Budgeted Prices) (3)
Class III	$(1,575 \times 0.34921^a) \times \$12 = \ \$\ 6,600$	$(1,575 \times 0.33333^b) \times \$12 = \ \$\ 6,300$	$1,500 \times 0.33333^b \times \$12 = \$\ 6,000$
Class II	$(1,575 \times 0.41270^c) \times \$10 = \ \ 6,500$	$(1,575 \times 0.33333^d) \times \$10 = \ \ 5,250$	$1,500 \times 0.33333^d \times \$10 = \ \ 5,000$
Class I	$(1,575 \times 0.23810^e) \times \$\ 8 = \ \ 3,000$	$(1,575 \times 0.33333^f) \times \$\ 8 = \ \ 4,200$	$1,500 \times 0.33333^f \times \$\ 8 = \ \ 4,000$
All Inputs	\$16,100	\$15,750	\$15,000

$$\underbrace{\qquad}_{\text{\$350 U}} \quad \underbrace{\qquad}_{\text{\$750 U}}$$
Total mix variance   Total yield variance

$$\underbrace{\qquad\qquad}_{\text{\$1,100 U}}$$
Total efficiency variance

F = favorable effect on operating income; U = unfavorable effect on operating income.

Actual Input Mix:
  [a]Class III = 550 ÷ 1,575 = 34.921%
  [c]Class II = 650 ÷ 1,575 = 41.270%
  [e]Class   I = 375 ÷ 1,575 = 23.810%

Budgeted Input Mix:
  [d]Class III = 500 ÷1,500 = 33.333%
  [f]Class II = 500 ÷ 1,500 = 33.333%
  [f]Class I = 500 ÷ 1,500 = 33.333%

24-22 (20 min.) Partial productivity measurement.

1. Partial productivity ratios for each input in 19_8:

$$\text{Direct manufacturing labor partial productivity} = \frac{\text{Quantity of output units produced during 19\_8}}{\text{Direct manufacturing labor-hours used to produce output in 19\_8}}$$

$$= \frac{400,000}{10,000}$$

$$= 40 \text{ units of output/direct manufacturing labor-hour}$$

$$\text{Direct materials partial productivity} = \frac{\text{Quantity of output units produced during 19\_8}}{\text{Tons of direct materials used in 19\_8}}$$

$$= \frac{400,000}{160}$$

$$= 2,500 \text{ units of output/ton of direct materials}$$

Partial productivity ratios for each input in 19_9:

$$\text{Direct manufacturing labor partial productivity} = \frac{\text{Quantity of output units produced during 19\_9}}{\text{Direct manufacturing labor-hours used to produce output in 19\_9}}$$

$$= \frac{520,000}{13,875}$$

$$= 37.48 \text{ units of output/direct manufacturing labor-hour}$$

$$\text{Direct materials partial productivity} = \frac{\text{Quantity of output units produced during 19\_9}}{\text{Tons of direct materials used in 19\_9}}$$

$$= \frac{520,000}{190}$$

$$= 2736.84 \text{ units of output /ton of direct materials}$$

2. Direct materials partial productivity increased from 19_8 to 19_9. Direct manufacturing labor partial productivity decreased from 19_8 to 19_9. We, therefore, cannot tell whether total factor productivity increased from 19_8 to 19_9. Partial productivities can change if one input is substituted for another. Total factor productivity helps evaluate the efficiency of these substitutions.

24-24 (40 min.) Analysis of cost changes.

Solution Exhibit 24-24 presents the analysis of cost changes in columnar form.

1. Actual costs incurred by Hanover Corporation is $770,000 in 19_8 and $1,000,000 in 19_9 (see columnar presentation).

2. Of the total change in costs of $230,000, the output adjustment component is $231,000 U; the price change component is $39,000 U; and the productivity change component is $40,000 F (see columnar presentation).

3. The output adjustment component measures the increase in costs attributable solely to increases in output assuming 19_8 prices and 19_8 productivities. The input price change component evaluates the increase in costs due solely to increases in the prices of inputs in 19_9, based on the inputs that would have been used in 19_8 to produce the 19_9 output. These two components would have resulted in Hanover Corporation costs increasing by $270,000 ($231,000 + $39,000) in 19_9 relative to 19_8. Hanover Corporation costs changed by a total of $230,000 because of a $40,000 gain in productivity. Hanover Corporation used fewer inputs and a cheaper mix of inputs to produce output in 19_9.

SOLUTION EXHIBIT 24-24
Analysis of Change in Actual Costs from 19_8 to 19_9

	Actual Costs for 19_9: Actual Units of Inputs Used To Produce 19_9 Output × 19_9 Prices (1)	Actual Units of Inputs That Would Have Been Used in 19_8 to Produce 19_9 Output × 19_9 Prices (2)	Actual Units of Inputs That Would Have Been Used in 19_8 to Produce 19_9 Output × 19_8 Prices (3)	Actual Costs for 19_8: Actual Units of Inputs Used to Produce 19_8 Output × 19_8 Prices (4)
Direct Manuf. Labor	13,875 × $25 = $ 346,875	13,000[a] × $25 = $ 325,000	13,000[a] × $26 = $ 338,000	10,000 × $26 = $260,000
Direct Materials	190 × $3,437.50 = 653,125	208[b] × $3,437.50 = 715,000	208[b] × $3,187.50 = 663,000	160 × $3,187.50 = 510,000
All inputs	$1,000,000	$1,040,000	$1,001,000	$770,000

$40,000 F — Productivity change

$39,000 U — Price change

$231,000 U — Output adjustment

$230,000 U — Total change in costs

F = Favorable effect on operating income; U = Unfavorable effect on operating income.

[a]Direct manufacturing labor that would have been used in 19_8 to produce 19_9 output $= \frac{\text{Direct manufacturing}}{\text{labor used in 19\_8}} \times \frac{\text{19\_9 output}}{\text{19\_8 output}}$

$$13,000 = 10,000 \times \frac{520,000}{400,000}$$

[b]Direct materials that would have been used in 19_8 to produce 19_9 output $= \frac{\text{Direct materials}}{\text{used in 19\_8}} \times \frac{\text{19\_9 output}}{\text{19\_8 output}}$

$$208 = 160 \times \frac{520,000}{400,000}$$

24-26 (30–40 min.) **Direct materials efficiency variance, mix and yield variances; working backward.**

1, 2 and 3. Solution Exhibit 24-26 presents the direct materials efficiency, yield and mix variances for the Base and Grade inputs and in total for Agrichem Enterprises. The steps to fill in the numbers in Solution Exhibit 24-26 follow:

Step 1: Base required per ton of fertilizer   = 75% × 1.20   0.90 tons
Grade required per ton of fertilizer   = 25% × 1.20   0.30 tons
All inputs   1.20 tons

Step 2: Fill in the flexible budget column (Column 3) for Base, Grade and in total for the 2,000 tons of fertilizer produced.

Step 3: Consider Column 2 of Solution Exhibit 24-26. The total of Column 2 in Panel C is $875,000 (the total flexible-budget direct materials costs of $840,000 + the unfavorable total direct materials yield variance of $35,000 which was given in the problem).

We need to find the actual quantities of all direct material inputs used, which we denote by m. The budgeted input mix is Base, 75%; Grade, 25%. From Column 2, we know that

$$(m \times 0.75 \times \$400) + (m \times 0.25 \times \$200) = \$875,000$$
$$300\,m + 50\,m = \$875,000$$
$$m = \$875,000 \div 350 = 2,500 \text{ tons}$$

Hence, the total quantity of all direct materials inputs is 2,500 tons. This computation allows us to fill in all the numbers in Column 2.

Step 4: Fill in all the numbers in Column 1 of Solution Exhibit 24-26, using actual quantities of all direct materials, the actual mix of inputs and budgeted prices of materials.

Solution Exhibit 24-26 displays the following total direct materials mix, total direct materials yield and direct materials efficiency variances:

1. Direct materials yield variances:
   Base $30,000 U
   Grade   5,000 U
   Total direct materials yield variance $35,000 U

2. Direct materials mix variances:
   Base $250,000 F
   Grade   125,000 U
   Total direct materials mix variance $125,000 F

24-26 (cont'd.)

3. Direct materials efficiency variances:

Base	$220,000 F
Grade	130,000 U
Total direct materials efficiency variance	$ 90,000 F

4.   Agrichem Enterprises has a total favorable efficiency variance of $90,000 F, largely because of a favorable mix variance of $125,000. The favorable mix variance arises because Agrichem uses a greater proportion of the cheaper Grade input in its direct materials mix. Using more of Grade may have caused the unfavorable yield variance, but this unfavorable variance is more than offset by the favorable mix variance.

SOLUTION EXHIBIT 24-26
Columnar Presentation of Direct Materials, Efficiency, Yield and Mix Variances for Agrichem Enterprises

	(Actual Total Quantity of All Inputs Used × Actual Input Mix) × Budgeted Prices (1)	(Actual Total Quantity of All Inputs Used × Budgeted Input Mix) × Budgeted Prices (2)	Flexible Budget: (Budgeted Total Quantity of all Inputs Allowed for Actual Outputs × Budgeted Input Mix × Budgeted Prices) (3)
Base	(2,500 × 0.50) × $400 = $500,000	(2,500 × 0.75) × $400 = $750,000	(2,000 × 0.90) × $400 = $720,000
Grade	(2,500 × 0.50) × $200 = 250,000	(2,500 × 0.25) × $200 = 125,000	(2,000 × 0.30) × $200 = 120,000
All Inputs	$750,000	$875,000	$840,000

$125,000 F   Total mix variance

$35,000 U   Total yield variance

$90,000 F   Total efficiency variance

F = favorable effect on operating income; U = unfavorable effect on operating income.

24-28 (40 min.) **Direct manufacturing labor price and efficiency variances, direct manufacturing labor yield and mix variances.**

1.   Actual output = 20,000 units

$$\text{Standard hours of actual output} = \frac{20,000 \text{ units}}{8 \text{ units per hour}} = 2,500 \text{ hours}$$

$$\text{Artisans:} \quad 2,500 \times \frac{2}{5} = 1,000 \text{ hours}$$

$$\text{Helpers:} \quad 2,500 \times \frac{3}{5} = 1,500 \text{ hours}$$

Solution Exhibit 24-28A presents the total direct manufacturing labor price and efficiency variances for Midwest Industries.

The total direct manufacturing labor price variance can also be computed as follows:

$$\begin{array}{l} \text{Direct manuf. labor} \\ \text{price variance} \\ \text{for each input} \end{array} = \left(\begin{array}{cc} \text{Actual} & \text{Budgeted} \\ \text{price} & \text{price} \end{array} \right) \times \begin{array}{c} \text{Actual} \\ \text{inputs} \end{array}$$

Artisans	= ($23 − $22) ×	900	=	$ 900 U
Helpers	= ($11 − $12) × 2,000		=	2,000 F
Total direct manufacturing labor price variance				$1,100 F

The total direct manufacturing labor efficiency variance can also be computed as follows:

$$\begin{array}{l} \text{Direct manuf. labor} \\ \text{efficiency variance} \\ \text{for each input} \end{array} = \left(\begin{array}{cc} \text{Actual inputs} & \text{Budgeted inputs allowed} \\ \text{used} & \text{for actual output achieved} \end{array} \right) \times \begin{array}{c} \text{Budgeted} \\ \text{price} \end{array}$$

Artisans	= (900 − 1,000) × $22	=	$2,200 F
Helpers	= (2,000 − 1,500) × $12	=	6,000 U
Total direct manufacturing labor efficiency variance			$3,800 U

The favorable price variance by hiring more helpers was more than offset by the unfavorable efficiency variance of using more helpers.

24-28 (cont'd.)

SOLUTION EXHIBIT 24-28A
Columnar Presentation of Direct Manufacturing Labor Price and Efficiency Variances for Midwest Industries

	Actual Costs Incurred: (Actual Inputs × Actual Prices) (1)	Actual Inputs × Budgeted Prices (2)	Flexible Budget: (Budgeted Inputs Allowed for Actual Outputs Achieved × Budgeted Prices) (3)
Artisans	900 × $23 = $20,700	900 × $22 = $19,800	1,000 × $22 = $22,000
Helpers	2,000 × $11 = 22,000	2,000 × $12 = 24,000	1,500 × $12 = 18,000
All Inputs	$42,700	$43,800	$40,000

$1,100 F $3,800 U

Total price variance   Total efficiency variance

$2,700 U

Total flexible-budget variance

F = favorable effect on operating income; U = unfavorable effect on operating income.

2.   Solution Exhibit 24-28B presents the total direct manufacturing labor yield and mix variances for Midwest Industries.

The total direct manufacturing labor yield variance can also be computed as:

$$
\begin{pmatrix} \text{Direct} \\ \text{manuf. labor} \\ \text{yield variance} \\ \text{for each input} \end{pmatrix} = \begin{pmatrix} \text{Actual total quantity} \\ \text{of all direct manuf.} \\ \text{labor inputs used} \end{pmatrix} - \begin{pmatrix} \text{Budgeted total quantity} \\ \text{of all direct manuf.} \\ \text{labor inputs allowed} \\ \text{for actual output achieved} \end{pmatrix} \times \begin{pmatrix} \text{Budgeted} \\ \text{input} \\ \text{mix} \end{pmatrix} \times \begin{pmatrix} \text{Budgeted} \\ \text{price of} \\ \text{direct manuf.} \\ \text{inputs} \end{pmatrix}
$$

Artisans	=	(2,900 × 0.40 – 1,000) × $22	= (1,160 – 1,000) × $22	= $3,520 U
Helpers	=	(2,900 × 0.60 – 1,500) × $12	= (1,740 – 1,500) × $12	= 2,880 U
Total direct manufacturing labor yield variance				$6,400 U

The total direct manufacturing labor mix variance can also be computed as:

$$
\begin{pmatrix} \text{Direct} \\ \text{manuf. labor} \\ \text{mix} \\ \text{variance} \\ \text{for each input} \end{pmatrix} = \begin{pmatrix} \text{Actual} \\ \text{direct manuf.} \\ \text{Labor input mix} \\ \text{percentage} \end{pmatrix} - \begin{pmatrix} \text{Budgeted} \\ \text{direct manuf.} \\ \text{labor input mix} \\ \text{percentage} \end{pmatrix} \times \begin{pmatrix} \text{Actual total quantity} \\ \text{of all} \\ \text{direct manuf.} \\ \text{labor inputs used} \end{pmatrix} \times \begin{pmatrix} \text{Budgeted} \\ \text{price of} \\ \text{direct manuf.} \\ \text{labor inputs} \end{pmatrix}
$$

$$\text{Artisans} = \left(\frac{900}{2,900} - 0.40\right) \times 2,900 \times \$22 = -0.08965 \times 2,900 \times \$22 = \$5,720 \text{ F}$$

$$\text{Helpers} = \left(\frac{2,000}{2,900} - 0.60\right) \times 2,900 \times \$12 = 0.08965 \times 2,900 \times \$12 = \underline{3,120} \text{ U}$$

Total direct manufacturing labor mix variance $\qquad\qquad\qquad\qquad \underline{\underline{\$2,600}}$ F

The total mix variance was favorable because a greater proportion of the cheaper helper labor was employed. However, the favorable mix was probably more than offset by the lower yield of the helper labor.

3. Assume that 2,900 hours of input were used at the standard mix of 40% for artisans and 60% for helpers. Using the actual direct manufacturing labor prices of $23 and $11, respectively:

Artisans:	$0.40 \times 2,900 \times \$23$	=	$26,680
Helpers:	$0.60 \times 2,900 \times \$11$	=	19,140
All Labor:			$45,820

These costs are higher than those actually incurred because the actual mix of hours was approximately 31% artisans instead of 40%.

SOLUTION EXHIBIT 24-28B
Columnar Presentation of Direct Manufacturing Labor Yield and Mix Variances for Midwest Industries

	(Actual Total Quantity of All Inputs Used × Actual Input Mix) × Budgeted Prices (1)	(Actual Total Quantity of All Inputs Used × Budgeted Input Mix) × Budgeted Prices (2)	Flexible Budget: (Budgeted Total Quantity of All Inputs Allowed for Actual Outputs × Budgeted Input Mix) × Budgeted Prices (3)
Artisans	$2,900 \times \frac{900}{2,900} \times \$22 = \$19,800$	$(2,900 \times 0.40^a) \times \$22 = \$25,520$	$2,500 \times 0.40^a \times \$22 = \$22,000$
Helpers	$2,900 \times \frac{2,000}{2,900} \times \$12 = \underline{24,000}$	$(2,900 \times 0.60^b) \times \$12 = \underline{20,880}$	$2,500 \times 0.60^b \times \$12 = \underline{18,000}$
All Inputs	$43,800	$46,400	$40,000

$\qquad\qquad\qquad\qquad$ $2,600 F $\qquad\qquad\qquad$ $6,400 U

$\qquad\qquad\qquad\qquad$ Total mix variance $\qquad\qquad$ Total yield variance

$\qquad\qquad\qquad\qquad\qquad\qquad\qquad$ $3,800 U

$\qquad\qquad\qquad\qquad\qquad\qquad\qquad$ Total efficiency variance

F = favorable effect on operating income; U = unfavorable effect on operating income.

Budgeted Input Mix:
[a]Artisans = 2 hours ÷ 5 hours = 40%
[b]Helpers = 3 hours ÷ 5 hours = 60%

24-30 (30 min.) **Total factor productivity, its comparison between two time periods, and analysis of cost changes.**

1.   19_8 total factor productivity using 19_8 prices :

Quantity of output produced = 525,000 units

$$
\begin{pmatrix} \text{Costs of} \\ \text{inputs used} \\ \text{in 19\_8} \\ \text{based on} \\ \text{19\_8 prices} \end{pmatrix} = \begin{pmatrix} \text{Direct} \\ \text{manufacturing} \\ \text{labor hours used} \\ \text{in 19\_8} \end{pmatrix} \times \begin{pmatrix} \text{Direct} \\ \text{manufacturing} \\ \text{labor rate} \\ \text{in 19\_8} \end{pmatrix} + \begin{pmatrix} \text{Direct} \\ \text{materials} \\ \text{used} \\ \text{in 19\_8} \end{pmatrix} \times \begin{pmatrix} \text{Direct} \\ \text{materials} \\ \text{prices} \\ \text{in 19\_8} \end{pmatrix}
$$

$$= (9{,}500 \times \$25) + (610{,}000 \times \$1.25)$$

$$= \$237{,}500 + \$762{,}500 = \$1{,}000{,}000$$

$$
\begin{pmatrix} \text{Total} \\ \text{factor} \\ \text{productivity} \end{pmatrix} = \frac{\text{Quantity of output}}{\text{Costs of inputs used in 19\_8 based on 19\_8 prices}}
$$

$$= \frac{525{,}000}{\$1{,}000{,}000} = 0.525 \text{ units of output per dollar of inputs}$$

By itself, the 19_8 TFP of 0.525 handles per dollar of input does not provide insight on efficiency. We cannot tell if the manager used fewer physical inputs to produce output, or if the manager wisely substituted one input for another to take advantage of changes in input prices in 19_8 relative to 19_7. We need something to compare the 19_8 TFP against. We use, as a comparison, the output per dollar of input that the manager would have achieved in 19_7 based on the inputs used and output produced in 19_7, calculated using 19_8 prices.

2.   19_7 total factor productivity using 19_8 prices:

Quantity of output produced = 375,000 units

$$
\begin{pmatrix} \text{Costs of} \\ \text{inputs used} \\ \text{in 19\_7} \\ \text{based on} \\ \text{19\_8 prices} \end{pmatrix} = \begin{pmatrix} \text{Direct} \\ \text{manufacturing} \\ \text{labor hours used} \\ \text{in 19\_7} \end{pmatrix} \times \begin{pmatrix} \text{Direct} \\ \text{manufacturing} \\ \text{labor rate} \\ \text{in 19\_8} \end{pmatrix} + \begin{pmatrix} \text{Direct} \\ \text{materials} \\ \text{used} \\ \text{in 19\_7} \end{pmatrix} \times \begin{pmatrix} \text{Direct} \\ \text{materials} \\ \text{prices} \\ \text{in 19\_8} \end{pmatrix}
$$

$$= (7{,}500 \times \$25) + (450{,}000 \times \$1.25)$$

$$= \$187{,}500 + \$562{,}500$$

$$= \$750{,}000$$

24-30 (Cont'd.)

$$\text{Total factor productivity} = \frac{\text{Quantity of output}}{\text{Costs of inputs used in 19\_7 based on 19\_8 prices}}$$

$$= \frac{375,000}{\$750,000} = 0.50 \text{ units of output per dollar of inputs}$$

TFP has increased from 0.50 in 19_7 to 0,525 in 19_8, an increase of 5% [(0.525 − 0.50) ÷ 0.50]. This is the overall effect of improvements in the use of each input as well as changes in the mix of inputs chosen in response to input prices prevailing in 19_8.

3.   Solution Exhibit 24-30 presents the analysis of cost changes in columnar form.

Actual costs incurred by Pittsburgh Industries is $690,000 in 19_7 and $1,000,000 in 19_8 (see columnar presentation).

Of the total change in costs of $310,000, the output adjustment component is $276,000 U; the price change component is $84,000 U; and the productivity change component is $50,000 F (see columnar presentation).

4.   The output adjustment component measures the increase in costs attributable solely to increases in output, assuming 19_7 prices and 19_7 productivities. The price change component evaluates the increase in costs due solely to increases in the prices of inputs in 19_8, based on the inputs that would have been used in 19_7 to produce the 19_8 output. These two components would have resulted in Pittsburgh Industries costs increasing by $360,000 ($276,000 + $84,000) in 19_8 relative to 19_7. Pittsburgh Industries costs changed by a total of $310,000 because of a $50,000 gain in productivity. Pittsburgh Industries used fewer inputs and a cheaper mix of inputs to produce output in 19_8.

SOLUTION EXHIBIT 24-30
Analysis of changes in actual costs from 19_7 to 19_8

	Actual Costs for 19_8: Actual Units of Inputs Used To Produce 19_8 Output × 19_8 Prices (1)	Actual Units of Inputs That Would Have Been Used in 19_7 to Produce 19_8 Output × 19_8 Prices (2)	Actual Units of Inputs That Would Have Been Used in 19_7 to Produce 19_8 Output × 19_7 Prices (3)	Actual Costs for 19_7: Actual Units of Inputs Used to Produce 19_7 Output × 19_7 Prices (4)
Direct Manuf. Labor	9,500 × $25.00 = $ 237,500	10,500^a× $25.00 = $ 262,500	10,500^a× $20.00 = $210,000	7,500 × $20.00 = $150,000
Direct Materials	610,000 × $ 1.25 = 762,500	$630,000^b× $ 1.25 = 787,500	630,000^b× $ 1.20 = 756,000	450,000 × $ 1.20 = 540,000
All inputs	$1,000,000	$1,050,000	$966,000	$690,000

$50,000 F $84,000 U $276,000 U

Productivity change   Price change   Output adjustment

$310,000 U

Total change in costs

F = Favorable effect on operating income; U = Unfavorable effect on operating income.

^{a}Direct manufacturing labor that would have   Direct manufacturing   19_8 output
been used in 19_7 to produce 19_8 output   =   labor used in 19_7   × 19_7 output

10,500   = $7,500 \times \dfrac{525,000}{375,000}$

^{b}Direct materials that would have been used   =   Direct materials   19_8 output
in 19_7 to produce 19_8 output   used in 19_7   × 19_7 output

630,000   = $450,000 \times \dfrac{525,000}{375,000}$

24-21

24-32 (30 min.) **Total factor productivity and analysis of cost changes.**

1. $\underline{\text{19\_8 total factor productivity using 19\_8 prices}}$

Quantity of carpet cleaned = 15,000,000 square feet.

$$
\begin{aligned}
\begin{pmatrix}\text{Costs of} \\ \text{inputs used} \\ \text{in 19\_8} \\ \text{based on} \\ \text{19\_8 prices}\end{pmatrix} &=
\begin{pmatrix}\text{Direct} \\ \text{cleaning} \\ \text{labor-hours used} \\ \text{in 19\_8}\end{pmatrix} \times \begin{pmatrix}\text{Direct} \\ \text{cleaning} \\ \text{labor rate} \\ \text{in 19\_8}\end{pmatrix} + \begin{pmatrix}\text{Cleaning} \\ \text{solution} \\ \text{used} \\ \text{in 19\_8}\end{pmatrix} \times \begin{pmatrix}\text{Cleaning} \\ \text{solution} \\ \text{prices} \\ \text{in 19\_8}\end{pmatrix} \\
&\quad + \begin{pmatrix}\text{Machine-} \\ \text{hours} \\ \text{used} \\ \text{in 19\_8}\end{pmatrix} \times \begin{pmatrix}\text{Machine-} \\ \text{hour} \\ \text{rate} \\ \text{in 19\_8}\end{pmatrix}
\end{aligned}
$$

$$= (15{,}000 \times \$22) + (10{,}000 \times \$12) + (6{,}000 \times \$45)$$

$$= \$330{,}000 + \$120{,}000 + \$270{,}000 = \$720{,}000$$

$$
\begin{pmatrix}\text{Total} \\ \text{factor} \\ \text{productivity}\end{pmatrix} = \frac{\text{Quantity of output}}{\text{Costs of inputs used in 19\_8 based on 19\_8 prices}}
$$

$$= \frac{15{,}000{,}000}{\$720{,}000} = 20.8333 \text{ sq. ft. of carpet per dollar of inputs}$$

By itself, the 19_8 TFP of 20.83 square feet of carpet per dollar of input does not provide insight about efficiency. For example, we cannot tell if the manager used fewer physical inputs to produce output. We need something to compare the 19_8 TFP against. We use, as a comparison, the output per dollar of input that the manager would have achieved in 19_7 based on the inputs used and output produced in 19_7, calculated using 19_8 prices.

2. $\underline{\text{19\_7 total factor productivity using 19\_8 prices}}$

Quantity of carpet cleaned = 12,000,000 square feet (12,000 labor-hours × 1,000 sq.ft. per labor-hour)

$$
\begin{aligned}
\begin{pmatrix}\text{Costs of} \\ \text{inputs used} \\ \text{in 19\_7} \\ \text{based on} \\ \text{19\_8 prices}\end{pmatrix} &=
\begin{pmatrix}\text{Direct} \\ \text{cleaning} \\ \text{labor-hours} \\ \text{used} \\ \text{in 19\_7}\end{pmatrix} \times \begin{pmatrix}\text{Direct} \\ \text{cleaning} \\ \text{labor rate} \\ \text{in 19\_8}\end{pmatrix} + \begin{pmatrix}\text{Cleaning} \\ \text{solution} \\ \text{used} \\ \text{in 19\_7}\end{pmatrix} \times \begin{pmatrix}\text{Cleaning} \\ \text{solution} \\ \text{prices} \\ \text{in 19\_8}\end{pmatrix} \\
&\quad + \begin{pmatrix}\text{Machine-} \\ \text{hours} \\ \text{used} \\ \text{in 19\_7}\end{pmatrix} \times \begin{pmatrix}\text{Machine-} \\ \text{hour} \\ \text{rate} \\ \text{in 19\_8}\end{pmatrix}
\end{aligned}
$$

$$= (12{,}000 \times \$22) + (10{,}000 \times \$12) + (4{,}800 \times \$45)$$
$$= \$264{,}000 + \$120{,}000 + \$216{,}000$$
$$= \$600{,}000$$

$$\text{Total factor productivity} = \frac{\text{Quantity of output}}{\text{Costs of inputs used in 19\_7 based on 19\_8 prices}}$$

$$= \frac{12,000,000}{\$600,000} = 20 \text{ sq. ft. of carpet per dollar of inputs}$$

Using 19_8 prices, total factor productivity increases from 20 square feet of carpet cleaned per dollar of inputs in 19_7 to 20.83 square feet of carpet cleaned per dollar of inputs in 19_8. The increase in total factor productivity from 19_7 to 19_8 is 4.167% ([20.8333 – 20.00] ÷ 20.00). The change in Quick Clean's total factor productivity could arise for two reasons : (1) an increase in the productivities of the individual inputs, and (2) the use of *relatively more* of direct materials whose prices have not increased as much as direct manufacturing labor. Quick Clean's gain in total factor productivity can be attributed to the increase in the partial productivity of the cleaning solution while maintaining the partial productivities of the other two inputs, cleaning labor and machine time. Mary Costas' ability to substitute among inputs is somewhat restricted because she has only a limited supply of cleaning labor. In order to maximize profits, Mary uses as much of the cleaning labor as she can.

3.   Solution Exhibit 24-32 presents the analysis of cost changes attributable to productivity gains in columnar form. Solution Exhibit 24-32 uses only the first two columns of Exhibit 24-8 of the text, since the requirement for this question focuses only on cost changes attributable to productivity changes between 19_7 and 19_8. Note that the computations of input price changes and output adjustment requires knowledge of the input prices in 19_7 which are not given in the question. Solution Exhibit 24-32 indicates that Quick Clean's actual costs decreased by $30,000 as a result of productivity gains between 19_7 and 19_8. The exhibit calculates the productivity change component to equal $30,000 F. As described in requirements 1 and 2 of this question, the reduction in cost arises because of the gain in total factor productivity between 19_7 and 19_8. This gain arises because of the increase in the partial productivity of the cleaning solution between 19_7 and 19_8.

The cost savings from productivity gains can also be computed as follows:

$$\begin{array}{ccc} \text{Costs savings} & & \text{Percentage change} & & \text{Actual costs} \\ \text{from} & = & \text{in productivity} & \times & \text{of all inputs} \\ \text{productivity gains} & & \text{from 19\_7 to 19\_8} & & \text{in 19\_8} \end{array}$$

$$= 4.167\% \times \$720,000$$
$$= \$30,000$$

SOLUTION EXHIBIT 24-32
Analysis of Change in Actual Costs Due to
Changes in Total Factor Productivity from 19_8 to 19_7

	Actual Costs for 19_8: Actual Units of Inputs Used To Produce 19_8 Output × 19_8 Prices (1)	Actual Units of Inputs That Would Have Been Used in 19_7 to Produce 19_8 Output × 19_8 Prices (3)
Cleaning labor	$15,000 × $22 = $330,000	15,000[a] × $22 = $330,000
Cleaning solution	10,000 × $12 = 120,000	12,500[b] × $12 = 150,000
Machine time	6,000 × $45 = 270,000	6,000[c] × $45 = 270,000
All inputs	$720,000	$750,000

$$\$30,000 \text{ F}$$
Productivity change

F = Favorable effect on operating income; U = Unfavorable effect on operating income.

[a]Direct cleaning labor that would have been used in 19_7 to produce 19_8 output $= \dfrac{\text{Direct cleaning}}{\text{labor used in 19\_7}} \times \dfrac{\text{19\_8 output}}{\text{19\_7 output}}$

$$15,000 = 12,000 \times \dfrac{15,000,000}{12,000,000}$$

[b]Cleaning solution that would have been used in 19_7 to produce 19_8 output $= \dfrac{\text{Cleaning solution}}{\text{used in 19\_7}} \times \dfrac{\text{19\_8 output}}{\text{19\_7 output}}$

$$12,500 = 10,000 \times \dfrac{15,000,000}{12,000,000}$$

[c]Machine-hours that would have been used in 19_7 to produce 19_8 output $= \dfrac{\text{Machine-hours}}{\text{used in 19\_7}} \times \dfrac{\text{19\_8 output}}{\text{19\_7 output}}$

$$6,000 = 4,800 \times \dfrac{15,000,000}{12,000,000}$$

24-34 (40 min.) **Direct manufacturing labor price and efficiency variances, direct manufacturing labor yield and mix variances, productivity measures, externally based standard costs.**

1.   Choshu Engineering is attempting to increase the pressure on its plants to become more cost-competitive. The Tokuyama plant assembles the same product as the Memphis plant. It appears reasonable to assume that the Memphis plant could learn from the efficiencies that the Tokuyama plant achieves.

Companies that use this approach to setting standards invest considerable resources in transferring knowledge from its most efficient plant its other plants—for example, by sending plant managers from Memphis to Tokuyama to study operations.

2.   Solution Exhibit 24-34A presents the total direct manufacturing labor price and efficiency variances for the Memphis plant in 19_8.

The total direct manufacturing labor price variance can also be computed as:

$$\begin{array}{c}\text{Direct manufacturing}\\\text{labor price variance}\\\text{for each input}\end{array} = \left(\begin{array}{cc}\text{Actual} & \text{Budgeted}\\\text{prices} & \text{prices}\end{array}\right) \times \begin{array}{c}\text{Actual}\\\text{inputs}\end{array}$$

Assembly labor = ($25 – $24) × 18,000   = $18,000 F
Testing labor = ($16 – $17) × 12,000   =   12,000 F
Total direct manufacturing labor price variance $ 6,000 U

The total direct manufacturing labor efficiency variance can also be computed as:

$$\begin{array}{c}\text{Direct manufacturing}\\\text{labor efficiency variance}\\\text{for each input}\end{array} = \left(\begin{array}{cc}\text{Actual} & \text{Budgeted inputs allowed}\\\text{inputs} & \text{for actual outputs achieved}\end{array}\right) \times \begin{array}{c}\text{Budgeted}\\\text{price}\end{array}$$

Assembly labor = (18,000 – 22,000) × $24   = $96,000 F
Testing labor = (12,000 – 10,000) × $17   =   34,000 U
Total direct manufacturing labor efficiency variance $62,000 F

24-34 (Cont'd.)

SOLUTION EXHIBIT 24-34A
Columnar Presentation of Direct Manufacturing Labor Price and Efficiency Variances for Choshu Engineering for 19_8

	Actual Costs Incurred (Actual Inputs × Actual Prices) (1)		Actual Input × Budgeted Price (2)		Flexible Budget (Budgeted Inputs Allowed for Actual Outputs Achieved × Budgeted Prices) (3)	
Assembly labor	$18,000^a \times \$25$	= $450,000	$18,000^a \times \$24 =$ $432,000		$22,000^b \times \$24 =$ $528,000	
Testing labor	$12,000^c \times \$16$	= 192,000	$12,000^c \times \$17 =$ 204,000		$10,000^d \times \$17 =$ 170,000	
		$642,000		$636,000		$698,000

$6,000 U
Total price variance $62,000 F
Total efficiency variance

$56,000 F
Total flexible-budget variance

Note that U = unfavorable effect on operating income; F = favorable effect on operating income.

^{a} 36 × 500 = 18,000 hours ^{b} 44 × 500 = 22,000
^{c} 24 × 500 = 12,000 hours ^{d} 20 × 500 = 10,000

3a.

	Actual direct labor mix percentage	Budget direct labor mix percentage
Assembly department	$\dfrac{18,000}{30,000} = 0.60$	$\dfrac{22,000}{32,000} = 0.6875$
Testing department	$\dfrac{12,000}{30,000} = 0.40$	$\dfrac{10,000}{32,000} = 0.3125$

b.   Solution Exhibit 24-34B presents the total direct manufacturing labor yield and mix variances for the Memphis plant in 19_8.

The total direct manufacturing labor mix variance can also be computed as the sum of the direct manufacturing labor mix variances for each input.

$$\begin{array}{c}\text{Direct manuf.}\\\text{labor}\\\text{mix variance}\\\text{for each input}\end{array} = \left(\begin{array}{cc}\text{Actual} & \text{Budgeted}\\\text{manuf. labor} & \text{manuf. labor}\\\text{input mix} - \text{input mix}\\\text{percentage} & \text{percentage}\end{array}\right) \times \begin{array}{c}\text{Actual total quantity}\\\text{of all}\\\text{manuf.}\\\text{labor inputs used}\end{array} \times \begin{array}{c}\text{Budgeted}\\\text{price of}\\\text{manuf.}\\\text{labor input}\end{array}$$

Assembly Labor = (0.60 – 0.6875) × 30,000 × $24 = – 0.0875 × 30,000 × $24 = $63,000 F
Testing Labor   = (0.40 – 0.3125) × 30,000 × $17 = 0.0875 × 30,000 × $17 = 44,625 U
Total direct manufacturing labor mix variance $18,375 F

The total direct manufacturing labor yield variance can also be computed as the sum of the direct manufacturing labor yield variances for each input

$$
\begin{pmatrix} \text{Direct manuf.} \\ \text{labor} \\ \text{yield variance} \\ \text{for each input} \end{pmatrix} = \begin{pmatrix} \text{Actual total quantity} \\ \text{of all direct manufacturing} - \\ \text{labor inputs used} \end{pmatrix} \begin{pmatrix} \text{Budgeted total quantity} \\ \text{of all direct manufacturing} \\ \text{labor inputs allowed} \\ \text{for actual output achieved} \end{pmatrix} \times \begin{pmatrix} \text{Budgeted direct} \\ \text{manufacturing} \\ \text{labor input} \\ \text{mix percentage} \end{pmatrix} \times \begin{pmatrix} \text{Budgeted} \\ \text{price of} \\ \text{direct manufacturing} \\ \text{labor input} \end{pmatrix}
$$

Assembly Labor	=	$(30,000 - 32,000) \times 0.6875 \times \$24$	=	$-2,000 \times \$0.6875 \times \$24$	= $33,000$ F
Testing Labor	=	$(30,000 - 32,000) \times 0.3125 \times \$17$	=	$-2,000 \times \$0.3125 \times \$17$	= $\underline{10,625}$ F
Total direct manufacturing labor yield variance					$\underline{\underline{\$43,625}}$ F

The manufacturing labor mix variance is favorable because Choshu used more of the low cost Testing Department labor than the budgeted mix. The total quantity of all manufacturing labor used was lower than budgeted resulting in a favorable yield variance.

SOLUTION EXHIBIT 24-34B
Columnar Presentation of Direct Manufacturing Labor Yield and Mix Variances for Choshu Engineering for 19_8

	(Actual Total Quantity of All Inputs Used × Actual Input Mix) × Budgeted Prices (1)		(Actual Total Quantity of All Inputs Used × Budgeted Input Mix) × Budgeted Prices (2)		Flexible Budget (Budgeted Total Quantity of All Inputs Allowed for Actual Output Achieved × Budgeted Input Mix) × Budgeted Prices (3)	
Assembly						
Labor	$30,000 \times 0.60 \times \$24 =$	$432,000	$30,000 \times 0.6875 \times \$24 =$	$495,000	$32,000 \times 0.6875 \times \$24 =$	$528,000
Testing						
Labor	$30,000 \times 0.40 \times \$17 =$	$\underline{204,000}$	$30,000 \times 0.3125 \times \$17 =$	$\underline{159,375}$	$32,000 \times 0.3125 \times \$17 =$	$\underline{170,000}$
		$636,000		$654,375		$698,000

$\uparrow$ $18,375$ F $\uparrow$ $43,625$ F $\uparrow$

Total mix variance   Total yield variance

$\uparrow$ $62,000$ F $\uparrow$

Total efficiency variance

Note that F = favorable effect on operating income; U = unfavorable effect on operating income

4.

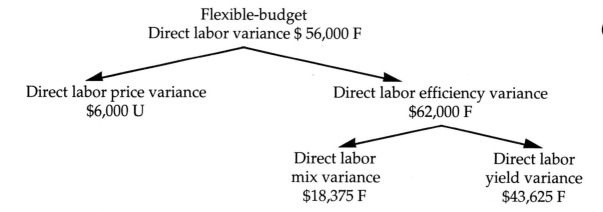

Flexible-budget
Direct labor variance $ 56,000 F

Direct labor price variance
$6,000 U

Direct labor efficiency variance
$62,000 F

Direct labor
mix variance
$18,375 F

Direct labor
yield variance
$43,625 F

The Memphis plant has made dramatic strides in increasing efficiency in 19_8. The major source of the increase is the direct labor yield variance of the assembly department.

5.

	19_7	19_8

Direct manufacturing labor partial productivity

Assembly $\quad \dfrac{500}{26,000} = \dfrac{0.0192}{\text{systems/hour}} \qquad \dfrac{500}{18,000} = \dfrac{0.0278}{\text{systems/hour}}$

Testing $\quad \dfrac{500}{14,000} = \dfrac{0.0357}{\text{systems/hour}} \qquad \dfrac{500}{12,000} = \dfrac{0.0417}{\text{systems/hour}}$

6.

$$\begin{aligned}
\text{Cost of inputs used in 19\_8 based on 19\_8 prices} &= \left(\begin{array}{c}\text{Direct}\\\text{manufacturing}\\\text{assembly labor}\\\text{used in 19\_8}\end{array} \times \begin{array}{c}\text{Direct}\\\text{manufacturing}\\\text{assembly labor}\\\text{rate in 19\_8}\end{array}\right) + \left(\begin{array}{c}\text{Direct}\\\text{manufacturing}\\\text{testing labor}\\\text{used in 19\_8}\end{array} \times \begin{array}{c}\text{Direct}\\\text{manufacturing}\\\text{testing labor}\\\text{rate in 19\_8}\end{array}\right)\\
&= (18,000 \times \$25) + (12,000 \times \$16)\\
&= \$450,000 + \$192,000\\
&= \$642,000
\end{aligned}$$

Total factor productivity for 19_8 using 19_8 prices $= \dfrac{\text{Quantity of output produced in 19\_8}}{\text{Cost of inputs used in 19\_8 based on 19\_8 prices}}$

$= \dfrac{500}{\$642,000} = 0.00078$ systems per dollar of input

or $1,284 per system

$$\begin{aligned}
\text{Cost of inputs used in 19\_7 based on 19\_8 prices} &= \left(\begin{array}{c}\text{Direct}\\\text{manufacturing}\\\text{assembly labor}\\\text{used in 19\_7}\end{array} \times \begin{array}{c}\text{Direct}\\\text{manufacturing}\\\text{assembly labor}\\\text{rate in 19\_8}\end{array}\right) + \left(\begin{array}{c}\text{Direct}\\\text{manufacturing}\\\text{testing labor}\\\text{used in 19\_7}\end{array} \times \begin{array}{c}\text{Direct}\\\text{manufacturing}\\\text{testing labor}\\\text{rate in 19\_8}\end{array}\right)\\
&= (26,000 \times \$25) + (14,000 \times \$16)\\
&= \$650,000 + \$224,000\\
&= \$874,000
\end{aligned}$$

24-34 (Cont'd.)

Total factor
productivity
for 19_7 using $\quad =\quad \dfrac{\text{Quantity of output produced in 19\_7}}{\text{Cost of inputs used in 19\_7 based on 19\_8 prices}}$
19_8 prices

$$= \dfrac{500}{\$874,000} = 0.00057 \text{ systems per dollar of input}$$

or $1,748 per system

7.   Both the efficiency and the productivity measures indicate the tremendous improvements Memphis has made in its manufacturing operations. Note, however, that the efficiency variances and the productivity measures use different benchmarks. The sharp gains in partial and total factor productivity indicate the improved performance of the Memphis plant in 19_8 compared to its own performance in 19_7. The favorable efficiency, mix and yield variances compare the Memphis plant's performance in 19_8 to the standards set for 19_8, in this case the 19_7 performance of the Tokuyama plant, the most efficient plant operated by Choshu Engineering. The favorable efficiency variances indicate that the Memphis plant's performance in 19_8, in addition to being better than in 19_7 (as evidenced by the productivity measures), was also better than the 19_7 performance of the most efficient plant.

CHAPTER 25
CONTROL SYSTEMS, TRANSFER PRICING, AND MULTINATIONAL CONSIDERATIONS

25-2 To be effective, management control systems should be (a) closely aligned to an organization's strategies and goals, (b) designed to fit the organization's structure and the decision-making responsibility of individual managers, and (c) able to motivate managers and employees to put in effort to attain selected goals desired by top management.

25-4 The chapter cites five benefits of decentralization:
1. Creates greater responsiveness to local needs
2. Leads to quicker decision making
3. Increases motivation
4. Aids management development and learning
5. Sharpens the focus of managers

The chapter cites four costs of decentralization:
1. Leads to suboptimal decision making
2. Results in duplication of activities
3. Decreases loyalty toward the organization as a whole
4. Increases costs of gathering information

25-6 No. A transfer price is the price one subunit of an organization charges for a product or service supplied to another subunit of the same organization. The two segments can be cost centers, profit centers, or investment centers. For example, the allocation of service department costs to production departments that are set up as either cost centers or investment centers is an example of transfer pricing.

25-8 Transfer prices should have the following properties. They should
1. promote goal congruence,
2. promote a sustained high level of management effort, and
3. promote a high level of subunit autonomy in decision making.

25-10 Transferring products or services at market prices generally leads to optimal decisions when (a) the intermediate market is perfectly competitive, (b) interdependencies of subunits are minimal, and (c) there are no additional costs or benefits to the corporation as a whole in using the market instead of transacting internally.

25-12 Reasons why a dual-pricing approach to transfer pricing is not widely used in practice include:
1. The manager of the division using a cost-based method does not have sufficient incentives to control costs.
2. This approach does not provide clear signals to division managers about the level of decentralization top management wants.
3. This approach tends to insulate managers from the frictions of the market place.

25-14 Yes. The general transfer-pricing guideline specifies that the minimum transfer price equals the additional *outlay costs* per unit incurred up to the point of transfer *plus* the *opportunity costs* per unit to the supplying division. When the supplying division has idle capacity, its opportunity costs are zero; when the supplying division has no idle capacity, its opportunity costs are positive. Hence, the minimum transfer price will vary depending on whether the supplying division has idle capacity or not.

25-16 (10 min.) **Goals of public accounting firms.**

If public accounting firms stress that each individual should have a high percentage of chargeable time, individuals will attempt to both maximize the percentage of their time charged to clients and minimize the time spent on nonchargeable tasks. Many accounting firms now recognize that their goals (growth, profitability, intellectual challenge, and so on) may not be promoted if all individuals focus on maximizing the percentage of their day-to-day time charged to clients. Aspects critical to promoting goals that are not chargeable to clients include:
    a.   Bidding for new clients
    b.   Superiors providing training to juniors
    c.   Continuing education to keep personnel up-to-date
    d.   General public relations aimed at promoting the profile of a well-known, reputable, and professional firm

25-18 (35 min.) **Multinational transfer pricing, effect of alternative transfer-pricing methods, global income tax minimization.**

1.   This is a three-country, three-division transfer pricing problem with three alternative transfer-pricing methods. Summary data in U.S. dollars are:

China Plant
> Variable costs: 1,000 Yuan ÷ 8 Yuan per $ = $125 per subunit
> Fixed costs: 1,800 Yuan ÷ 8 Yuan per $ = $225 per subunit

South Korea Plant
> Variable costs: 240,000 Won ÷ 800 Won per $ = $300 per unit
> Fixed costs: 320,000 Won ÷ 800 Won per $ = $400 per unit

U.S. Plant
> Variable costs: = $100 per unit
> Fixed costs: = $200 per unit

Market prices for private label sale alternatives:
> China Plant: 3,600 Yuan ÷ 8 Yuan per $ = $450 per subunit
> South Korea Plant: 1,040,000 Won ÷ 800 Won per $ = $1,300 per unit

The transfer prices under each method are:

a.   Market price
   - China to South Korea   = $450 per subunit
   - South Korea to U.S. Plant   = $1,300 per unit

b.   200% of full costs
   - China to South Korea
     2.0 ($125 + $225) = $700 per subunit
   - South Korea to U.S. Plant
     2.0 ($700 + $300 + $400) = $2,800 per unit

c.   300% of variable costs
   - China to South Korea
     3.0 ($125) = $375 per subunit
   - South Korea to U.S. Plant
     3.0 ($375 + $300) = $2,025 per unit

	Method A Internal Transfers at Market Price	Method B Internal Transfers at 200% of Full Costs	Method C Internal Transfers at 300% of Variable Costs
1. CHINA DIVISION			
Division revenues per unit	$ 450	$ 700	$ 375
Deduct :			
Division variable costs per unit	125	125	125
Division fixed costs per unit	225	225	225
Division operating income per unit	100	350	25
Income tax at 40%	40	160	10
Division net income per unit	$ 60	$ 190	$ 15
2. SOUTH KOREA DIVISION			
Division revenues per unit	$1,300	$2,800	$2,025
Deduct:			
Transferred-in costs per unit	450	700	375
Division variable costs per unit	300	300	300
Division fixed costs per unit	400	400	400
Division operating income per unit	150	1,400	950
Income tax at 20%	30	280	190
Division net income per unit	$ 120	$1,120	$ 760
3. UNITED STATES DIVISION			
Division revenues per unit	$3,200	$3,200	$3,200
Deduct:			
Transferred-in costs per unit	1,300	2,800	2,025
Division variable costs per unit	100	100	100
Division fixed costs per unit	200	200	200
Division operating income per unit	1,600	100	875
Income tax at 30%	480	30	262.5
Division net income per unit	$1,120	$ 70	$ 612.5

2.   Division net income:

	Market Price	200% of Full Costs	300% of Variable Cost
China Division	$ 60	$ 190	$ 15.00
South Korea Division	120	1,120	760.00
U.S. Division	1,120	70	612.50
User Friendly Computer Inc.	$1,300	$1,380	$1,387.50

User Friendly will maximize its net income by using the 300% of variable cost, transfer-pricing method. This is because the 300% of full cost method sources most income in the countries with the lower income tax rates.

25-20 (30 min.) **Effect of alternative transfer-pricing methods on division operating income.**

	Internal Transfers at Market Prices Method A	Internal Transfers at 110% of Full Costs Method B
1. MINING DIVISION		
Revenues:		
$90, $66[1] × 400,000 units	$36,000,000	$26,400,000
Deduct:		
Division variable costs:		
$52[2] × 400,000 units	20,800,000	20,800,000
Division fixed costs:		
$8[3] × 400,000 units	3,200,000	3,200,000
Division operating income	$12,000,000	$ 2,400,000
METALS DIVISION		
Revenues:		
$150 × 400,000 units	$60,000,000	$60,000,000
Deduct:		
Transferred-in costs:		
$90, $66 × 400,000 units	36,000,000	26,400,000
Division variable costs:		
$36[4] × 400,000 units	14,400,000	14,400,000
Division fixed costs:		
$15[5] × 400,000 units	6,000,000	6,000,000
Division operating income	$ 3,600,000	$13,200,000

[1] $66 = $60 × 110%

[2] Variable cost per unit in Mining Division = Direct materials + Direct manufacturing labor + 75% of Manufacturing overhead = $12 + $16 + 75% × $32 = $52

[3] Fixed cost per unit = 25% of Manufacturing overhead = 25% ×$32 = $8

[4] Variable cost per unit in Metals Division = Direct materials + Direct manufacturing labor + 40% of Manufacturing overhead = $6 + $20 + 40% × $25 = $36

[5] Fixed cost per unit in Metals Division = 60% of Manufacturing overhead = 60% × $25 = $15

2.   Bonus paid to division managers at 1% of division operating income will be as follows:

	Method A Internal Transfers at Market Prices	Method B Internal Transfers at 110% of Full Costs
Mining Division manager's bonus (1% × $12,000,000; 1% × $2,400,000)	$120,000	$ 24,000
Metals Division manager's bonus (1% × $3,600,000; 1% × $13,200,000)	36,000	132,000

25-20 (Cont'd.)

The Mining Division manager will prefer Method A (transfer at market prices) because this method gives $120,000 of bonus rather than $24,000 under Method B (transfers at 110% of full costs). The Metals Division manager will prefer Method B because this method gives $132,000 of bonus rather than $36,000 under Method A.

3.   Brian Jones, the manager of the Mining Division, will appeal to the existence of a competitive market to price transfers at market prices. Using market prices for transfers in these conditions leads to goal congruence. Division managers acting in their own best interests make decisions that are also in the best interests of the company as a whole.

Jones will further argue that setting transfer prices based on cost will cause Jones to pay no attention to controlling costs since all costs incurred will be recovered from the Metals Division at 110% of full costs.

25-22 (25 min.) Multinational transfer pricing, global tax minimization.

1.   Solution Exhibit 25-22 shows the after-tax operating incomes earned by the U.S. and Austrian divisions from transferring 1,000 units of Product 4A36 using (a) full manufacturing cost per unit, and (b) market price of comparable imports as transfer prices.

2.   There are many ways to proceed but the first thing to note is that the transfer price that minimizes the total of company import duties and income taxes will be either the full manufacturing cost or the market price of comparable imports.

Consider what happens every time the transfer price is increased by $1 over say the full manufacturing cost of $500. This results in the following

a.	an increase in U.S. taxes of 40% × $1	$0.400
b.	an increase in import duties paid in Austria 10% × $1	0.100
c.	a decrease in Austrian taxes of 44% × $1.10 (the $1 increase in transfer price + $0.10 paid by way of import duty)	(0.484)
	Net effect is an increase in import duty and tax payments of	$0.016

Hence, Mornay Company will minimize import duties and income taxes by setting the transfer price at its minimum level of $500, the full manufacturing cost.

25-22 (Cont'd.)

SOLUTION EXHIBIT 25-22

Division incomes of U.S. and Austrian divisions from transferring 1,000 units of Product 4A36

	Method A: Internal Transfers at Full Manufacturing Cost	Method B: Internal Transfers at Market Price
U.S. DIVISION		
Revenues:		
$500, $650 × 1,000 units	$500,000	$650,000
Deduct:		
Full manufacturing cost:		
$500 × 1,000 units	500,000	500,000
Division operating income	0	150,000
Division income taxes at 40%	0	60,000
Division after-tax operating income	$ 0	$ 90,000
AUSTRIAN DIVISION		
Revenues:		
$750 × 1,000 units	$750,000	$750,000
Deduct:		
Transferred-in costs:		
$500, $650 × 1,000 units	500,000	650,000
Import duties at 10% of transferred-in price		
$50, $65 × 1,000 units	50,000	65,000
Division operating income	200,000	35,000
Division income taxes at 44%	88,000	15,400
Division after-tax operating income	$112,000	$ 19,600

25-24 (20 min.) Transfer-pricing dispute.

This problem is similar to the Problem for Self-Study in the chapter.

1. Company as a whole will not benefit if Division C buys on the outside market:

Purchase costs from outsider, 1,000 units × $135	$135,000
Deduct: Savings in variable costs by reducing	
Division A output, 1,000 units × $120	120,000
Net cost (benefit) to company as a whole by	
buying from outside	$ 15,000

2. Company will benefit if C purchases from the outsider supplier:

Purchase costs from outsider, 1,000 units × $135		$135,000
Deduct: Savings in variable costs,		
1,000 units × $120	$120,000	
Savings due to A's equipment		
and facilities assigned		
to other operations	18,000	138,000
Net cost (benefit) to company as a whole by		
buying from outside		$ (3,000)

3. Company will benefit if C purchases from the outside supplier:

Purchase costs from outsider, 1,000 units × $115	$115,000
Deduct: Savings in variable costs by reducing	
Division A output, 1,000 units × $120	120,000
Net cost (benefit) to company as a whole by	
buying from outside	$ (5,000)

The three requirements are summarized below (in thousands):

	(1)	(2)	(3)
Total purchase costs from outsider	$135	$135	$115
Total relevant costs if purchased from Division A			
Total incremental (outlay) costs if purchased from A	120	120	120
Total opportunity costs if purchased from A	–	18	–
Total relevant costs if purchased from A	120	138	120
Operating income advantage (disadvantage) to			
company as a whole by buying from A	$ 15	$ (3)	$ (5)

Goal congruence would be achieved if the transfer price is set equal to the total relevant costs of purchasing from Division A.

25-26 (30 min.) **Transfer-pricing, goal congruence.**

1. The transfer price that achieves a 20% return on sales can be computed as follows:

Costs to make airbags:	
Direct materials costs	$ 40
Direct manufacturing labor costs	55
Variable manufacturing overhead costs	10
Fixed manufacturing overhead costs	25
Variable marketing costs	5
Fixed marketing costs	15
Fixed administrative costs	10
Total costs	$160

The desired operating income ratio is 20% on sales. Therefore, the transfer price can be determined by dividing total costs of $160 by 80% (1 – 20%), which equals $200.

2. Because the current market price from external suppliers for the airbag is $130 per unit, the Letgo Division cannot ask for more than the outside market price of $130 because the Igo Division will otherwise purchase the airbags from outside suppliers. If Letgo Division is interested in maximizing its own operating income, a transfer price equal to the current outside market price of $130 will achieve this objective.

3. The relevant costs for this decision are as follows:

Direct materials costs	$ 40
Direct manufacturing labor costs	55
Variable manufacturing overhead costs	10
Variable marketing costs	5
Relevant costs	$110

The other costs are fixed (manufacturing $25, marketing $15, and administrative $10), and are irrelevant to the decision. These costs are unavoidable because they will continue whether Letgo Division sells the airbags to Igo Division or to outsiders or decides not to sell at all. Since Letgo has surplus capacity, the transfer price to Igo should cover the variable costs of $110. This transfer price should be used for Letgo's make-or-buy decision. If the outside market price is less than $110, Igo Division should buy the product from outside suppliers. However, the product should be produced internally by Letgo Division since the variable costs of $110 are less than the market price of $130. This decision will maximize the company's overall operating income. Any transfer price between $110 and $130 will lead to goal congruence. Both the Letgo Diviion and the Igo Division would like to transact internally, which is also in the best interests of Nogo Motors.

25-28 (30–40 min.) **Pricing in imperfect markets.**

An alternative presentation, which contains the same numerical answers, can be found at the end of this solution.

1. Potential contribution from external intermediate
       sale is $1,000 \times (\$195 - \$120)$ $75,000
    Contribution through keeping price at $200 is
       $800 \times \$80$.   64,000
    Forgone contribution by transferring 200 units $11,000

Opportunity cost per unit to the supplying division by transferring internally:

$$\frac{\$11,000}{200} = \$55$$

Transfer price = $120 + $55 = $175

An alternative approach to obtaining the same answer is to recognize that the incremental or outlay cost is the same for all 1,000 units in question. Therefore, the total revenue desired by A would be the same for selling outside or inside.

Let X equal the transfer price at which Division A is indifferent between selling all units outside versus transferring 200 units inside

$$1,000\ (\$195) = 800\ (\$200) + 200X$$
$$X = \$175$$

The $175 price will lead to the correct decision. Division B will not buy from Division A because its total costs of $175 + $150 will exceed its prospective selling price of $300. Division A will then sell 1,000 units at $195 to the outside; Division A and the company will have a contribution margin of $75,000. Otherwise, if 800 units were sold at $200 and 200 units were transferred to Division B, the company would have a contribution of $64,000 plus $6,000 (200 units of final product $\times$ $30), or $70,000.

A comparison might be drawn regarding the computation of the appropriate transfer prices between the preceding problem and this problem:

$$\begin{pmatrix}\text{Minimum} \\ \text{transfer price}\end{pmatrix} = \begin{pmatrix}\text{Additional \textit{incremental costs}} \\ \text{per unit incurred up} \\ \text{to the point of transfer}\end{pmatrix} + \begin{pmatrix}\textit{Opportunity costs} \\ \text{per unit to} \\ \text{Division A}\end{pmatrix}$$

Perfect markets: = $120 + (Selling price – Outlay costs per unit)
                   = $120 + ($200 – $120) = $200

25-28 (Cont'd.)

$$\text{Imperfect markets:} \quad = \$120 + \frac{\text{Marginal revenues} - \text{Outlay costs}}{\text{Number of units transferred}}$$

$$= \$120 + \frac{\$35,000^a - \$24,000^b}{200} = \$175$$

[a] Marginal revenues of Division A from selling 200 units outside rather than transferring to Division B
= ($195 × 1,000) − ($200 × 800) = $195,000 − $160,000 = $35,000.
[b] Incremental (outlay) costs incurred by Division A to produce 200 units
= $120 × 200 = $24,000.

Therefore, selling price ($195) and marginal revenues per unit ($175 = $35,000 ÷ 200) are not the same.

The following discussion is optional. These points should be explored only if there is sufficient class time:

Some students will erroneously say that the "new" market price of $195 is the appropriate transfer price. They will claim that the general guideline says that the transfer price should be $120 + ($195 − $120) = $195, the market price. This conclusion assumes a perfect market. But, here, there are imperfections in the intermediate market. That is, the market price is not a good approximation of alternative revenue. If a division's sales are heavy enough to reduce market prices, marginal revenue will be less than market price.

It is true that either $195 or $175 will lead to the correct decision by B in this case. But suppose that B's variable costs were $120 instead of $150. Then B would buy at a transfer price of $175 (but not at a price of $195, because then B would earn a negative contribution of $15 per unit [$300 − ($195 + $120)]. Note that if B's variable costs were $120, transfers would be desirable:

Division A contribution is:
800 × ($200 − $120) + 200 ($175 − $120) = $75,000
Division B contribution is:
200 × [$300 − ($175 + $120)]   =   1,000
Total contribution $76,000

Or the same facts can be analyzed for the company as a whole:

Sales of intermediate product,
800 × ($200 − $120)   = $64,000
Sales of final products,
200 × [300 − ($120 + $120)]   =   12,000
Total contribution $76,000

If the transfer price were $195, B would not accept the transfer and would not earn any contribution. As shown above, Division A and the company as a whole will earn a total contribution of $75,000 instead of $76,000.

2. a. Division A can sell 900 units at $195 to the outside market and 100 units to Division B, or 800 at $200 to the outside market and 200 units to Division B. Note that, under both alternatives, 100 units can be transferred to Division B at no opportunity cost to A.

Using the general guideline, the minimum transfer price of <u>the first 100 units</u> [901–1000] is:

$$TP_1 = \$120 + 0 = \$120$$

If Division B needs 100 additional units, the opportunity cost to A is not zero, because Division A will then have to sell only 800 units to the outside market for a contribution of $800 \times (\$200 - \$120) = \$64,000$ instead of 900 units for a contribution of $900 (\$195 - \$120) = \$67,500$. Each unit sold to B in addition to the first 100 units has an opportunity cost to A of $(\$67,500 - \$64,000) \div 100 = \$35$.

Using the general guideline, the minimum transfer price of <u>the next 100 units</u> [801–900] is:

$$TP_2 = \$120 + \$35 = \$155$$

Alternatively, the computation could be:

Increase in contribution from 100 more units, $100 \times \$75$	$7,500
Loss in contribution on 800 units, $800 \times (\$80 - \$75)$	4,000
Net "marginal revenue"	$3,500 $\div 100$ units $= \$35$

(Minimum) transfer price applicable to first 100 units offered by A is $120 + $0	=	$120 per unit
(Minimum) transfer price applicable to next 100 units offered by A is $120 + ($3,500 ÷ 100)	=	$155 per unit
(Minimum) transfer price applicable to next 800 units	=	$195 per unit

b. The manager of Division B will not want to purchase more than 100 units because the units at $155 would decrease his contribution ($155 + $150 > $300). Because the manager of B does not buy more than 100 units, the manager of A will have 900 units available for sale to the outside market. The manager of A will strive to maximize the contribution by selling them all at $195.

25-28 (Cont'd.)

● This solution maximizes the company's contribution:

$$900 \times (\$195 - \$120) = \$67,500$$
$$100 \times (\$300 - \$270) = \underline{\quad 3,000}$$
$$\$70,500$$

which compares favorably to:

$$800 \times (\$200 - \$120) = \$64,000$$
$$200 \times (\$300 - \$270) = \underline{\quad 6,000}$$
$$\$70,000$$

ALTERNATIVE PRESENTATION (by James Patell)

1.   Company Viewpoint

a: Sell 1,000 outside at $195		b: Sell 800 outside at $200, transfer 200	
Price	$195	Transfer price	$200
Variable costs	120	Variable costs	120
Contribution	$ 75 × 1,000 = $75,000	Contribution	$ 80 × 800 = $64,000

Total contribution given up if transfer occurs[*]
    = $75,000 − $64,000 = $11,000

● On a per-unit basis, the relevant costs are:

$$\text{Incremental costs to point of transfer} + \text{Opportunity costs to Division A of transfer} = \text{Transfer price}$$

$$\$120 + \frac{\$11,000}{200} = \$175$$

By formula, costs are:

$$\begin{bmatrix} \text{Incremental costs} \\ \text{to point} \\ \text{of transfer} \end{bmatrix} + \begin{bmatrix} \text{Lost opportunity to} \\ \text{sell 200 at \$195, for} \\ \text{contribution of \$75} \end{bmatrix} - \begin{bmatrix} \text{Gain when 1st 800} \\ \text{sell at \$200} \\ \text{instead of \$195} \end{bmatrix}$$

$$= \quad \$120 + \frac{200 \times \$75}{200} - \frac{[(\$200 - \$195) \times 800]}{200}$$

$$= \quad \$120 + \$75 - \$20 = \$175$$

[*]Contribution of $30 per unit by B is not given up if transfer occurs, so it is not relevant here.

25-28 (Cont'd.)

2. a. At most, Division A can sell only 900 units and can produce 1,000. Therefore, at least 100 units should be transferred, at a transfer price no less than $120. The question is whether or not a second 100 units should be transferred.

Company Viewpoint

a: Sell 900 outside at $195

Transfer price	$195
Variable cost	120
Contribution	$ 75 × 900 = $67,500

b: Sell 800 outside at $200, transfer 100

Transfer price	$200
Variable cost	120
Contribution	$ 80 × 800 = $64,000

Total contribution foregone if transfer of 100 units occurs
= $67,500 − $64,000 = $3,500 (or $35 per unit)

$$\begin{array}{ccccc} \text{Incremental costs to} & & \text{Opportunity costs to} & & \\ \text{point of transfer} & + & \text{Division A of transfer} & = & \text{Transfer price} \\ \$120 & + & \$35 & = & \$155 \end{array}$$

b. By formula:

$$\begin{bmatrix} \text{Incremental costs} \\ \text{to point} \\ \text{of transfer} \end{bmatrix} + \begin{bmatrix} \text{Lost opportunity to} \\ \text{sell 100 at \$195, for} \\ \text{contribution of \$75} \end{bmatrix} - \begin{bmatrix} \text{Gain when 1st 800} \\ \text{sell at \$200} \\ \text{instead of \$195} \end{bmatrix}$$

$$= \quad \$120 + \frac{100 \times \$75}{100} - \frac{[(\$200 - \$195) \times 800]}{100}$$

$$= \quad \$120 + \$75 - \$40 = \$155$$

Transfer Price Schedule (minimum acceptable transfer price)

Units	Transfer Price
0 – 100	$120
101 – 200	$155
201 – 1,000	$195

25-30 (30 min.) **Goal congruence problems with cost-plus transfer-pricing methods, dual-pricing methods.**

1. Two examples of goal congruence problems are:
   a. Division managers using an outside supplier when Oceanic Products' operating income is maximized by buying from an internal division.
   b. Division managers selling to an outside purchaser when it is better for Oceanic Products to further process internally.

2. Transfers to buying divisions at market price
   Harvesting Division to Processing Division   = $1.00 per pound of raw tuna
   Processing Division to Marketing Division   = $5.00 per pound of processed tuna

   Transfers out to selling divisions at 150% of full costs
   Harvesting Division to Processing Division
           = 1.5 ($0.20 + $0.40) = $0.90 per pound of raw tuna
   Processing Division to Marketing Division
           = 1.5 [($1.00 × 2)* + $0.80 + $0.60] = $5.10 per pound of processed tuna

   *The transferred-in cost is $1.00 per pound of raw tuna. It takes two pounds of raw tuna to produce one pound of tuna fillets.

   Tuna Harvesting Division
Division revenues: $0.90 × 1,000	$ 900
Division variable costs: $0.20 × 1,000	200
Division fixed costs: $0.40 × 1,000	400
Division total costs	600
Division operating income	$ 300

   Tuna Processing Division
Division revenues: $5.10 × 500	$2,550
Transferred-in costs: $1.00 × 1,000	1,000
Division variable costs: $0.80 × 500	400
Division fixed costs: $0.60 × 500	300
Division total costs	1,700
Division operating income	$ 850

   Tuna Marketing Division
Division revenues: $12 × 300	$3,600
Transferred-in costs: $5 × 500	2,500
Division variable costs: $0.30 × 300	90
Division fixed costs: $0.70 × 300	210
Division total costs	2,800
Division operating income	$ 800

3.

	Division Operating Income
Tuna Harvesting Division	$ 300
Tuna Processing Division	850
Tuna Marketing Division	800
Oceanic Products	$1,950

The overall company operating income from harvesting 1,000 pounds of raw tuna and its further processing and marketing is $2,000 (see Problem 25-29, requirement 1).

A dual transfer-pricing method entails using different transfer prices for transfers into the buying division and transfers out of the supplying division. There is no reason why the sum of division operating incomes should equal the total company operating income.

4.   Problems which may arise if Oceanic Products uses the dual-transfer pricing system include:

a.   It may reduce the incentives of the supplying division to control costs since every $1 of cost of the supplying division is transferred out to the buying division at $1.50. It may also reduce the incentives of the supplying divisions to keep abreast of market conditions.

b.   A dual transfer-pricing system does not provide clear signals to the individual divisions about the level of decentralization top management seeks.

25-32 (30–40 min.)   **Multinational transfer pricing and taxation.**

1.   Anita Corporation and its subsidiaries' operating income if it manufactures the machine and sells it in Brazil or in Switzerland follows:

	If sold in Brazil	If sold in Switzerland
Revenue	$1,000,000	$950,000
Costs		
Manufacturing costs	500,000	500,000
Transportation and modification costs	200,000	250,000
Total costs	700,000	750,000
Operating income	$ 300,000	$200,000

Anita Corporation maximizes operating income by manufacturing the machine and selling it in Brazil.

2.   Anita Corporation will not sell if the transfer price is less than $500,000 — its outlay costs of manufacturing the machine.

The Brazilian subsidiary will not agree to a transfer price of more than $800,000. At a price of $800,000, the Brazilian subsidiary's incremental operating income from purchasing and selling the milling machine will be $0 ($1,000,000 – $200,000 – $800,000).

The Swiss subsidiary will not agree to a transfer price of more than $700,000. At a price of $700,000, the Swiss subsidiary's incremental operating income from purchasing and selling the milling machine will be $0 ($950,000 – $250,000 – $700,000).

Any transfer price between $700,000 and $800,000 will achieve the optimal actions determined in requirement 1. For prices in this range, Anita Corporation will be willing to sell, the Brazilian Corporation willing to buy, and the Swiss subsidiary not interested in acquiring the machine.

Where within the range of $700,000 to $800,000 that the transfer price will be set depends on the bargaining powers of the Anita Corporation and the Brazilian subsidiary managers. Anita Corporation's main source of bargaining power comes from the threat of selling the machine to the Swiss subsidiary. If the transfer price is set at $700,000, then

Anita's operating income, $700,000 – $500,000	$200,000
Brazilian subsidiary's operating income, $1,000,000 – $700,000 – $200,000	100,000
Overall operating income of Anita and subsidiaries	$300,000

Note that the general guideline could be used to derive the minimum transfer price.

25-32 (Cont'd.)

$$\begin{matrix} \text{Minimum} \\ \text{transfer price} \end{matrix} = \begin{pmatrix} \text{Additional } incremental \text{ costs} \\ \text{per unit incurred up} \\ \text{to the point of transfer} \end{pmatrix} + \begin{pmatrix} Opportunity \text{ costs} \\ \text{per unit to the} \\ \text{supplying division} \end{pmatrix}$$

$$= \$500,000 + \$200,000 = \$700,000$$

Anita's opportunity cost of supplying the machine to the Brazilian subsidiary is the $200,000 in operating income it forgoes by not supplying the machine to the Swiss subsidiary. Note that competition between the Brazilian and Swiss subsidiaries means that the transfer price will be at least $700,000.

3. Consider the optimal transfer prices that can be set to minimize taxes (for Anita and its subsidiaries) (a) for transfers from Anita to the Brazilian subsidiary and (b) for transfers from Anita to the Swiss subsidiary.

    a.   Transfers from Anita to the Brazilian subsidiary should "allocate" as much of the operating income to Anita as possible, since the tax rate in the United States is lower than in Brazil for this transaction. Therefore, these transfers should be priced at the highest allowable transfer price of $700,000 to minimize overall company taxes.

Taxes paid:

Anita, 0.40 ($700,000 – $500,000)	$ 80,000
Brazilian subsidiary, 0.60 ($1,000,000 – $700,000 – $200,000)	60,000
Total taxes paid by Anita Corporation and its subsidiaries on transfers to the Brazil	$140,000

After-tax operating income:

Anita, ($700,000 – $500,000) – $80,000	$120,000
Brazilian subsidiary ($1,000,000 – $700,000 – $200,000) – $60,000	40,000
Total after-tax operating income for Anita Corporation and its subsidiaries on transfers to Brazil	$160,000

    b.   Transfers from Anita to the Swiss subsidiary should "allocate" as little of the operating income to Anita as possible, since the tax rate in the United States is higher than in Switzerland for this transaction. Therefore, these transfers should be priced at the lowest allowable transfer price of $500,000 to minimize overall company taxes.

Taxes paid:

Anita, 0.40 ($500,000 – $500,000)	$ 0
Swiss subsidiary, 0.15 ($950,000 – $500,000 – $250,000)	30,000
Total taxes paid by Anita Corporation and its subsidiaries on transfers to Switzerland	$30,000

25-32 (Cont'd.)

After-tax operating income
Anita,($500,000 – $500,000) – $0	$	0
Swiss subsidiary ($950,000 – $500,000 – $250,000) – $30,000		170,000
Total net income for Anita Corporation		
and its subsidiaries on transfers to Switzerland		$170,000

From the viewpoint of Anita Corporation and its subsidiaries together, overall after-tax operating income is maximized if the machine is transferred to the Swiss subsidiary (after-tax operating income of $170,000 versus after-tax operating income of $160,000 if the machine is transferred to the Brazilian subsidiary). Note that the corporation and its subsidiaries trade off the lower overall before-tax operating income achieved by transferring to the Swiss subsidiary with the lower taxes that result from such a transfer. Hence, (a) the equipment should be manufactured by Anita, and (b) it should be transferred to the Swiss subsidiary at a price of $500,000.

4. As in requirement 2, the Brazilian subsidiary would be willing to bid up the price to $800,000, while the Swiss subsidiary would only be willing to pay up to $700,000. Anita Corporation, acting autonomously, would like to maximize its own after-tax operating income by transferring the machine at as high a transfer price as possible. As in requirement 2, the price would end up being at least $700,000. Since the taxing authorities will not allow prices above $700,000, the transfer price will be $700,000. At this transfer price, the Swiss subsidiary makes zero operating income and will not be interested in the machine. Hence, Anita Corporation will sell the machine to the Brazilian subsidiary at a price of $700,000.

The answer is not the same as in requirement 3 since, acting autonomously, the objective of each manager is to maximize after-tax operating income of his or her own company rather than after-tax operating income of Anita Corporation and its subsidiaries as a whole. Goal congruence is not achieved in this setting.

Can the company induce the managers to take the right actions without infringing on their autonomy? This outcome is probably not going to be easy.

One possibility might be to implement a dual pricing scheme in which the machine is transferred at cost ($500,000), but under which Anita Corporation is credited with after-tax operating income earned on the machine by the subsidiary it ships the machine to (in this example, $170,000 of net income earned by the Swiss subsidiary). A negative feature of this arrangement is that the $170,000 of after-tax operating income will be 'double counted' and recognized on the books of both Anita Corporation and the Swiss subsidiary.

Another possibility might be to evaluate the managers on the basis of overall after-tax operating income of Anita Corporation and its subsidiaries. This approach will induce a more global perspective, but at the cost of inducing a larger noncontrollable element in each manager's performance measure.

25-34 (30–40 min.) **Transfer prices, goal congruence, external markets, capacity constraints.**

1.   The revenue from selling Aldon in a competitive market is $0.33 per pound, so Division A should transfer Aldon to Divisions B and C so long as the incremental net revenues (revenues – processing costs) in Divisions B and C exceed $0.33. From Solution Exhibit 25-33, this means that Division A will transfer

- 2,000 pounds of Aldon to Division B
- 3,000 pounds of Aldon to Division C

Note that for this decision, the variable costs of manufacturing Aldon equal to $0.18 per pound are irrelevant since the same variable costs will be incurred under all three alternatives of transferring to B, transferring to C or selling in the external market.

Since Division A earns a positive contribution margin of $0.15 ($0.33 – $0.18) from selling Aldon, it should use all its remaining capacity of 5,000 pounds (10,000 pounds – 5,000 pounds transferred to Divisions A and B) to produce and sell Aldon in the external market. Therefore, the production allocation that maximizes Cheap Shot's operating income is (1) transfer 2,000 pounds to B, (2) transfer 3,000 pounds to C, and (3) sell 5,000 pounds of Aldon in the external market.

2.   Division A will only be interested in transferring Aldon to Divisions B and C if the transfer price is at least $0.33 per pound (otherwise Division A would be better off selling Aldon directly in the open market).

Division B will demand 2,000 pounds of Aldon at any transfer price between $0.25 and $0.35 per pound. In this price range, the incremental net revenue of $0.35 per pound for the 2,000 pounds will exceed the transfer cost. If the transfer price is above $0.35 per pound, B will demand no more than 1,000 pounds; if the transfer price is below $0.25 per pound, B will demand 3,000 pounds or more.

Using a similar argument to the one described for Division B, Division C will demand 3,000 pounds of Aldon at any transfer price between $0.30 and $0.60.

Any transfer price for Aldon between $0.33 and $0.35 per pound satisfies the three conditions described for Divisions A, B and C, and will result in Division A producing 10,000 pounds, and Divisions B and C demanding 2,000 and 3,000 pounds, respectively; Division A will sell 5,000 pounds of Aldon in the external market.

The transfer price range that satisfies all these requirements is $0.33 to $0.35 per pound of Aldon.

3.   To maximize Cheap Shot's operating income, Division A should transfer all the 4,000 pounds it produces to Divisions B and Division C according to the highest incremental net revenue rule. So, Division A should transfer

> 3,000 pounds of Aldon to Division C (incremental net revenue of $0.60 per pound).
> 1,000 pounds of Aldon to Division B (incremental net revenue of $0.50 per pound).

It should not sell any pounds of Aldon in the external market because Cheap Shot would earn more by transferring Aldon to Divisions B and C rather than selling it in the external market. As in requirement 1, the variable costs of manufacturing Aldon equal to $0.18 per pound are irrelevant since the same variable costs per pound will be incurred under all alternatives.

4.   Division C will demand 3,000 pounds of Aldon at any transfer price between $0.30 and $0.60 per pound. In this price range, the incremental net revenue of $0.60 per pound for the 3,000 pounds will exceed the transfer cost. At a price above $0.60 per pound, Division C will demand zero pounds of Aldon, and if the transfer price is below $0.30 per pound, C will demand 4,000 or more pounds of Aldon.

Using a similar argument to that described for Division C, Division B will demand 1,000 pounds of Aldon at any transfer price between $0.35 and $0.50 per pound.

At any transfer price above $0.33 per pound, Division A will not sell directly in the open market.

Any transfer price for Aldon between $0.35 and $0.50 per pound satisfies the three conditions described for Divisions A, B, and C, and will result in Division A supplying 4,000 pounds, and Divisions B and C demanding 1,000 and 3,000 pounds, respectively; Division A will not sell any Aldon in the external market.

25-34 (Cont'd.)

SOLUTION EXHIBIT 25-33
Incremental Revenues Minus Processing Costs per Pound
from Selling Baxon and Calmite

DIVISION B

Pounds of Aldon Processed in B	Revenues – Processing Costs from Selling Baxon	Incremental Revenues – Processing Costs per Pound from Selling Baxon
1,000	$ 500	$0.50
2,000	850	0.35[a]
3,000	1,100	0.25
4,000	1,200	0.10

DIVISION C

Pounds of Aldon Processed in C	Revenues – Processing Costs from Selling Calmite	Incremental Revenues – Processing Costs per Pound from Selling Calmite
1,000	$ 600	$0.60
2,000	1,200	0.60
3,000	1,800	0.60
4,000	2,100	0.30
5,000	2,250	0.15
6,000	2,350	0.10

[a]For example, $\dfrac{\$850 - \$500}{2,000 - 1,000} = \$0.35$

25-36 (40–50 min.)   **Goal congruence, taxes, different market conditions.**

1.

	New Engine	Existing Engine Used by Assembly
Sales price	$375	
Savings in purchase costs by making engines in-house		$400
Manufacturing costs:		
Direct materials	$100	$125
Direct manufacturing labor	40	50
Variable manufacturing overhead	25	25
Total costs of manufacturing	165	200
Contribution margin from New Engine	$210	
Net savings in costs by making existing engine in-house		$200

If order for the new engine is accepted, San Ramon earns a contribution margin of $210 × 2,000 units. $420,000

In this case, Engine Division will only be in a position to supply 2,000 units to Assembly and Assembly will have to purchase 1,200 engines from outside. The incremental cost of buying engines from outside is $200 × 1,200   240,000

Net benefit from accepting order $180,000

An alternative approach is to compare relevant costs of the accept order and reject order alternatives.

	Accept Order	Reject Order
1. Contribution margin from selling 2,000 units of new engine $210 × 2,000	$(420,000)	
2. Incremental cost of making and transferring 2,000 units of old engine $200 × 2,000	400,000	$640,000
3. Incremental costs of purchasing 1,200 units from outside $400 × 1,200	480,000	
	$460,000	$640,000

San Ramon Corporation should
    a.   make 2,000 units of the new engine in the Engine Division
    b.   make 2,000 units of the existing engine for the Assembly Division
    c.   have the Assembly Division purchase 1,200 engines that it requires from the outside market

2.   The options facing the Engine Division manager are (a) to sell 2,000 units of the special order engine and make 2,000 units for the Assembly Division, or (b) to make 3,200 units for the Assembly Division. The contribution margin per unit from accepting the special order is $210 per unit. Let the transfer price be $X. Then we want to find X such that

$$\$210 \times 2{,}000 + (\$X - \$200)\,2{,}000 = (\$X - \$200)\,3{,}200$$
$$(\$X - \$200)(3{,}200 - 2{,}000) = \$420{,}000$$
$$\$X - \$200 = \frac{\$420{,}000}{1{,}200} = \$350$$
$$X = \$550$$

For transfer prices below $550, the Engine Division gets more by selling 2,000 units outside and transferring 2,000 units to Assembly Division. It will not transfer more than 2,000 units to Assembly even though the transfer price is greater than the variable costs of manufacturing the existing engine, $200 plus the contribution margin per unit from accepting the special order of $210 equal to $410 ($500, say). Why? Because by transferring an additional 1,200 units (say) it will have to give up $420,000 ($210 × 2,000) of contribution margin by not accepting the special order. The Engine Division manager would be willing to transfer the remaining 2,000 units for which it has capacity to the Assembly Division provided the transfer price covers the Engine Division's variable costs. So the range of transfer price that will induce the Engine Division manager to implement the optimal solution in requirement 1 is:

$$\$200 \le TP < \$550$$

The Assembly Division manager would be willing to buy from the Engine Division so long as the transfer price is less than or equal to the price at which the Assembly Division can buy the engines on the outside market.

$$TP \le \$400$$

It will not buy the engines from the Engine Division if TP > $400. The range of TP that will result in both managers favoring the optimal actions in requirement 1 are TPs that satisfy the respective constraints described above.

$$\$200 \le TP \le \$400 \text{ for the first 2,000 units}$$

$$\$400 < TP < \$550 \text{ for any additional units}$$

This transfer pricing scheme will induce both managers to transfer 2,000 units between the Engine and Assembly Divisions, but no more.

25-36 (Cont'd.)

3a.   The full manufacturing costs of the engines transferred to the Assembly Division are:

Direct materials	$125
Direct manufacturing labor	50
Variable manufacturing overheads	25
Fixed manufacturing overheads	
$(\dfrac{\$520,000}{2} = \$260,000 \div 2,000 \text{ engines})$	
since the engines transferred to the Assembly Division use up half the Engine Division's capacity	130
Total manufacturing cost	$330

b.   A transfer price of $330 is in the optimal range identified in requirement 2 and, so, will achieve the optimal actions of selling 2,000 engines under the outside offer and transferring 2,000 engines to the Assembly Division as identified in requirement 1. (If we also want the Assembly Division manager to not ask for any additional engines beyond 2,000 units, the transfer price for any additional engines would have to be set such that $400 < TP < $550.) If the transfer price is set at $330, the Assembly Division manager will want more engines but the Engine Division manager will not be incented to transfer anything more than 2,000 units, preferring to supply 2,000 units for the special order.

c.   One advantage of full cost transfer pricing is that it is useful for the firm's long-run pricing decisions.

One disadvantage of full cost transfer pricing is that costs that are fixed for the corporation as a whole look like variable costs from the viewpoint of the Assembly Division manager. This is because by choosing not to have a unit transferred from the Engine Division, the Assembly Division manager would appear to save both the variable and fixed costs of the engine. This could lead to suboptimal decisions.

4a.   To minimize taxes, San Ramon should transfer the engines at the market price of $400. The Engine Division would pay no taxes on any income that it would report. By setting the transfer price as high as possible, the Assembly Division would minimize the income it would report and, hence, the taxes it would pay.

b.   Yes, as in part 3b, the transfer price of $400 is also within the range identified in requirement 2 and so will achieve the outcome desired in requirement 1 (sell 2,000 engines under the outside offer and transfer 2,000 engines to the Assembly Division).

5.   San Ramon should use a transfer price of $400 for transferring engines from the Engine Division to the Assembly Division. This transfer price minimizes tax payments for the San Ramon Corporation as a whole and also achieves goal congruence. That is, at a transfer price of $400 for all engines transferred from the Engine Division to the Assembly Division, both Divisions will be content with the following arrangement

   a.   The Engine Division will make 2,000 engines for outside customers and 2,000 engines for the Assembly Division

   b.   The Assembly Division will take 2,000 engines from the Engine Division and 1,200 engines from the outside market

Of course, the Assembly Division manager would like to negotiate a price lower than $400 (but greater than $200) for the 2,000 engines from the Engine Division, but this would increase San Ramon's tax payments.

At a transfer price of $400, it would still be alright to evaluate each division's performance on the basis of division operating income because the transfer price of $400 approximates the market prices for the engines transferred from the Engine Division to the Assembly Division. Market-based transfer prices give top management a reasonably good picture of the contributions of the individual divisions to overall companywide profitability.

CHAPTER 26
SYSTEMS CHOICE: PERFORMANCE MEASUREMENT, COMPENSATION, AND MULTINATIONAL CONSIDERATIONS

26-2   The five steps in designing an accounting-based performance measure are:
1.   Choosing the variable(s) that represents top management's financial goal(s)
2.   Choosing definitions of the items included in the variables in Step 1
3.   Choosing measures for the items included in the variables in Step 1
4.   Choosing a target against which to gauge performance
5.   Choosing the timing of feedback

26-4   Yes. Residual income is not identical to ROI. ROI is a percentage with investment as the denominator of the computation. Residual income is an absolute amount in which investment is used to calculate an imputed interest charge.

26-6   Definitions of investment used in practice when computing ROI are:
1.   Total assets available
2.   Total assets employed
3.   Working capital (current assets minus current liabilities) plus other assets
4.   Stockholders' equity

26-8   Special problems arise when evaluating the performance of divisions in multinational companies because
   a.   The economic, legal, political, social, and cultural environments differ significantly across countries.
   b.   Governments in some countries may impose controls and limit selling prices of products.
   c.   Availability of materials and skilled labor, as well as costs of materials, labor, and infrastructure may differ significantly across countries.
   d.   Divisions operating in different countries keep score of their performance in different currencies.

26-10   Moral hazard describes contexts in which an employee is tempted to put in less effort (or report distorted information) because the employee's interests differ from the owner's and because the employee's effort cannot be accurately monitored and enforced.

26-12 Measures of performance that are superior (measures that change significantly with the manager's performance and not very much with changes in factors that are beyond the manager's control) are the key to designing strong incentive systems in organizations. When selecting performance measures the management accountant must choose those performance measures that change with changes in the actions taken by managers. For example, if a manager has no authority for making investments, then using an investment-based measure to evaluate the manager imposes risk on the manager and provides little information about the manager's performance. The management accountant might suggest evaluating the manager on the basis of costs, or costs and revenues, rather than ROI.

26-14 When employees have to perform multiple tasks as part of their jobs, incentive problems can arise when one task is easy to monitor and measure while the other task is more difficult to evaluate. Employers want employees to intelligently allocate time and effort among various tasks. If, however, employees are rewarded on the basis of the task that is more easily measured, they will tend to focus their efforts on that task and ignore the others.

26-16 (30 min.) **Return on investment; comparisons of three companies.**

1.   The separate components highlight several features of return on investment not revealed by a single calculation:
    a.   The importance of investment turnover as a key to income is stressed.
    b.   The importance of revenues is explicitly recognized.
    c.   The important components are expressed as ratios or percentages instead of dollar figures. This form of expression often enhances comparability of different divisions, businesses, and time periods.
    d.   The breakdown stresses the possibility of trading off investment turnover for income as a percentage of revenues so as to increase the average ROI at a given level of output.

2.   (Filled-in blanks are in bold face.)

	Companies in Same Industry		
	A	B	C
Revenue	$1,000,000	$ 500,000	$10,000,000
Income	$ 100,000	$ 50,000	$ 50,000
Investment	$ 500,000	$5,000,000	$ 5,000,000
Income as a % of revenue	10%	10%	0.5%
Investment turnover	2.0	0.1	2.0
Return on investment	20%	1%	1%

Income and investment alone shed little light on comparative performances because of disparities in size between Company A and the other two companies. Thus, it is impossible to say whether B's low return on investment in comparison with A's is attributable to its larger investment or to its lower income. Furthermore, the fact that Companies B and C have identical income and investment may suggest that the same conditions underlie the low ROI, but this conclusion is erroneous. B has higher margins but a lower investment turnover. C has very small margins (1/20th of B) but turns over investment 20 times faster.

26-16 (Cont'd.)

I.M.A. Report No. 35 (p. 35) states:

"Introducing revenues to measure level of operations helps to disclose specific areas for more intensive investigation. Company B does as well as Company A in terms of income margin, for both companies earn 10% on revenues. But Company B has a much lower turnover of investment than does Company A. Whereas a dollar of investment in Company A supports two dollars in revenues each period, a dollar investment in Company B supports only ten cents in revenues each period. This suggests that the analyst should look carefully at Company B's investment. Is the company keeping an inventory larger than necessary for its revenue level? Are receivables being collected promptly? Or did Company A acquire its fixed assets at a price level that was much lower than that at which Company B purchased its plant?"

"On the other hand, C's investment turnover is as high as A's, but C's income as a percentage of revenue is much lower. Why? Are its operations inefficient, are its material costs too high, or does its location entail high transportation costs?"

"Analysis of ROI raises questions such as the foregoing. When answers are obtained, basic reasons for differences between rates of return may be discovered. For example, in Company B's case, it is apparent that the emphasis will have to be on increasing turnover by reducing investment or increasing revenues. Clearly, B cannot appreciably increase its ROI simply by increasing its income as a percent of revenue. In contrast, Company C's management should concentrate on increasing the percent of income on revenue."

26-18 (10–15 min.) ROI and residual income.

$$\text{ROI} = \frac{\text{Operating income}}{\text{Investment}}$$

$$\text{Operating income} = \text{ROI} \times \text{Investment}$$

[No. of menhirs sold (Selling price – Var. cost per unit)] – Fixed costs = ROI × Investment

Let X = minimum selling price per unit to achieve a 20% ROI

1. $10,000 (X - \$300) - \$1,000,000 = 20\% (\$1,600,000)$
    $10,000X = \$320,000 + \$3,000,000 + \$1,000,000 = \$4,320,000$
    $X = \$432$

2. $10,000 (X - \$300) - \$1,000,000 = 15\% (\$1,600,000)$
    $10,000X = \$240,000 + \$3,000,000 + \$1,000,000 = \$4,240,000$
    $X = \$424$

26-20   (25 min.)   **Financial and nonfinancial performance measures, goal congruence.**

1.   Operating income is a good summary measure of short-term financial performance. By itself, however, it does not indicate whether operating income in the short run was earned by taking actions that would lead to long-run competitive advantage. For example, Summit's divisions might be able to increase short-run operating income by producing more product while ignoring quality or rework. Harrington, however, would like to see division managers increase operating income without sacrificing quality. The new performance measures take a balanced scorecard approach by evaluating and rewarding managers on the basis of direct measures (such as rework costs, on-time delivery performance, and sales returns). This motivates managers to take actions that Harrington believes will increase operating income now and in the future. The nonoperating income measures serve as surrogate measures of future profitability.

2.   The semi-annual installments and total bonus for the Charter Division are calculated as follows:

Charter Division Bonus Calculation
For Year ended December 31, 19_7

January 1, 19_7 to June 30, 19_7

Profitability	(0.02) ($462,000)	$ 9,240
Rework	(0.02 × $462,000) − $11,500	(2,260)
On-time delivery	No bonus – under 96%	0
Sales returns	[(0.015 × $4,200,000) − $84,000] × 50%	(10,500)
Semi-annual installment		$ (3,520)
Semi-annual bonus awarded		$ 0

July 1, 19_7 to December 31, 19_7

Profitability	(0.02) ($440,000)	$ 8,800
Rework	(0.02 × $440,000) − $11,000	(2,200)
On-time delivery	96% to 98%	2,000
Sales returns	[(0.015 × $4,400,000) − $70,000] × 50%	(2,000)
Semi-annual installment		$ 6,600
Semi-annual bonus awarded		$ 6,600
Total bonus awarded for the year		$ 6,600

The semi-annual installments and total bonus for the Mesa Division are calculated as follows:

Mesa Division Bonus Calculation
For year ended December 31, 19_7

January 1, 19_7 to June 30, 19_7

Profitability	(0.02) ($342,000)	$ 6,840
Rework	(0.02 × $342,000) – $6,000	0
On-time delivery	Over 98%	5,000
Sales returns	[(0.015 × $2,850,000) – $44,750] × 50%	(1,000)
Semi-annual bonus installment		$10,840
Semi-annual bonus awarded		$10,840

July 1, 19_7 to December 31, 19_7

Profitability	(0.02) ($406,000)	$ 8,120
Rework	(0.02 × $406,000) – $8,000	0
On-time delivery	No bonus - under 96%	0
Sales returns	[(0.015 × $2,900,000) – $42,500] which is greater than zero, yielding a bonus of	3,000
Semi-annual bonus installment		$11,120
Semi-annual bonus awarded		$11,120
Total bonus awarded for the year		$21,960

3.　The manager of the Charter Division is likely to be frustrated by the new plan as the division bonus is more than $20,000 less than the previous year. However, the new performance measures have begun to have the desired effect—both on-time deliveries and sales returns improved in the second half of the year while rework costs were relatively even. If the division continues to improve at the same rate, the Charter bonus could approximate or exceed what it was under the old plan.

The manager of the Mesa Division should be as satisfied with the new plan as with the old plan as the bonus is almost equivalent. However, there is no sign of improvements in the performance measures instituted by Harrington in this division; as a matter of fact, on-time deliveries declined considerably in the second half of the year. Unless the manager institutes better controls, the bonus situation may not be as favorable in the future. This could motivate the manager to improve in the future but currently, at least, the manager has been able to maintain his bonus without showing improvements in the areas targeted by Harrington.

26-20 (Cont'd.)

Ben Harrington's revised bonus plan for the Charter Division fostered the following improvements in the second half of the year despite an increase in sales
- increase of 1.9 percent in on-time deliveries.
- $500 reduction in rework costs.
- $14,000 reduction in sales returns.

However, operating income as a percent of sales has decreased (11 to 10 percent).

The Mesa Division's bonus has remained at the status quo as a result of the folllowing effects
- increase of 2.0 percent in operating income as a percent of sales (12 to 14 percent).
- decrease of 3.6 percent in on-time deliveries.
- $2,000 increase in rework costs.
- $2,250 decrease in sales returns.

This would suggest that there needs to be some revisions to the bonus plan. Possible changes include:

- increasing the weights put on on-time deliveries, rework costs, and sales returns in the performance measures while decreasing the weight put on operating income.
- a reward structure for rework costs that are below 2 percent of operating income that would encourage managers to drive costs lower.
- reviewing the whole year in total. The bonus plan should carry forward the negative amounts for one six-month period into the next six-month period incorporating the entire year when calculating a bonus.
- developing benchmarks, and then giving rewards for improvements over prior periods and encouraging continuous improvement.

26-22 (25 min.) **Residual income, economic value added.**

1.

	Truck Rental Division	Transportation Division
Total assets	$650,000	$950,000
Current liabilities	120,000	200,000
Investment		
(Total assets – current liabilities)	530,000	750,000
Required return		
(12% × Investment)	63,600	90,000
Operating income before tax	75,000	160,000
Residual income		
(Optg. inc. before tax – Reqd. return)	11,400	70,000

2. After-tax cost of debt financing = $(1 - 0.4) \times 10\% = 6\%$
   After-tax cost of equity financing = 15%

$$\text{Weighted average cost of capital} = \frac{\$900,000 \times 6\% + 600,000 \times 15\%}{\$900,000 + 600,000} = 9.6\%$$

	Truck Rental Division	Transportation Division
Required return for EVA		
9.6% × Investment		
(9.6% × $530,000; 9.6% × $750,000)	$50,880	$72,000
Operating income after tax		
0.6 × operating income before tax	45,000	96,000
EVA (Optg. inc. after tax – Reqd. return)	(5,880)	24,000

3.   Both the residual income and the EVA calculations indicate that the Transportation Division is performing better than the Truck Rental Division. The Transportation Division has a higher residual income ($70,000 versus $11,400) and a higher EVA [$24,000 versus $(5,880)]. The negative EVA for the Truck Rental Division indicates that on an after-tax basis the division is destroying value—the after-tax economic return from the Truck Rental Division's assets is less than the required return. If EVA continues to be negative, Burlingame may have to consider shutting down the Truck Rental Division.

26-24 (20 min.) **Multinational performance measurement, ROI.**

1. U.S. Division's 19_7 ROI $= \dfrac{\$1,200,000}{\$8,000,000} = 15\%$

2. Swedish Division's 19_7 ROI in kronas $= \dfrac{6,552,000 \text{ kronas}}{42,000,000 \text{ kronas}} = 15.6\%$

3. Convert total asset into dollars at December 31, 19_6 exchange rate, the rate prevailing when assets were acquired (6 kronas = $1)

$$42,000,000 \text{ kronas} \quad = \quad \dfrac{42,000,000 \text{ kronas}}{6 \text{ kronas per dollar}} \quad = \quad \$7,000,000$$

Convert operating income into dollars at the average exchange rate prevailing during 19_7 when operating income was earned equal to

$$\dfrac{6,552,000 \text{ kronas}}{6.5 \text{ kronas per dollar}} = \$1,008,000$$

$$\text{Comparable ROI for Swedish Division} \quad = \quad \dfrac{\$1,008,000}{\$7,000,000} = 14.4\%$$

The Swedish Division's ROI calculated in kronas is helped by the inflation that occurs in Sweden in 19_7. Inflation boosts the division's operating income. Since the assets are acquired at the start of the year on 1-1-19_7, the asset values are not increased by the inflation that occurs during the year. The net effect of inflation on ROI calculated in kronas is to use an inflated value for the numerator relative to the denominator. Adjusting for inflationary and currency differences negates the effects of any differences in inflation rates between the two countries on the calculation of ROI. After these adjustments, the U.S. Division shows a higher ROI than the Swedish Division.

26-26 (20–30 min.) **Risk sharing, incentives, benchmarking, multiple tasks.**

1a. An evaluation of the three proposals to compensate Marks, the general manager of the Dexter Division follows:

(i) Paying Marks a flat salary will not subject Marks to any risk, but will provide no incentives for Marks to undertake extra physical and mental effort.

(ii) Rewarding Marks only on the basis of Dexter Division's ROI would motivate Marks to put in extra effort to increase ROI because Marks' rewards would increase with increases in ROI. But compensating Marks solely on the basis of ROI subjects Marks to excessive risk, because the division's ROI depends not only on Marks' effort but also on other random factors over which Marks has no control. For example, Marks may put in a great deal of effort, but despite this effort, the division's ROI may be low because of adverse factors (such as high interest rates, or a recession) which Marks cannot control.

   To compensate Marks for taking on uncontrollable risk, AMCO must pay him additional amounts within the structure of the ROI-based arrangement. Thus, compensating Marks only on the basis of performance-based incentives will cost AMCO more money, on average, than paying Marks a flat salary. The key question is whether the benefits of motivating additional effort justify the higher costs of performance-based rewards.

   Furthermore, the objective of maximizing ROI may induce Marks to reject projects that, from the viewpoint of the organization as a whole, should be accepted. This would occur for projects that would reduce Marks' overall ROI but which would earn a return greater than the required rate of return for that project.

(iii) The motivation for having some salary and some performance-based bonus in compensation arrangements is to balance the benefits of incentives against the extra costs of imposing uncontrollable risk on the manager.

1b. Marks' complaint does not appear to be valid. The senior management of AMCO is proposing to benchmark Marks' performance using a relative performance evaluation (RPE) system. RPE controls for common uncontrollable factors that similarly affect the performance of managers operating in the same environments (for example, the same industry). If business conditions for car battery manufacturers are good, all businesses manufacturing car batteries will probably perform well. A superior indicator of Marks' performance is how well Marks performed relative to his peers. The goal is to filter out the common noise to get a better understanding of Marks' performance. Marks' complaint will only be valid if there are significant differences in investments, assets and the business environment in which AMCO and Tiara operate. Given the information in the problem, this does not appear to be the case.

26-26 (Cont'd.)

2.   Superior performance measures change significantly with the manager's performance and not very much with changes in factors that are beyond the manager's control.   If Marks has no authority for making capital investment decisions, then ROI is not a good measure of Marks' performance—it varies with the actions taken by others rather than the actions taken by Marks. AMCO may wish to evaluate Marks on the basis of operating income rather than ROI.

ROI, however, may be a good measure to evaluate Dexter's economic viability. Senior management at AMCO could use ROI to evaluate if the Dexter Division's income provides a reasonable return on investment, regardless of who has authority for making capital investment decisions. That is, ROI may be an inappropriate measure of Marks' performance but a reasonable measure of the economic viability of the Dexter Division. If, for whatever reasons, bad capital investments, weak economic conditions, etc., the Division shows poor economic performance, as computed by ROI, AMCO management may decide to shut down the division even though they may simultaneously conclude that Marks performed well.

3.   There are two main concerns with Marks' plans. First, creating very strong sales incentives imposes excessive risk on the sales force, because a salesperson's performance is affected not only by his or her own effort, but also by random factors (such as a recession in the industry) that are beyond the salesperson's control. if salespersons are risk averse, the firm will have to compensate them for bearing this extra uncontrollable risk. Second, compensating salespersons only on the basis of sales creates strong incentives to sell, but may result in lower levels of customer service and sales support (this was the story at Sears auto repair shops where a change in the contractual terms of mechanics to "produce" more repairs caused unobservable quality to be negatively affected). Where employees perform multiple tasks, it may be important to "blunt" incentives on those aspects of the job that can be measured well (for example, sales) to try and achieve a better balance of the two tasks (for example, sales and customer service and support). In addition, the division should try to better monitor customer service and customer satisfaction through surveys, or through quantifying the amount of repeat business.

26-28 (30–40 min.) **Alternative measures for the investment base of gasoline stations.**

1. For decisions concerning the disposal of any one or more of the currently owned gasoline stations, the relevant comparison is:
    a. the present value (PV) of cash inflows from continuing to operate the gasoline station, with
    b. the current disposal price (DP) or current selling price of the gasoline station.

If PV > DP, ARCO should retain the gasoline station. Thus, current disposal price is the only one of the three measures (historical cost, current cost, and current disposal price) provided in the problem that is relevant to the disposal decision.

2.	Fresno Station	Las Vegas Station	Modesto Station
$\dfrac{\text{Operating income}}{\text{Historical cost}}$	$\dfrac{\$100,000}{\$400,000} = 25.0\%$	$\dfrac{\$120,000}{\$200,000} = 60.0\%$	$\dfrac{\$ 60,000}{\$260,000} = 23.1\%$
$\dfrac{\text{Operating income}}{\text{Current cost}}$	$\dfrac{\$100,000}{\$640,000} = 15.6\%$	$\dfrac{\$120,000}{\$480,000} = 25.0\%$	$\dfrac{\$ 60,000}{\$290,000} = 20.7\%$
$\dfrac{\text{Operating income}}{\text{Disposal price}}$	$\dfrac{\$100,000}{\$600,000} = 16.7\%$	$\dfrac{\$120,000}{\$2,500,000} = 4.8\%$	$\dfrac{\$ 60,000}{\$300,000} = 20.0\%$

3. For evaluating the performance of a gasoline station as an investment activity, ARCO is concerned with the sum of:
    (a) the operating income from the gasoline station, and
    (b) the change in disposal price of the gasoline station over the period for which performance is being evaluated.
The sum of (a) and (b) represents the return from retaining the gasoline station. This return should be compared with the opportunity cost of the best alternative use of investing the disposal proceeds had the gasoline station been sold at the start of the performance evaluation period.

4. The choice of an appropriate measure depends on how ARCO judges the managers of its service stations.
    If ARCO uses a single benchmark (say 16%) in judging the performance of each manager, the current cost measure will promote comparability among managers who are in charge of gasoline stations bought at different times or in areas with different real estate markets. Both historical cost and current disposal price will give rise to differences in ROI among gasoline stations that are unrelated to differences in operating efficiency.

26-28 (Cont'd.)

If ARCO tailors the performance benchmark for each gasoline manager in its budgeting process, then the choice of a specific investment measure is less contentious. For example, if historical cost is used, the budgeted ROI benchmark for the Las Vegas station could be, say, 55% whereas the budgeted ROI benchmark for the Fresno station could be, say, 20%. One benefit of tailoring the budget to each manager is that more incentives are provided to managers who are put in charge of poorly performing stations or stations in highly competitive markets. The measures for judging the performance of the manager differ from the measure used for deciding whether to dispose of a gasoline station (requirement 1) and the measure used to judge the performance of the gasoline station as an investment activity (requirement 3).

5.   Alternative measures to ROI can be divided into two categories: (a) financial, and (b) nonfinancial. Examples include:
   - a.   Financial measures
     Operating income
     Residual income
     Cash flow

   - b.   Nonfinancial measures
     Volume of gasoline pumped
     Customer service indicators (e.g., customer waiting time, and cleanliness of station)
     Customer satisfaction indicators (e.g., based on consumer surveys or complaint letters)

26-30   (40–50 min.) **Evaluating managers, ROI, value-chain analysis of cost structure.**

1.

	$\dfrac{\text{Revenues}}{\text{Total Assets}} \times$	$\dfrac{\text{Operating Income}}{\text{Revenues}} =$	$\dfrac{\text{Operating Income}}{\text{Total Assets}}$
Computer Power			
19_6	1.111	0.250	0.278
19_7	0.941	0.125	0.118
Peach Computer			
19_6	1.250	0.100	0.125
19_7	1.458	0.171	0.250

Computer Power's ROI has declined sizably from 19_6 to 19_7, largely because of a decline in operating income to revenues. Peach Computers' ROI has doubled from 19_6 to 19_7, in large part due to an increase in operating income to revenues.

2.

Business Function	Computer Power 19_6	Computer Power 19_7	Peach Computer 19_6	Peach Computer 19_7
Research and development	12.0%	6.0%	10.0%	15.0%
Design	5.0	3.0	2.0	4.0
Production	34.0	40.0	46.0	34.0
Marketing	25.0	33.0	20.0	23.0
Distribution	9.0	8.0	10.0	8.0
Customer Service	15.0	10.0	12.0	16.0
Total costs	100.0%	100.0%	100.0%	100.0%

Business functions with increases/decreases in the % of total costs from 19_6 to 19_7 are:

	Computer Power	Peach Computer
Increases	Production Marketing	Research and development Design Marketing Customer service
Decreases	Research and development Design Distribution Customer service	Production Distribution

Computer Power has decreased expenditures in several key business functions that are critical to its long-term survival—notably research and development and design. These costs are (using the Chapter 8 Appendix terminology) discretionary and can be reduced in the short run without any short run effect on customers, but such action is likely to create serious problems in the long run.

3.　Based on the information provided, Provan is the better candidate for president of User Friendly Computer. Both Computer Power and Peach Computer are in the same industry. Provan has headed Peach Computer at a time when it has considerably outperformed Computer Power:

a.　The ROI of Peach Computer has increased from 19_6 to 19_7 while that of Computer Power has decreased.
b.　The computer magazine has increased the ranking of Peach Computer's main product, while it has decreased the ranking of Computer Power's main product.
c.　Peach Computer has received high marks for new products (the lifeblood of a computer company), while Computer Power new-product introductions have been described as "mediocre."

26-32 (20–30 min.) Division manager's compensation.

Consider each of the three proposals that Rupert Prince is considering:

1. <u>Compensate managers on the basis of Division ROI.</u>
    The benefit of this arrangement is that managers would be motivated to put in extra effort to increase ROI because managers' rewards would increase with increases in ROI. But compensating managers largely on the basis of ROI subjects the managers to excessive risk, because each division's ROI depends not only on the manager's effort but also on random factors over which the manager has no control. A manager may put in a great deal of effort, but the division's ROI may be low because of adverse factors (high interest, recession) that the manager cannot control.

    To compensate managers for taking on uncontrollable risk, Prince must pay them additional amounts within the structure of the ROI-based arrangement. Thus, using mainly performance-based incentives will cost Prince more money, on average, than paying a flat salary. The key question is whether the benefits of motivating additional effort justify the higher costs of performance-based rewards. The motivation for having some salary and some performance-based bonus in compensation arrangements is to balance the benefits of incentives against the extra costs of imposing uncontrollable risk on the manager.

    Finally, rewarding a manager only on the basis of division ROI will induce managers to maximize the division's ROI even if taking such actions are not in the best interests of the company as a whole.

2. <u>Compensate managers on the basis of companywide ROI.</u>
    Rewarding managers on the basis of companywide ROI will motivate managers to take actions that are in the best interests of the company rather than actions that maximize a division's ROI.

    A negative feature of this arrangement is that each division manager's compensation will now depend not only on the performance of that division manager but also on the performance of the other division managers. For example, the compensation of Ken Kearney, the manager of the Newspaper Division, will depend on how well the managers of the Television and Film studios perform, even though Kearney himself may have little influence over the performance of these divisions. Hence, compensating managers on the basis of companywide ROI will impose extra risk on each division manager.

3. <u>Compensate managers using the other divisions' average ROI as a benchmark.</u>
    The benefit of benchmarking or relative performance evaluation is to cancel out the effects of common noncontrollable factors that affect a performance measure. Taking out the effects of these factors provides better information about a manager's performance. What is critical, however, for benchmarking and relative performance evaluation to be effective is that similar noncontrollable factors affect each division. It is not clear that the same noncontrollable factors that affect the performance of the Newspaper Division (cost of newsprint paper, for example) also affect the performance of the Television and Film studios divisions. If the noncontrollable factors are not the same, then comparing the ROI of one division to the average ROI of the other two divisions will not provide useful information for relative performance evaluation.

A second factor for Prince to consider is the impact that benchmarking and relative performance evaluation will have on the incentives for the division managers of the Newspaper, Television and Film studios Divisions to cooperate with one another. Benchmarking one division against another means that a division manager will look good by improving his or her own performance, or by making the performance of the other division managers look bad.

26-34 (20–30 min.) Division manager's compensation, risk sharing, incentives.

1. Consider each of the three proposals that the management of Mason Industries is considering:

a. <u>Compensate Grieco on the basis of a fixed salary without any bonus</u>.
Paying Grieco a flat salary will not subject Grieco to any risk, but will provide no incentives for Grieco to undertake extra physical and mental effort.

b. <u>Compensate Grieco on the basis of Division residual income (RI)</u>.
The benefit of this arrangement is that Grieco would be motivated to put in extra effort to increase RI because Grieco's rewards would increase with increases in RI. But compensating Grieco largely on the basis of RI subjects Grieco to excessive risk, because the division's RI depends not only on Grieco's effort but also on random factors over which Grieco has no control. Grieco may put in a great deal of effort, but the division's RI may be low because of adverse factors (high interest rates, recession) that the manager cannot control. For example, general market conditions will influence Grieco's revenues and costs.

To compensate Grieco for taking on uncontrollable risk, Mason Industries must pay him additional amounts within the structure of the RI-based arrangement. Thus, only using performance-based incentives costs Mason more money, on average, than paying a flat salary. The key question is whether the benefits of motivating additional effort justify the higher costs of performance-based rewards.

c. <u>Compensate Grieco using other companies that also manufacture go-carts and recreational vehicles as a benchmark</u>.
The benefit of benchmarking or relative performance evaluation is to cancel out the effects of common noncontrollable factors that affect a performance measure. Taking out the effects of these factors provides better information about management performance. However, benchmarking and relative performance evaluation are only effective when similar noncontrollable factors affect each of the companies in the benchmark group. If this is the case, as it appears to be here, benchmarking is a good idea. If, however, the companies in the benchmark group are not exactly comparable because, for example, they have other areas of business that cannot be separated from their go-cart and recreational vehicle business, or they operate under different market conditions, benchmarking may not be a good idea. If the noncontrollable factors are not the same then comparing the RI of Grieco's division to the RI of the other companies will not provide useful relative performance evaluation information.

26-34 (Cont'd.)

2. Mason should use a compensation arrangement that includes both a salary component and a bonus component based on residual income. The motivation for having some salary and some performance-based bonus in Grieco's compensation is to balance the benefits of incentives against the extra costs of imposing uncontrollable risk on the manager. If similar noncontrollable factors affect the performance of the benchmark companies that also manufacture and sell go-carts and recreational vehicles, I would recommend that the bonus be based on the JSC Division's residual income relative to the residual income earned by the benchmark companies.

26-36 (50 min.) ROI, residual income, investment decisions, division manager's compensation.

1. Average investment in operating assets employed

Balance at December 31, 19_8	$15,750,000
Balance at December 31, 19_7 ($15,750,000 ÷ 1.05)	15,000,000
Beginning balance plus ending balance	$30,750,000
Average balance ($30,750,000 ÷ 2)	$15,375,000

$$\text{ROI} = \frac{\text{Income from operations before income taxes}}{\text{Average operating assets employed}}$$

$$= \frac{\$1,845,000}{\$15,375,000}$$

$$= 0.12 \text{ or } 12\%$$

2.

Income from operations before income taxes	$1,845,000
Minimum return on average operating assets employed:	
Average operating assets employed ($15,375,000)	
× Required rate of return on invested capital (0.11)	1,691,250
Residual income	$ 153,750

3. Yes, Reigis Steel's management probably would have accepted the investment if residual income were used. The investment opportunity would have lowered Reigis Steel's 19_8 ROI because the expected return (11.5%) was lower than the division's historical returns (11.8% to 14.7%) as well as its actual 19_8 ROI (12%). Management rejected the investment because bonuses are based in part on the performance measure of ROI. If residual income were used as a performance measure (and as a basis for bonuses), management would accept any and all investments that would increase residual income (i.e., a dollar amount rather than a percentage) including the investment opportunity it had in 19_8. Using residual income to reward management would create incentives for managers to accept all investments which have a rate of return in excess of 11%, decisions that are in the best interests of the company as a whole. The investment considered by management in 19_8 had a rate of return of 11.5%.

4.   Consider each of the four proposals that James Chen is considering:

a.   <u>Pay division managers a flat salary independent of division RI.</u>

Paying division managers a flat salary has the advantage that it will not subject division managers to any uncontrollable risk. But this arrangement also suffers from the disadvantage that it will not provide division managers with any incentives to undertake extra physical and mental effort.

b.   <u>Compensate managers only on the basis of division RI.</u>

The benefit of this arrangement is that managers would be motivated to put in extra effort to increase RI because managers' rewards would increase with increases in RI. But compensating managers largely on the basis of RI subjects the managers to excessive risk, because each division's RI depends not only on the manager's effort but also on random factors over which the manager has no control. A manager may put in a great deal of effort, but the division's RI may be low because of adverse factors (high interest rates, recession) which the manager cannot control.

To compensate managers for taking on uncontrollable risk, Chen must pay them additional amounts within the structure of the RI-based arrangement. Thus, using only performance-based incentives will cost Chen more money, on average, than paying a flat salary. The key question is whether the benefits of motivating additional effort justify the higher costs of performance-based rewards.

Finally, rewarding a manager on the basis of division RI will induce managers to maximize the division's RI even if taking such actions are not in the best interests of the company as a whole. This is an important consideration because the two divisions are vertically integrated with the output of the Steel Division used by the Machinery Division. For example, to maximize the Steel Division's RI, the manager of the Steel Division may prefer to produce premium alloy steel plates demanded by outside customers which generate a higher return for the division but hurt the interests of the Machinery Division and Raddington Industries as a whole.

c.   <u>Compensate managers largely on the basis of company wide RI.</u>

Rewarding managers on the basis of companywide RI will motivate managers to take actions that are in the best interests of the company rather than actions that maximize a division's RI. This issue is particularly relevant because the two divisions are vertically integrated and, hence, highly interdependent.

A negative feature of this arrangement is that each division manager's compensation will now depend not only on the performance of that division manager but also on the performance of the other division manager. For example, the compensation of the manager of the Reigis Steel Division will depend on the Machinery Division manager's performance, even though the manager of the Reigis Steel Division may have little influence over the performance of the Machinery Division. Hence, evaluating division managers on the basis of companywide RI will impose extra risk on them and increase the cost of compensating them.

d. <u>Compensate each division manager using the other division's RI as a benchmark</u>.

The benefit of benchmarking or relative performance evaluation is to cancel out the effects of common noncontrollable factors that affect a performance measure. Taking out the effects of these factors provides better information about management performance. However, for benchmarking and relative performance evaluation to be effective, it is critical that similar noncontrollable factors affect each division. It is not clear that the same noncontrollable factors that affect the performance of the Reigis Steel Division (industrywide steel capacity, for example) also affect the performance of the Tool and Die Machinery Division. If the noncontrollable factors are not the same then comparing the RI of one division to the RI of the other division will not provide useful relative performance evaluation information, will only add noise to division performance measures, and, hence, impose extra risk on the division managers. Raddington would then have to compensate the managers for bearing this extra risk.

A second factor for Chen to consider is the impact that benchmarking and relative performance evaluation will have on the incentives for the division managers of the Steel and Machinery Divisions to cooperate with one another. Benchmarking one division against another means that a division manager will look good by improving his or her own performance, or by making the performance of the other division manager look bad.

5. Raddington should use a compensation arrangement that builds on the various elements described in requirement 4. The arrangement should include (a) a salary component to reduce the risk the division manager is subjected to; (b) a bonus based on division residual income to provide managers with incentives; (The motivation for having some salary and some performance-based bonus in compensation arrangements is to balance the benefits of incentives against the extra costs of imposing uncontrollable risk on the manager.) (c) a small bonus based on companywide residual income to encourage cooperation and coordination among managers given the integrated and interdependent nature of the two divisions; and (d) bonus based on the performance of each division manager relative to other steel and tool and die machinery companies.

For reasons outlined in requirement 4, I would not use one division's performance as a benchmark for the other division in this situation.